How to

[hairy bottom not required]

Build Money Saving DIY Skills,
Create a Unique Home and
Properly Look After Your Stuff

Ian Anderson MSc LCGI

HANDYCROWD MEDIA

How to be Handy
[hairy bottom not required]

Build Money Saving DIY Skills,
Create a Unique Home and
Properly Look After Your Stuff

Ian Anderson MSc LCGI

Copyright © 2017 by Ian Anderson

Published by handycrowd media Reg No. 995979268 Norway

ISBN 978-82-93249-05-4

Disclaimer: The author has made every effort to ensure that the information in this book is accurate. However, since it cannot be determined what you intend to do with this information or how competent you are, it shall be your own responsibility to ensure this information meets your specific requirements. The author is a professional builder educated in the UK and the working practises and observations in this book reflect this. It is your responsibility to ensure the advice given in this book is suitable for your country or situation as working practises and rules differ from country to country. It is your responsibility as the homeowner to ensure you have permission to carry out alterations and additions to your home.

Seek local professional advice if you are in any way unsure.

I dedicate this book to my father,
Michael Anderson, the most ingenious man I
know and an inspiration for us all to do more
with what we have to hand.

p.s... and apologies to Julia and William who want me to get
off the computer now and do some fun stuff with them...

THE BARE MINIMUM

Enough? No? Keep reading for the full Monty, the whole caboodle, the whole enchilada, or we can ditch the clichés and just call it what it is...
The Whole Works ... (or feel free to jump forward 8 pages or so if you're just super keen to start at the beginning).

THE WHOLE WORKS

PREFACE

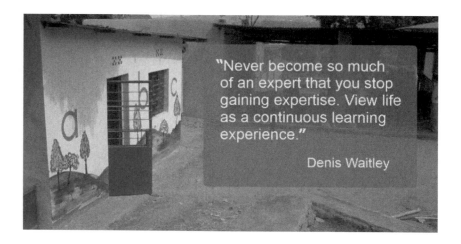

"Never become so much of an expert that you stop gaining expertise. View life as a continuous learning experience."

Denis Waitley

When this book was first suggested, I feared it would be impossible to write, because after more than 30 years of looking at the world through practical eyes, it's like breathing to me. How do I get down on paper this apparently intuitive process? Then it dawned on me; it wasn't totally intuitive, because *I* hadn't stopped learning either. This book describes what I do *every single day* on my own jobs. Sure, I'm applying *some* existing knowledge, but I'm always building that knowledge by learning new skills and looking for solutions when I'm stuck.

People say 'Oh, it's easy for you, you're a born handyman!' But of course, that's nonsense, I wasn't born handy; I just never stopped being curious about things, (although I have stopped putting things in my mouth...well, except the odd nail or two...).

Handy people gain their 'superpower' through a childlike curiosity to learn and understand how things work. And here's the thing, because this childlike process is so 'built in'; it means it's never too late to access it and use it to make you handy; and yes, that means even you!

I understand you're worried; you might even fear to start a practical task or feel it's beyond you, but I'm going to show you how easy it is to overcome your fears and learn a few simple skills. No matter who you are, or how little you think you know; you'll get there. Trust me, I'm a builder... (and yeah, I know that doesn't have the same ring as, 'trust me I'm a doctor' but I'm working with what I've got, okay?).

I was born lucky in one sense though; because both my parents have great common sense and are pretty good with their hands. All learned through necessity, growing up in the frugal post war years. It rubs off. I started with Lego and Meccano and worked my way up to building stuff in the fields and woods around my home. I don't ever remember not having a penknife in one pocket and string in the other.

Naturally enough, being interested in the physical workings of the world turned into my living. For decades now, I've been building houses, extensions, carrying out renovations, refurbishments, improvements and maintaining stuff, plus teaching in the UK and in developing countries. I'm drawn to renovating or repairing stuff, recycling, and reusing materials or repurposing things. Oh, and of course I love buying and learning to use tools!

As for *why* I wanted to write this book. Well, I love what I do, and through this book I want to encourage *you* to live a more practical life and experience the deep satisfaction you'll get though Doing It Yourself. Being handy is part of who I am, right here in my hands, in my head and in my heart. I hope it rubs off on you too.

But enough about me, what about you? What do you want to learn how to do? What new and exciting project is bouncing around in that head of yours? Well then, let's get to it!

(Well actually, you'll have to wait a minute, since apparently, the acknowledgements etc. must follow the preface...)

ACKNOWLEDGEMENTS

"With realisation of one's own potential and self-confidence in one's ability, one can build a better world."

Dalai Lama

Thanks to all the incredible people scribbling away in the blogosphere whose observations about life 'as it happens', continue to inspire me to add mine. Even though our subjects and approaches vary, we are more alike than different. Most are way smarter (and prettier) than me; but hanging on to their coat-tails is quite a ride and I learn something new every day.

A book I'm reading right now lists 39 people on their publishing team, oh how I wish! I'd also like to be able to thank the multitude of folks who helped me put this book together, but nope, it was just me, stubbornly wrestling with it all in a pig headed, self-defeating fashion. It is a book about DIY after all... so the mistakes (and there are bound to be a few), are mine alone.

However, I do give a large rhetorical thankyou to the burgeoning independent publishing fraternity, without whom, doing this would be much more difficult, thanks for knocking down the walls guys. People like Joel from The Book Designer, Emilie from Puttytribe, Dave from Kindlepreneur and Jeff Goins to name a few; plus of course the folks at amazon via Kindle Publishing.

But the most thanks go to my wife Cecilia, who believed I could do this right from the start, even when faced with an overwhelming lack of evidence. She never put me under any pressure to finish this book, not even when she had to work so hard to bring home most of the bacon. Thanks again for your continuing encouragement and confidence, especially during the times when I wondered if it was worth all the time and effort...

DULL BUT IMPORTANT SAFETY NOTICE

This book talks about using tools, working with electrical items, climbing on ladders, roofs, or scaffolding etc. It also talks about working with heavy or potentially dangerous materials and machines. Staying safe **must** be your **No.1 priority**. You should wear the right personal protection equipment for the job and get into the habit of working safely, *every time*.

I can't recommend highly enough the importance of reading the *Health and Safety* chapter in this book *before* starting any work. Go online and seek the specific advice you need to stay safe during your planned project, the hse.gov.uk and osha.gov websites are good places to start.

Every minute of every day, somebody somewhere is suffering an accident; whether or not that is you one day, is nearly always your choice. I don't ever want to hear that you hurt yourself because you did something reckless or dumb, because then I'd feel bad and you don't want that.

Always take your time, be careful and for goodness sake *use your common sense*, **because if it feels unsafe or dangerous... it probably is!**

So be careful, this stuff can hurt... a lot.

INTRODUCTION

"One of the greatest and simplest tools for learning more and growing, is doing more."

Washington Irving

'Only a third of people actually feel confident in their ability to carry out DIY repairs and maintenance around the home,' according to a recent AA Home Emergency Response study.

I want to get you into that confident group of DIY'ers by sharing with you a simple approach to learning practical things which will, over time, automatically develop your handy ability. I'll show you how real handy people approach new practical tasks. How to kick-start your own learning process and build up your handiness. You'll be able to get your house sorted; your car fixed, or even start your dream project.

You'll start slowly, you don't even have to lift a screwdriver until you're ready. And when you're done with reading and are ready to try a little practising, we'll start with something simple, because early success is essential to boost your confidence. I'll be gentle, so don't worry; plus, I'll be here to hold your hand if you're a bit out of your depth, so keep in touch okay?

You'll notice as you read on, that this isn't your normal step-by-step DIY manual. Nope, instead, consider this book an introduction, an attempt to explain common sense and gumption, to show you a way of looking at the physical world around you so that it makes sense, and above all I want it to inspire you and motivate you; to give you that gentle nudge into handiness.

It's also a bit eclectic, maybe even a bit of a jumble of thoughts sometimes, but that's me, practising what I preach, teaching myself about writing, battling with my tenses, learning about fonts, line spacing and playing with images etc. I hope you'll forgive me if I fumble a word or two, as I'll forgive you when you drop your screwdriver or cut something too short.

We're in this together, just me and you, no one looking over our shoulders, no one judging us for what we know or don't know. No one taking the mickey at our attempts to learn new things. Me as I expand my learning about bookish things and you as I show you how to connect your head, hands, and heart to create something wonderful, fix something you treasure or maintain something you want to keep. I'm looking forward to the journey and I hope you are too.

Now, we're going to spend some hours together (and I don't want us to fall out), but to be honest, I don't know you very well, or what you're capable of. So please forgive me if you think I'm patronising you, I'm truly not. I've written the book from a simple standpoint, so I hope you can be thankful for any obvious parts and learn from the parts which are new to you.

To add to the inspirational flavour, I've liberally scattered some of my favourite words of wisdom throughout the book, so you'll know you're in good company as we head down the path to your handiness (I hope you don't mind this indulgence, but I do so I love inspirational quotes!).

THE STORY SO FAR...

"All things are difficult Before they are easy."

Thomas Fuller

You've probably said, 'I can't do DIY' in the past, but let's stop and ponder that for a second. Why do you say that? Or more specifically, what exactly went wrong on your last project? I talk to people every day who consider themselves walking DIY disasters and I hear three common complaints; see if you recognise any of them...

I DON'T KNOW WHERE TO START...

They, (whoever 'they' are), say 'if you fail to prepare, you are preparing to fail' and in this case 'they' are right. Planning and preparation are important (so I'll show you how to do it properly a bit later on).

I'll show you how to find out what materials, skills, or techniques you'll need for your project. Help and advice is out there, and I'll show you how to find it, in books, on the internet and from the folks around you. Armed with facts and knowhow, you can prepare for your project properly and avoid failures. You'll learn how in the *Developing Practical Knowledge* and *Preparation and Planning* chapters.

I ALWAYS MAKE A RUBBISH JOB...

Practise on scrap materials first (yes really, practise. I know, I mean, who knew?!). But seriously, I'll show you how to use some tools and how to practise. Everyone goes through this 'apprenticeship' where they make mistakes, (yes, even me!) Be smart and make your mistakes on scrap materials. Practise will make you consistent, improve your accuracy, and reduce the likelihood of mistakes on the real work.

Be fussy about your results and aim to produce good quality work (it'll look better and last longer) and the only way you'll achieve this is to practise, practise, practise and then practise some more. Learn how in the *Developing Practical Skills* chapter. Did I mention you'll need to practise? Yes? Good.

IT TAKES ME TOO LONG...

No worries, going slower is actually BETTER! Because getting a step right, makes the NEXT step that much easier. Each logical step on a job is inextricably tied to the *previous one* AND the *next one* (like a chain). Rushing creates small inaccuracies which compound; they get bigger, they get complicated and they swallow loads of *time* to fix or overcome. But most importantly, they often lead to *failure* or *poor end results*; (i.e. the chain snaps...).

Time and quality are inseparable. Many people rush into jobs believing faster is better, even tradesmen, (I blame DIY makeover TV!). Sure, professionals look like they're working fast, but speed plus accuracy takes years of familiarity and experience to master. Remember; you don't need to *work fast*, you're not making a living at this, (well not yet at least!), fight the urge to rush, dig deep to find the patience to carry out each step carefully and care about the quality of the finish.

Getting it *right* and making a *good job* is your first priority (sorry, that should be second priority, safety is first remember, but I'll get to that in a bit!). Seriously, ignore the time it takes; a year from now you'll have long forgotten the time it took, but the end results are right in front of you. If you make a good job, you'll be happy, if you make a rubbish job, it'll annoy you every time you look at it. Not only do rushed jobs look bad (to you and others), they'll knock your confidence too.

The only caveat about allowing plenty of time is when it interferes with daily living. Being without a kitchen or a bathroom for a week is doable, just. But if it's going to take you a month of Sundays and then some, you might hear some grumbling from the ranks. Tackle bigger projects during time away from work so you can put in some long days to finish in a reasonable time. Alternatively, try collaborating with friends or even hiring in a friendly professional to work alongside you to shorten the timescale.

Can you see how these three things tie together? *Preparation, good quality work and time* are the basic building blocks for success on your project. Be honest about what *your weaknesses* are and focus on improving them. Next time you feel or hear yourself shutting down and saying, "I can't do this", stop. What are you really saying? Find the real reason behind your fear and read around it to find a solution. I sometimes spend hours reading up on a new material, technique, or skill before going to get my tools and if I need to do it as an experienced professional, why shouldn't you? At the moment, I'm learning how to climb trees via ropes, to carry out pruning and to fell difficult trees from the top down. It's technical, physically difficult, and potentially lethal if I get it wrong. I'm spending many tens of hours reading up... (just sayin').

Remember also there's no such thing as easy or difficult, because we're all unique, with lots of different experiences; what one person finds easy, another can find difficult. See what I mean with this joke.... Yes?

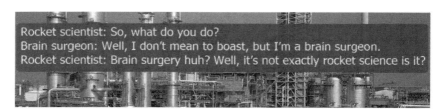

Rocket scientist: So, what do you do?
Brain surgeon: Well, I don't mean to boast, but I'm a brain surgeon.
Rocket scientist: Brain surgery huh? Well, it's not exactly rocket science is it?

I'M REALLY, REALLY HOPELESS AT DIY...

Okay okay, I hear you. But fear not apprentice handy one, because here's the secret; you don't need to learn all this stuff overnight. Your DIY abilities will develop just as you learned all your other skills; s l o w l y . Remember, you had to learn how to use a spoon once...

Many everyday items are actually quite simple to assemble, maintain or even repair. Even complicated things fail in spectacularly simple ways sometimes. Remember, most of the hard work's done by the designers and manufacturers, leaving you with a much easier job (maintenance or repair).

And don't believe the rubbish that you're not a handy person because 'it's just not in your genes'. Being handy is not about your genes, or what your father did, or how clever you are. It's time to kick that *can't do it* 'troll' out of your head pronto!

Nido Qubein, (an extremely successful businessman who started with nothing) once said; "Your present circumstances don't determine where you can go; they merely determine where you start." Clever chap...

BUT I'M NOT CLEVER ENOUGH...

R u b b i s h ! Some of the *least* academic people I know (and I mean that in the nicest possible way) are brilliantly handy. To attempt some little jobs around the home doesn't mean you need to come from a long line of practical folk or have a genius IQ. Albert Einstein once said its imagination which is the true sign of intelligence, not knowledge. So, don't worry about how smart you think you are, *you can do this stuff* I promise you, I've never met anyone who's not amazed at how easy some DIY jobs are once they've started...

WILLING TO LEARN AND HAVE A GO

"Nothing great was ever achieved without enthusiasm"

Ralph Waldo Emerson

Being handy is not particularly hard, learning how to use a few tools is not particularly hard, what is hard is having the right attitude. So of course, it's not enough to be a little bit interested, I mean you've got to *want* to learn this stuff; enthusiastically ideally! Half-hearted, ill-prepared attempts will destroy your confidence as well as your project. Like learning *any other skill or hobby*, you need the *inspiration* and *motivation* to try, to *commit* to the *learning process* and *enough time* to *persevere* and *make progress*, (even when it gets difficult or complicated). As Benjamin Franklin said, 'Energy and persistence conquer all things.' Another clever chap...

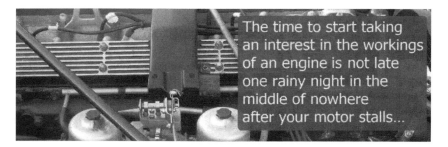

The time to start taking an interest in the workings of an engine is not late one rainy night in the middle of nowhere after your motor stalls...

FINDING THE CONFIDENCE

I understand you're probably new to DIY, but as I said, I hope the approach outlined in this book will inspire and motivate you to 'have a go.' I totally understand if you feel you're not capable of great things just yet, but remember what Napoleon Hill said; '*If you can't do great things; do small things in a great way*'. That sounds doable, doesn't it? It doesn't matter how big the first thing you do is, just that *you do it*. For example, do something as small as making your tarnished front door knocker beautiful again by polishing it up with a metal cleaner/restorer. Don't discount how important such small successes are, because they will give you the confidence to try other things.

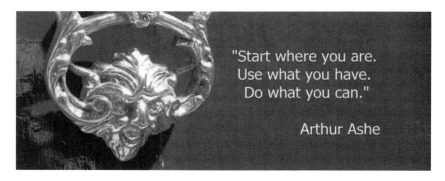

"Start where you are.
Use what you have.
Do what you can."

Arthur Ashe

So, don't let fear of making a mistake prevent you from starting. Remember Samuel Johnson's words; he said that "Nothing will ever be attempted if all possible objections must first be overcome" ...

PERSEVERANCE VS LIFE

Learn to persevere, but don't be a slave, because you have a life too! DIY is work (even if you enjoy it) and it takes time. So, it's important to develop a strategy that works for you and fits into your lifestyle. Don't let the project take over every aspect of your life. Create a sanctuary, somewhere that you can retreat to if necessary, to escape the mess and recharge your batteries. This can be a room you're not working on in the house, a place in the garden, or even a place nearby, like a park or the beach. Take your favourite drink, grab whatever it is you like to do to relax and take an hour or two if need be. Put the chaos behind you for a little while. Like I said, time rarely matters; (if only I could convince some of my clients!) because it's all forgotten in the end.

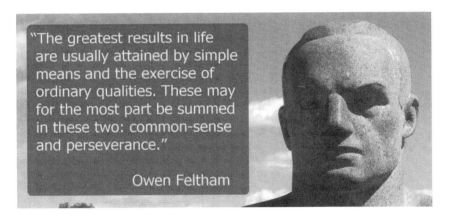

"The greatest results in life are usually attained by simple means and the exercise of ordinary qualities. These may for the most part be summed in these two: common-sense and perseverance."

Owen Feltham

WHAT'S DIFFERENT ABOUT THIS DIY BOOK?

Many DIY books are huge and intimidating, full of step-by-step instructions, '*how to fix a leaky tap*', for example; but what happens if your tap doesn't look like the one in the book? What happens if you get stuck? What happens if the guide's instructions don't work? What if the step-by-step guide was written by a journalist or an academic and not a tradesman, or it's simply out of date? You get my drift...

I want this book to teach you the principles of being handy, because once you understand the principles, the details you can find out for yourself. And the details matter, (critically sometimes). For example, I could show you how to fix a particular thing in detail, but then if you took those very same details and applied them to something else, the end result could be disastrous.

So let's take you way beyond following step-by-step instructions, let's get you *thinking* and *acting* like a handy person; and then you'll be able to do anything you set your mind to, absolutely anything, seriously.

Sticking with the fictional tap analogy, the approach in this book will show you how to look at your imaginary tap, figure out *how it goes together*, spot the details showing you *how to get it apart*, to notice *where the seal fits* and to understand *how it seals* and *stops the tap from leaking*. Figuring out how the tap works makes *repairing the leaky bit* a cinch, because you'll *understand the problem*, you'll know *where to go to find a replacement seal* and 'hey presto', you've just come up with a workable *solution* and *solved the problem*.

LEARNING 'ON THE FLY'

Running a construction business, I see new things all the time, and I wondered, how do I do this? I realised that I approached new stuff in a particular way, Microsoft call it "integrating new information and skills to enhance personal performance", i.e. Learning on the fly...

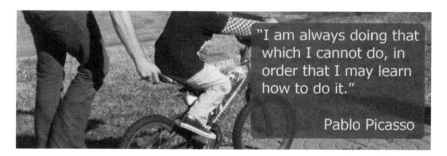

"I am always doing that which I cannot do, in order that I may learn how to do it."

Pablo Picasso

Learning as we go is as important as it is inevitable, because of change. Manufacturers alter specifications, suppliers come and go, imports from abroad and progress introduces new technology and materials. And professional need to learn it all (usually without any official extra training). It might look like handy people instinctively know what to do, but it's not all instinct, it's more 'learned' than that. Of course, I do *start* by comparing the new task with any remotely similar previous experiences I've had and adapting any applicable existing skills. But critically, the important thing to remember is that I'm always learning. By using all my senses in a way that I'd been unconsciously honing my entire life, plus researching just *enough* to fill in the gaps and get the job done.

In this book, I'll explain how *you* can train your senses, build up your knowledge of the physical world, practise some simple skills and critically, teach *yourself* just enough to get the job done. Yes, you read correctly, that's '*teach yourself.*' But before you rush to ask for your money back, give me a chance; let me show you, read the book and start-taking notice of the physical world that surrounds you. I think you'll surprise yourself how easy it's to learn once you practise this simple approach.

You'll have no doubt heard the cheesy old proverb which says:

'*Give a man a fish and you feed him for a day.*
Teach a man how to fish and you feed him for a lifetime.'

Most DIY guides give you the fish, but I hope this book will teach you *how* to fish! Erm, well, I'm not *actually* going to teach you how to *fish* ....Oh, you know what I mean!

WHAT'S IN IT FOR ME?

"Not only must we be good, but we must also be good for something."

Henry David Thoreau

What? Being rock star handy isn't enough? Dude! Okay then, here's the thing; it's a universal truth that there is ALWAYS something to do in any kind of house, even a tree house or a mud hut. From eradicating unwanted traces of the previous occupiers, to getting it how you want it. Then you've got maintenance to think about to protect yourself and your investment.

No matter whether you're a homeowner, tenant, first time buyer, independent, newly independent or a long-suffering partner; learning a few practical skills will come in handy. Even if you're turning your back on the rat race to live in a mud hut, you'll need to know how to repair those cracks and maintain those banana leaves on the roof before the monsoon season starts... (I talk from experience here...).

As you go through the book you'll start to *think* and *act* like a handyperson. Picture yourself being able to do some of these things...

- Fix simple failures on your everyday items.
- Look after and maintain stuff you want to keep.
- Repair stuff that breaks down.
- Assemble new stuff you buy and with no parts left over.
- Breathe new life into tired things and be creative.
- Find free information you need online and offline.

Actually, we can be more succinct, being handy means being able to *do stuff*, any kind of stuff! Still need convincing that learning this stuff is worth the effort? Let's look at some more benefits...

SHOW ME THE MONEY

Property experts say you should spend around *one percent* your properties value *every year* on maintenance to keep it looking good and properly protected. Work out one percent of the average house price in your street (dang, I know I should have charged more for this book!) Hiring people to improve, repair or maintain your home or vehicle costs a lot because craftspeople demand good salaries, shiny 4x4 trucks, short days, and sunny holidays in exchange for their considerable skills (quite rightly so!).

This means DIY could save you hundreds or even thousands every single year; giving you more money to spend on more exciting stuff like your own sunny holidays.

OH, THE PERSONAL SATISFACTION

Home insurance experts report one in ten DIY jobs end in disaster.

But wait, that means 90% are successful!

We can live with that.

Don't underestimate the satisfaction and the intense feeling of pride you'll get when working with your hands. I can recommend Matthew Crawford's book "The Case for Working with Your Hands: Or Why Office Work is Bad for Us and Fixing Things Feels Good" to understand more about this.

You'll also enjoy the feeling of being able to cope when everyday items 'wobble', fixing them on the spot or preventing them from failing altogether by recognising what's happening. Even nicer is the feeling of maintaining something you treasure or improving your home. No matter how small the job, the sense of achievement is hugely satisfying and rewarding.

GETTING YOUR WORK DONE ON YOUR TERMS

Hiring people can be a lottery because of variations between your expectations and what the other person thinks is acceptable.

Besides, for many people, having big hairy blokes* tramping through the house can be inconvenient or upsetting even, especially if they are less than professional in their management of any mess.

Whereas, being handy and doing-it-yourself, you get your jobs finished on your terms, exactly how you want them done and no waiting weeks or months to start. You also have complete control over how much it costs and the quality of the work. *Apologies for the stereotype, but I'm most definitely hairy...

DIY, FUN AND KEEPING FIT

Your savings on gym membership is worth the price of this book alone, *and* it's more fun than going to the gym. Fun? Yes, fun. Anything's more fun than staring out of the window on a treadmill, isn't it? Come on!

For example; I use my practical skills to cut down and chop up unwanted trees for the local authority. Lugging logs through the woods, swinging an axe and stacking, turns my hard work out into valuable firewood, (I live in Norway now and winters are long and cold...), warming me twice as they say.

Many other DIY jobs are physically demanding too; paint preparation and painting usually involves lots of climbing up and down (steps?) Bending up and down to lay a wooden floor (aerobics?) Knocking down brick walls or digging foundations (weights?) Consider mowing the lawn with a push mower (cardio?), which saves money as well as entertaining the neighbours and keeping you fit. Oh, and don't forget the little victory dance when you finish a project or fix the washing machine... (Zumba?).

SAVING THE WORLD

We all like to do our bit to protect the environment. As a handy person, you'll save valuable resources by keeping your stuff in good repair and avoid the untimely purchase of replacements. Handy people understand the importance of quality, buying things that will last a long time with some simple mainte-nance. Fashion, peer pressure or obsolescence is less likely to persuade you to buy replacements for things you have that still work just fine.

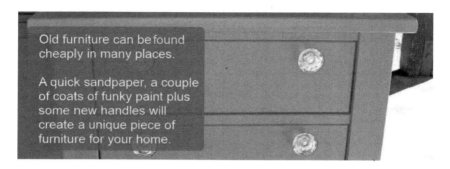

Old furniture can be found cheaply in many places.

A quick sandpaper, a couple of coats of funky paint plus some new handles will create a unique piece of furniture for your home.

Plus, there's charm in building relationships with something you hope is going to be around forever. For example, the good quality tools I bought as a teenage apprentice, now fit me like a glove...

In addition, you'll be able to make 'new' things by reusing or re-purposing stuff other people don't want anymore, gaining interesting characterful things for your home. There many cheap things, furniture especially, that will love a new lease of life in an alternative setting after a few easy modifications or im-provements.

HOW TO USE THIS BOOK

You can of course choose to read the book from cover to cover wearing comfy pyjamas in your favourite armchair, or you could cherry pick chapters sitting on the toilet (eww!). Either way, will you do it? Will you follow through? Remember Jim Rohn's words; "The book you don't read won't help." So, use the book as a starting point, but make the effort to practise what you learn as well; it's the only way to improve your skills. I know you want to be handy or you wouldn't be here, but will you do the work? Do you have what it takes, huh? Huh? Yes, of course you do... Excellent!

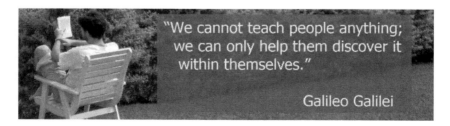

"We cannot teach people anything; we can only help them discover it within themselves."

Galileo Galilei

A NOTE ABOUT STUFF

I like the word stuff. It covers a lot of, well, erm.......stuff! Because this book isn't a step-by-step guide, I'll refer to lots of things as simply 'stuff.' Just replace the word 'stuff' with tap washer, toaster, tractor or whatever else you're working on beginning with 'T'!

DON'T FORGET I'M HERE TO HOLD YOUR HAND

You'll not be alone. You'll find me pottering around on the companion website 'handycrowd.com', where you can ask questions if you get stuck.

Have I managed to convince you that this DIY stuff is going to be cool? (with the longest introduction to ever grace the front of a DIY book!). Are you still with me?

Then you're a superstar and good to go, read on...

DEVELOPING PRACTICAL KNOWLEDGE

"Never neglect an opportunity for self-improvement."

Sir William Jones

Behind the scenes and deep in the sub-conscious, your mind is a swirl of inputs as it views the physical world around you. Going about your business, your brain is aware of thousands of things, from the horizon in the far distance, the airplane above your head to the little bird in the bush. It's like data pouring into a supercomputer, and like a super-computer, there is an algorithm. A set of parameters the brain uses to sift through all this data to determine what's important to save, and what to discard. You won't even register most of this stuff, unless your brain recognises something amiss or you notice something of interest, something you like, something the brains algorithm picks up.

Some things you see, you stop and pick up, to touch and feel, to use. you hear the noises things make and you notice some things smell good and some bad. All these sensory inputs bombard your brain with huge volumes of infor-mation, some identifiable and some not, some interesting and some not. Most of this goes on outside of your conscious knowledge, otherwise your mind would drown in minutiae.

Most folks drift along like this, oblivious to large parts of the world, the world outside of their interests. The inputs you choose to notice make up your known world (or the world as you choose to know it), because you only actively notice the things you're looking for and are interested in. Conversely, it means you also ignore things you are not (at this moment in time) interested in or looking for.

This explains the rapid progress a person makes once they set their mind to learning something new; interest redirects the flow of previously ignored details from the constant river of data into the consciousness. From this it's possible to learn, (over time) what things are made from, how they function, and how to use new tools or develop new skills.

Thankfully the world is also largely reliable and predictable; which means anomalies stick out, i.e. they become noticeable (if you're looking for them...). And when you notice something new and unusual, you get to decide. The untrained brain might choose to ignore it and do nothing, but a trained brain might start to think about what happened and what needs doing to correct the anomaly. In short, *practically minded people learn to notice the little things,* It's a bit like the following word cloud...

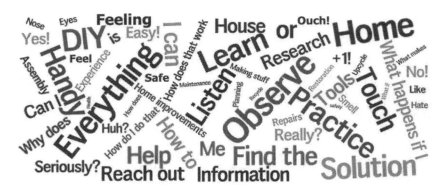

I know it might look chaotic, but buried in there, is the cognitive process that leads a person to handiness; because a practical and handy person needs to **Observe, Listen, Feel,** and **Smell** everything! They also know (when faced with a problem) to gather extra **Information** to add to their **Experience** to find a **Solution.**

Right then, we need a name for this process, don't we? So, let's see... the first letter of the above words is OLFSIES. Oh dear, that doesn't exactly roll off the tongue, does it? I was hoping for a brilliantly witty acronym not a clumsy initialism. Let's rearrange the word order a little, and that gives; FLOSSIE.

Nope; I don't think that's going to fly either.

R.E.L.E.A.R.N

Okay, let's be a little more creative with which letter we use... Hmm, how about RELEARN? Hmm, yup, that works because as you read this book, you'll 'relearn' how to interact with the physical world. And then; just as you did when you were a child, you'll use all that new information to forge new practical skills. Let's make a pretty picture...

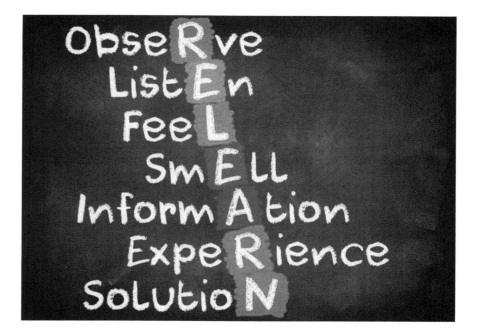

I know, I know, it's a stretch, but work with me here okay, and at least it's easier to remember than OLFSIES, so give it a try huh?

In minute we'll go through each one in more detail to get you started on the path to handiness. And don't worry, it's not too difficult. In short, to begin with, I want you to start building your practical awareness by taking notice of the physical stuff you use every day. Allow a little extra time to wonder about how they work and see if you can identify the materials used to make them. It doesn't matter if you have no idea right now, just be curious, pick them up, (not the photocopier obviously!) explore them and take in some of the details.

These details are potentially useful nuggets of practical information which are currently bouncing off your sub consciousness; you're ignoring them because you hadn't appreciated their value. However, if you recognise them and file them away, they'll morph into real knowledge and understanding of how things work. But first, you need to start noticing them...

Psychologists call this 'immersion', where constant exposure to stimulus builds awareness, understanding and ability. Add some practise to this new knowledge and then you're building experience. Experience, plus finding new information from other resources will eventually make this process intuitive.

OBSERVE

Eighty percent of what we learn is visual, so to start your journey into hand-iness, begin to *observe* precisely the physical world surrounding you.

Remember how you can never get things back into the box?

That's because you forgot to notice how everything was arranged in your excitement to get at the contents.

Think like a detective, notice and remember little details.

NOTICING THE PHYSICAL WORLD WITH PRACTICAL EYES

Even the simplest of things can teach you something about material or function. But you'll have to make a little effort to do this, because your brain is a super computer with filters. It cherry picks the things you're interested in and throws them in front of you like roadkill. It pretty much ignores everything else. (I know, shocking, isn't it?).

So change your brains mental algorithm and re-write your internal code. In other words, fine tune your mental radar to remind yourself to actually notice the stuff you're using. In other words, fine tune your mental radar (stick post-it notes up to jog your memory if it helps).

Remember how you can never get things back into the box they came in? That's because you forgot to notice how everything was arranged in your excite-ment to get at the contents. I'm sure you'll also recognise the scenario where you've bought something new, a car for example, and then you start seeing them everywhere? That's your radar working; those cars were there before, but your brain ignored them because you were not looking for them.

For example, as you go about your day, you'll see many electrical or mechanical machines, gadgets, furniture, and vehicles, plus the buildings you live, work, or play in as well as the great outdoors. Right now, you probably take many of these things for granted and barely notice this stuff, (especially when everything is working okay). So, change your habits; next time you're using an everyday thing, look at it closely and think about...

- How does it work or operate generally?
- How does it close or open, what holds it etc.?
- How do the components fit or sit, in relation to each other?
- What parts move and which parts are static?
- Where does the power come from?
- How do you use it, hold it, direct it, etc.?
- What material is it made from?
- Start to wonder, how is it made?

Pay particular attention to the things you normally do on autopilot or without much thought. For example, don't wait for the toast to pop up idly, take a proper look at the toaster! From putting more paper in the photocopier to driving your car, start noticing the details. This will get you thinking about the way physical things work: Look out for motion or movement, leverage, force, power, and alignment; especially how it relates to your body or how it's used. All these observations will make more sense when you start to use tools.

Honing your observation skills will also enable you to notice and register how things *look, sound,* and *feel* when *everything is working okay.* This'll alert you to change (hardly ever good in this context), which is important because stuff rarely fails without displaying some kind of symptom, however small. These often-tiny changes are advance warnings, which might help you diagnose a problem before something fails completely.

IT'S ALL IN THE DETAILS

To supercharge your general observations of the practical world, look very *closely* at the small *details* in, on or under the things you use. Look to see how stuff physically holds together; look for joins, fasteners, fixings, holes, gaps, slots, dimples, indentations, or casting seams etc. Wonder how those things relate to what's holding the parts together, a seam indicates a join for example. This might help you figure out how they might come apart. Look also at how the parts operate, notice each parts function and how the parts work together to create the desired outcome.

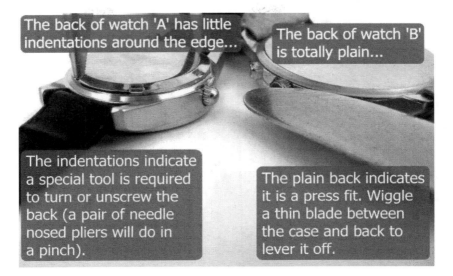

As designs get ever more complex, not everything is obvious or clear. Often there is hidden stuff or multiple things happening. Don't expect some things to give up their secrets easily; you might have to try a little probing, pulling, flexing, and poking. Look to see which bits don't move, because any bits that don't move or flex a little, may be hiding a fastener of some kind (a missed screw for example).

A PROCESS OF ELIMINATION OR LOGIC

Sometimes you've looked at a few things, but nothing is obvious, you just can't see what it is you're looking at. So, cross some things off the list by eliminating the things you know are not a part of the solution. You might even have to try a few things to determine what they are. For example, I had a call out recently where a dishwasher door was hitting the kicking boards underneath and preventing the door from opening. Bear in mind that I know nothing about this model (or even dishwashers in particular, although I have fitted quite a few in new kitchens) and had never seen this door mounting method before. So, what did I do...?

- I tried opening the door and saw that it was in fact, hitting the kicking board (duh!).

- I looked for movement in the kicking board but no, it looked to be in its original position, properly clipped to the cabinet legs.

- I checked the position of the dishwasher machine itself and no, the screws holding the machine were still in place and tight.

- I checked the position of the vanity wooden door on the door of the actual machine. And ah ha; I saw signs that the door had moved downwards because there was bright white strip at the bottom, (okay, the newly exposed parts of the door were dirty!).

- Closing the door again, I now notice it needs adjusting upwards a little to bring it in line with the neighbouring units' doors.

- I examined the inside of the machine to look for the screws which hold the door in place. Nothing jumps out at me immediately but there are screws down each side of the door...

- I unscrewed one of the screws and found it was just a short machine screw holding the metal door parts together. Okay, no other screws are visible on the inside of the door.

- I looked further afield and noticed two small holes on the sides of the dishwasher door, and inside the holes were two T20 screws (T20 is a common screw for adjusting and fitting stuff to white goods).

- I slackened the T20 screws and I felt the door move. The screws controlled a 'pinch' mechanism and the door slid up and down on a ratchet slide mechanism.

- I slackened off both sides, pulled the door up a few millimetres and re-tightened the screws. Hey presto, the door now clears the kicking board and lines up better with the doors on the neighbouring unit.

We'll look at this in more detail in the *Repairing Stuff* chapter, but I hope this example illustrates the process of elimination, or the logic of looking at something new and unknown. One, by one I eliminated the first things I looked at, but I kept on looking until I found something useful I could use to push me in the right direction towards the solution.

COLOUR

From the colour of the milk bottle top for your tea, to the antifreeze in your car*. Colours make great identifiers. Here are some examples...

- Of course, we all know *green* means go, on or 'all clear' and *red* means off, stop or danger.

- Wire or cable colours (mostly *red* or *brown* is live, and often *blue* is neutral, *green,* and *yellow* is almost always earth or ground etc.)

- Electrical fuses, e.g. automobile blade fuses are different colours according to their load rating. (Red=10A, Blue=15A, Yellow=20A etc.)

- Wall plugs. *Brown* is 7mm, *red* is 6mm, *yellow* is 5mm etc. (varies from place to place and manufacturer to manufacturer though, so use a tape measure if unsure).

- Electrical resistors on circuit boards have a whole bunch of colour codes to indicate their function.

*green antifreeze is inorganic additive technology/IAT, the orange stuff is organic acid technology/OAT),

RANDOM STUFF TO LOOK OUT FOR

Observe everything critically. If something stops working, look for anomalies, missing parts, burnt areas or broken parts. Look for stuff which appears out of place. Is anything disconnected, a lever or wire only fastened one end for example? If there's a free wire floating around, can you see where it might have come from? (logic dictates it to be within an arc of its own length). Or can you see any obvious place where a dislocated part should be? Are drive belts tight, (twist them through 90°, not more)? Give wires a wiggle to check they are secure. Is there any corrosion anywhere, especially on connections or fasteners? Look for loose screws or bolts or even an empty hole which might indicate a missing fastener.

Look for illogical stuff, things which are definitely not supposed to be there; dirt, stones, corrosion, hair, sticky drinks (think remote controls), mice in engine bays etc...

In the depths of a cold winter, some mice thought my nice warm engine bay would make a cozy home...

Sometimes stuff will fight you, so take your time. If something bursts open because you pulled too hard, it may be impossible for you to see how the internal components fitted together. This is especially true for anything that contains springs or sprung loaded stuff like locks. Be extremely careful with springs at all costs... trust me on this!

HIDDEN THINGS

A section on things you can't see in the Observation section... yes, well, it kind of makes sense if you think about it! Your house is full of hidden things, primarily services like pipes and electrical wires but also parts of the structure like floor joists or studs in a wall.

Electrical wiring 'should' be in presumed *safe zones*; i.e. places where it's considered okay for tradesman to place their cables. However, this may only apply to newer constructions and of course it assumes the work's done by competent tradesmen, (search Google images for 'safe zones for electric cables' for more info in your area). Pipes should also run in logical places according to relevant rules and regulations etc. This means that wires and pipes usually go up or down from outlets and occasionally sideways, but never at an angle (in theory at least...).

However, in an old house, all bets are off and you might find services in the most unlikely or improbable places, depending on who did the work and when. Always try to check for hidden cables and pipes, especially before drilling holes in the structure. Eventually your honed and experienced observations skills will tell you if there's likely to be any services in a particular place in a wall, but it's still good practise to check using a detector to be safe.

Look all around for outlets which obviously point towards wires and pipes etc. then it's just to figure out which direction the wires or pipes come into the outlet. Don't forget that wires etc. can sometimes come into an outlet from the rear, i.e. from the other side of the wall, in another room...

Learn how to isolate the main power in your house in case of emergency. As part of learning about your house you need to open up that scary cupboard under the stairs (or wherever yours is etc.) and learn what each circuit does in your fuse box. Then you'll be able to flip the switch (breaker) and isolate any area of the house in an emergency or before working on it. Take any power you need from a non-isolated part of the house via a sturdy extension lead plugged into a safety breaker such as an RCD (Residual Current Device). RCD's protect you from electrical shock by switching off your device in a few milliseconds if it detects a problem. Remember to place a strip of tape over any closed breakers to warn others not to switch them back on. Alternatively, hit your main breaker and borrow power from a neighbour's place via an extension lead and RCD.

Finding and damaging a water pipe is the most likely hidden thing to cause a surprise DIY disaster. Be prepared, go and find out how to switch off (isolate) the water supply to your house *right now*, go on, this is important, I'll not write another word till you do...

p.s. (Most likely it will be somewhere stupid like under the kitchen sink, buried under a load of stuff, or in some random cupboard somewhere...)

... good, you found it? That's called a stopcock, and now you know what it looks like and what it does. You'll thank me for this if you're ever unlucky enough to nail through a stupidly positioned, hidden pipe (plumbers eh!?).

Whilst we're on the subject, it's a good idea to keep a few emergency repair supplies in the house if there's even a remote possibility you could damage your water pipes. Ask *Google* about *emergency pipe repairs* or go to the local plumbers' merchant and ask for the same. Emergency repairs range from a roll of special (very!) sticky tape you wind around the pipe to seal the hole, right up to a clever gadget you simply clamp onto the pipe over the hole and fasten the clip.

One last hidden thing is... everything. Huh, what's that supposed to mean? I mean light, or rather a lack of light, (of course), hides all manner of things. Never struggle in poor lighting conditions, you'll miss something important. It's amazing how much better it is to work in good light. Always make sure you have good light, buy an LED stick lamp, head torch, regular torch and even flood lights on tall stands if you can afford them.

RECORD YOUR OBSERVATIONS

Part of observation is remembering what you've seen and learned; so, whenever you're looking at something, remember to make notes or take snapshots (phones are brilliant for this) to help you understand it all, especially if the job will take several days or if you expect interruptions or delays. It's amazing how easy it is to forget details once you take your eyes and mind away from a task for a few days. Use an app (I like *Evernote*) to store images and add notes to clarify them. If you're more old school, make a sketch and label the parts to go with your notes and store them all in a big folder.

STORE OBSERVATIONAL INSPIRATIONS

Related to recording your observations of work in progress, also store the inspirational stuff you see, call it an 'inspiration file' if you like.

Adding a timber frame around some scrap reinforcing mesh makes a great trellis.

I noticed flowers (okay, it was mostly weeds!) growing through some leftover reinforcing mesh at the roadside and it inspired me to make this trellis out of some scrap mesh I had kicking around for my own garden...

Tear articles you like out of magazines (not in the doctor's surgery or newsagent obviously!) etc. Alternatively use your phone (or camera) like a copier to take photos of pictures in magazines or newspapers, billboards, shop window displays, in the library, the bookshop and even the TV (if you're quick!). Snap away on the street, at work, in friends' houses and well, you can work it out...

When you see something awesome that stops you in your tracks, get as many photos as you can from different angles. Use these to incorporate aspects of the design you love into your own projects. Again, you can use an organisational tool like *Evernote, or* even better, a content sharing service like *Pinterest,* to store any cool stuff you might want to make one day (I even have a folder called 'one day').

Meet Fred the Moai Head.

Carved with a chainsaw and an axe from an old Ash tree that had to come down for safety reasons.

He is actually hollow, you can see if you look in his mouth!

A carving I saw online inspired me to make 'Fred the Moai Head' from a rotten old Ash tree I took down in my garden for safety reasons. Rather disconcertingly, birds often fly in and out of Fred's mouth as they feed on the insects that live in there!

Designers in the media are always dressing up old stuff, making new, clever, and sometimes useful things out of stuff other folks have thrown away. Don't be afraid to borrow and re-shape their ideas by adding a few twists of your own. My folder of 'one day' projects is huge and given the time and cash, I would build them all. From rustic art to fun stuff for the kids...

Stretch yourself: don't be afraid to ask or get up close. Knock on doors and say, 'sorry to bother you but I just love your XYZ, do you mind if I take a picture of it?' It will flatter most people and they'll have no problem with you taking a quick snap. Close-ups are so much better if you're going to replicate something and need to know how it goes together. If they do object, well then politely say sorry to have bothered you (and then zoom in anyway from the roadside, grumpy so and so's!).

Check out the online resources section in appendices one for some cool design websites. Look for inspiration everywhere you go and get creative with anything you're thinking of throwing away.

LISTEN

Everything makes some noise, however small, so keep your ears open (is that even possible?) and really *listen* to stuff! Listen out for the 'normal' sounds your stuff makes when things are working okay. Knowing exactly how stuff *should sound* will make you more aware of new or unusual sounds. Treat any new sound as a warning, because inevitably it does mean there's a problem. Remember each bump, creak, squeeeek, groan, tap, knock, squeal, and rattle *means something*. It means something's changed and although change might be good for us, it's terrible for most machines or physical things because it usually indicates a problem such as wear or even an impending failure.

As the surfaces of moving parts gradually wear, the tolerance or the space between the parts increases, which leads to more movement, and more movement means more noise. This extra movement is usually microscopic and so the increase in noise might be small and constant, a low-level drone or wine, or even just a different pitch to normal for example. Some wear related noise might only be apparent when under a particular load. i.e. the noise is worse when under a light or a heavy load. Heavy loads can tighten up some things and quieten them and conversely some things become noisier when under a heavy load (I never said this was going to be easy!).

Alternatively, intermittent sounds might indicate something is moving around unexpectedly. If something has broken rather than worn for example, if parts are in alignment one minute, but not the next or if something works in one position okay but not in another.

Generally, most sounds are uniform, timber should sound solid if tapped (not dull) and a motor should run free and constant with no stutters. Heavy things sound dense, hollow things ring and good things sound different to rotten things etc.

A good brick or tile will 'ring' like a bell when tapped, but a cracked one will sound dull.

Motors or mechanical movements like levers, cogs, pulleys, drivebelts, wheels etc. often sound rhythmic, melodic even, when they're working fine. It's a bit like the *clickety clack* of a train, you soon start to notice when something is disharmonious... if you're listening for it and recognise something has changed. Even Harley Davidson motorcycle engines, which produce a cacophony of crackles, clatters, and pops when you first hear them, have a uniformity and rhythm to their sound if you actually listen to them.

Sound (and touch to a degree) is particularly good for developing your inner gut feeling, if something doesn't sound (or feel) right, it's very likely there's a problem. Learn to trust it, stop, and investigate.

THE SOUNDS OF DOOM

You can often diagnose failing components as they break up internally using a simple stethoscope. I often use a special stethoscope for cars (very cheaply available) to identify failing bearings or difficult to trace noises on machines. The sounds a stethoscope reveals are miraculous in their ability to show whether moving parts are happy or not. Why do you think they are a favourite for doctors? You don't even need any special tools to take advantage of this, wise mechanics used to touch a long screwdriver tip or wooden dowel onto a suspected bad part, pop their thumb over the top press their ear to it. Try it, it works! Just be careful if you're near any moving parts, you don't want to get pulled into an engine by your ears!

BLAH, BLAH, BLAH

Tune in when you hear people talk about their DIY projects. Listen out for any DIY related problems, to learn what happened and what they did to fix it. Listening to other people's DIY stories will also help you identify who is knowledgeable about DIY in your circles, these are the guys to ask for help in the future if you're stuck and need help on your own project.

For example, don't tune out the neighbour complaining about his lawn mower not starting, because one day, your lawnmower might not start. Then the neighbour's little nugget about the air filter getting oily because he tipped the mower over, will race back into your consciousness and might be the problem you're having with your lawnmower. Information is all around us every day; tune in and think about how it might relate to future problems with your own stuff.

Also, listen out for advice from seasoned handy people in the media. TV, radio etc. often have practical advice columns or shows. I know some home makeover shows can be irritating, but you'll probably learn useful nuggets that might help you one day.

FEEL AND TOUCH

Touchy, feely stuff works, and not just on your partner, it's handy for DIY too. Closely linked to the listen technique above, is how things feel. Reach out and touch things, hold them, get a sense of how they feel in operation. BUT FIRST, think about what you're going to touch, is it safe? I know it's mostly obvious, but I'll say it anyway, be especially careful around...

- Electricity, even static or low volts (isolate or ground).

- Hot things, elements, bulbs etc. (wait until cool).

- Things that move or could potentially move (secure first).

- Anything sharp and not just actual cutting blades etc.

- Chemicals, including dry powders like cement, plaster etc.

- Heavy or awkward objects or materials (support well).

- Unstable, loose, or unsecured stuff.

- Angry or annoyed partners, because you didn't fix that thing...

If you're going near moving parts, especially any running rotating things like drivebelts, shafts or fan blades etc. always tuck in and secure lose hair/clothing. Fingers are very fragile so please use your head before going in with your hands. Oh, and gloves are nearly always a good idea if appropriate.

Take notice of and familiarise yourself with how things feel. Mechanical components have a distinctive feel to them when they're running smoothly. You can feel the vibrations of the gearbox in a car through the gear lever or the workings inside your cordless drill during use, for example.

Often the first inkling that something is about to fail or break, is a slight difference in the 'feel' or vibration. You might even notice a 'missing' feeling (as in misfiring or rapid on/off), or even a definite and distinct roughness in the running. You can even feel the contact a vehicle has with the road through the tyres, if you really concentrate!

Try turning rotary things when they're switched off to see how they feel. Because when things start to break up internally you can often feel a grinding or roughness as you turn them, this usually means failing bearings. A hit and miss or on/off feel might mean a problem with gears, missing or worn teeth (causing them to not mesh properly).

Many things get warm in use and some too hot to touch, (heaters, engines, exhaust pipes etc).

But if something is hotter than normal, shows scorch marks or is blackened, then something is wrong (like the cracked and dry joints on this PCB for example).

Most things get warm when running or in use; but try to compare with how hot you'd expect it to be in normal use. Faulty electrical parts often increase current load, causing overheating of wires or components. Also, check for proper lubrication, because something running tight creates extra friction which produces heat.

You can also *feel movements*, even tiny ones barely visible to the eye. If you have a car, try jacking up a front wheel (use an axle stand under the chassis). Then grasp the wheel and try to move it from side to side (3 and 9 o'clock) and you'll feel the steering mechanism move. Now try moving the wheel from top to bottom (12 and 6 o'clock); on modern vehicles, you shouldn't feel anything. Try spinning the wheel round and round, what do you feel? It should be smooth, if you can feel roughness something is catching or worn.

Your sense of touch when handling materials can also tell you a lot about them; if a length of timber feels unusually heavy it may have high moisture content and could shrink excessively. If cement feels lumpy inside the bag, (wear gloves when touching cement though, as it can really dry out or even burn your skin) it's soaked up moisture from somewhere and is now useless.

Learn what's normal by noticing how your stuff feels before there's a problem. Develop a 'sixth sense' for when things are 'off' and file all this touchy-feely stuff away to use as a reference for that 'it feels different somehow' moment in the future.

THUMPING THE TV

It used to be a classic scenario on TV shows that when the picture has a problem, you'd thump the top of the TV set and it would miraculously 'fix' the picture quality. Electrics have moved on from those days, but strangely enough thumping the top of things is still often the first resort of many folks, and here's the thing; they might just be onto something there.

It doesn't always need to be a thump either, I forget the amount of times I've picked up a malfunctioning 'something', only for it to start working again as if by magic. Often stuff with broken wires will start working again, (if only intermittently), because movement temporarily reconnects the wire ends.

Always touch things, pick them up, and turn them around and over, give them a wiggle or a shake, or dare I even say it... a gentle thump or two on the top, (common sense applies here of course, don't try this with your great grandfather's gold carriage clock).

Now I'm not suggesting, (even for a second), that this will 'fix' the problem permanently, but it might just give you an idea where to look in order to find out what the real problem is. That wiggle might just free up a sticking lever or moving something around might reveal a break in the power cable. Recently for example, our washing machine's display would flicker and click alarmingly, a sharp tap on the top of the machine just above the display stopped it immediately. Further investigation inside found a dry connection on the PCB, easily fixed with a soldering iron and a blob of solder...

YIELD!

No, not you, come on, up off your knees, I'm not the Queen. But related to touch, strength and feelings is the fact that everything eventually yields under stress. Sometimes under your tools, and sometimes even just in your hands. The problem is learning to feel when you've reached that yield point. Not enough power and the work won't get done, but too much power and you'll break something. Robert Pirsig in his famous *Zen and the Art of Motorcycle Maintenance* (not a book about motorcycle maintenance incidentally) calls it a *mechanics feel for the elasticity of a material*. We don't tend to think of metal being elastic, but it's very elastic when compared to glass for example, i.e. you'll need to be very careful fastening that mirror to the wall, one tiny bit too far and crack; seven years' bad luck.

Many materials are strong in one sense and weak in another. Hard but brittle for example. Concrete is an example we'll look at in more detail later, which is strong in compression but very weak in tension. We utilise a materials strength to achieve what we want to do. But we also need to learn a materials particular weaknesses to avoid accidental breakage whilst working with them. On the flip side, we can exploit those very same weaknesses to deliberately break the material, i.e. when we need to remove it etc.

Learning about yield is not just about feelings though. It combines all of the RELEARN method down to one single point, drawing inputs from all your senses, plus your knowledge and experience. And that single point is: when is enough, enough? Learning when a material has reached a point of so much stress it's going to fail, is about using your brain to constantly process (and evaluate) the inputs from your eyes, your ears, and your sense of touch.

Ultimately, it's experience which teaches you the yield point of each material, simply lifting up a piece of drywall the wrong way will cause it to snap on you (under its own weight) and you'll not likely do it again. Wood will bend a lot before yielding, unless there is a knot and then it'll snap in a heartbeat. Plastics; like chocolates, vary. Some are hard and snap easily and some are so soft you can bend them in half easily. And then there is metal. Well, metal is the hardest thing, until it's not. Then that feeling when you've gone too far and the threads yield and sheer off into nothingness is heart-breaking. Not to mention leaving you with a new and big problem to solve.

BEING CAREFUL

This Way Up. Handle with Care. Think Before You Act. Be careful. Watch Your Step etc. etc., are all quotes taken from workplace safety signs and all relate to how you handle stuff. Most stuff you'll be working with is easy to damage, either by handling it roughly or by holding it incorrectly whilst working on it. Some things are very heavy and made from extremely hard materials and yet their surfaces are very delicate and even tiny damage will render it useless. Anything inside an engine for example, all hard steel but clamp a part in a metal vice and scratch a surface which has been finely machined to a thousandth of an inch, game over, part ruined. A heavy door or worktop etc., also tough material, but put a tool down in a hurry and you've scratched the surface and are in trouble.

Be merciless in using dustsheets or thin sheet material to protect stuff. Use soft jaws in a vice to hold delicate items, use soft hammers made from hide, copper, plastic or even wood to gently tap stuff in to place. Never dump stuff or tools onto hard surfaces, always put scraps of something on the floor or surface first, i.e. timber, cardboard or old carpet etc. This protects both the item and the surface.

SMELL (NO, NO, NOT YOU; I MEAN ALL THE OTHER STUFF...)

Drains shouldn't smell too bad believe it or not!

Pipes should "fall" away from the house towards the larger main drains, taking water (and the yucky stuff!) away completely.

Bad smells can indicate poor falls or a blockage.

Learn to recognise and identify how things *smell*, because it's especially good in conjunction with your other senses i.e. smells can often reinforce your diagnosis. For example, you might *see a leak* first, but you might need to use your sense of smell to *identify the liquid*. For example, is it engine oil (smells almost burnt with a hint of fuel), normal air conditioning water discharge (no smell) or engine coolant/ antifreeze (odd fishy smell) on the driveway?

Alternatively, you might not be able to see anything, but your sense of smell tells you there's a hidden leak somewhere. For example, a musty smell in a bathroom might mean there's a small leak in the sealant around the bath or shower. Oh, and never ignore small leaks, as all leaks eventually cause additional problems...

Overheated stuff smells because all materials give off vapours when they get very hot, even metal. Train your nose to recognise how different things smell and mentally file away the smells of the everyday things you use or want to learn more about. Many things have quite characteristic and distinctive smells, such as...

- Burning plasticky smells from stuff means it's getting hot or starting to char. Dangerous, do not inhale.

- Burning or hot oil / lubricant smells mean excess friction is overheating the lubricant. Failure or seizure could be imminent.

- Fishy smells inside a vehicle might mean leaking coolant (and subsequent overheating once the coolant level drops).

- Musty or mouldy smells indicate that moisture is soaking into fabric, timber, insulation, walls, or floors or is getting past seals.

- Fishy or odd smells from electrical stuff, cables, plastic, insulation etc. could mean overheating problems (plastic smells when hot).

- Ozone smells can mean badly running electric motors, damaged contacts, worn out brushes or armatures etc., (often described as the 'electric train smell').

Use smell to identify different materials, remember how you check new shoes to see if they are leather or manufactured materials, yup, a good sniff is quicker than reading the label! This also works on stuff in unlabelled jars (but only until you remember to always label stuff you put in jars...) the different solvents used in paints for example. Only inhale a tiny amount from a safe distance though, because solvent fumes are dangerous to your health. Read ingredient lists on stuff you buy and learn to identify the solvent or active ingredients. Identifying the type of solvent or chemical will help you choose a suitable cleaning agent (oil paint = white spirit, acrylic paint = water etc.).

Again, be very careful here, almost all gasses and fumes are dangerous to your health. Use your common sense and take notice of any bad smells, but don't get up close and inhale like a smoker after a ten-hour flight!

Oh, and be aware that your brain is very good at ignoring smells after its registered them. You might think the smell has 'gone away,' but it might just be your brain deciding it's no longer important or relevant and has filtered it out of your consciousness. Remember when you first go into a house and you are immediately 'hit' by a smell? Yet the smell seems to 'disappear' after a while. The smell is probably still there, but your brain has filtered it out as uninteresting and not needed. Dog owners, cigarette or pipe smokers and scruffy buggers beware...

INFORMATION

I'm hesitant to use the other "I" word here as I don't want you to run away gibbering like an eejit, but use it I must, because instructions (wince) are a biggie. If the thought of instructions fills you with dread, please persevere because following instructions will help you in the end. Now I don't mean glancing at them and then waving them around saying 'I don't understand them'. I mean actually sitting down and reading them, several times if necessary. Because instructions and any other information you find is the knowledge which fills the gaps in your understanding. This isn't just because you're new to all this practical stuff either, even someone with 30 years' experience has not done every type of job (or even close) or can remember all the facts and figures you sometimes need (and yes that includes me!). Instructions and further research to find information is a key part of the process of understanding what it is you're about to undertake.

Find instructions and information to help you...

- *Diagnose* problems. Check to see if other owners report similar symptoms and if it's common.

- Find potential *solutions* from others who have fixed their own problems on similar stuff.

- Find *technical data*. Find torque wrench settings for a specific bolt, wiring diagrams, tyre pressures etc.

- Find exploded diagrams to illustrate how stuff goes together.

- Find 'How to' information when you're learning a new skill. Plastering a wall or how to paint plastic for example.

- Find spare parts or repair kits etc.

Don't try to learn it all, there's no need to know or learn how to do every-thing, instead, target *just what you need to learn* to *do the task in hand*. Harness-ing the expertise of others is a smart way to work, utilise their knowledge for your own needs, let them make your mistakes for you. Treat your research as a DIY 'app' or giant USB stick drive you can plug into your brain whenever you need to find answers for your DIY queries.

Woodrow Wilson commented that he not only used all the brains that he had, but all that he could borrow.

For example, a few years ago, when I had my first meeting with the Profes-sor running a masters course I wanted to do, he asked me to bring something I'd written. I took a huge three month report I'd done documenting the lessons learned on a £10M aid project in Uganda I'd worked on. He flipped straight though it to the end and read *only* the lessons learned and conclusion sections (less than 5% of the report). Smart, because to be honest, everything else was just setting the scene. The only real 'take away' value in the report was in those last two sections. So, during your own research copy my old professor and look out for words like...

- Conclusions and lessons learned.
- Downloads, PDF's etc.
- How to Videos.
- Installation guides, (usually from manufacturers).
- Summaries.
- Technical details (manufacturers spec sheets, safety data sheets etc.).
- Technical support lines or emails.
- Techniques and 'how to...'
- Tips and tricks.

- Top ten lists or top 'xyz' lists.
- Troubleshooting.
- Tutorials.

Don't forget to *cherry pick only the facts you need* and don't get distracted! Once you find the information you need...

- Favourite or bookmark using long descriptive tags.
- Make notes: online, notebook or folder, post it notes etc.
- Photocopy, scan, or photograph (see apps next).
- Use an app: Evernote, OneNote, Google Keep etc.
- Save, save as, homegroups, libraries, cloud drives, share.
- Tear out and save (don't try this in the library...).

It doesn't matter how you store this information and you'll know what works for you. The important thing is that you squirrel it all away for future reference where you can easily find it. All this information is out there right now waiting for you. Info from local repair shops, service centres, local tradesmen, manufacturers, books, newspapers, magazines, brochures and of course increasingly accessible on the internet.

Your research might be to discover; 'where to find spare parts' or 'what is the torque setting for a specific bolt' etc. Or it might be job specific, 'how to' information, e.g. 'how to drive drywall screws home properly' etc.

Let's look at a few different places to find information...

BROCHURES AND THE DREADED INSTRUCTIONS

Always, *always* keep the brochures, guarantees and instructions which come with the stuff you buy, (I know, I know, the horror of it!). Because seriously, if you bin them, you're sure to need them one day. Stick them in a folder.

Tech folks talk a lot about the infamous phrase 'Read the Instructions Stupid', because it really is the best place to start. Even if they're in the worst 'Chinglish'* possible, it's likely they'll still point you in the right direction or at least get you started. Don't just use the instructions as a last resort when you're already stuck. * 'Chinglish' is the rather derogatory term for badly translated instructions from Chinese to English, hence 'Chin-glish'

For example, the instructions for a chainsaw sharpening tool I recently bought were indecipherable. Therefore, I searched on YouTube.com and watched a video showing a similar machine to help me understand the principles. I then applied what I had seen to my own machine and got it sorted out in less than half an hour.

Especially keep any parts list or diagrams and exploded images as these become invaluable if you need to *go inside* to carry out repairs once the guarantee period has expired. If it's going to rescue you and save the day in some future crisis, first you'll have to be able to find it.

Go and grab a cup of coffee or cup of tea and organise your own half-heartedly stored pile of instructions and guarantees etc. I use a ring binder and plastic inserts or pockets which are ideal for the little booklets many things come with.

ONLINE: THE 'ALL SEEING' INTERNET

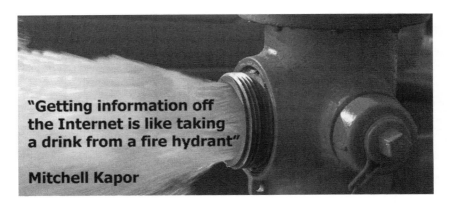

"Getting information off the Internet is like taking a drink from a fire hydrant"

Mitchell Kapor

People post a truly enormous amount of ~~useless rubbish~~ practical information online every day. The only slight problem sometimes is finding it among all the irrelevant or inaccurate stuff.

If you've never done a particular task before and worry about staying safe (and you should!) plus you want to make a good job; search online for a tutorial or better still, a video or three to show you how. Find them, watch them, take it all in and then you're ready to have a practise go yourself.

Search engines like Google allow you ask questions and then you can filter whether to see web pages, images, videos etc. Simply click on the tab or format you want to see. Here's how to find the most accurate stuff for your query on the web...

IT'S ALL ABOUT KEYWORDS

Google's chrome browser works well for me, but you can use your favourite flavour of search engine if you're a little bit indie. Forgive me if you already know all this, but for those that don't.... the words you use to search for something on the internet are *keywords* and search engines understand little else. Be very specific with your choice of words or you'll get irrelevant results, millions of them probably. Here are some *keywords* you could try adding to your query or search, depending what you're looking for...

- The manufacturers name, Bosch, Siemens, Volvo, Kitchen Aid etc.

- The specific model name, type, or number.

- Actual serial numbers taken from the label or box.

- Use words to identify parts affected, e.g. switch, handle, motor, etc.

- Use words that describe your problem, e.g. not working, stopped, makes noise, does a specific thing etc.

- Try informal names for your item or slang words.

- Try different regional words, e.g. tire vs. tyre or silencer vs. muffler or fixing vs. fastener etc.

- Try trade or brand names which have become generic terms or even verbs. Formica, Hoover, Jet Ski, Q-tips, Scotch tape, Sellotape, Sharpie, Tupperware, Velcro etc. etc. are all brand names which are now a part of common language.

- Try alternative words which have similar meanings: *fix* or *mend* or *repair* or *adjust* or *overhaul or rectify,* and so on.

- Try words like 'exploded parts diagram' or 'parts list'.

- Try adding 'tutorial' to your keywords.

- Start your search with 'How to fix [insert item here]'

- Try adding 'owners club' or 'fan club',

- Try adding 'blog' or 'forum'.

- Try adding 'customer service' or 'help' or 'online support' or 'advice line' or 'reviews' or 'technical help' etc.

- Last but definitely not least, look for the word 'FAQ'; and nope, it's not cockney wordplay for "what the faq's gone wrong?" it means 'frequently asked questions' and they are frequently asked for a reason... (i.e. it's a common failure point etc.).

You can combine *any* of the above, try adding serial numbers to manufacturers to forums for example. The order of keywords can be important too. Search engines add importance to the words at the beginning of your search query, so put the important stuff first, like the manufacturer and model numbers etc.

Also, be accurate; don't use *two* if everyone else uses *II* or *2*. Remember that search engines are stupid* and will return exactly what you ask for, whether it's relevant to your search or not. To some search engines, *2* and *two* and *II* can be as different to each other as *dog*, *duck,* and *dingbats.*
*Sorry Larry and Sergey, still you're getting better all the time...

If you're getting too many non-relevant results because your search keywords can mean different things, try adding the non-relevant results to your search with the *minus symbol* in front. Search engines will then ignore this word in their results, well mostly! Although search engines are getting better at recognising phrases, sometimes it's still worth joining words together by putting *quotation marks* around the phrase you're looking for. Then the search engine will only look for that phrase specifically.

Try to think what someone else would write when looking for whatever it is you need. Try phrasing your query as a question someone is likely to ask, 'how to fix a leaky tap' or even 'my faucet is leaking' for example. Remember that more words are often better (up to about ten) and try omitting the small connecting or *stop* words (a, and, of, to etc.) as search engines often ignore them anyway.

For example, after hitting a rock whilst mowing my lawn I broke the blade holder, and could I find a new one? Nope. In addition to the make and model of the lawn mower, I tried 'blade holder', I tried 'blade mount', 'blade adapter' and even 'blade hub' but nope, I just wasn't hitting the right one for my machine. Eventually I found one using the keywords 'blade boss', I mean, who would have though it? Finding the right keyword is an exercise in experimentation sometimes, try to think laterally in addition to the 'obvious' stuff...

SEARCHING IMAGES

One of the best and quickest ways to find great content and results on the web is to hit the *images* tag on your search engine, limiting the results to just images. Your brain can take in huge amounts of information visually, much faster than reading the text excerpts of each website. The end result is that on the internet, a picture really is worth a thousand words.

If an image on a website has a title and a properly detailed description which matches the words you searched for, there's a high chance the image (and the page it's on) will provide relevant and useful information to you.

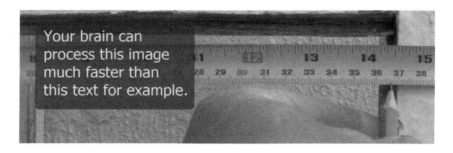

Your brain can process this image much faster than this text for example.

SEARCHING VIDEOS

Video is fast becoming the 'most searched for' form of info. And that's because it's the perfect medium for instructional tutorials. However, with content ranging from the fantastically useful to the downright pointless, you have rather a lot of searching and filtering to do. Use the same keyword rules to find useful videos as you would when searching the web generally, (don't forget YouTube is a search engine itself). If someone has described his or her video properly, there's a high chance it will be relevant and show you what you want to learn.

Try to find videos made by professionals (in the field you're researching). Sure, there is a lot of useful amateur content out there, but you can't beat the stuff from the pros. Always take a few seconds to look at the video publishers 'about' tab. On YouTube, click the publishers name and then you'll find the 'about' tab on the right in the menu bar under the header image.

Don't just search for videos on YouTube either, although the biggest, they are not the only ones hosting useful videos. You can add the word *video* to any of your search queries or use the dedicated video section of your preferred search engine, which should produce results from across all the video hosting websites.

JOIN ONLINE FORUMS

Forums are where folks go these days to rant about stuff they love and more often, about stuff that's gone horribly wrong. Regular web searches include results from most open forums, but to ask questions and get help from more experienced members, you'll have to join. All are free.

Forums are one of the best ways to ~~waste time~~, I mean find a solution to your problem. Because from what I've seen, there is a forum for everything no matter how obscure. You'll wade through a lot of irrelevance and silly stuff on some forums, but eventually you'll find the information you need in one of them.

First some do's and don'ts regarding forums if you're new to them. Although forums aim to be friendly places, folks can be very prickly if you violate forum etiquette (and I don't mean that nastily). It's because most forums are populated by real enthusiasts and they don't suffer fools gladly; especially if you sign up today asking a question that's in the FAQ (frequently asked questions). This labels you as lazy, i.e. too lazy to do a quick search to see if the answer is in the archives. The moral is *always use the forum search box first!* Pop in your query and check to see if there are already answers to your problem before posting your own question. If the forum archive answers your question, you might consider posting a thankyou on the general board... It all puts you in good stead for the next time.

In addition, before posting a question on a forum or board, double check it's in the right part of the forum, some forums are huge with lots of specific sub-forum boards. It's also a good idea to politely introduce yourself or take a few minutes to fill in the forum profile page so that other people know you're real and not a robot or some pesky spammer.

When describing your problem, it's great to be descriptive, but if it's difficult to explain, consider including photos rather than a thousand-word story. And don't bother with the self-depreciating stuff like 'Sorry, I am a noob' because they'll know that as soon as you open your mouth. Just be nice and don't forget to give a little back. If someone helps by posting a solution, pop back, thank them and say whether it worked or not, because someone else in the future stumbling across the thread might find it useful.

Many forum threads end up dangling because people don't make the time to go report back about how they got on and how the problem was finally resolved. The more help you give back, the more likely you are to receive help next time. It's called karma...

CONTACT TECHNICAL DEPARTMENTS

Some of the better/bigger manufacturers have excellent technical departments, where you can get free help and advice about your specific machine. Quality varies, but I've used these to great effect on many different projects from fixing washing machines to learning how to install high tech building materials etc.

Normally contact is through a phone number and it can take a few attempts to get though. Email addresses are getting increasingly common, but the response time varies from a day or two to 'never'. Follow up with a phone call if they 'forget' to reply to your query.

If you can't find a technical department number on the literature or online, try calling any numbers you do find, (sales usually) and ask the person to transfer you to a technical representative or give you their direct number.

Same rules apply to technical departments as forums though; make sure you've read the instructions first. You'll get short shrift if you ask a question that's in the instructions, although I guess you can still call if you don't understand the said instructions. Also make sure you have any paperwork you have in front of you because they may ask for model or serial numbers etc.

BOOKS, LIBRARIES, JOURNALS, MAGAZINES, AND TV

Once there was a time before the internet and do you know, it ticked along pretty well, so don't dismiss the offline world when it comes to finding information. Books are of course a prime resource for learning about DIY, either in general or for task specific stuff, take this book for example *cough*! The cheapest way is to try your local library and don't forget to ask if they have access to a bigger database of books (this is why you need to plan ahead!), because many have inter-library lending schemes, hugely increasing the number of books available to you.

Additionally, offline sources like libraries (especially in universities) often have access to mind bogglingly massive amounts of information in databases as well, in what's often called the 'deep web'. This is information not indexed and therefore not accessible by public search engines (unless you are a CIA hacker...), but this info is accessible via a browser and specific websites once you have the access details etc. Information stored in the deep web includes current thinking from trade journals (there are thousands), research, microfiche records, old physical archives and much, much more. It's estimated that the deep web is 500 times larger than the 'surface web'...

Ask library staff for more info and if there's any information available that's not physically in the library. Note: Part of the *deep web* includes the *dark web*, which is the parts of the internet deliberately hidden from the outside world, mostly for legal reasons, but you don't want to go wandering around in there, nope, best not, because there are all sorts of funny folks in there...

Don't discount old-fashioned encyclopaedias either if you just want to read up on general principles about how something in the world works.

Magazines cover the most popular practical subjects of the day to tempt you to buy them. This means there are magazines on every topic imaginable, and they have one great advantage, the information is current. However, don't forget to check the back catalogue as well, since many DIY "how to" topics stay relevant for a long time. Even as a professional, I regularly learn something new, some tip, trick, or way of working from a great magazine article.

Check for an online version of the magazine as well or take advantage of any 'free' or introductory subscriptions to check out what they have and get access to all the back copies, a huge resource. Don't forget to cancel it at the end of the free period if it's not what you need though. To see if there is a magazine that caters for your interests, visit the *yahoo magazines directory*, or just do a web search for your interest plus the word magazine (e.g. wooden boat + magazine etc.)

TV is awash with home improvement shows these days and although they can be a little unrealistic on timescales and work involved, they can provide interesting inspiration for your own projects. Keep a notebook handy to record anything that interests you. Great for those evenings where you just need a break from your own project.

Check your TV listings for home improvement, home makeover or self build re-runs and copy the tips and techniques they use on your own projects.

ASK PEOPLE YOU KNOW FOR HELP

I know this is obvious, but I also know you don't like to bother anyone because you think your questions are 'stupid', but here's the thing. People LOVE talking about their projects, what they did and how much money they spent or saved. In fact, I find people are only too willing (too much sometimes!) to talk about, what went wrong and often what a PITA it all was!

So, learn from their experience and avoid making the same rookie mistakes they made. Need a new kitchen for example? Chances are some of your family or friends have already been there and have the paint splattered T-shirt. Ask around to see what they did and what they learned.

Colleagues at work are often a good resource too. Tune in next time someone starts a tale about his or her latest project at home. Listen to what went well and what went wrong on the job. Note down the places they went for good deals from useful suppliers. Don't be afraid to ask questions, because people are even more willing to chatter on about their projects at the coffee machine, just don't forget you're supposed to be at work...

"From the errors of others, a wise man corrects his own."

Publilius Syrus

Your neighbours are probably doing stuff too. Keep an eye open for the comings and goings of deliveries, materials, or tradesmen in the street. Visiting other houses of a similar design is incredibly useful in helping you decide how you want your own place to look. You'll be amazed how different each house is on your street, even if outwardly they all look similar.

Keep your eyes open when you're out and about too, if you pass someone doing something you're interested in, don't be shy, approach them and ask if you can watch them for a moment or to ask a question or two. Just say 'Wow that looks great-interesting-clever, how do you do that?'

Just about everyone I've ever worked with likes a bit of flattery and appreciation of their skills, who wouldn't? Be sensible if the person is using power tools though, wait for a suitable pause before approaching and make sure the person can see you clearly as you approach. Startling someone using a chainsaw is not going to make you any friends!

That leaves any 'older' people you know, and no, I don't mean someone over thirty, I mean someone who is a genuine senior. Because regardless of what people under twenty think about older folks; many older people are a goldmine of knowledge and often have useful skills or experience to share. Just imagine, all that experience...

And all you need to do is ask, and sometimes you don't even need to ask... (my father tells me *ALL* the time...). In my experience, folks love to talk about what they have done or learned on a project. So why not take advantage of all that knowledge, all that experience and lessons learned to help you avoid making the same mistakes? Treat the knowledge of others as a resource; a tool to be used, just like any other.

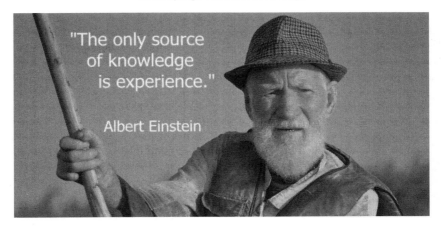

"The only source of knowledge is experience."

Albert Einstein

Your family and friends can also help indirectly as well. They might know what you like and could act as a sounding board for your ideas or they can babysit if you have very young children, so you can concentrate fully on your project etc. This can also make sense for safety reasons and will definitely make the job go quicker, well worth a bottle of wine or two! Once your children get older though, include them by giving them something to do. Kids just love painting, but are less keen on sandpapering and preparation work for some reason...

ASK A LOCAL PROFESSIONAL FOR ADVICE

Not always easy to do and it will depend on your confidence to walk into a place and ask your questions, especially once it becomes clear to the staff you're not buying anything today. But don't forget, the worst-case scenario is they'll say *'sorry, can't help you'* which only takes you back where you started. Sometimes though, you might need a spare part, and many places will give you helpful advice on how to fit it etc. In addition, there is always the potential to sell you replacement parts etc. in the future; smart businesses know this and should look after you to ensure you come back. Build relationships by always using the same supplier if you can, then they won't mind answering your questions from time to time.

LEARNING ABOUT YOUR HOME

Armed with all your tingling senses, now's a good time to explore your home and develop a good understanding of how it's constructed. Examine all the nooks and crannies, and yes, especially the scary places like under the floorboards, that dark cupboard under the stairs and in the attic! It's important you understand your home intimately to avoid nasty surprises during any work you do.

Start with these simple things...

- Check which way the floor boards run because this tells you which way your floor joists run, (joists run perpendicular or 90° to the floor boards).

- Find which walls have floor joists going into them (usually the joists go into the walls parallel to the floor boards, as noted above) this means the wall is load bearing.

- Follow the wires from your fuse box and find out where the main routes are around the house. Look for *runs* (removed or disturbed floorboards etc.) or access panels and ducts if you're lucky.

- Follow any water and any heating pipes you can see and learn how to isolate them. Again, look for runs and feel for warm floorboards (probably a pipe under there). Access panels might reveal shut off valves etc.

- Examine your walls to find out what materials they used and how thick they are etc. (measure them at doorways or windows).

- Look in any basements, crawl spaces or attics; what can you see? Pipes, wires, tops of walls, timberworks etc.

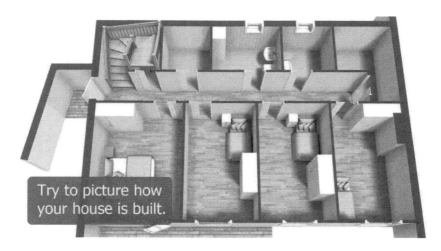

Try to picture how your house is built.

Try to picture your home as an empty shell, ignore all the finished stuff. Picture the walls, the floors, the ceilings, and roof, how does it all sit together?

Does everything make sense? What sits on top of what? If you find parts that don't look logical, you might have hidden structural things like steel beams supporting stuff. Try to get copies of the original builder's drawings (try the local planning and building control dept.).

Solid masonry walls or bigger timber stud work walls carrying upper floors or walls are often load-bearing. Lighter timber walls or studwork internally is often non-loadbearing as they carry only their own weight.

Also, be aware that not everyone is as good as they should be, i.e. there are very poor tradesmen and unscrupulous homeowners abound. Don't assume that everything is exactly as it should be, always uncover things carefully and constantly evaluate what you find. Stop at the first sign that something is amiss and seek advice.

Building up a basic understanding of how your house goes together will help you make sensible decisions about what is feasible to do without spending the earth. They say you can do anything with enough money and time, but if your plans require that much money and time, maybe you should stop and ask yourself "is this the right house for me?".

EXPERIENCE

Your own experience is the most reliable tool in your arsenal. You are a great source of information about your own stuff because no one knows it like you do. I guess we've all taken the car to the mechanic only for it to behave faultlessly, but you know, deep down, that something is not working properly, and you are most likely right.

All the previous sections come together here. All the little inputs you have over time might help you diagnose a problem (which is often half the battle) and thus a solution. Practise is also experience (the *Developing Practical Skills* chapter is next), do it, remember what you learn and keep on doing it!

Plus, if something happened once, it might happen again (especially with computers...). "But I forgot what I did last time" you say; so, remember what I said about keeping records earlier? Either file away handwritten notes or leverage technology and make notes online via *Evernote* or such like. I love Evernotes ability to handle lots of different formats, from a quick photo to a hand-written note. Just jot down what you did, what you just saw or stuff which inspires you and click save. Job done.

I also have a folder on my computer called *lessons learned* where I start a new page on anything I've fixed where it was tricky to find information or where the solution was a little complicated. Make notes on the solution you used and list any sources etc. Easy and it'll be soooo useful next time...

It's often quoted that Michelangelo was 87 years old when he uttered the words "I am still learning" ... He probably didn't say that according to the academics, but semantics aside, be like Michelangelo! Always be learning and adding to your experience.

DON'T IGNORE THE WARNING BELLS

As much as we like to personalize machines and property, they do not have bad days or moods or personalities (arguably, some old stuff does, but that's another book). If something looks, sounds, or feels different, then something *has* changed. Occasionally these tiny changes are insignificant, but more often they signal that something 'not nice' is going to happen. It could mean something extra's in the works (a foreign body like grit or water), or you're losing something (metal wearing away or something is leaking). The actual failure point might be far in the future and undramatic, like a dry and squeaking door hinge for example. Or, it could be in a split second and problematic; like a key snapping off in your neglected front door lock for example (and yes, you do need to lubricate them once in a while...).

We use such a huge variety of stuff every day, fast stuff (engines), slow stuff (doors), little stuff (jewellery clasps), big stuff (wardrobes), plus all the stuff in the workplace. It's easy for something small that's new or different to drown in the everyday melee.

Train your sub-conscious to notice and register tiny details as you go about your routine, consciously think about them to put them on the mental radar we talked about earlier. Don't ignore these small changes in case it's a warning of impending doom; don't be that guy driving down the street on a flat tyre who says at the end of his journey, "Well I did think it felt a bit funny" (but ignored it). Your sub-conscious is powerful and largely idle, so tell it to monitor the clickity clack for that one time when it goes clackity click; because it might just save the day.

INTUITION IS USUALLY RIGHT (SO DON'T IGNORE IT!)

Closely related to the above I know, but in addition to watching out for the actual physical changes around you, also listen to the little voice inside you. Even if you think you don't know very much right now, believe me, your intuition is constantly learning and growing from your experiences, even if you don't recognise it yet.

Intuition or insight is the initial little flash of *knowing* that might just stop you from making a mistake. It doesn't even come as a fully-fledged thought, but rather as a little niggle in the back of your mind. It's easy for the uninitiated to ignore but learn to recognise it and act. First, stop what you're doing and think for a moment, trust your instincts, and let it come to you. If nothing comes, mentally go through what you're doing again to encourage the niggle to turn into something concrete you can act on. Learn to listen to your intuition and you'll have a powerful ally in your camp to avoid screw-ups, big and small.

With experience, intuition, and a little dollop of luck, maybe you'll avoid making a mistake or you'll identify a failing part early on, maybe you'll even prevent a catastrophic failure from happening at all. Just by stopping and listening to the inner you and carrying out a few simple tweaks, maintenance or repairs before things get out of hand.

SOLUTIONS

Solutions are simple, once you've arrived at them, as they say. Prior to that, it's not always so easy. But don't panic if you don't see a solution straight away and never fear getting stuck. Sometimes getting stuck leads you to that quiet point where you just need to sit and stare at the problem (or even go away and leave it for a while). Only then will some little overlooked or ignored nugget of information bob to the surface of your consciousness. And sometimes that little nugget is all you need to figure out a solution, call it an 'Ah ha' moment if you like. And that's what the RELEARN method is all about, showing you the principles or way of looking at stuff, so you can work out for yourself, the specific details of your task or project in hand.

By harvesting all sorts of 'data' through the RELEARN way of looking at the world, you'll avoid *rigid thinking*, that crippling condition which switches off the more creative and inventive parts of your brain, which also happens to be your solution finding powerhouse! The RELEARN method is about noticing all those previously ignored little details and drawing them all together to a logical point where you can look at it all, draw some conclusions, and come up with a plan to move forward, or find a solution to whatever problem the project has thrown at you.

Over time, practising and utilising the RELEARN method will train your *common sense*, your *horse sense*, or (my favourite), your *gumption,* or whatever folks call it in your part of the world, (thanks again Mr Pirsig for reminding me about the word). Gumption is an unshakable belief that there is a solution, a belief that you can find it, and a belief that you can carry out that solution. With enough gumption, you'll find workable solutions for all your practical problems. Whether it's figuring out what went wrong with the lawn mower or deciding whether the wall between the lounge and dining room is load bearing or not.

Has all that theory sent you to sleep yet? No? Wow; then you're ready to try some practical stuff... roll up those sleeves and let's go...

DEVELOPING PRACTICAL SKILLS

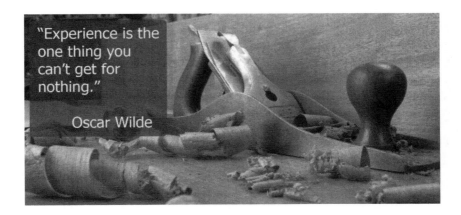

"Experience is the one thing you can't get for nothing."

Oscar Wilde

Being handy is more than just understanding the theory about how the practical world works though. To actually build, fix, improve or maintain something you're going to have to apply your growing theoretical knowledge and translate it into practical action. That means learning how to use tools and working with materials.

PRACTISE MAKES PERFECT (CORNY BUT OH, SO TRUE)

And yes, I know you don't want to hear this part, but bear with me, it'll save you time in the end. Clarence Day once said that *'information's pretty thin stuff unless mixed with experience,'* and the best way to gain experience is to practise (if you don't like the word practise, call it *studying* or *training* instead... is that better?). If you don't believe me, watch this TED talk first, Youtube.com/watch?v=f2O6mQkFiiw to learn what happens to the brain when you practise. The video also shows mentally practising stuff improves your skills nearly as much as physically practising, how awesome is that?

And yet, most folks seem bemused by the concept of practising DIY skills as if it's an incredulous notion; they just want to get straight on with the job. Can you think of anything else you'd do without a few trial runs first? What do you think your chances are of producing perfect work with no experience and no practise? I'll tell you; not very good. Think back to the first time you did anything in your life (from learning to walk, to learning to drive). All things improve with practise; (come on, you know this makes sense!).

As an apprentice, I had to 'practise' *for years* at college before building something on site unsupervised. I gained experience slowly, starting with tiny (often horrible!) jobs building up in size and responsibility over the years.

Play around with scrap materials, practising sawing straight (over and over again), by cutting a length of timber up like a bread loaf, hammer in a bunch of nails or drive in a load of screws; all this will pay off enormously in building your confidence and skills over time.

"Practice yourself in little things, and thence proceed to greater"

Epictetus

Recently I had to supervise a bunch of kids hammering in nails at a school open day. Age ranged from 5 to 12 and that's pretty much how they scored too. Some kids got it after a few nails and were hammering nails in like a pro, but for some, it took a whole lot more instruction and practise before they'd stop bending every nail. What I'm trying to say is that we all start close to zero, but with practise, (either a little or a lot) you'll make very rapid progress. Anything you do which trains your hand and eye co-ordination, will help build useful DIY skills.

PRACTISE BY HELPING OTHERS

If you're not quite ready to work on your own projects just yet, consider offering to help a handy friend out. Not many people would turn down the offer of an extra pair of hands on a project, regardless of your current skill level. Even if all you can do is pass tools, carry material, or help to clear up, you'll get to learn what each tool is and what it does and how important a clean and tidy workplace is.

You'll also learn about the different materials involved on a real job, especially if you go and help pick them up from the store (great introduction). You'll learn about choosing materials, loading them into or on top of a vehicle, getting them home safe and storing them properly once you get there. You'll learn about the process and order of work. You could also volunteer to make the vast quantities of coffee all properly planned projects need...

Most importantly, when helping, treat nothing as irrelevant or boring... *ever*; because there's always something to learn. Even the most mundane task will teach you something about procedure or technique, but only if you're receptive enough to notice it. Remember the 'wax on, wax off' lessons in The Karate Kid movie?

For example, sweeping up should teach you that...

- A clean and tidy workplace is a safe workplace (you'll have no accidents because you're not falling over stuff).

- A tidy workplace is more productive (because you know where everything is and access to tools and materials is good).

- A clean workplace gives you a more pleasant working experience.

- A clean workplace keeps your clothes cleaner and stops dust and muck spreading throughout the rest of your place.

- A tidy site makes other people 'on site' happy (read the other half/client/neighbours/children etc.).

And that's just from sweeping up, absolutely amazing huh... 'Watch and copy' is how we figure out most things in life; from learning how to hold a pencil to learning how to use a computer; being handy is *exactly* the same. Pay attention to what's happening around you; what tools can you see and how are they used? What materials can you see and how are they handled? What techniques or little tips or tricks do you notice? Ask questions if you don't understand, my 'master' used to tell me "it's better to ask a 'stupid' question than to make a stupid mistake" and he's right. Remember 'she who asks a question is a fool for five minutes; she who does not ask a question remains a fool forever'... so ask away!

Regardless of how handy you are, you'll learn from those around you. I've worked with hundreds of people over the years and I've learned something from *all* of them, (sometimes something small and occasionally something revelatory). Take advantage of the fact that everyone's knowledge or experience is unique and learn from them.

WARNING: DO TRY THIS AT HOME

When you're ready, just like learning to ride a bicycle, there comes a point where you just need to start the job. Afterwards, it's normal to feel it could have gone better, been quicker or have been easier. Whether you miscalculated or forgot something (like reading the instructions!) or you pushed too hard on a tool and slipped or damaged something because you didn't handle it properly. Learning from mistakes and experimentation is an important part of learning most things, and DIY is no different.

Accept that you will make mistakes, (even I do, very occasionally), but I always know why I made a mistake (usually failing to think far enough ahead on a design of my own at home) and although frustrating, it's rarely disastrous. Most things are 'rescuable'. Just suck it up and carry on. It might take a little longer or use a little extra material, but rarely is a screw up disastrous. The biggest damage might be to your ego or confidence, but that doesn't cost you a penny (it's best if no one else finds out though...).

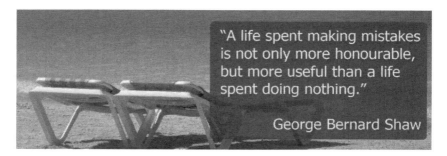

"A life spent making mistakes is not only more honourable, but more useful than a life spent doing nothing."

George Bernard Shaw

Even professionals are fallible when working on new or challenging stuff. There's not a professional in the world who's never made a mistake on a client's job, (except me of course, *whistles innocently*).

Every little project will teach you a little more about what works or doesn't work with each tool and material. You'll learn where your weaknesses are and what tool or material needs more work come practise time. Remember also that, 'nothing is a waste of time if you use the experience wisely'.

Learn from your experiences (or mistakes) and study to plug any gaps ready for next time. Dramatically improve the odds in your favour by preparing well beforehand. Research thoroughly, practise lots and then take the time to think things through before starting. It's better to learn from a mistake than let fear stop you doing something because you *might* make a mistake.

However, I will be honest; there might be times when you'll think, 'why the heck did I not get someone in to do this?' You just have to pick yourself up, dust yourself off (literally sometimes) think about what *exactly* went wrong, research some more and learn from it. If you persevere and see it through to the finish, you'll be twice as proud once the jobs done *and* you'll have gained valuable *experience*.

"Anyone who's never made a mistake has never tried anything new."

Albert Einstein

You could make a start by taking apart something that's going into the recycle bin? (i.e. where it doesn't matter if you break something). Open it up and have a look inside. Try to identify the different components; where does the power come in for example, or try to figure out what each part does. Read the *Repairing Stuff* chapter for more help with this.

Or you could take a look at something simple, have a gentle fiddle with a cabinet door hinge for example. Turn each screw half a turn and watch to see what it does to the door and then back again. Adjust that catching one and even up the gaps while you're at it! Remember, getting to know how stuff works when things are good *will* help you diagnose failures or problems later.

If you're feeling more adventurous, you could try to make something small from scratch, something not too complicated or time consuming. Something where you can simply start over if it goes horribly wrong. Bird nest boxes are ideal incidentally, or a cool bird table or bird feeder for example (I'm detecting a little bird theme here...). Search for "nest box plans" using Google images to find lots of very simple, easy to follow free plans.

Incidentally, you'll be doing your bit to help the birds; modern houses are nearly impenetrable for birds and so nesting opportunities are dwindling. Plus, I'll show you how to saw square, and use a hammer later on in this chapter, so there is no excuse and what perfect timing!

Lastly here, make yourself comfortable (nope, not on the sofa...) I mean don't struggle. Make the time to look after yourself, eat well, take a hot drink (or a cold one) when you want one and wear the right clothes, i.e. be comfortable. If you're too cold and can't feel your toes, how likely is it you'll spot that tiny thing in your rush to get finished and back in the warm? Not very likely I'd say. If you're too warm you're likely to be snappy and irritable too and more prone to impatience and having an accident. Keep cool. If it's scorching hot start real early in the morning and take the afternoons off and go do something fun to cool down. There is nothing better than an early start in the summertime now is there?

UNDERSTANDING HOW TOOLS WORK

Understanding the basic operation of a tool is fundamental in mastering it.

Always remember...
let the tool do the work!

(Let's get the boring bit out of the way). Before using any newly acquired or borrowed tool, *first read any instruction manual or operating instructions* on the box etc. (and yes, I really do mean it!) Then pick up the tool and relate it to what you've just read, i.e. identify what the different parts are, how to hold it properly and which part actually does the work.

For example, most handsaws have teeth that cut on the front edge, so put the effort into the push stroke to cut the timber and don't waste energy putting pressure on the return or pull stroke because there's no cutting action there (unless it's a Japanese pull saw of course...). But most tools need multiple inputs to operate correctly; for example, you need to *align* it properly, to apply a suitable *force* and use it at a suitable *speed*. Let's look at these briefly...

ALIGNMENT

Holding tools at (even slightly) the wrong angle means one of two things, either they will not work at all or they will slip. This could damage the tool itself, the workpiece or worse still, you. Practice holding tools so the working parts are in the best position related to your workpiece. Some tools such as screwdrivers need to be perfectly in line with the fasteners you're using and other tools such as drills, hammers (kind of, the head is in line though), saws, spanners, and wrenches etc. need to be 90° to the work surface or fastener.

Push tools such as spanners and wrenches fully down onto the nut/ bolt head or there's a high risk of slipping and *rounding off* the corners of nut/ bolt heads, which makes them very difficult to remove. Slipping will skin your knuckles too... Ring spanners are less likely to slip than open-ended ones and never use the wrong size, even if you think it's close enough (it will slip). Save adjustable spanners for emergencies only and never use them on tight fasteners, as they are very prone to slipping off.

To ensure correct tool alignment, first clean any debris away. For example, clean out screw slots with a pointed bradawl and wire brush away oily build up from around nuts & bolts etc. Then position the tool and look down it from a couple of different viewpoints, make adjustments to find the optimum angle for the tool and task. Your eyes are very good at judging when a screwdriver lines up with a screw for example, (it's the same with a picture hanging on the wall, you see even if it's a tiny bit out of level...).

Most tools need proper alignment because only then are all the working surfaces of the tool in full contact with the workpiece. This is what gives maximum grip or optimum cutting angle etc. Even a few degrees out of line will cause tools to lose grip or slip, ouch!

Alignment is especially critical when using the majority of power tools, spinning blades need to be free with only the cutting edge touching the workpiece, if you push the tool out of alignment it can jam or worse, kick back at you. Kickback is scary and very dangerous.

FORCE

No young Jedi, not that kind of force, I mean the force that does the work. Usually by transferring the power of your muscles or a motor into motion of some kind.

Picking screwdrivers as an example; if you put a screwdriver into a screw head and simply turned it, the screwdriver pops straight back out again, likely damaging the relatively soft screw head. It's only when you apply a *downward force* and at the *right angle* to prevent the screwdriver from lifting out, as well as *a turning force,* that the screw turns instead of lifting out. This is even more important when using fast and powerful power screwdrivers.

Learn to judge just how much force is enough for each tool and the task in hand. Too little and it won't do the work, too much and the tool can slip as the force exceeds the grip of the tool, again especially important with cordless power screwdrivers (set the safety clutch mechanism to slip).

Tools with blades need two forces, one to hold the tool in place securely and a second to push the blade into the material. One trick with power tools is to hold firmly and push steadily and listen to the motor/ blade.

Listen to motors. Don't push too hard, most tools should only slow down a little (guestimate around 10%) for best results. Let the tool do the work!

Here you'll start to learn the relationship between bad/blunt tools and force/effort. For example, worn, blunt or chipped screwdrivers, chisels, saws, files, or snips need much more force to do the same work than their sharp or well-fitting counterparts. This excessive force in conjunction with the blunt edges and poor gripping surfaces increases the likelihood of the tool slipping. When a tool slips, remember all that excessive force must go somewhere (usually uncontrollably) and you'll likely damage the workpiece or yourself.

Sometimes you need more power. A wrecking or crow bar is a great example. These massively multiply the pressure you can bring to bear on an object by using a long lever over a fulcrum to move a short lever.

In the same way, the turning force of a wrench is easily multiplied by slipping a length of tube or pipe over the handle, lengthening it, and thus the force it applies (careful again though, it often exceeds the fasteners breaking point).

Lever the spanners against each other and break the lock

Lost your key?

A rather naughty example of the power of a lever, is the trick with two spanners to break open a padlock if you've lost the key. Choose a pair of spanners which just fit into the hasp (U shaped bit) and with the spanner heads together, push the other end of the spanners together like a pair of scissors. The force is easily enough to break the lock open. Closely followed by the sound of sirens if it's not your padlock, you have been warned...

SHOCK

Another type of force you can use is shock. If you multiply force with a lever, you have a slow application of power, but if you use a heavy and sharp application of force, this can shock things loose. A tap or three on and around the nut or bolt head with a small hammer can help *break* the hold of a tight fastener (especially if it's corroded). But, never hit any exposed threads (not even once!), especially on the end of the bolt, or you'll damage them. You can also use a combination; try pulling sharply on a long lever. The combined shock of the sudden pull and the extra power from the lever often works where a steady pull will not.

Use force to free stuck screws; put the screwdriver into the screw and tap the end of the screwdriver with a small hammer a few times. There is also a tool called an *impact driver*. This goes onto the fastener like a regular driver and you hit the other end with a hammer, which shocks and turns the fastener at the same time; hopefully 'breaking' the rusty seal and undoing it. Unfortunately, you need a lot of room to use an impact driver and if you're working on something in situ, you might struggle.

A hammer and a cold or masonry chisel also uses shock to break up bricks or concrete. A powerful hammer blow transmits an exponentially magnified force through the chisel to a tiny area on the very tip of the chisel.

The third (and last resort) to force super tight stuff apart is to use physics, on metal things at least (don't try this on anything else!) Gently heat up the offending part with a small heat source, like a plumber's blowtorch or in a pinch, that 'Crème Brulee' blowtorch you got for Christmas. Never try this near anything remotely flammable and remember that heat travels. Be especially careful near any kind of fuel or fuel tank, even if it's empty, (several people every year die working with naked heat sources near empty fuel tanks). Concentrate the heat onto the offending part (usually a nut) until it starts to glow. Removing the heat, quickly try again to undo the nut using a wrench and of course thick gloves, (heat travels up wrenches too remember!). The heat forces the nut to expand at a different rate to the bolt, breaking the tightness... hopefully.

Incidentally, cold, heat, and pressure are forces of nature often used to fix parts together. Cold parts shrink and hot parts expand. Combine the two and they will slide together easily and yet bond tightly at room temperature. These forces create a method of fixing stuff together called an interference fit, or a press or friction fit, (they fit train wheels this way). Alternatively, huge amounts of pressure will force two parts together. It's common to use a hydraulic (or manual screw) press to push a bearing onto a shaft for example.

SPEED, GLORIOUS SPEED

Ah, the *need for speed!* Everybody wants to get the job done as quickly as possible (again blooming 'makeover' TV!). However, just as a car tyre can cope with just so much water before it starts to skid; many tools also have an optimum speed. Excessive speed, often along with excessive force wastes effort and can go badly wrong because you'll lose accuracy and/or grip. This nearly always leads to damage to you or your workpiece (so slow down!).

MECHANICAL SYMPATHY

Noticing how your tools sound and feel at speed will help develop your *mechanical sympathy*, another kind of *sixth sense* for recognising when a machine is struggling to cope because it's overloaded. Some novice DIY'ers have notoriously bad mechanical sympathy, often thinking the harder they push a tool, the more work they'll do. Overloading tools usually produces less work, because it quickly blunts sharp edges and can really shorten the lifespan of motors etc. Pushing tools too hard can also lead to dangerous breakages, damaging the workpiece or yourself.

Concentrate on your technique and accuracy first (see alignment and force above) and aim to be consistent. Go at a pace that feels controllable and comfortable, gently experimenting with different speeds or pressures to find what works best for the material (and you).

Usually, tools or tasks which need high pressure, need a slower speed, undoing a screw for example, or drilling a hole in metal. Faster speeds usually need less pressure as the speed is doing the work, drilling into wood or masonry for example.

"There is time for everything."

Thomas A.Edison

Being slow and steady rarely causes any problems and you're way less likely to make time consuming or expensive mistakes, saving you time and grief in the end. One last time, all together now... *Let the tool do the work!*

USING TOOLS CORRECTLY

When you use tools, there's a learning curve as your brain adapts to the new eye to hand configuration. Try watching a good artisan at work (videos or on the job) and notice the techniques or rhythm they use. Once you have an idea about how the tool works, pick up your own and practise, s l o w l y, preferably on a test piece, (we looked at the practise thing earlier yes...?)

Oh, and it's normal to struggle at first, some tools take many hours (if not years) of practise to master. Being able to work a little quicker will come automatically with practise and experience I promise you, (it's every 'apprentices' constant chagrin the world over, believe me, I know!). And remember, practise will make you better and faster, plus it's a 'no-brainer' to make your mistakes on scrap material, right?

If something slips or doesn't work out, stop and back up a step. Try asking yourself some of these questions to figure out what caused *'the incident'*...

- Did you read the tools operating instructions (duh)?
- Was the tool sharp and/or in good condition?
- Was the tool properly adjusted for the task?
- Were you physically holding the tool properly?
- Did you hold the tool in the proper place, i.e. using the moulded grips if it has them?
- Was the tool aligned correctly with the workpiece?
- Did you look at it from different angles to check?
- Were you pressing too hard or not hard enough?
- Were you positioned comfortably and not over reaching?
- Could you clearly see what you were doing or working on?
- Were you being careful or rushing a little?
- Where did the tool go when it slipped or moved?
- What did the tool do at the point it *let go*?
- What were *you* doing at the point when the tool let go?

Obviously, this a long, generic list of questions that obviously won't apply to every task or tool, but the point is to get you thinking about some of the things to watch out for. Always ensure you're standing in a comfortable position with a good 'footing' (i.e. not on debris etc.) and easily able to reach the task in hand (preferably on a workbench etc.), then...

- ➤ Make sure that you can see the *business end* of the tool and what it's doing. Use extra lighting if necessary.

- ➤ Prepare for the point at which something changes, a plane at the end of a run for example, or a drill bit approaching the back of the material and the classic, a saw blade just about to go all the way through.

- ➤ Practise using the tool carefully and deliberately, ensuring the two points above are uppermost in your mind, (support stuff properly!).

- ➤ Take your time, rushing about nearly always spoils something or other, either the tool, the material or you...

Now you've started to think a little more about how tools work, let's take a quick look at a few of the simplest and most common tools you'll be able to get the hang of pretty quickly...

HAND TOOLS, AND SOME EXAMPLES

But first; SAFETY. Yeah, yeah, yada yada yada! But wait, although considered less dangerous than their power tool cousins, most injuries I see are from hand tools; chisels, screwdrivers, and hammers in particular, (understandably), and spanners (maybe surprisingly). Just sayin'...

Plus, folks seem to have a particular fascination with sharp stuff; for example, I can tell you that the moon is 238,900 miles away and you'll believe me, but if I tell you to be careful, that chisel is sharp (or the paint is wet!), for some inexplicable reason you feel *compelled to touch it* to find out if I am telling the truth! Mindboggling really...

Of course, some hand tools are more dangerous than others, a new wood chisel for example will be wickedly sharp, straight out of the packet, but even the humble screwdriver can pierce you and make you swear if you slip trying to use one at an awkward angle. In fact, most hand tools make pretty good gouges on humans. Ouch...

Don't forget you're all soft, squidgy, full of precious liquid and are very, very easy to damage. Whereas most hand tools are sharp, heavy (or both) and made from hard, unforgiving materials.

Minimise the risk...

- Store your tools in a safe and practical manner. Plunging bare hands into toolboxes to 'root through' piles of tools is asking to find the craft knife in a very unpleasant way.

- Don't overcrowd your toolboxes, because it'll frustrate you and waste time as you try to find that particular small tool which always ends up at the bottom.

- Keep your tools in good condition; clean and sharp.

    NOTE: If sharp tools come with edge protectors, use them. Alternatively, buy a tool roll to store sharp tools safely.

- Be aware of alignment, force, and speed (as talked about above) when using all hand tools, even screwdrivers.

- Don't leave tools lying around at the workplace. If you've finished with it, put it away. Keeping a 'day' bucket handy helps.

- Wear gloves where appropriate.

- Wear goggles where appropriate and even when you think the risk is tiny.

Now I've slightly terrified you, lets step back a little and take a look at the humble pencil...

HOW TO USE A PENCIL

Don't laugh! I said we'd start slowly didn't I, and anyway, there's a real skill to marking out accurately, honestly. First, practise storing your pencil behind your ear until you can bend down without it falling off... No? Okay, try sharpening it with a razor-sharp wood chisel then, still no? well, I'm afraid there is no hope for you then...

Only joking. Just sharpen it with your Minnie Mouse pencil sharpener and keep it in your back pocket, I'm not judging...

You'll need a pencil nearly all the time, they are brilliant for all sorts of marking out from bracket hole positions for your new shelves to a marking out a new doorway in a wall. But let's start with something simple, say you want to cut a piece of timber to length...

- Sharpen your pencil. I know you just did it but do it again for good practise; and anyway, I want to see that Minnie Mouse sharpener again! Plus, a blunt pencil will ruin your accuracy.

- Measure the length and place a pencil mark exactly on the measurement you need. This makes the exact size in the *middle* of the pencil mark. Use a carpenter's square to extend the mark across or even all around the workpiece.

- Indicate on the workpiece which side is 'scrap', using a cross, wiggly line, a smiley face or whatever you like.

- Indicate which direction the cut is going if cutting mitres.

- Cut on the waste side of your pencil mark, aiming to have half the pencil mark still showing on your work piece.

- Measure the workpiece afterwards and adjust your 'marking style' next time to increase your accuracy in future.

I should point out that this is only one way of doing it, sometimes you need to mark totally on the waste or scrap side, cutting the pencil mark out completely with the saw, leaving the workpiece clean for example.

Pinch your fingers together to hold them tight and slide down the workpiece with your pencil

Mind out for splinters!

Another marking tip you can do with a pencil is to use it like a marking gauge... (I'll just wait whilst you nip to the glossary) ...

... all good? Right, hold the pencil between your thumb and index finger and pop your ring finger on the edge of the material. Adjust the point of the pencil until it's where you want it, and then squeeze all your fingers together to kind of 'lock' them in place. Now slide your hand down the material in a parallel motion (mind out for splinters if it's wood). The ring finger acts as a guide and then; oh, this is way too difficult to describe here, just look at the previous image and have a practise!

MARKING HOLE POSITIONS WITH A PENCIL

When you mark the position of holes, take the time to be accurate, really accurate. Sometimes tiny differences in position can be a real problem, especially on things with no built-in adjustment, (such as simple shelf brackets).

If you're mounting a bracket of some sort, hold it in position on the wall and mark the holes through the fixing points on the bracket. Be sure to mark the full circle so that you will know where the centre of the hole is. You might need to use a *deep hole marker* or shave a pencil down for brackets made from thicker material. Be consistent, either drill your marks all in the exact centre of the mark or all closer to the top of the mark, not one at the top of one mark and at the bottom or side of the next mark, as this will cause things to be slightly out of line, level or plumb.

Mark out all the holes at once using a spirit level or laser level (they are getting cheaper all the time) for the most accurate results.

Snapped your pencil again? That's the trouble with keeping them in your back pocket, buy some proper work trousers with side pockets. Or cut your pencils in half to start with, or 'borrow' some from IKEA...

HOW TO USE A TAPE MEASURE

'Measure twice; cut once' is a folk law for a reason (it prevents mistakes) but to help, try keeping a little notepad in your back pocket to write down measurements when you're working. Double-check the measurement on the notepad with the one in your head before cutting. This is especially useful if you got to cut several pieces, whilst fitting skirting boards around a room for example and the power saw is outside...

It doesn't matter what measuring units you use (although I'd avoid *palms* or *thumbs*, no really, we've come a long way in the past few hundred years...), and generally I'd recommend being consistent, i.e. if you like cm's stick to cm's, then you'll not get confused and make mistakes using mm's or inches. However, I must confess to using whichever mark is convenient, I'd choose 10 feet for example, instead of measuring out 3.048 metres any day. As a builder, we use metres (m) or millimetres (mm) mostly, so apologies for that...

Most people (including me) find it difficult to calculate in imperial feet and inches, so stick to working out material volumes and quantities in cubic metres to be on the safe side, plus then you can 'cheat' and use a calculator!

The hook on the end of a tape measure 'floats' to allow you to take external (and internal) measurements. The amount of float equals the thickness of the metal hook you see.

If you want to measure inside something (a cupboard for example), hold the tape blade itself and push the hook end of the tape up to one side and then push the body of the tape measure itself to the other side; press the lock button and read the measurement as it comes out of the casing. Add the width of the tape itself (printed on the side of the case) to get the total. This is more accurate than trying to estimate the exact figure from the radius of the metal tape as it curls up against the side. Also, never hold the hook against the inside of something with your thumb and then pull the tape out and measure, you'll be the thickness of the hook short. Always push the tape up to the surface when measuring inside for the best accuracy.

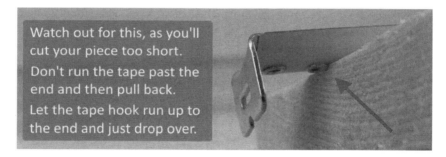

Watch out for this, as you'll cut your piece too short.
Don't run the tape past the end and then pull back.
Let the tape hook run up to the end and just drop over.

Also, be aware that it's possible with some retractable tape measures (notably the cheaper ones) for the rivets holding the floating hook at the end of the tape blade to catch the material instead of the hook proper. This means you'll cut the material short... very annoying. Get into the habit of pushing the tape along until the hook just drops over the end (rather than shooting the tape past the end of the material, drawing it back) and then pulling it tight.

You can draw circles by hooking the little slot in the end of the tape over a convenient nail in the centre of your circle and use an elastic band to hold a pencil at your desired radius, (and you always wondered what that little slot was for huh?).

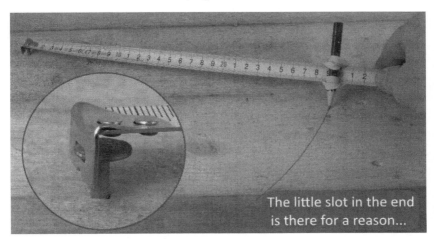

The little slot in the end is there for a reason...

Similar to 'using a pencil as a marking gauge' tip above, you can mark (or even cut) parallel cuts by pinching the blade of the tape at your desired width. Using your fingers as a guide, slide along the workpiece, holding a pencil (or a craft knife) at the end of the tape with your other hand. A common method to cut drywall. Hmm, much easier to explain this using a picture...

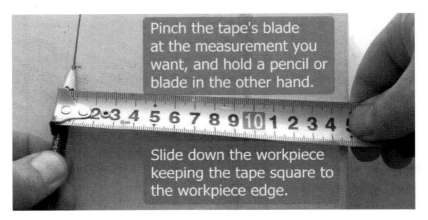

Pinch the tape's blade at the measurement you want, and hold a pencil or blade in the other hand.

Slide down the workpiece keeping the tape square to the workpiece edge.

Finally, if you get a tape measure wet, grab a dry rag, pull out the whole tape, and run it all back in slowly through the rag to dry it off. Store it somewhere warm overnight too if you can. It'll go rusty in hours if you don't.

Digital or laser measures have come a long way recently and make a useful addition to the kitbag, especially if you often work alone. They are especially useful for measuring internal dimensions or long lengths of trims in awkward locations like up near the ceiling for example.

HOW TO USE A SCREWDRIVER

Again, I know you might think this too basic, and yet every single day on the job I lose time trying to remove damaged screws, which shows that many people (including pros'), can't drive in screws without damaging them (especially since power drivers became the norm). Whether you use a power driver or a plain old humble screwdriver, the tip (or bit) needs to be clean and in great condition, throw away any with rounded or chipped edges. Screwdriver bits cost peanuts; replace them often to avoid damaging screw heads.

Never use brute force to drive in screws because once they get too tight the tip of the driver will twist out of the screw head, called 'cam out'. This damages the head of the screw and/or rounds off the edges of the tool, making it nearly impossible to drive them further in. Trust me when I say that removing damaged screws is tricky work...

Countersink
The countersink provides space for the screw head to sit flush (or below) the surface.

Clearance Hole
The clearance hole allows the screw to pass through the piece being fastened and to be pulled down tight to the substrate. The threads do not hold in this part.

Pilot Hole
The pilot hole in wood (or plastic etc.) locates and guides a screw into the material allowing the threads to bite into the sides of the hole.

Without a pilot hole, the screw may get too tight and either burst the material or snap the screw completely.

To use a screwdriver properly and to avoid cam out, make the time to do three things: drill countersink, clearance, and pilot holes...

- In the timber you're *fastening,* carefully position and drill a shallow *countersink hole.*

- In the centre of the countersink hole, drill a *clearance hole,* just wide enough to push/drive the screw through.

In line with the clearance hole, drill a *pilot hole* in the timber you're *fastening to* (see table below for diameters but a little more than half the shank diameter in a pinch).

Some folks like to drill the clearance hole first and then the countersink hole, but it's easy for the countersink bit to chatter if you do that, and then you'll end up with hexagonal shaped countersink holes!

There are tools available that can drill all three of these things in one go and they include the screwdriver bit. Search for *flip driver* for a great way to install screws, they are well worth the outlay.

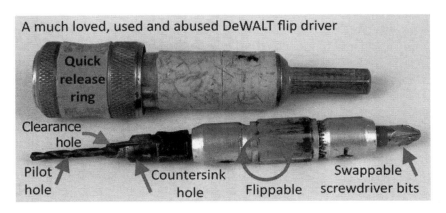

A much loved, used and abused DeWALT flip driver

Quick release ring — Clearance hole — Pilot hole — Countersink hole — Flippable — Swappable screwdriver bits

You'll know when you've got it right because the screw will pull up the timber you are fastening nice and tight, plus the screw head will pull itself into the wood a little. If the going is too tight it will be difficult to get the screw head all the way in and if the going is too loose the screw head will spin around and around once it hits the surface of the workpiece. Both situations leaves the screw with very little holding power.

Gauge	Metric equiv.	Pilot hole	Clearance hole	Masonry plug size
3	2.5mm	1.0mm	3.0mm	Yellow (5mm hole)
4	3.0mm	1.5mm	3.5mm	Yellow (5mm hole)
6	3.5mm	2.0mm	4.0mm	Red (6mm hole)
8	4.0mm	2.5mm	4.5mm	Red (6mm hole) or Brown (7mm hole)
10	5.0mm	3.0mm	5.5mm	Brown (7mm hole)
12	5.5mm	3.5mm	6.0mm	Brown (7mm hole)
14	6.5mm	4.0mm	7.0mm	Blue (10mm hole)

The previous table is a rough guide to drilling suitably sized holes to avoid problems when driving in screws. Remember these pilot hole recommendations are typical for softwoods. Hardwoods may well need a larger pilot hole. Always stop and back out if the screw gets too tight or you risk breaking the screw (disastrous!). Simply drill a larger pilot hole and try again or use a smaller gauge screw.

Special screws like timber decking and other slender, self-cutting screws often drive straight in, but I'd still recommend drilling clearance holes for the screws close to an edge (or end) to avoid splitting on better quality work.

Be especially careful if you're using any kind of particleboard, chipboard, MDF and the like. These often have a harder wearing surface and are softer in the middle. The tightest hold is when the screw head is exactly flush with the board top (where the board is hardest). Screw heads sunk deep into the softer middle part of chipboard for example, don't hold nearly so well.

Otherwise, finish off your screws one of several ways...

- Leave screws flush with the timber surface on out of sight, non-face work, it's stronger that way.

- Especially leave all external and especially decking screws flush with the surface. If you sink these screws deep into the wood, water sits on the top of them and accelerates corrosion of the screw and allows more water into the timber itself, rotting it. And yes, even treated wood rots eventually, surprisingly quickly sometimes.

- On internal work, drive them below the surface a little and fill the hole with a suitable filler. Paintable/stainable ones are available as are matching coloured fillers etc. Fill twice, the first lot will shrink.

- Drive the screw into a counter-bored hole (a deeper version of the countersink hole) and glue a matching (or even contrasting) wooden plug into the hole. Shave the plug flush with the surface using a very sharp chisel or block plane after the glue has dried (watch the grain of the plug or you'll pull out wood fibres from deeper than the workpiece surface).

And finally, after 786 words, we get to the part where you can put the blooming screw in...

- Hold the screwdriver firmly with the butt of the handle in your palm, OR grip the drill driver properly with your index finger over the trigger and perfectly in line with the screw (look down it from two sides, 90° apart).

- Push quite firmly to ensure good grip and avoid it slipping out. Use both hands if necessary.

- Hold the screw under the head on the part with no threads with your forefinger and thumb, to stop the screw wobbling when you start to turn it.

- Turn or power the screw fast enough to bite into the wood, letting go with our fingers once the screw has stabilised and drawing into the workpiece.

- Slow down as the screw head approaches the surface.

- Slowly drive the screw in the last little bit until the head sits tightly into the countersink.

- Don't let the tip or bit twist out or it will damage both the screw tip and screwdriver end (especially power drivers).

- Alternatively, some powered screwdrivers have a clutch, set it to slip just as the screw fully sits in the countersink (your mileage may vary using the clutch as wood density varies in individual pieces of timber which can affect how deep each screw goes before triggering the drills clutch mechanism).

Avoid over tightening the screw, which can strip the new threads cut into the substrate by the screw as it drives in, especially if you haven't drilled countersink holes and are trying to get the screw head under the surface.

REMOVING SCREWS

I guess this is as good a place as any to talk about how to remove screws! Removing screws is often a pain because they tighten over time, especially if corroded. If they are too tight to move, stop before you damage the screw head and try a short sharp tap or two on the end of a firmly held screwdriver with a mallet (it's okay, I know you'll use your hammer...). This often 'breaks' the hold the material has on the threads. Follow this up with a LOT of downwards pressure (perfectly in line of course) with your screwdriver or drill driver on slow and 'pulse' the trigger to have a fighting chance of removing it.

If the screw is just too tight and you damage the head, you're going to need a little ingenuity...

- If you've got good access, cut a slot into the damaged screw head using a hacksaw or Dremel type tool. Then tap in a big slotted screwdriver and remove the screw.

- A long shot is to try a rubber band underneath the driver tip.

- If the damaged head is clear of the surface, use a pair of pliers or mole grips to grip the damaged head and unscrew it (you'll never be that lucky though...).

- The last resort is to use a special 'screw extractor' which digs into the damaged head and drives it out but to be honest these will not always work and often end up snapping the head off smaller screws.

Which leads nicely to... If you actually break off the head or snap a screw inside the wood, you're in serious doo doo because your options are limited...

- Using a small drill bit of say 3 or 4mm (⅛″) drill down all around the sides of the broken screw, through the first part of the material. Pull off the top material. Remove the screw that's left sticking out of the substrate with a pair of pliers or mole grips. OR.

- Use a hollow, small diameter core drill and likewise drill down and around the broken screw. Be very careful when starting up, because without a centre guide drill bit, the drill bit will try to walk all over the workpieces surface (I did say this is difficult!).

- Repair both the above large holes by drilling out and gluing in a short piece of dowel to replace the damaged area.

- As a last resort, use brute strength and a long bar to prise apart the material. Obviously not an option if you need to keep all the parts in good condition.

HOW TO USE SPANNERS AND WRENCHES

Spanners (also read socket, wrench, driver etc) tighten and remove threaded fasteners like nuts and bolts. If you can see both the nut and the head of the bolt, remove the nut first (if it's accessible). Often though, there is no nut because the threads are a part of the machine itself. Then you'll only see the bolt head as the bolt shank disappears through a part deep into the machine. Be careful with nuts and bolts, they are tight (duh!) and often difficult to remove, watch your positioning and clean rust and muck away first.

REMOVING NUTS & BOLTS

Spanners etc. are the single biggest cause of skinned knuckles around because unless everything is the optimum position, they easily slip off the nut or bolt head. Often oil or corrosion exacerbates the problem. Plus, sometimes you'll need a lot of force to undo a nut or bolt; so, if it does slip, that force will release explosively, throwing your soft, squidgy hand into the nearest hard, sharp metal surface with very predictable and painful results.

To avoid unpleasantness and blood, follow the golden rules...

1. Always use a socket before spanner (if there is space), a socket wrench gives more control, especially on tight fasteners.
2. Always use the right (and I mean exactly right) size socket/ spanner etc. It should be a tight fit. If you can move the spanner handle left and right more than a fraction, it's the wrong size.
3. Always apply the force at exactly 90° to the fasteners shaft. The wrench head (even if it's cranked slightly) must sit perfectly flat and down around the nut or bolt head. If one side is even slightly lifted up, it will slip under force.

EXTREME FORCE FOR TIGHT OR CORRODED FASTENERS

Fasteners like screws or nuts & bolts are sometimes impossibly tight (often because of corrosion), causing colourful cursing and skinned knuckles. Because a tight fastener under load becomes too tight to undo by normal means, try soaking it with a penetrating fluid (like WD40) and walk away for a while. Go get a cup of coffee, walk the dog, or just sit in the sunshine and ponder the mysteries of the universe. When you get back the fluid will have miraculously sorted out the problem, no? Okay, then you're going to need much more force or power, (without resorting to eating a can of spinach...).

Two spanners doubles the turning force...

The turning force of a tool multiplies by applying some basic physics, i.e. lengthening the size of a lever multiplies the force. Increasing the length of any tool applying a turning motion will dramatically increase the force applied. A common way to increase leverage (on a wrench for example), is to slide a long metal tube over the handle to increase the turning force. Be careful though, as you'll soon reach or exceed the breaking point of the spanner and/or fastener. If the fastener is that tight you might want to think about trying to loosen it first (penetrating fluid, shock, or heat).

Some screwdrivers have a 'hex' on the shaft to use a spanner or grips to increase the turning torque (don't forget to press down equally as hard though). Be a little careful though, as this extra force can easily break the tool (or fastener). You'll learn by experience (and by breaking the odd tool) to feel when there is enough strain.

It often takes a lot of force to 'start' undoing a fastener but once started it will get easier and easier as it works its way out. Often, once a fastener is part way out, you'll be able to remove it the remainder of the way by hand if you want (faster than using the wrench).

Occasionally though, a fastener will start to undo okay and then become tight once the protruding rusted threads on the bolt hit the nut clogging it up. Either wire bush the protruding threads to remove the rust before starting to undo it or keep working the nut back and forth as you undo it to clear any rust off the threads.

Be careful once you feel the fastener getting to the very end though, (i.e. almost out), hold onto it firmly; dropping it will invoke another universal law; it will either end up far from where you dropped it, or end up stuck on an inaccessible ledge, or drop down a crack in the floor or at the very least get covered in grit. Guaranteed...

Incidentally, that reminds me, never put fasteners on the floor. Always pop them into a receptacle of some kind to keep them safe. I use a variety of empty plastic tubs such as ice cream tubs (plus you get to eat ice cream...). Don't forget to thoroughly clean any dirty or dropped fasteners before re-assembly, grit on threads is a nightmare. A wire brush and a degreaser is useful here. On older machines a smear of copper grease is beneficial when re-assembling most kinds of fasteners.

CROSS THREADING

Hold your horses, are you sure that fastener has started properly? I can't stress enough how important it is when refitting bolts to start them properly. Even a slight angle or a single thread misalignment will cause a terrible and nasty thing called 'cross-threading'.

Crossed threads are where the threads on the fastener don't align properly with the threads in the nut or worse still, in the component. Instead of following the existing threads, the male part (e.g. the bolt) tries to 'cut' a new way into the female part (e.g. the nut or part), quickly getting very tight. Keep going and the fastener will either get stuck, snap or 'strip' the threads, ruining either the fastener or the nut (not too bad as easily replaced), but if the other female threads are in a component, it means drilling out the damage and then cutting some new oversize threads. Then you'll need a new larger fastener etc. Tricky enough work if the part is easily accessible and impossible if down the side of a machine with 50mm of work space.... Trust me when I say that you'll really be having a bad day if you strip threads in anything important like an engine...

Fortunately, it's very simple to make sure it *never* happens to you. First, pop the bolt or screw back into the top of its hole and gently turn it anti-clockwise as if you were undoing it again (or clockwise for rare left-hand threads). You will feel a small 'click' as the thread on the fastener (bolt for example) drops over the thread in the hole (in the nut for example). Once it clicks, gently start turning the fixing in the opposite direction, (tightening it). Second, keep going by hand as far as possible, because it's near impossible to cross-thread a fastener by hand (unless you're a meta-human with super strength...). Once you've completed a few turns you're probably 'safe' from the risk of cross threading and can reach for the wrench to tighten the fixing fully home. If it becomes tight early, stop, and investigate why before reaching for the wrench. Better to double check than strip a thread.

REPLACING FASTENERS: HOW TIGHT IS TIGHT ENOUGH?

Okay, we touched on this a little talking about 'yield' earlier, so let's see how it applies here. Imagine you've got your threads started straight and the fastener is all the way in, when do you stop? Judging how tight to tighten nut and bolts is different to screws for example, as mostly the material is metal and so the fasteners will not sink into the workpieces surface. Generally, you'd run up a fastener until what's called hand tight and then either turn it a further part of a turn and this varies (see the problem). Large fasteners in hard metal might only need a further $1/8^{th}$ of a turn to fully tighten. But a small fastener in a soft metal like aluminium, well, you're in the tighten by feel zone and I think it's something you'll either develop or you won't.

No matter though, if you are planning to work on a few mechanical things, I'd seriously consider getting a small torque wrench, because they are brilliant. Torque wrenches accurately tighten to a specific torque (tightness) and then you'll never need to worry about over tightening anything or stripping threads ever again.

The amount of torque or power required to hold something in place is specific to the size of the fastener and the load it carries. Stuff that's heavy, fast moving or vibrates, need to be very tight indeed. Stationary or lightweight or small things obviously don't need to be so tight. (NOTE: The above applies to most screws as well). Think about this on the things you're working on, will the fastener be under stress and if so, how much?

When you tighten a nut or bolt, the force you apply does two things: first, it overcomes the friction between the threads on the fastener and the threads in the hole, PLUS the friction between the underside of the bolt head and the component. And second, tightening a fastener stretches it, and it's this stretching which creates the clamping force (picture the pull you feel when you stretch a big elastic band, just imagine the pull when you stretch a 12mm (½″) bolt, yup, it's a huge force...).

However, the tightness of a fastener has little to do with the clamping force it's exerting, (I know, doesn't make sense huh?). But just because a bolt is tight, it doesn't necessarily mean it's holding okay, that's a myth. A rusty fastener or one with debris on the threads, will still pull up tight and trigger the torque setting on the wrench. But half the force you applied was fighting the friction caused by the rusty or dirty threads or the friction between the underside of the bolt head and the components surface. The result? A bolt with way too little clamping force. Laboratory testing of the actual clamping force of factory bolts vs 'on site' bolts has proven this time and time again.

Two things you need to do: first, it's very important to clean up any dirty or rusty threads with a wire brush and under the bolt head. Second, I like to use a light lubricant on old bolts. This helps the torque wrench get the fastener all the way up to the proper torque without losing too much tension due to friction. However, adding lubrication does have a slight risk. It's easier to over tighten a fastener if it's all slippery with lubricant, so don't go crazy with the lubricant and don't exceed the torque settings, in fact some folks say you can go a little lower if you've lubed the fastener...

If the nut or bolt is in an inaccessible location and it keeps dropping off the wrench as you lower it into place; place a small strip of paper over the nut or bolt head first. The extra tightness stops the bolt from dropping out whilst you manoeuvre it into place.

TIGHTENING IN SEQUENCE AND STAGES

On flanges or multiple fastener items it's wise to tighten them in a particular sequence and in particular stages.

For example, replacing a four-bolt car wheel (replace wheel with a multi fastener item of your choice). First pick a bolt (or nut) and tighten it up until it's just snug, preferably by hand, or with the socket in your hand (from the socket wrench) for a little added leverage (hand tight). Then do the same to the bolt opposite. Then you have a choice of bolts (left or right), but the point is to move around the wheel working on opposite sides each time. This helps settle the wheel (read component) in exactly the right place.

In addition to the component being in the right place it's important not to distort some items whilst tightening them up. This is especially important on anything with a sealing gasket. Tightening the bolts in stages spreads out the load and avoids building up too much stress in one place. To finish the wheel analogy; once you have gone around the wheel once and all the bolts are snug. Repeat the process applying a little load on the wrench. Now you can lower the wheel to the ground and do the final tightening up to the set torque using your properly calibrated torque wrench.

A similar although much more critical procedure happens when replacing something large like a cylinder head on the top part of an engine for example. There is a proper sequence to ensure the head doesn't twist out of shape (usually going from side to side working from the centre outwards). Following the sequence, you'd tighten the bolts up to a specific torque and then again to another specific torque and so on until the head is properly tightened down to the full torque. And even then, you'd need to check the bolts torque again, after the engine has run for a specific number of hours.

And lastly, did I mention putting a small torque wrench on your wish list? I did? Jolly good.

HOW TO USE A HAMMER

The statement "anyone can hammer in a nail" is a falsehood soon discovered by those who try it for the first time. That said, I think most folks find hammering in nails is very satisfying; once you get the hang of it. Hitting your thumb with a hammer, not so much... Fortunately it takes so little practise to get the hang of it, an hour tops and you'll be an expert, I promise you.

First, to properly direct and control a hammers force, it's essential the size of the hammer (thus force) matches the situation, i.e. small stuff = small hammer, bigger stuff needs, yup, you guessed it, a dirty great big hammer. Never use a large hammer lightly or a little hammer aggressively. It's worth taking the time to go and get the right hammer, because big hammers inevitably break small stuff and little hammers are dangerously ineffective on big stuff because they can break or ricochet.

Oh, and don't use any other tool as a hammer either, because you'll struggle and might damage the workpiece (not to mention the tool). Right that's the boring stuff out of the way, now pass me that hammer!

Start by holding the hammer at the proper place on the handle, i.e. not too close to the head of the hammer. Start in the middle somewhere and work your way to the end as you improve. Then, picture hitting the nail with the head (top part) of the hammer completely in line with the nail, as this ensures the actual face of the hammer is 90° to the nail head, i.e. hitting it squarely. Practise just touching the nail like a golfer practises his swing...

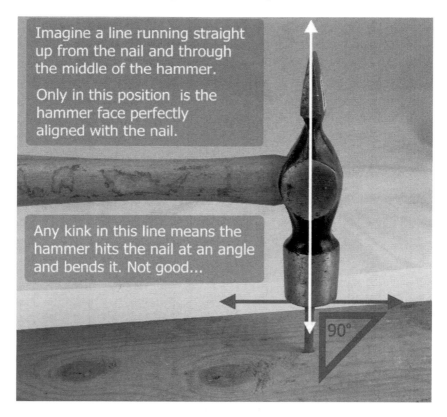

Imagine a line running straight up from the nail and through the middle of the hammer.

Only in this position is the hammer face perfectly aligned with the nail.

Any kink in this line means the hammer hits the nail at an angle and bends it. Not good...

90°

Try keeping a hold of the nail (if you dare!) and (relatively gently) tap the nail until it's about a *quarter of its length* in, then the nail will be sturdy and less likely to bend if you slightly miss-hit it; mind your fingers though...

Let go of the nail and carry on hitting it, relatively gently again until the nail is about half way in or more, be deliberate and accurate with your blows. Try increasing the force (if you want), to drive the nail in the last half, but slow down again just before the nail head hits the surface.

Finish off the last few blows carefully to avoid unsightly 'half-moons' where the hammer hits the wood on the last stroke. Once the nail head is flush, or almost flush with the timbers surface, consider using a nail punch to drive the nail below the surface for mark free results.

Thrashing away like a heavy metal guitarist is going to make hitting the nail squarely virtually impossible. If you're bending the nail each time, it usually means the hammer is hitting the nail at a slight angle (or too big a hammer!) The head *must* hit the nail head perfectly flat to drive it in straight.

If you very slightly miss hit a nail and it bends slightly one way, make the next blow slightly more towards the side in which the nail is leaning to send it back over the other way to straighten it.

If you've bent a nail, use your claw hammer to straighten up the worst of it. Here, like this...

Grab the nail in between the claw and twist the hammer in a rotating, upwards motion.

Concentrate your effort on the nail above the bend, not the bottom part of the nail.

And then use a club hammer on one side and your claw hammer on the opposite side to 'dress' the nail straight again before continuing. Like so...

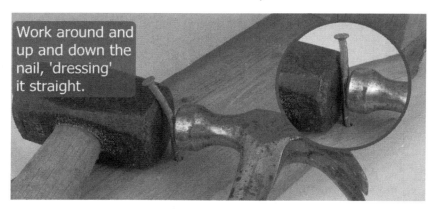

Work around and up and down the nail, 'dressing' it straight.

If you find the hammer is skidding off the nail and you're convinced you're hitting it squarely... try the tradesman's' trick and sandpaper the striking face of the hammer to remove the polished surface before trying again.

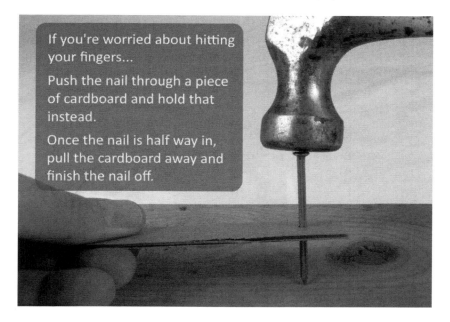

If you're worried about hitting your fingers...

Push the nail through a piece of cardboard and hold that instead.

Once the nail is half way in, pull the cardboard away and finish the nail off.

If you're nailing close to the end of a piece of wood, try tapping the point on a nail to flatten it. This works because the now flat top punches a hole through the timber fibres (breaking and tearing them) whereas the original point drives through them like a wedge, creating stress and pressure, often enough to split the timber, especially if you're nailing within 25mm (1″) of the end of the workpiece.

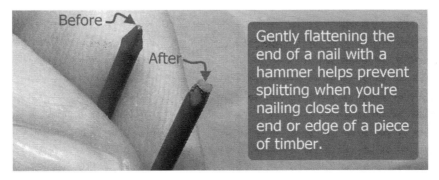

Before

After

Gently flattening the end of a nail with a hammer helps prevent splitting when you're nailing close to the end or edge of a piece of timber.

A downside to hitting something with a hammer is that it might move and holding two workpieces securely is often difficult. It's best to hammer the nail well into the first timber and then check your alignment before carrying on into the second timber.

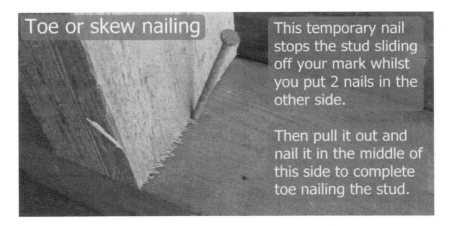

Toe or skew nailing

This temporary nail stops the stud sliding off your mark whilst you put 2 nails in the other side.

Then pull it out and nail it in the middle of this side to complete toe nailing the stud.

On 90° joints, (toe or skew nails), either hold your boot on the back side of the stud or use a temporary nail (driven in 12.5mm or ½" or so) to stop the timber moving.

If nailing something which is not sturdy, hold something heavy (a heavy hammer) on the opposite side. This acts as a counter weight and absorbs some of the force of your blows.

PULLING OUT NAILS

Stuff that's nailed together requires more care to dismantle because often the only way to dismantle it is by using a pry bar or crow bar to lever the pieces apart, either fully or just enough to 'pop' the nail heads out of the surface so that you can pull out the nails with the other end of the bar.

Sometimes when you lever the item out a little, the nail head 'pops out', but promptly disappears again when you release the bar, try levering it out again and then use a second claw hammer or bar and 'tap' the part of the nail that emerges from the back piece of timber to dent or bend it slightly. This often stops it disappearing back into the hole when you let go, popping the nail head out the face side in the process.

Nailed stuff in general is crude and messy to dismantle and needs more than a little brute strength. But if you're saving something, be a little 'clever' and think about which way you lever the bar. Try to lever away from the 'face' surface and into the piece you're throwing away if you can (e.g. pull instead of push).

Don't lever against the wall when taking off trims like skirting or base boards, cornices etc., because it'll put a dent in the plasterworks, or even make a hole in drywall. Use offcuts of timber behind the bar, minimum 25mm × 100mm × 300mm (1"×4"×12") on masonry and much bigger on drywall (to span between two studs). The timber will spread the point load out and stop the bar digging into the plaster. Consider buying one of the modern flat, thin pry bars too, as the fine end makes getting into the smallest of gaps a cinch.

Start by driving a pry bar into the end of any seams or joints between parts (don't start in the middle). Two prying implements are good for this, leapfrogging over each other as you work your way down the joint or seam.

Split small stuff apart using your 'No. 2' tools (read *Putting Together a Tool Kit* in *Appendices One*), an old wood chisel or screwdriver and the 'claw' part of your hammer for example.

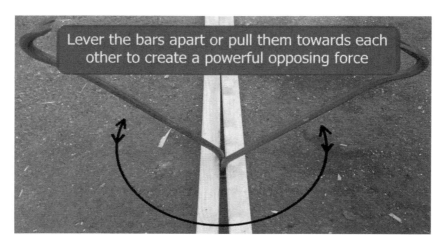

Lever the bars apart or pull them towards each other to create a powerful opposing force

Sometimes you'll need to separate stuff that will not stay put, like the two timbers nailed together in the previous image. To separate these, use two bars and lever in opposite directions. The longer the levers, the easier it is. According to Mr Newtons third law, one bar cancels out the force of the equal and opposite bar, keeping the workpiece still whilst still opening out the joint.

Make it a habit to 'make safe' any protruding nails as you work because handling stuff full of sharp nails is almost impossible to do without hurting yourself. You don't necessarily have to remove the nail from the timber, just knock them through from the backside to make the nail point safe

If you intend reusing trims etc. try experimenting with pulling the nails through from the backside with a pair of pincers. Imagine a nail punched into the trim and then filled and painted over, then imagine knocking it through from the back side, what's going to happen? Yup, like a bullet hole it's going to make a mess on the 'exit'. Pulling small gauge wire or 'air gun' nails through from the rear is especially easy and leaves the front unmarked...

Pull small nails out from the back using a pair of pincers. Tapping them through from the back with a hammer will splinter the front face.

HOW TO USE A HANDSAW

The 'Daddy' of all tool alignment issues is being able to saw timber squarely with a handsaw. Fortunately, it's also the easiest to practise until you get it right. Buy one of the, multi-purpose hardpoint saws and throw it away when it gets blunt, it'll last years if you keep it dry and hang it up when you're done, (oh and not catching nails or masonry with it helps no end...).

To give yourself the best chance of sawing squarely, mark the *top, back and front edges* of your timber using a carpenters' square or the handle of your saw (most have a 'square' and 45° built into the handle). Then, starting at the front top corner, carefully rest the edge of your hand on the timber and use your thumb to support the saw blade (above the teeth!) at 90° to the timber.

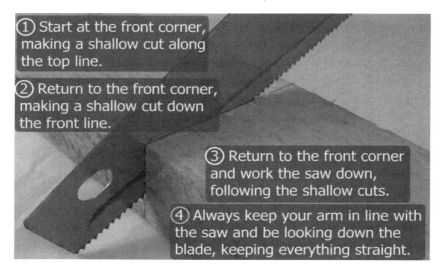

1 Start at the front corner, making a shallow cut along the top line.

2 Return to the front corner, making a shallow cut down the front line.

3 Return to the front corner and work the saw down, following the shallow cuts.

4 Always keep your arm in line with the saw and be looking down the blade, keeping everything straight.

Starting at a shallow angle to the top of the timber (nearly horizontal), slowly draw the saw backwards and form a shallow cut, first on the corner and then extend it along the top line. Return to the front corner and then, holding the saw nearly vertical, form another shallow cut down the front line, following your pencil mark.

Then, returning to the front top corner and start sawing, holding the saw between 30° and 60°, moving alternately between and following the two shallow cuts, working deeper into the body of the timber. The saw will follow your two shallow cuts and once you get deeper into the timber the cut itself acts as a guide for the blade as you progress through the bottom half of the cut. Remember to slow right down for the last few strokes and support the offcut to prevent it falling and tearing away the last section. Either reach over and hold the offcut with your other hand (awkward) or better still, work on sawhorses or a bench.

If your saw is sharp you shouldn't need to press very hard at all; apply a *gentle downwards pressure* and a *steady back and forth* motion, it'll cut better if you do. In fact, a brand-new saw will be 'scary sharp' and you'll need to be very careful with it as even a slight touch will cut you badly.

The little guy in the next image used to get super frustrated because his saw cuts went in all different directions in a 'frenzy' of short strokes. If he slows down, doesn't press so hard, concentrates on his alignment, (keeping his lower arm and saw blade roughly in line) and keeps the saw in his shallow cuts, he manages just fine...

And don't forget you paid for the whole saw, so use all of it; don't just use the middle bit. Seriously, using the whole saw, i.e. long strokes really helps keep the saw in a straight line...

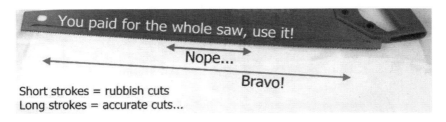

Short strokes = rubbish cuts
Long strokes = accurate cuts...

EXIT STRATEGY

While we're looking at saws you also need to be mindful about where the saw blade 'exits' the work piece. This is because toothed blades tear splinters where they exit the workpiece. The saw blade needs to go *into* the *face side* of the workpiece and out of the rear, (this applies to powered saws as well). Note that if you're using a hand held circular saw, this means cutting from the rear side, (face side down) because the blade rotates up through the workpiece and out of the top.

If you have some small splintering on the back edge, run a small hand plane or sandpaper at 45° to the cut edges afterwards to create a tiny chip hiding chamfer (works well on laminated boards like melamine or worktops).

HOW TO USE A METAL SAW (HACKSAW)

Cut metal using a hand-held saw called a hacksaw, which is an elongated D shaped frame with a thin, small toothed blade made out of very hard metal (as you can imagine). First make sure that the teeth on the saw are facing away from the handle so that you're cutting on the push stroke. Second, make sure the blade is tight by screwing in the wing nut on the front end, the blade needs to be very tight to prevent buckling during sawing (the blade heats up and expands slightly). Oh, and always have a spare blade, because you'll definitely break the blade if you don't have a spare one. If you have a spare blade, the one you have will last forever., it's called *Murphy's law...*

Three things to remember when cutting metal...

- Support or hold the workpiece very, very securely, a vice usually. Alternatively, quick clamp the metal to a piece of wood.

- Cut close to the support to prevent excessive noise and vibration.

- Slow down when you're nearly all the way through and make sure you support the offcut.

On rough work, you might not need to go all the way through, saw ¾ of the way through or so and then bend the offcut back and forth a couple of times to snap it off, (most metals fatigue quickly to failure point).

One last point, on fine work you might need to protect the metal from clamping damage. For example, an engineer's vice has a rough pattern on the inside face of the jaws to better grip smooth metal. This will leave an imprint on the workpiece, so use special *soft jaws* that slip over the regular metal ones if you need to keep the workpiece unmarked. Or pop a couple of pieces of wood either side of the workpiece or consider a woodworker's vice which have wooden jaws suitable for holding a wide range of different material.

POWER TOOLS (PLUS A COUPLE OF EXAMPLES)

Okay, time to take a step up. Power tools. But first; you know what I'm going to say by now don't you? Yup. Although new power tools can make folks drool in anticipation, never forget that tools like circular saws, mitre saws, routers etc. can cause you permanent, catastrophic, personal, physical damage. In short, you could lose valuable parts of your anatomy, ask anyone who works in the local Accident & Emergency Dept. at your local hospital...

So, minimise the risk... (don't worry, it's easy...)

- Read the instructions before using a new tool (Duh!).

- Watch videos online to familiarise yourself with how the tool works, (check out the manufacturers site first).

- Look at the blade and figure out how it cuts and which way it runs (with the tool unplugged). Be careful with any sharp blades.

- Create an un-crowded workspace, free from distractions and debris. Route power cables safely to avoid trip hazards.

- Work out the best way to hold the workpiece firmly and safely.

- Always be aware of the tool, where it is, whether it's plugged in and if the power is live.

- Familiarise yourself with the tools controls before starting it up.

- Position yourself comfortably and practise the best way to hold the tool once it's in operation.

- Start the tool up a few times and familiarize yourself with its motion, feel and sound.

- Consider what happens if it snatches the workpiece, which way will it go? (Shouldn't happen if you support the workpiece properly).

- Following the instructions, slowly and steadily, but firmly use the tool for the first time.

- After cutting, be very careful when you put the tool down, usually you should wait until it has completely stopped to be safe.

- Phew! Still in one piece? Great, but never, ever get complacent, always work safely.

And just in case it all goes horribly wrong, remember to wrap any accidentally removed body parts in a clean damp cloth, pop it into a sealable plastic bag, and place the bag in ice cold water or the bottom of the fridge (not freezer). Cooling the severed part will keep it viable for half a day or so, but without cooling, that reduces to as little as a few hours. Never put body parts directly on ice as this tends to make stitching them back on much more difficult. Seriously, I'm not joking. Oh, and call an ambulance, if you still have enough fingers left...

But you can easily avoid all the above unpleasantness by working safely (and I know I keep 'beating this drum' but it's important!). Please, only use tools for their designed purpose and for the love of God, practise slowly and gently on some well secured scrap material until you've gotten the hang of the tool, it's time well invested.

Now I've totally terrified you, lets step back a little and look at the ever so slightly gentler art of drilling holes...

HOW TO DRILL HOLES

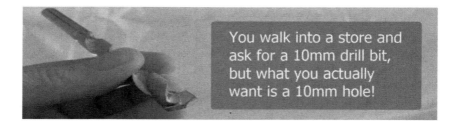

You walk into a store and ask for a 10mm drill bit, but what you actually want is a 10mm hole!

Your house is full of holes, literally. And no, it's not going to leak next time it rains. But you might want to make even more holes to put up new shelves or run new wiring cables etc. You'll need to learn how to make different sized holes in different materials.

The secret to drilling holes is in three parts...

- *Knowing your material*, i.e. what you're drilling into.

- Choosing the *right drill bit* for that material.

- Using the *right technique* for *that bit* in *that material*.

KNOWING YOUR MATERIAL

Of course, some materials are obvious to identify, but for arguments sake, lets practise using the RELEARN method to confirm what you're drilling into...

- *Observe* the surface; can you identify the material visually? Additionally, check for nearby electrical items or water pipes. Look for anything that disappears into a wall, floor, or ceiling. Use a suitable tester if at all unsure.

- *Touch it*. Can you feel what it is? Concrete and plaster are hard, whereas plasterboard on studs might give slightly when pushed.

- *Listen* to the material. If you tap it with your knuckles or the handle of a screwdriver; is it hollow? (plasterboard?). Is it dense? (plaster or concrete?). Sometimes plasterboard sounds hollow in places because it's stuck to a masonry wall (dot and dab in the UK), keep tapping and see if you can find the hard areas of 'dabs' or adhesive. Hollow-dense-hollow-dense at a regular spacing? Could be you're finding the timber studs behind a partition or stud wall.

- *Smell it.* Okay, just joking, your sense of smell might not help you with this, unless you live in a gingerbread house of course...

- *Information.* You might have the original plans that give you the build specifications, materials used etc. Also, what was it your neighbour said the other week? If your houses are similar, he might have useful information to share.

- *Experience.* Have you drilled holes in this house before? What happened? What material was it? etc.

- *Solution.* Once you have an idea what the material is, search online for *drilling holes + your material*, to find specific advice on what methods/drill bits to use (or keep reading!).

CHOOSING THE RIGHT DRILL BIT

These drill bits are from my own drill box. And yes, if you get them wet, most of them will go rusty, as you can see...

Choosing the right drill bit is important because they only work properly in the material they're designed for (except HSS metal drill bits, which also work fine in wood and plastic).

Some holes might need to go all the way through like clearance holes in timber or holes for bolts in metal, but some holes must stop before exiting the backside, pilot holes for instance. In masonry, always go a little deeper than the fastener you're going to use to prevent the fastener hitting the bottom of the hole, in timber it's not so critical, so you can go about the same depth as the length of your fastener.

MATERIAL DRILLING TIPS & TECHNIQUES

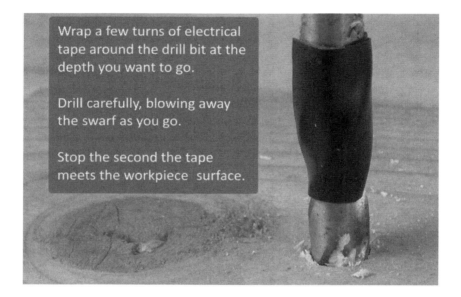

Wrap a few turns of electrical tape around the drill bit at the depth you want to go.

Drill carefully, blowing away the swarf as you go.

Stop the second the tape meets the workpiece surface.

A simple way to create a 'depth stop' is to wrap a few turns of electrical tape around the bit at the depth you want to stop at. Keep a close watch on the tape as you drill, stopping just before the tape hits the surface of the workpiece or you'll push the tape up the bit and drill too deep, potentially ruining your perfectly good day...

Starting very slowly works well in all materials, at least until the drill bit has cut a shallow depression exactly over your mark. Watch for the drill bit twisting up and away from your mark if you start too fast.

As the hole deepens, you may gradually apply more speed and/or pressure. Listen and get a feel for when the drill bit is clogging up, (it will slow down and sound different). Clear clogged drill bit flutes by backing the bit almost all the way out to allow the swarf (bits of wood you've drilled out) to clear before plunging back in again. Repeat as often as necessary.

Drill gently, letting the sharpness of the bit do its work; then you'll get a split seconds warning if the drill bit hits something unexpected. If you are leaning into the tool like a sumo wrestler, you'll be through the obstruction (or the other side of the wall) before you know it. Bad news if it's a thin capping over an unexpected wire...

Always be ready for when the drill bit breaks through the other side (when applicable, don't do this when drilling into a party wall...), listen and feel for the bit as it approaches the underside, it'll start to feel and sound different, maybe slowing down a little and a deeper note. Ease off on the pressure and be ready to pull up the millisecond it goes through, to avoid the drill chuck slamming into your workpiece.

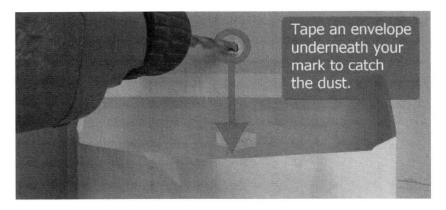

Tape an envelope underneath your mark to catch the dust.

Keep things clean; tape an open envelope beneath the hole on a wall or drill through a small plastic pot (aerosol top etc.) if the hole is on the ceiling to catch the dust, or best of all, simply hold a vacuum cleaner nozzle close by as you drill the hole.

DRILLING TIMBER

Many different types of drill bits will cut in wood; even a masonry bit will roughly force its way through a piece of timber when pushed on the hammer setting. Generally, though, most folks use HSS or twist bits for holes up to 10mm ($^3/_8$") and flat or auger bits between 10mm and 25mm ($^3/_8$" to 1") or so and then hole saws for large holes from 25mm (1") up to around 100mm (4") or so. Anything bigger than 100mm (4") or so, it's easier to use a jigsaw.

Simple plastic hole jig
or make your own out
of thin plywood.

Starting holes in timber with a regular twist or HSS bit is tricky as the bit will try to move off your mark slightly (normally twist bits are for drilling metal in fixed drill presses). Either practise and be careful with twist bits or for perfect hole positioning make (or buy) a drilling jig out of scrap plywood or plastic and clamp it to the workpiece where you want your holes. Drill through the jig and into your workpiece.

Try to avoid drilling damp or sappy wood as it will really clog up the flutes (spiral parts) on twist drill bits, causing them to slow down and smoke.

Also, consider using flat bits for timber, which have sharp points to ensure good starting accuracy in wood (they start around 6mm or ¼″ in diameter and go up to around 25mm or 1″ or so). Lastly and best for deeper holes are auger bits which pull themselves into wood via a small screw lead point.

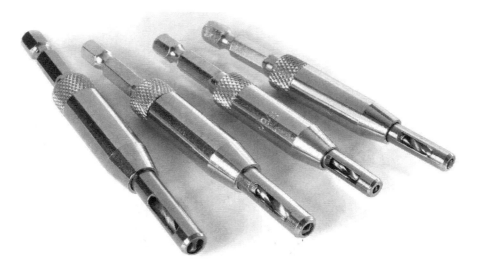

For super accurate drilling of small mounting holes, such as through a hinge for example, treat yourself to a set of self-centring drill bits (previous image). These have a pilot drill inside a spring-loaded chamfered tube. Simply locate the tube into the countersunk hole in the hinge (etc.) and press. The tube self-centres itself and ensures the pilot drill hits the exact centre of the hole. Brilliant!

Like a bullet, any drill bit will exit with a big splash of torn wood around the hole if you're not careful. Tear out on smaller holes using a twist bit is less of a problem, although you'll mostly use these bits for blind holes (not all the way though).

For the cleanest holes use flat or auger bits and drill into the timber until just the tip of the bit shows through on the backside. Then withdraw the bit, turn the workpiece over and carry on from the other side to remove the last part of the hole.

Another way of avoiding tear out on the backside is to clamp some scrap timber to the backside and drill through the whole thing. This way the tear out occurs in the scrap timber and not your finished work piece.

Be a little wary when using auger drill bits as the little lead screw on the front literally pulls the auger into the wood and it's difficult to stop before you're all the way through sometimes! I'd recommend you start with spade bits first as these require you to push them into the wood which makes it easy to regulate the depth. Once you're used to drilling holes, progress to auger bits as they do cut much faster and leave cleaner holes.

If you make a mistake with an auger, a spade bit or a hole-saw and drill a 'too small' hole, you're in trouble. Because now there is no centre timber to hold the lead point or guide drill bit. But don't fear, there is a solution. Grab a piece of scrap wood bigger than the hole you want and drill the right sized hole through it. Then clamp the new hole over the original 'too small' hole, drill through your new template and it will guide the bit into the original hole. Once you are part way into the original hole you can stop and remove the template and the part hole will guide you the rest of the way through. You're welcome... Oh, and if you've drilled a hole that's too big... you're on your own.

DRILLING CONCRETE, MASONRY, AND DRYWALL

Masonry drill bits are not sharp in the same way as other drill bits because they don't cut away material, instead they chip and break it away like a hammer and chisel (in fact this is how stone carvers used to form holes in ancient times, rotating by hand a star shaped, fluted chisel and a hammer...).

Light hammer drills are not terribly effective though, as they only wobble the drill bit at high speed. They work reasonably well in soft masonry such as soft bricks or blocks, but the straight bits will quickly blunt in anything remotely hard like concrete or engineering brick.

The SDS drill bit system however, is effective and robust, making it the only serious choice for drilling harder masonry and concrete. SDS and its derivatives use a true percussive impact design, literally hammering out and quickly removing material. In addition, SDS drill bits last a very, very long time due to the effective way they work (i.e. good design rather than applying lots of pressure). In fact, I mostly lose drill bits before wearing them out!

As with timber, the exit hole is significant when drilling masonry and concrete, only more so probably, (because of the hammer action). Always drill from the 'face' side and never from the backside (inside) or you'll end up with a very large hole in the face of the wall where the drill bit exits. It's easier to patch up plaster (or cover it with an electrical or cover plate etc.) on the inside than it is to repair a damaged brick on the outside.

Occasionally when drilling into old masonry the drill bit will hit air, in other words there is nothing to drill into. This is because of hidden voids in the mortar joints, or bad sections of brick, block, concrete etc. If there's no possibility of moving the location of the hole (common if it's a bracket etc.) you'll need to fill the void with something that will set hard. Vacuum out the hole and fill the void with a mortar/ filler, pushing it in repeatedly until it's full and firm, allow to fully dry and try to re-drill the hole. For smaller voids, it's sometimes possible to pump a grab adhesive (no-nails or liquid nails type) into the hole followed by the wall plug (push the plug well in and scrape away an excess that squeezes out). Allow the adhesive to set overnight before fitting and tightening the screw.

Also, occasionally when drilling into masonry the drill bit will veer off at an angle. This is usually when the bit hits something unexpectedly hard like a stone in an old brick or block for example. This is difficult to correct and if possible, just move along a few inches and try again. If the hole absolutely must be in that spot, then fill the hole with mortar (and allow a couple of days for it to dry) and try again using a thin timber template to hold the drill bit true as it enters the wall. Hold the template onto the wall (or ask a friend), remark your hole onto the timber and then drill through the timber and into the wall. Rubber strips stapled onto the back of plywood makes a good template.

Large diameter holes in masonry are possible using diamond tipped hollow core drills, hired from your local tool hire store. Installing ventilation fans in kitchens and bathrooms often use a 117mm (4½″) core drill mounted into a large, powerful drill for example. It's not a job for the faint hearted though, as a drill powerful enough to drill holes this big is quite a beast to handle.

Drywall is so soft you can make holes in it using almost anything; in fact, some types of drywall fittings drill their own hole. HSS bits are popular to drill drywall materials, but don't expect to be able to drill metal with them afterwards (mark them with some electrical tape and save for the next time you need to drill into drywall). Otherwise a normal masonry bit is the 'official' bit for drilling holes in drywall (although not terribly accurate).

DRILLING METAL

For most small diameter holes in metal, use HSS or *twist* drill bits, (HSS stands for high speed steel). For holes in thin metal over 13mm use special hole saws with hardened teeth.

Because metal is hard, drill bits find it difficult to start and *wander* or *walk* all over the place. To avoid this, place a *centre punch* dead centre of your proposed hole and give it one (and only one) sharp tap with a hammer. The tiny depression gives something for the drill bit to bite into as it starts up.

Centre punch exactly on your pencil marks. The drill bit follows your punch marks. Without centre punch the drill bit wanders.

Although metal is hard stuff to drill holes into, if you follow these rules it's relatively easy to drill holes for nuts and bolts, screws, or rivets etc...

- Use a vice or clamps to hold the metal. *Never, ever* hold metal in your hands (or feet) when drilling holes. Drill bits' snag as they go through the back side *every single time,* and if the workpiece is not well secured, it turns into a propeller, a very sharp propeller, just picture a lawnmower blade, i.e. it's going to get bloody...

- Sharp drill bits are essential. You'll need to press a blunt bit harder to get it to cut which causes it to overheat. The more it overheats the blunter it gets and the harder you must press, blunting it further still and… you can see where this is going can't you? Use sharp bits!

- Drill bits must not overheat (see above) because it alters their hardness. Watch the tip for smoke, which means it's getting too hot. Use a coolant for all but the smallest holes in thin material…

- Engineers use a special coolant, a thin cutting fluid dripped onto drill bits. You can use WD40 or light oil. In a pinch use water in an old washing up liquid bottle or spray bottle (dry off afterwards to prevent corrosion).

- Remember: the above fluid act as a coolant first and a lubricant second. But it doesn't mean you will get away with using blunt bits!

- Use a slow drill speed and high feed (press quite hard), the bigger the bit, the slower the speed.

- The drill bit must be 90° to the work surface. The cutting edge of a drill bit works like a rotating plane blade, if the angle isn't perfect the cutting-edge lifts off the metal and stops cutting.

If you intend to do a lot of drilling, cheap pillar drills are the way to go as they hold the drill bit perfectly perpendicular to the material (see the last point above). Plus, a pillar drill incorporates a small vice like mechanism to securely hold the workpiece. Drilling using a hand-held drill is haphazard by comparison (although possible with care) and it blunts drill bits much quicker.

You can easily see when a drill bit is sharp and you've got the angle right because as with a wood plane, the shavings (called swarf when drilling) will peel off in long-ish pieces (in steel). If you're getting small chips when drilling steel then the drill bit is not sharp enough (small chips are normal in some types of metal though, e.g. brass).

For larger holes, drill a small 'lead hole' first. This makes it much easier for the larger drill bit. For example, if your goal is an 8mm hole, start with a 4mm one first (appx. half the final hole size); then follow with the 8mm bit. For even bigger holes, you can step them in a similar way; 4mm, 8mm, and finally 12mm etc.

Some metals require special drill bits,

- Brass needs a bit which has a 90° cutting edge. In effect, the cutting edge scrapes the brass off like a milling machine (in a pinch you can file a small flat on the cutting edge of a regular HSS bit). A regular HSS bit will bite too far into brass and become stuck.

➤ Stainless steel needs harder bits made using cobalt, titanium, carbide, or diamond etc. plus lots of feed in combination with a slow drilling speed and lots of cooling lubricant, (SS is super hard!).

➤ Aluminium is comparatively soft and clogs drill flutes easily, so try *pecking* (backing in and out) during drilling to clear the swarf etc.

DRILLING TILES, CERAMICS, AND GLASS

Tiles and ceramics are amongst the most difficult materials to drill as they have very hard surfaces and some, like porcelain or glass for example are very hard all the way through. Hard materials like this require special tile/glass drill bits made from carbide or increasingly diamond tips.

Another challenge is stopping the drill bit from wandering all over the hard surface when starting to drill. Try using masking tape on the tile for small holes. Personally, I use a non-slip guide/template which is pre-drilled with some common hole sizes. I simply hold the hole size I need over my perfectly measured and marked holes and use the guide to get the hole started. Once there is a shallow depression, I remove it and finish the rest of the hole off normally. You can make your own template guide out of thin plywood with self-adhesive rubber 'feet' on the back (or put flat lines of silicone on the back of the template and then let it dry).

Regular masonry drill bits (with tungsten carbide tips) will drill small holes in some ceramic glazed tiles (e.g. 6mm holes for a toilet roll holder etc.). Remember to switch off the hammer action off and remember you run the risk of overheating the tip and melting the brazing that holds the tungsten carbide tips in place. It's unlikely a masonry bit will drill harder tiles though, porcelain for example.

Take care to keep all drill bits cool. Either keep removing the bit and dipping it into water (small risk of chipping hole edges by continuously removing the bit) or spray water onto the drill bit using a pump or trigger spray bottle every few seconds (pop a towel underneath to catch the overspray).

If drilling horizontally, make a small ring of putty, blue tack or plasticine type material around the drill bit tip to act as a moat, keeping water around the tip as you drill.

Drilling hard material like this takes a while. Don't apply too much feed, tile is the opposite of metal, a medium to high speed and very light feed is usually best for tile.

Drilling clean, through holes in glass utilises a similar technique we looked at when drilling a piece of timber; drill into the glass until the tip shows through the backside, then turn over and continue from the backside to minimise chipping around the hole. Incidentally, remember that you will not be able to drill holes (or cut) safety, tempered or toughened glass.

Lastly, are you sure you need to drill the hole in the first place? Just that small and lightweight stuff easily hangs from special adhesive pads. Alternatively, we hang small and lightweight stuff using silicone sealant. Stick the backing plate to the wall with a little silicone and tape up to hold until the silicone sets. Then go around the edges with more silicone to reinforce it. Leave to cure fully and then pop the item onto the bracket. This works well for lightweight stuff such as toothbrush holders, loo roll holders and the like.

DRILLING PLASTIC

Although plastic is soft, you'll still need sharp drill bits, or you'll just 'burn' your way though. And because it's soft, a standard HSS drill bit will pull strongly into the material as you drill, possibly dangerously yanking it up the drill bit and out of your clamp. A drill bit with a flattened cutting edge also works well in plastic (like the ones we looked at for drilling brass).

It's not always easy to hold plastic firmly as some sections are not strong enough to clamp properly and it's often an unusual shape (pipe, L shaped angles, T pieces, C pieces, etc. etc.). Try clamping an offcut of timber onto or into the section if possible to hold the plastic rigid over a longer length.

It's best to drill through plastic into a piece of wood if possible. This lowers the risk of the bit cracking the plastic if the bit snatches the plastic as it exits. I tend to drill plastic slowly to avoid heat build-up causing a problem.

DRILLING RUBBER

Of course, I'm half joking, you can't really drill rubber because, well, it's rubbery! It is possible to drill small holes using a regular twist bit, but they tend to be very raggedy inside and much smaller than the diameter of the drill bit you used. Instead of a drill bit, try using a hollow punch or make one out of a sharpened piece of pipe or similar. Pop the rubber sheet onto a solid block of wood and hold the punch very firmly on your mark. One sharp hit with a hammer works best for the cleanest holes. This should punch a hole straight through the rubber sheet. To make rubber washers you'll need two stamps, one for the inside diameter and then another for the outside diameter (or use scissors for the outside cut on bigger washers).

MAKING HOLES IN FABRIC, CARPETS ETC.

You can't drill holes in fabric as such either, but occasionally you might need to make holes in carpet, fitting sliding door rail runners for example. You'll need to be very careful not to use anything rotary or you'll run the risk of pulling a thread and believe me if the drill bit, or even a screw, 'catches' a carpet thread, it'll run across the whole carpet in a flash, long before you can stop the drill...

Use the same technique as mentioned above for rubber, (a hollow punch or in a pinch, a slightly sharpened pipe). Some folks like to melt holes using a pipe (or even a socket wrench etc.) heated with a blowtorch (seems a little risky to me though). I've regularly stamped holes through carpet where I've needed to get a fixing into concrete subfloors (where the client wanted carpet wall to wall under built in wardrobes etc.). It does create a problem in the future though for whoever is replacing the carpet (when they find it goes underneath things), but still, the client is always right and all that...

Any nylon or plastic based fabric (or rope/cord incidentally) responds well to melting holes as the heat automatically seals the edges. It's best to test the method on a scrap workpiece first though to see what happens. Obviously, take care when using naked flames around flammable objects. Oh, and the fumes will be dangerously nasty too...

HOW TO CUT TIMBER WITH A MITRE SAW

There are dozens of different power tools you could buy, (depending on your first project or two), but for many folks, the mitre saw is probably No.2 on the list after a drill. I know we've looked at this before but, as always, the maxim you get what you pay for rules supreme on power saws. The cheap mitre saws around these days are scarily bad, and if you can't afford one from a reputable manufacturer; seriously, you'd be better spending your cash on a regular hand saw instead. Cheapo mitre saws usually don't have soft starts and will scream at you as you chew your way through the wood with a wobbly blade etc. Branded saws, especially the smaller ones are not terribly expensive these days either. Stick to the 'big' three (in the UK at least), Bosch, DeWalt and Makita. I have tools from all three and I've never had a bad one. There are of course, plenty of other manufacturers, but do your due diligence and research before buying to avoid buying a lemon.

Most mitre saws don't come with legs which means either buying a proper stand, building yourself a workbench (temporary or permanent) or using it on the floor. Using a mitre saw on the floor is possible, but it's tiring, and it will get old really quick. Either buy a stand or use a length of stout timber (e.g. a scaffold plank) and pop it onto a pair of trestles etc. (to stop the saw from moving, either bolt it down or drill some shallow holes big enough to hold the saws rubber feet). Measure the height of the saws cutting bed and cut some support blocks, fixing them to the plank along either side of the saw to hold the workpiece at the exact height of the saw bed. Why? Because supporting the workpiece makes life easy.

The blade runs downwards which pushes the workpiece backwards towards and against the rear support on the saws bed. Thus, you must make sure you hold the workpiece firmly against the rear support or the blade will snatch it and yank it back for you, pinching your fingers in the process.

For square or 90° cuts on a mitre saw you should…

- Properly support the timber along most of its length. Including the offcut side (often overlooked).

- Hold the timber with your left hand firmly, pushing it down onto the bed and back hard against the saw's rear upstand.

- Most folks like to hold the actual workpiece with the left hand and have the waste or offcut to the right (it depends on the size of the workpiece.

- Workpieces too small to hold safely with the left hand (because it ends up too close to the blade) need to swap cutting sides. Instead hold the waste or offcut side and position the blade to the left of your pencil mark, workpiece to the right.

- With your right hand, release the blade guard mechanism and gently lower the stationary blade and position it to the right (waste or offcut side) of the pencil mark or where you want it. Nudge the workpiece left of right to adjust and lower the blade again to check. Repeat until the blade is perfectly positioned on your pencil mark.

- Once happy with the blade position, gently but firmly allow the saw to return to the upright position until the blade guard re-engages.

- Still holding the workpiece very firmly with your left hand, start the saw. If the workpiece moves, switch off the saw, wait for it to stop spinning and repeat the above process, only holding more firmly (this is why soft start saws are so good and the 'screaming banshee' saws are so bad).

- With your right hand, release the blade guard mechanism again and gently but firmly, lower the now running blade onto and steadily through your work piece. Don't labour the blade speed, slow and gentle is good.

- Pay special attention to the moment the saw blade exits the rear of the workpiece as this means there is a loose offcut on the right-hand side of the blade which may move.

- Gently raise the saw to the upright position and switch off the saw and remain still until the blade stops spinning. You can whistle while you wait if you want...

- Recover your workpiece and offcut. Rinse and repeat.

The first few times will be scary and probably feel a bit dangerous (because it potentially is. But practise will help and after a few cuts you'll be fine. If you stick to working safely and never, (and I mean never) try to do anything remotely stupid, like cutting a tiny workpiece or not supporting the timber properly or crossing your hands, holding the workpiece the wrong way etc., you'll survive unscathed.

A couple of extra things to note when you're cutting mitres...

- Hold the workpiece especially firmly as the blade is obviously not square to the saw bed now. This means it will try to pull the workpiece along the direction of the blade a little causing it to snatch. (especially if the blade is a little dull).

- Keep your hands well out of the way, don't forget the blade is coming across you now at 45° as well.

If you're cutting profiled trims, try a practise cut first and note where the blade chips the edge. Usually you'll need to cut the trim front to back to avoid chipping the often-thinner front edge. Fine trims really need a special blade with many more teeth than a standard multipurpose cutting blade. The more teeth, the finer the cut.

You might hear the term combination mitre saws; these are where the saw head tilts in both planes; 45° left and right plus 45° from perpendicular. This is useful for cutting mitres on trims and stock taller than 60mm or so (cut lying flat on the saw bed instead of standing upright).

One last tip, if you've used the saw to cut something slightly out of square, don't forget to return the saw to its 90° setting or you risk cutting something out of square the next time you use the saw (I did this earlier today actually, cutting a board with a 5° angle when I wanted it square. Oops.).

Okay, that's enough with the power tool stuff or we'll be here forever! Just make time to slowly practise with each one until you have some experience and are confident to use it without fear.

STRAIGHT, LEVEL, PLUMB & SQUARE

To be truly handy you need to master the dimensions, and no, not in a Doctor Who kind of way, although a sonic screwdriver would come in handy... No, I mean you must learn how important it is to get things absolutely; *straight, level, plumb and square.* Most things need to be correct in *all* of these *planes.* Anything significantly *out of true* or inaccurate, (in any of these planes), may operate poorly and be difficult to adjust correctly.

Honestly, I just can't stress this enough, it's such a common failing for newbies to think 'it's near enough', but it never is, leaving stuff slightly out in one plane or another, will nearly always bite you on the butt later in the project. Either the last part won't fit properly, or you won't be able to adjust a component properly, or a component won't work properly, or it just looks bad. Take the time to get stuff exactly straight, level, plumb and square because then everything will fit much better with only minimal adjustments needed, saving you lots of time. Let's go through them...

STRAIGHT (IN LINE OR FLAT)

Getting things straight, inline, or flat is important for them to look good to the naked eye. Anything out of line will visually jump out at the beholder, highlighting or even exaggerating any errors and thus spoiling the look (remember that wonky picture frame?). Installing stuff straight or parallel to a wall, floor, or ceiling for example, leads the eye towards the item itself in all its glory, no distractions from tapered gaps, curves, hollows, bumps, lumps, or kinks.

To check for flatness or straightness, use something you know to have a true straight edge. For small things, a spirit level makes a great straight edge, or you can make a longer one from a straight piece of timber, 50mm × 100mm (2″ × 4″) is common. For truly straight, you can buy proper aluminium straight edges, which are the bee's knees of straightness and cost less than you think.

Move your straight edge around to find, curves, bumps, or high spots, it will rock, and not in a good way! Look for gaps between the straight edge and your surface indicating hollows or low spots. When everything touches the straight edge, it's straight and in line. Hold the straight edge at different angles such as corner to corner to check different planes.

Use the humble builder's string line to check longer distances for straightness, because a taut line stretched between two points is always perfectly straight. To check for parallel, measure equal distances from a straightedge or string line.

LEVEL (HORIZONTAL)

It is very important to make sure everything you build or fit is truly level because errors in level will likely cause impossible adjustment problems later on, (even if you don't see how right now). This is especially true when fitting any kind of cabinets (kitchen, bathrooms & bedrooms etc), or ceramic tiling, brickwork, patios and so on.

For example, I've built houses, level from top to bottom hardly using a spirit level to measure horizontals. How? Because I set up the foundations exactly horizontal and measured my brickwork up from that foundation level using my tape measure. If it's level to start with, (and each corner is the same height), it will still be level at the roof. Whereas we have laughed at teams who threw the concrete into their trenches in a rush, wasting valuable time trying to get the brickwork level in time to put the first-floor windows in.

If you're marking fixing points onto a wall ready for drilling holes, they should be absolutely level, even if there's adjustment within the fixings themselves (slots or other adjusters). Use a spirit level or a laser level. Measure down from a ceiling or up from the floor as a last resort if you don't have anything else (newish houses only, don't try this in a period cottage...).

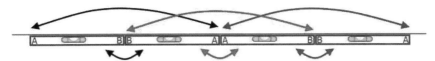

Turn the spirit level around each time you move to counteract any inaccuracy in the spirit level.

If you're marking out a level line along a wall you must flip the level around, end to end each time you move. This way any inaccuracy within the spirit level itself will even out. If you keep the spirit level the same way each time you move (and it's 1mm inaccurate), your line could be several mm's out of level by the time you get across the room.

Remember there's not much margin for error with a spirit level; the bubble really *must* be in the middle of the lines. Many spirit levels are only accurate between ½ to 1mm per metre, which means a small spirit level on top of a 4m long straight edge can be quite inaccurate, but still show 'exactly level'.

You can double-check a spirit level for accuracy by placing it on something horizontal and turning it around through 180° lengthways. The bubble should be in the middle both ways to be truly level. If it shows correct one-way but slightly out when turned around, there may be a problem with the spirit level.

RISE AND FALL

Maybe it's strange to include gradients in the level section, but when you look at their construction, you'll see it makes sense... Rise and fall are essentially the same thing, just from the opposite direction, so for now let's just say fall. If you want a rise, just flip it around.

Mentioning patios earlier reminds me, sometimes a surface needs to be absolutely flat (i.e. no hollows or bumps etc. which could puddle), but built with a gradient, either along the length (end or longitudinal fall) or across the length (cross or transverse fall). Sometimes a surface will fall in multiple directions, especially if the lowest point is a single spot like a drain. Imagine a shower floor for example which falls four ways to a central point.

Some other examples of fall you'll see are...

- Paved areas and roads fall to drainage points (soft landscaping or pipes to soakaways or storm drains) to prevent water puddling.

- Wheelchair ramps fall from doorways to the ground outside to enable easy access.

- Outdoor steps need falls to avoid holding water (which freezes in the winter or encourages slippery algae to grow in the summer).

- Roof guttering works better with a small fall towards the downpipe to prevent water sitting on the joints.

- Waste pipes need falls to carry their contents (no need to go there!) to the drains, sewers, or storage tanks etc.

- Shower floors fall to a central drain to prevent puddles.

- And not forgetting the big one, your roof needs a fall to avoid turning your house into a swimming pool.

It's especially important to get small falls or slopes very accurate to avoid water pooling, falls such as the 1:60 for a stone patio or the minimum 1 in 90 gradient for a plastic pipe for example. Your roof at 1:1 (45°), not so much.

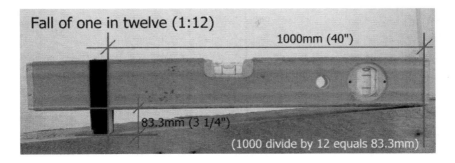

Fall of one in twelve (1:12)
1000mm (40")
83.3mm (3 1/4")
(1000 divide by 12 equals 83.3mm)

Rise and fall expressed as a gradient or ratio is common, but sometimes you'll see degrees or even percentages. Wheelchair ramps should be no steeper than one in twelve (4.8° or 8.3%) for example. 1:12 means that for every 12 units (mm, cm, inches, feet, metres) travelled, the rise (or fall) is one unit. This works with any unit you like, even the width of your thumb...

For example, if your spirit level is 1200mm (48") long, make a mark at 1m. Then divide 1000 by 12 which gives you 83mm or so. Either measure down from the bottom of your spirit level (at the 1m mark) or even better; fix an 83mm tall block of wood to the outside of the 1m mark you made. When the bubble is exactly, (and I mean exactly), in the middle between the lines, the spirit level is measuring an accurate 1 in 12 fall (or a rise if you turn the spirit level around).

Why 1000mm and not 1200mm? Mostly for clarity, but the math works for any length, the longer the better for accuracy. Just remember to measure to the upside of the block, as in the previous image (the side that's touching the slope), because the slope falls another 2mm over the width of the little block, which might matter on really accurate work.

Re-hash the math to make this work for any gradient. Laying a pipe in the basement to 1 in 40? Using the same example as above, 1000 divided by 40 equals 25. Pop a 25mm wooden block (or your thumb, a popular drain fall in-dicator!) above the 1000mm mark on your spirit level, and there you have it, a 1:40 fall. You can convert any gradient to a percentage by dividing it into itself e.g. 1÷12 is 0.083 and then multiplying it by 100 e.g. 0.083×100 is 8.3%.

PLUMB (TRULY VERTICAL OR STRAIGHT UP AND DOWN)

Things out of plumb are difficult to adjust and a bad fit performs poorly. Use a known accurate spirit level and make sure you take notice of what the bubble is telling you. You can check if a spirit level is accurate for plumb by turning it through 180° and using the 'other' side (box section levels only though), the bubble should read the same both ways if the level is accurate.

Optical illusions sometimes make things look bad, so *very occasionally* it's best to go with what *looks right*, regardless of what the spirit level bubble is saying. For example, a bookcase close to a doorway might look better fitted an equal distance from the architrave, creating a parallel gap, even if it's then slightly out of plumb. This is because stuff that tapers can draw the eye and look 'wrong'.

If you don't have a good spirit level or you want to check something from floor to ceiling (or higher) use a plumb line (a pointed weight suspended on the end of a thin string or line). You can make your own by tying anything small and heavy to the end of thin string and suspend it where it can hang completely free. Either measure from the line or place marks on the wall behind the string etc. Plumb lines are always 100% accurate, (well, until the planet really starts wobbling that is!)

A rough (and risky) way to check if something is plumb is to measure from a nearby corner or door frame etc., but plumb lines are so easy to make, there really is no excuse not to get it 100% right.

SQUARE (90°)

Square is when something is 90° or perpendicular to something else. Getting stuff square is vital because it affects your ability to fit something level and plumb. A kitchen cabinet for example should have 90° internal corners and therefore be square. However, if you rushed the assembly of your kitchen cabinet and the corners are not square, you'll find it physically impossible to get it both level (horizontal) *and* plumb (vertical). This tends to bite you on the butt later because it makes fitting the doors just a *l i t t l e* bit tricky... By the laws of the universe (cue dramatic music...), if something is perfectly level *and* plumb it *must* also be square (don't worry about this, it just is okay!).

Use a regular carpenters square to check small stuff for square and for general carpentry work. Set out medium sized things, using a framing/ roofing square or one of the popular foldable/ collapsible squares. Check big stuff (extensions, patios, decking etc.) for square using a tape measure and measuring the length of the diagonals, (remember that lesson from school?), if they are equal, it's exactly square.

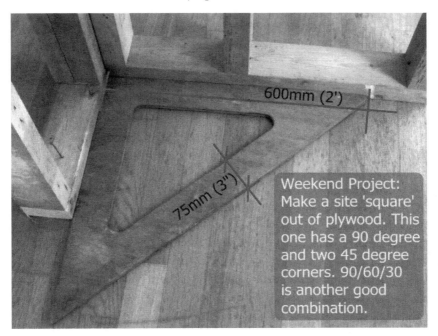

600mm (2')

75mm (3")

Weekend Project: Make a site 'square' out of plywood. This one has a 90 degree and two 45 degree corners. 90/60/30 is another good combination.

If you want to make your own square, grab an offcut of 9mm or 12mm plywood, around 600mm × 600mm (24″ × 24″) should do, or even MDF (medium density fibreboard) in a pinch. Cut your plywood into an accurate triangle and then take a small triangular section out of the middle. Make sure the external 90° angle is one of the original factory cut corners of the plywood sheet to ensure reasonable squareness. Give it a coat or two of wood preservative if you intend using it outdoors a lot.

If you like your maths, you'll also remember the 'power of Pythagoras' (cue dramatic music again!) The Pythagorean Theorem or 3:4:5 as it's often called on building sites.

Measure 3 units along one side and 4 along the adjacent side and then measure across the *hypotenuse* (long side). Drum roll please... if it's exactly 5 units, then it's square. It doesn't matter what units you use if you *keep to the ratio*, metres, centimetres, inches, feet etc. are all good.

Multiples work even better; (6:8:10 or 9:12:15 etc.) because longer lengths increase accuracy.

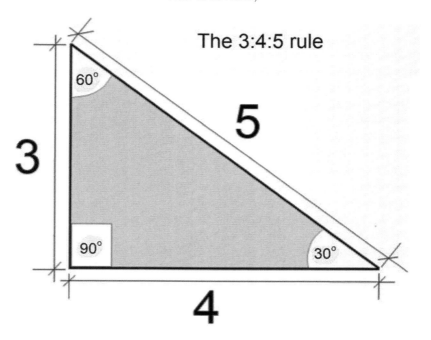

WORKING EFFICIENTLY & PRODUCTIVELY

We all want the job done as quickly as possible, especially if the work is hard or tedious, so here's a few things you can do to increase your efficiency and ability to get the job done a little quicker...

BREAK DOWN PROJECTS INTO TINY PIECES

Some DIY projects are tough and sometimes you'll just get fed up with the whole thing. You'll want the mess to go away and your nice quiet life back. The trick to avoid DIY burnout during bigger projects (or dare I say it, any boring bits), is to break up the job into much smaller tasks. Don't focus on the whole project. Focus instead on each small task, each step, each brick, each tile, or each coat of paint etc. At the end of each task look at it, saying 'Wow that looks fantastic; I made a really good job of that.' Then, move on to the next task and repeat. These small successes add up over time until one day it's finished. Will Smith, (actor) once said, "don't focus on the whole wall, focus on each brick, the wall will take care of itself". Great advice.

It works because viewing your project task by task, reduces the mental enormity of the whole project. By focusing instead on individual tasks, the mind can concentrate solely on the job in hand. Ignore the finish line, concentrate on *how far you've come, how much you've learned* and *how much you've done* rather than what's left to do. Then you'll be more confident of your success *plus* you'll enjoy the work much more.

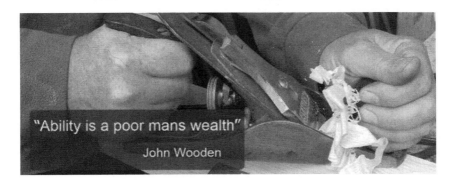

"Ability is a poor mans wealth"
John Wooden

ALWAYS BE FINISHING SOMETHING

Each day you plan to tackle a part of your project, it's essential to choose a task that fits the time you have available. For example, if you only have 30 minutes one day, choose to do something that takes 30 minutes to finish. Don't get 30 minutes into a job that's going to take 4 hours to finish, because when you come back to it next time you'll waste precious minutes wondering where it was you'd got to. Save the 4-hour job for a day when you have the full 4 hours.

Using this approach is efficient because it ensures you'll *always be finishing something* and that's a good thing! A steady stream of successfully finished tasks is great motivation. Plus, you'll not be tempted to leave half-finished stuff all over the place, annoying the heck out of everyone else in the house. The quality of your work will improve too, since stopping and starting is a poor technique for many DIY tasks, especially ceramic tiling, decorating etc.

As an example, as a teenager I fell in love with an old Daimler from the 1970's which I impulsively bought, naively thinking it would be an easy restoration project (I was 19 remember!). Sometimes it was too much for me though; because there was so much welding, painting, and fixing worn out stuff to do, I thought I'd never finish it. Then I started to focus just on *one part at a time*, all the while visualising them going back onto the car, thinking, 'this car is going to be soooo cool!' and eventually it was (and still is!).

Sure, it took some years to finish that car, sometimes work went slow (when the opposite sex or work got in the way!), but it doesn't matter, the one step at a time process guarantees you'll get there in the end. It's only when you stop, when you give up, that you fail to finish.

Saving this 1977 Daimler Two Door from the scrapyard was a huge project, and it taught me a lot about perseverance.

But I'll be honest with you, some days nothing works, and you'll wonder why the heck you even started. Then it's best to take a break and go do something else for a while. Get out of the house, visit a friend, or go for a walk. Try looking for inspiration as you go; for example, if the painting preparation gets too monotonous for you, head out and start the next phase by looking for paint colours. Or have a wander around the fabrics or furniture departments and think about what you want once all the hard work is finished.

When you come back, you'll have more energy and the inspiration you picked up will help you through the rest of the job. In a few months' time, you'll have completely forgotten about any hardships, but the satisfaction of a fantastic job well done and the cash saved, is yours to enjoy for as long as you want to.

Importantly, you should learn to recognise what stuff tests your limits or pushes you close to your breaking point. For me it's boring, physically hard stuff like digging etc. (yes, I'm getting to be a wuss in my old age!). Factor these things into your plan if need be, maybe you could arrange some help for those parts, (i.e. I'll provide the food and beer, you just bring a shovel...).

All these feelings are perfectly normal; we all have good days and bad days. DIY is sometimes hard work, or you might make a mistake, but when it goes right, (and it always does in the end) it's just so rewarding. Fortunately, most DIY jobs are enjoyable enough and even entertaining at times.

"When you reach the end of your rope, tie a knot in it and hang on."

Thomas Jefferson

WORKING EFFICIENTLY

Car manufacturers understood this decades ago, meshing man and machine into an efficient process akin to an ant farm. No wasted energy and every movement serves some part of the manufacturing process. Whilst I don't expect you to aim for such heady heights, (many professionals don't), you can start to think about how you approach the tasks you do. Working faster's not an option (it's hard work and leads to mistakes). But here are some ways you *can* improve your efficiency...

- Measure properly, don't estimate your material quantities. Going to pick up extra materials from the store wastes valuable time and ending up with excess materials wastes money.

- Place the materials close to the final fixing place. Obvious yes? But it's surprising how often I see badly placed materials and folks over reaching or even walking some distance to retrieve them for fixing.

- Plan the space required for the materials so you don't need to handle them more than necessary etc.

- Order materials for larger jobs in a logical flow as you need them, called 'just in time' in logistics speak. Utilise the stores delivery capability to save your time. This avoids clogging up your valuable storage space.

- Never walk *away* from the work place *empty handed*. Think about what stuff you've finished with. Pick it up and take it out as you go, even if it's just a piece of rubbish. This will save a dedicated trip out with it later.

- Never walk *towards* the workplace *empty handed* either. Is it possible to take the tools/material/etc. into the workplace for the next task? E.g. on one job, we all carried in a length of timber (for a big stud wall) each time we returned from coffee break. By Friday, all 150 lengths of timber were stacked next to the job ready for the chippie on Monday (saving me time and money for little effort).

- Sawing timber is easier on proper supports for example. Struggling in a badly prepared workplace loses more time than the time it takes to set up properly.

- Be methodical in your actions and less.... erm... random! Paint in a logical sequence for example, not waving your arms about like a man flagging down a bus...

- Mentally 'walk' though your project, daily if need be. Think about each task and what tools/materials you need. Have you thought about everything?

- If you have a known weakness, (i.e. sawing squarely), avoid doing it and spoiling work. Instead, either acquire a tool that will do it for you, or study and practise... a lot!

Batching is another way to improve your efficiency. Combine all similar tasks into one batch and tackle them in succession. Don't get distracted by urgency and forget to concentrate on efficiency. Every time you stop and change direction/tool/task, you lose time. In your plan group the same tasks together logically if possible. For example, an *inefficient* plan would be...

Joe's Bedroom

- Sandpaper skirting boards.
- Sandpaper the window and fill holes in walls.
- Paint window.
- Paint ceiling.
- Paint walls.
- Fit new carpet.

Jane's Bedroom

- Sandpaper skirting boards.

- Sandpaper the window and fill holes in walls.

- Paint window.

- Paint ceiling.

- Paint walls.

- Fit new carpet.

More efficient would be... Work on both bedrooms consecutively. I.e. do one task in Joe's room, and then immediately do the *same* job in Jane's room...

- Sandpaper skirting boards in Joe's and then Jane's room.

- Sand the window/ fill holes in Jane's room and then Joes.

- Paint window in Joe's room and then Janes.

- Paint ceilings in Jane's room and then Joes.

- Paint the walls in Joe's room and then Janes.

- Fit new carpet in Joe's room and then Janes.

That's a hypothetical example I know, but I hope it shows the important principle of a rolling process of tasks, of like following like and handling each group of tools and materials once as you zig-zag between the two rooms. And best of all, you only need to clean your paint roller once; at the end of each paint colour/job because all the painting is concentrated or 'batched' together (you can wrap rollers tightly in cling film or roll it into a plastic carrier bag for a day or two in-between coats if necessary).

THE TWO-MINUTE FIX

Consider keeping a couple of screwdrivers somewhere handy (in a kitchen drawer?) so you can employ the 'two-minute' rule' where anything taking less than two minutes or so to fix, you deal with on the spot. Then those small jobs don't pile up on you. Because you've dealt with it, you no longer need to think about it, which reduces stress. Next time you notice something amiss in your home, think about what you'd need (there and then) to fix it or stop it getting worse. How long would it take to go and get a screwdriver and fix that catching cabinet door before it gets worse? It might take less time than you think.

If you don't even have two minutes, make a note on your maintenance plan or list. This at least frees your mind and gives you a few tasks to start with when you do have time to catch up on your DIY.

AN ASIDE ABOUT PRODUCTIVITY

'I can lay a squillion bricks a day' said Bill the bricklayer. Bragging about technical prowess on building sites seems to be compulsory amongst bricklayers especially, with each claiming to be the 'best' and by best, I mean fastest. But what a load of old tosh! Producing work of a good standard is not like the Tour-de-France cycle race, although I do know one or two bricklayers who'd definitely benefit from some 'performance enhancing substances'...

I used to train many apprentices (as a lecturer at college plus on site as an employer) and all of them complained about their apparent lack of productivity. They all wanted to lay a thousand bricks a day, surely one of the most enduring of all urban myths. Sure, laying a thousand bricks a day is possible in straight runs on a large supermarket wall, but most bricklayers (if they're truthful) cannot consistently lay a thousand bricks a day, because there's more to most jobs than just laying bricks, plus you'd eventually ruin your back...

The point to remember is that speed comes naturally once you *become proficient*, because once you have developed a *good technique*, your *efficiency will improve* and ergo your speed. If you try to go fast before you've fully mastered the proper techniques, you'll produce shoddy work.

Productivity is an obsession with us bricklayers; because when you're head down and bottom up, laying one brick on top of another hour after hour, day after day, week after week, you just can't help but think 'how can I lay more bricks?' Because ultimately it means *more money*. Still, you'll never lay a thousand perfect bricks a day though, but if you can, call me and we'll talk...

Efficiency is intelligent laziness

QUALITY WORK AND COMPROMISE

Forgive me, I know I keep banging on about accuracy and quality etc. but making the effort to produce good work is important because you'll have enough to cope with (learning and practising all this stuff), without having to overcome problems caused by your own sloppy work. But I do understand it's not easy to do, especially if you're under pressure to finish.

Producing great work comes from *not compromising* your craft. It's about reading up on good working practises and then following them. It's about using the right fasteners or the right tool. It's about not leaving something out because it's inconvenient or because you want to finish quickly. It means going back again and again, making small adjustments until it's perfect. Plus, it's having the resolve to stop, abandon that particular piece and start over with a new one, if that's what it's going to take to get it right.

Quality is never an accident.
It is always the result of intelligent effort.
John Ruskin

Going back to Robert Pirsig and his *Zen and the Art of Motorcycle Mainte-nance* again, he comments that "to say craftspeople are not artists is to misun-derstand the nature of art" and that's how it feels to me. I can turn two things (a pile of bricks and a pile of mortar) into a house, or a BBQ or a pizza oven. Two materials! It sure feels like art as I work with the wet mortar together with the brick, adjusting and adjusting and adjusting until the brick is just so, I've satis-fied my eye, and I can reach for the next brick.

Whereas, less able workers often cut once and fit, even if it's not quite right. They compromise the quality in the name of speed or profit. Whereas, someone who cares about the finish will go back again and again, trimming, or adjusting until it's a great fit, I know I do.

Sadly, there is often an attitude on building sites that the minimum stand-ard is THE standard, and there is little interest (read profit) in building some-thing that exceeds the minimum standard. This culture comes from the very top though, it's not just shoddy workmanship (although sometimes it is). Time is money in construction and the margins (read prices and profit) are usually tight. There is a lot of competition out there and there just isn't room in the budget for folks to work at a relaxed pace and produce excellent results. Things are in a rush usually, deadlines need to be met and stuff is overlooked or even swept un-der the carpet in order to not fall behind and incur the punitive penalty fines for 'late delivery', which are built into many contracts.

On an individual level, each trade knows the limitations of the following trade and often you might hear, it's okay, 'the painters will get over it' and as good as they are, no trade should have to fix another trades mistake.

The reason you should be serious about producing high quality work is because it not only looks better but it's more durable too. It will also make you feel prouder of your efforts and achievements, especially if others notice. Actually, and this is really sad, but folks often only notice when the standard of work is poor. Read into that whatever you will about our society...

So never think, *it's near enough* when an exact fit is better. Small errors also have a nasty habit; they quickly magnify and trip you up. Cabinet runs in a kitchen are a good example of this; if your cabinets are all wonky, making the cabinet doors look good is incredibly difficult and time consuming. Finishing off badly fitted stuff to make it look good requires lots of experience, and even then, it's a compromise. It's much easier to take your time and ensure everything is accurate to start with.

Following plans or instructions and working to accepted standards makes your work predictable. You'll know for sure that the end results will be good and fit for purpose. Whereas it's difficult to predict what the consequences might be in the future if you cut corners today, the effects might not show for years. Leaving the fridge out of level might shorten it's working life; not washing down before painting those windows might take years off the paints ability to remain firmly stuck to the timberwork; leaving out a few fasteners on the IKEA furniture might mean wobbly bits a few years down the road; not using an earthing strap whilst working on electrical items might damage a component causing it to fail tomorrow, or in a years' time. This list could go on and on as you might imagine.

Remember what I said in the introduction; time and quality are inseparable and here you have a huge advantage over a hired tradesperson, *you have time*. You don't need to work fast, you're not on a fixed price, or working to another person's deadline (your other half excepted!) or making a living at this. So no excuses okay, make the time to do it properly, you'll not regret it 6 months from now I promise you.

Still with me? Cool, then let's make a plan...

PREPARATION AND PLANS

"planning is bringing the future into the present so you can do something about it now"

Alan Lakein

Now you're starting to get familiar with your tools and practising, it's time to look at the next step. Getting ready for a real project of your own. General Colin Powell once said there were no secrets to success; it's just the result of preparation, hard work, and learning from failure. Hard work we know all about and learning from failure we do from infancy, so that only leaves preparation to worry about.

After decades of preparing and planning work for clients, I've built up a good knowledge of what I need to finish a job to a high standard. I know how long the job is likely to take and what difficulties I'm likely to find (plus how much extra time I need to overcome them). I know where to go to buy materials and who to see to get good prices. I also have a lifesaving network of associated trades to call when I need extra help. This experience means I always know what I'm doing and what I'm going to do next. Well, bully for you I hear you think, but that doesn't help me now does it? So, what *can* you do?

What you *can do* in lieu of experience is to *make a plan*. A plan will help you to think through each part of the project to discover what you need to learn and what you need to buy. In short, it'll help you with the details. Oh, and don't think you can skip this part, because you really do need a plan, oh yes indeedy! Making even a simple plan will help you find any holes in your reasoning. Does making a plan frighten you a little bit? Well, don't call it a plan then, let's call it a list instead; and we all like making lists, don't we? Okay? Since you're so happy with one list, any objections to making it three lists, still okay?

Awesome...

- A list describing the project plus your notes, (overview).

- A list of what you need, (preparation).

- A list of what to do, (planning).

I've even been known to add things to my list just so I can cross them off and to make my wife think I've been super busy!

OVERVIEW

Once you have an idea for a project swirling around in your head, grab a sheet of paper or a notebook and write down an overview, a brief description simply detailing what you want to achieve. It doesn't have to be elaborate, just a sentence or two with a few details or a short bullet list about what you'd like. Writing it down gets your mind thinking about what you need and making a written plan counts as actually starting the project and we all know starting is the hardest part...

You can also use this sheet as a place to keep notes or reminders about the project too. It's also a good place to keep any clippings from magazines, websites, stores you visited or sample materials etc. Some people even keep a pin board for this part of the planning process.

PREPARATION

Now we have a brief description of what you want, it's time to start the preparation list, i.e. a record of what you need to buy or do before you start the physical work? Start your preparation by re-visiting your favourite places looking for specific information, details, prices, (shops, internet, library, magazines, friends etc.) This'll also give you a rough idea what some of the big costs are likely to be too. Then, armed with a head full of facts and figures...

MAKE A LIST OF WHAT YOU NEED

- Measure up accurately and record what materials you need and how much. Always allow 5-10% extra for wastage, cuts, breakages etc.

- Research and note available options. Different qualities, and how these affect your budget etc.

- List the places that stock what you need online and locally (materials and advice).

- Decide on a budget, allowing a reasonable amount for contingencies. Allow a realistic contingency sum, from 10% to 50% depending on how decisive you are and what your financial constraints are.

- Finalise or decide what you intend to buy within your budget and make a *pick-up list* store by store.

- Order ahead, anything that has a long delivery lead-time.

- Buy any new tools/equipment needed or book their hire.

- Clear the project area, remove stuff you're re-using and cover down everything else for protection.

- Gather everything you need (tools, materials etc.) and set up 'camp' in or close to the proposed working area.

- Start your planning or *what to do list,* but keep coming back to this list (esp. with forgotten things) to add detail and depth.

Careful measurement and calculation is not only essential to prevent waste, but it will also help you estimate how long the project might take; i.e. you'll know that laying 10 paving slabs is only going to take a few hours, but 100 paving slabs might take you a few days. Work these estimates into your planning list. Plus, careful measurements prevent the inevitable delay while you run to the store because you're short of materials.

PLANNING

Make a list detailing what *you need to do,* task by task which gives you a framework to follow on a daily basis. Use this list to guide you through each part of the job *in lieu of experience and routine.*

Leave a wide margin on this list so you can make notes when you stop for the day, note what stage you're at and what's next. Note also new discoveries and revelations you made that day, plus anything you'd forgotten about. These notes are important; especially as it's likely your work will be constantly interrupted, due to working evenings, odd days, and weekends. These side notes are especially helpful to track where you are if you're not able to work on the project for a while due to work, holidays, illness, or family stuff. Never under estimate the effect of interruptions to the work flow; stuff that's obvious to you when you put your tools down for the day are often totally incomprehensible to you when you pick them up again a week later after a busy week.

The planning list is essentially a '*to do*' list giving you checkpoints to follow, going from task to task in a logical order, plus it'll remind you of areas where you need more information. Lots of small details are often lost or forgotten in the everyday melee of life, so this is the place to quickly note them down before they disappear only to pop up inconveniently later on. I hope making a list like this will give you confidence, reassuring you that you're on the right path and making progress. Oh, and don't forget to cross off all your finished tasks because it's a great motivator.

BEFORE YOU START

- Decide on when to do the work. Remember to factor in suitable weather conditions and allow enough time to find and hire any outside help. Call tradespeople early (they hate last minute planners).

- Make sure your planning list includes all the steps you think are involved in a logical way (break it right down.) More about this in a few paragraphs...

- Estimates of how long it'll take to complete each step. Use the material quantities from your *preparation list* to help you estimate.

- Work through your list of things you need to research or learn, new skills etc., especially if you're unsure exactly what's involved to complete a particular step.

I use a template/plan that I designed combining the preparation and planning lists, which enables me to price larger jobs for clients. You're welcome to visit **handycrowd.com/workbook** online, to download a copy and see if it gives you any ideas for your own planning. I use the workbook to list my costs when building extensions and houses, but it's worth a look for you to get some ideas to make your own lists or workbook.

STICK TO THE PLAN (OR MAKE ANOTHER PLAN)

What do you mean you didn't stick to the plan? You *always* stick to the plan, even if it means screwing it up and making a new one.

In 'proper' project management, you *must* follow the plan, or the project falls apart, heads roll, and people don't get paid. The plan in your case might be very simple, but you must always have a plan, (okay, I'll even allow you to keep in your head for tiny projects). When you change your mind about what you want (and you will!) either modify the old plan or start over and make a new one. Seriously, sit down; note down the changes along with the new things you need. Do the research for the new stuff and find out their associated costs, including new time estimates. Then merge the new information into the original plan (think 'cut and paste') to make a brand new, shiny, up to date, actionable plan. Then you can revise your budget plus your *task by task* job list and carry on.

It's become such an overused phrase I almost can't write it because it's become so corny; but here's the thing, it's still just so true (watch a few episodes of Grand Designs if you don't believe me!). So, repeat after me, 'if you fail to plan, you are planning to fail'. Save the surprises for birthdays and Christmas, don't build them into your DIY projects.

HAVE A BACK-UP PLAN.

Just to be on the safe side, all good plans should have one, because of Murphy's Law, this safeguards you from ever needing to use it. I can't count how many times I uncover really, really dumb stuff left behind by previous owners or tradesmen. Cables going diagonally across a wall just under the wallpaper, a soldered gas pipe that was only in its fitting by 1mm (and had been like that for 20 years!), openings in structural walls with no means of supporting the floor loads above, chimney breasts taken out leaving tons of brickwork just hanging in the attic, cupboards hanging on a single nail (like a picture frame!), structural parts of cars filled with newspaper and filler, etc. This list goes on and on, they even make TV shows about this stuff...

Since you never know what you might find or what might happen, especially with an older house; it's essential to have a list of folks to call 'in case of emergency'. Get to know a plumber, electrician, or a builder etc., *before* you start. As usual, ask your friends and colleagues for a reliable contact in each trade. Don't, whatever you do call random guys from the local phone book or classifieds, especially when you are vulnerable in an emergency. Again, find good guys *before* you need them, and *personal recommendation* is the best way.

If you're new to an area and don't know anyone; go to the local builder's merchant during a quiet time of day (not first thing, lunchtime or at closing time) and ask at the counter for a recommendation. Sure, they might all joke and say 'no-one, they're all useless around here!' but then listen to what they say. Trust me, these guys see everyone and know exactly who the good guys are, or more importantly the guys to avoid. Always ask with a smile, or better still a box of chocolates...

Plan B consists of any good guys you hear about a call, or better still make an appointment to see them in person; perhaps you could call in and visit them on their current job? Just to introduce yourself, (tell them who sent you and say that you've heard nice things about their work etc!) Then briefly tell them what you plan to do and if it's okay for you to call them and hire them for a short while to help if you get stuck. Paying someone to come for an hour or three to avoid struggling with a problem is just smart; everyone needs a helping hand occasionally.

HALF AND HALF

Doing it all yourself or getting someone in to do it all for you are not the only options. As a house builder for example I would regularly carry out the time consuming (but less technical) parts of an installation and hire in the specialists to finish of the more skilled bits or those covered by regulations like electrical wiring or anything to do with gas for heating etc.

For example, here are some ways to leverage other people's skills...

- Set out a building accurately and mark exactly where the foundations need to be and then call in our local excavator company to do all the digging and carting away of soil.

- Cut and fix all the drywall and then hire in a busy plasterer just to do the finish plaster (skimming in the UK) or tape and fill the joints.

- Call your friendly plumber (who's likely to be tooooo busy), for a quick site visit to talk through what's needed. Then get on with the 'donkey work' like chopping holes in walls and running pipes etc (plastic is brilliant!). Once the pipes were all in place and the job ready for the next or second fix stage, back comes the plumber to fit all the expensive, complicated bits. Plus if you do the pipework, you're guaranteed really tidy pipework (sorry Mr Plumber, but sometimes your pipework is too untidy for me, especially under kitchen sinks!).

- Do the same with your tame electrician, chopping holes in walls, drilling holes through floor joists, fastening the backboxes, forming cable runs and even running cables. All to their specs though...

- Wash down the paintwork and sandpaper it all up ready for the painter to work their magic with a brush, (although that sounds pretty boring, I'd rather hire someone to wash down the paintwork and sandpaper it all up ready for me to paint it!).

- Some tradespeople will actually work alongside you, halving the time the job takes and you get to learn from them.

All the above can trim huge amounts off the final labour bill, because good tradesfolk are expensive (because you get what you pay for).

Sadly, not all tradesmen are happy to do this, but it's worth hunting down the friendly ones who appreciate what you're trying to do and are flexible enough to work with you. One electrician I use wishes all his clients did this, as drilling holes, finding cable routes, and running cables is the least interesting part of his job, not to mention the dirtiest. He's happy to 'second fix' all day long. Maybe that's how you should 'sell' it to your guy?

Consider hiring in some muscle to do the heavy lifting. Remodelling the garden and afraid of the heavy materials? Local teenagers are always looking to earn cash, hire one to work with you and bear the brunt of the heavy stuff.

Wow, so now you have a plan? Then let's go and buy the stuff...

BUYING STUFF

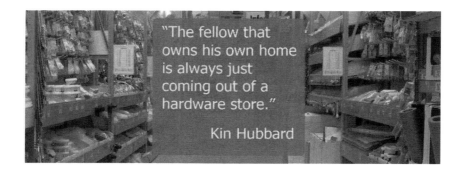

"The fellow that owns his own home is always just coming out of a hardware store."

Kin Hubbard

Although some folks do head into the store asking for a 'thingamajig' or a 'whatchamacallit', (especially on Saturday mornings), staff in the store will really appreciate it (and be more helpful) if you have at least some knowledge. Learning the proper names for the things you need for your project is the first step. Treat the store as a library, pick things up off the shelf and look at them; read what it says on the packaging and file it away, even if you don't have much idea what it all means just yet. Familiarise yourself with the store and the different departments to help build up your knowledge about what all these different things do. And yes, this will take some time...

Collect leaflets and brochures. Most stores have lots and they're pretty elementary, perfect in fact, if you're just starting out. If you like, take photos of things with your phone and when you get home, use the photos to search for the brand names you saw to find loads more info online. Add this information to your general online and other offline research, (like friends, neighbours, and colleagues), to build up your working knowledge about materials and tools (and even skills).

But first let's look at deciding a budget, because this helps determine what quality you can afford and in turn, where you should shop.

THE BUDGET

When talking about buying things the first thing that springs to most people's mind is *the budget*. In other words, *how much have I got to spend*? But people budget in different ways; some know exactly how much they want to spend, and some know exactly what it is they want. A subtle difference and two completely different approaches to buying stuff.

Two people looking to buy a new kitchen for example, one guy has a set budget and looks to get the most bang for his buck up to that limit. Another lady knows roughly what kitchen she would like but wants to do it for the least amount of money possible.

The guy with a set budget walks into a kitchen supply store and negotiates to include as much in the deal as possible. But the lady trying to save money needs to do much more legwork and research to find the best possible prices across a range of different suppliers, cherry picking the best deals for each part of the project. They may even end up with similar kitchens, but the lady will have traded more of her time in exchange for spending less money.

The simple truth is that the more time you invest in finding lower prices, the cheaper the project will be, but there is a law of diminishing returns. Note that I said 'lower' prices not 'lowest', because your own time also has a value, to you and especially to your family. Saving those last few bucks takes the most time, so don't spend hours tracking down a tiny saving right at the bottom of the pile. You should look for *good and fair prices*, not the *absolute cheapest* supplier on the planet. Life is too short and arguably, that time is better spent, either working on the project or earning overtime on your paying job.

Before you set yourself a budget though, think about...

QUALITY AND COMPROMISE

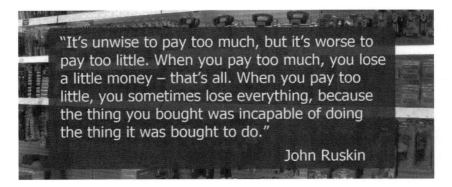

"It's unwise to pay too much, but it's worse to pay too little. When you pay too much, you lose a little money – that's all. When you pay too little, you sometimes lose everything, because the thing you bought was incapable of doing the thing it was bought to do."

John Ruskin

Before setting a budget for anything you buy in stone, remember that the price you pay, the quality you receive, and how long it all lasts, runs along a sliding scale of compromise. Mass-produced, budget quality stuff has a limited life expectancy, whereas well designed stuff made from high quality materials could last generations. Some clever clogs once said, '*If you buy quality, you only cry once*', he was right.

For example, I'm lucky to have a classic stainless-steel mechanical watch which I intend to maintain and repair indefinitely. I can do this because it's designed that way. Sure, it was horrendously expensive new, even all those years ago, but it's a masterpiece of engineering bordering on art. It will NEVER go 'out of fashion' or end up as land fill.

Next time your drawn so something 'fashionable', stop and think; is this a durable, classic design? Is it made from quality materials? Is it made by a leader in the field? Will it age well? Classics often get better and/or more valuable with age and patina. Someone once said that 'tomorrows antiques depend upon your purchases today'. Food for thought...

In contrast, items at the lower end of the price range make cost savings by using simpler designs with less features, using cheaper materials or by outsourcing the manufacture of certain components to cheaper countries. But these compromises don't just result in fewer features, poorer performance, and a shorter life expectancy; it's likely to affect their reparability too.

Repairing or even maintaining cheaply produced items is problematical if the manufacturer installed 'sealed for life' components or used glue instead of fasteners, making dismantling difficult. They might also have thinner, less durable high 'wear' areas or use weaker plastic parts for example (instead of metal) to cut costs. Spare parts might not be available or be prohibitively expensive (related to the purchase price). Plus, if you need to pay a professional to help with any aspect of the repair; it quickly becomes uneconomical. In short, budget items are just not designed for easy repairs.

"Good design doesn't date."

Harry Seidler

If you want to buy something and keep it indefinitely, you need to look for products with a long history and those that are a *core product* for the manufacturer. Products with good support from the manufacturers themselves and large, active communities or a fan base of people who love the product.

Great design with solid engineering, backed up with good quality materials is a winning combination. For example, the watch above has coped with more than twenty years of working in a heavy construction environment, including years in hot and dusty Africa, and yet it survives. I anticipate giving it to my son when I'm gone, I'm that confident in its strength. Prior to this, I used to buy watches costing about a day's wages and they'd all fail within a couple of years or so.

Now I'm not suggesting you buy everything at the top of the range, that's not affordable, but consider buying some of your most heavily used things at the mid to high end of the price scale. Often this even makes good financial sense, because you'll get reliability and durability plus reparability, which adds up to a long lifespan. High end stuff is by design, *easy to maintain or repair*. And in theory, some stuff could keep going indefinitely (or until spare parts run out, and even then, new ones could be made in theory by specialists).

The head designer over at Bentley (the luxury car makers), once said that "our cars have a product life span of 100 years" … It's probably a bad example, but it did make me start thinking, especially on heritage jobs; 'will this (whatever I am building) last another 100 years? And if it fails how will it fail?'. Thinking long term like this, really helps me to avoid 'building in' future problems by being sloppy or using poor materials or design. Be like Bentley...

However, be aware that some of the more expensive options are complicated, because fashion or exclusivity influences the price, but not necessarily the build quality. You want your extra cash to go into good design and better materials, not to keep up with the neighbours!

Fashion and changing circumstances also influence how long you live with stuff. You might buy the best quality current *hot thing*, but if in six months' time all your friends have something new and *possibly better*, it's tempting to follow them, leaving your recently acquired high quality item without a purpose or a place to live.

Okay, so the best quality stuff is expensive, that much we know, so what can we do? Well, buying second hand is sometimes an option for some things. For example, I have a manual, treadle type Singer sewing machine made in the year 1900 that's had many hundreds, if not thousands of hours of use judging by the wear marks on the casing. Nevertheless, with an occasional squirt of oil, it works just fine, *and* you can buy them for next to nothing. Second hand tools might need a little work to bring them up to scratch but compared against the price of high-quality new ones, it's still a good deal.

To further complicate things, some products are more reliable than others (irrespective of price), and the only way to find them is search the web for [*insert item name*] + *reviews* to learn about any specific shortcomings. This applies to everything from a new phone to a new house. Use the reviews to avoid buying a known *lemon* (technical term for a rubbish item!) or to negotiate an appropriate price, including little buffer to cover the cost of any potential repairs in the future. Keep a sense of perspective here though and remember negative reviews often form a tiny minority compared to the silent majority of folks who are happy with the product.

Personally, I want things to last forever, which is probably why I research the heck out of things before choosing what to buy (use 'vs' as a search term to compare two or more things online, i.e. Bosch vs Makita etc). I want my tools to perform perfectly and produce good results every time, because failure means wasted time and money for me.

Oftentimes cheap stuff performs poorly from the start as well. So, my advice is as the same as the old adage, '*always buy the best you can afford*', even if it means saving for a little while longer for the really special stuff you want. Someone once said that '*poor people can't afford to buy cheap*' (because they can't afford replacements) ... food for thought, if you're in it for the long run...

HOW MUCH IS THIS GOING TO COST ME?

More than you think, to be honest. Projects overspend or overrun because life gets in the way, folks change their minds and unexpected things happen, (and that's normal). Some DIY jobs end up costing more or taking longer than anticipated (often both) simply because there was no proper plan in place from the start. But it doesn't have to be that way, you can safeguard your cash by doing your research and following the advice in the *Planning and Preparation* chapter.

From your plan, anticipate the expected costs and add a small contingency sum into the plan to cover the unforeseen stuff, such as...

- Miscalculated material quantities (see next section).

- Items missed off the budget all together, usually smaller items like fasteners or consumables like blades etc.

- Unforeseen things once work is underway that require more work, tools, or materials to correct.

- Change of mind, circumstances, or plans.

- Time overruns increase the cost of hired tools, hired help, access or scaffolding costs, insurance, bridging loans etc.

- Bad weather can add protection costs or time overruns to projects with an exterior element.

- Hired in help can let you down leading to scheduling problems or time overruns.

- Delayed deliveries or wrong deliveries can cause scheduling problems or time overruns.

- Mistakes or accidents can break or spoil materials.

- Tools can break and need repairing or replacing.

- And the most expensive one of all.... you didn't make any plan whatsoever... (what am I going to do with you, huh?).

If any of this bad stuff doesn't happen and you don't need the contingency sum, then whoopee, the holiday fund just got a boost, don't complain. Too many projects grind to a halt because there's zero 'wiggle room' in the budget to cover these almost inevitable additional costs. A small job in a newish house might get away with a 5% contingency fund, but an extensive renovation of an old period cottage might need 30% or more. Opinion varies, but to allow 10-20% on top of your expected costs is not crazy by any means. On a sliding scale, the older or bigger the project, the bigger the contingency fund should be, plus the more likely it is that you'll need it.

BUYING INSUFFICIENT (OR EXCESS) MATERIALS

A big cost drain is failing to measure up your project properly. Calculate what you need accurately and keep your notes. Don't rely on stuff in your head or on the back of a cigarette packet. And don't guess! Always make the time to work it out properly; you'll save money and time if you do. Remember that most materials need an extra 5 to 10% or so added to cover breakages and natural waste from cutting etc.

Be especially careful with your quantities if you're hunting for bargains (and you should!) in the *clearance* or *bargain* part of the store, because it's unlikely you'll be able to return for a 'few extra to finish the job' if you have a shortfall. Plus, it's a universal truth that you'll only run out of materials after the store has closed...

AVOID UNSUITABLE MATERIALS

Another cost drain is using the wrong materials as a result of bad information. As already covered, research thoroughly; study similar work on and offline to find out exactly what materials you need. Trade stores will be able to recommend what to use for your specific job, this is especially true in places that sell spare parts, ceramic tiles, paint etc. In regular stores always read labels or any descriptions on stuff in the store and if you are still unsure double check by asking a knowledgeable member of staff.

HANDLING, TRANSPORTING, AND STORING TIPS

I'll mention this here because if you don't take care it's going to cost you money due to spoiled materials. Basically, don't be rough with stuff okay? Always prepare in advance when handling materials, Especially during collection and delivery to your home or workplace. It's easy during the stress of finding, buying, and paying for stuff to rush the loading in a rush to get out of the darn place (especially IKEA...). Don't. It's important to take your time.

Getting heavy or awkward stuff into the car or trailer without damaging it often needs two people (tip, take a friend or don't be shy, ask a passer-by). Don't rely 100% on the packaging to protect stuff either, a piece of cardboard or polythene isn't going to stop you scratching your new door if you slide it over the tailgate latch or a small stone in the bottom of the trailer bed... Padding, padding and more padding (old blankets, sheets, foam etc., which you need to bring with you), oh and some good straps to tie down properly.

Obey the rules for specific loads, for example fridges and freezers don't like it if you lay them down, but if you can't avoid it, stand them the right way up for a day or so afterwards before switching them on. Washing machines will have transport screws which you must remove before use etc... Anything covered with a tarpaulin or polythene needs special care (and many straps) to avoid flapping etc. Loose or light materials like garden waste need a net ideally, and dust, well, it'll all be gone by the time you get where you're going...

An unsecured load isn't a legal term, but dangerous driving is. If you lose part of your load or even if the load is too heavy for your vehicle or trailer, your insurance will be invalid. If you lose something from your vehicle or fail to stop because your vehicle is overloaded, and you hurt someone (or worse) you're in trouble, and I mean a lot of trouble. Like, even jail time trouble.

Learn how to tie stuff down properly with decent ratchet type straps (rope is hopeless unless you know how to tie the truckers hitch...). Knowing where to tie is quite an art form and it's vital you do it properly. Even then, it's a good idea to stop after driving for a few minutes, just to double check everything is still secure. Sometimes stuff moves after a few pull offs, corners and braking etc. (go easy on corners and try to avoid heavy starts or braking etc.). This is especially important if you have a loaded roof rack or towing a heavily loaded trailer.

Carrying thin sheet material. Thin stuff on a roof rack or sticking out of a trailer is prone to snapping under the wind load of driving. Try to get a curve in the sheet, which adds strength. Put a length of timber on the middle of the roof rack for example and bend the sheet over it.

The distance you're going to drive doesn't matter, always secure stuff properly, no matter how short the trip.

Always go under the roofrack bar and back over the material. Bring any loose ends back on itself and under the bar again to prevent it coming undone. Wrap any spare length around the load or tuck it into the vehicle and close the door on it. Strap beats rope every time.

Once you get home, put down a folded dustsheet or timber offcuts before stacking things on the floor, especially heavy stuff. Just putting a heavy door down onto a hard surface is likely to chip its bottom edge. Dirt, dust, and grit easily damages fine finishes, so look at stuff, note the vulnerable parts and make a special effort to protect them from scratches, scrapes, shocks, knocks, drops or excessive pressure. Stack and store stuff properly...

- Stack bagged powdered products covered in a dry area, off the ground on a pallet, away from sharp objects.

- Store timber flat, off the ground in a dry area away from direct heat and ensure plenty of airflow around it.

- Stack drywall materials flat and off the ground on pallets in a dry area. Cover with polythene if cold/ damp.

- Keep hardware, fixtures, and fittings in their boxes, preferably on a rack/shelf. Keep similar things together.

- Leave flat packs/doors/windows etc in their wrappers until fitting and store either flat or vertical in a dry area (don't lean).

WHERE TO SPEND YOUR MONEY

There are too many places to source materials, tools, hardware, furniture, and other stuff today and it's likely that you'll use a variety of places to find everything you need, even if the 'big box' stores appear to sell everything. Let's go through some of your options...

LOCAL SUPPLIERS

Obviously, your nearest city is likely to have DIY stores or builder's merchants, and even an auction house or specialist suppliers if you're lucky. Local suppliers have a huge advantage because their obvious accessibility makes damaged items or guarantee issues easy to sort out. In addition, you'll be able to ask a real person for advice.

Set aside some time to visit when you're not busy or desperately looking for something. Particularly look out for...

- Flatpack options for self-assembly (of almost anything).

- Fixings or fasteners such as: screws, plugs, bolts, staples, nails, and special fasteners and fittings etc.

- Glues, sealants, caulks, silicones etc. all have their intended uses printed on the packaging. Follow up with online research.

- Ironmongery and hardware such as, hinges, brackets, fixing plates, handles, bolts, and locks etc.

- 'First fix' or basic materials, e.g., timber, sheet materials, masonry, sand, cement, plaster, metal sections, etc.

- 'Second fix' stuff which goes in after the construction work is finished, e.g. kitchens, bathrooms, doors, trims, light fixtures, etc.

- Tools, oh so many tools! Time spent ~~drooling over~~ looking at tools is never wasted! Avoid 90% of gadgets though...

- Personal safety gear. Important you know what's available to keep yourself safe. You only get one chance here.

- Storage options. You've got to be able to find it to use it!

Build up a mental inventory of what's available locally to help when you're researching and planning projects, because then you'll be able to picture what you need and where to buy it. You'll also build your knowledge about prices and if they vary from place to place (handy also to compare with online prices). You can even keep a simple list (or spreadsheet if you're getting serious) detailing suppliers, what they stock and their prices.

Keep an eye on any building sites you pass day to day, and note where they get their materials from (look for delivery trucks, sign boards etc.) You can also note down any names on the workers' vehicles, because if they're local you could add them to your list of potential sources of help if you're stuck. If you notice that ABC builders always use XYZ Electrical for example; that might mean they're good and worth adding to your backup plan list of people to contact if you need to hire in extra help.

I have built good relationships with my local suppliers, (and I recommend you do the same) because as a professional I need places to support me and my business. In return, I trust and expect them to give me good service at a fair price. Plus, it only costs a big box of chocolates come Christmas, some friendly banter day to day and never being unreasonable (i.e. insisting on 'next to no notice' deliveries etc).

Building a relationship with a supplier is like any relationship though; it will have its ups and downs from time to time. Someone will screw up an order or delay a delivery. But when you're buying from a supplier several times a week you just have to roll with the occasional mistake. Deal with any problem politely, getting angry will just make future purchases difficult and embarrassing for everyone. You want staff to smile when you walk into a store, not run for cover muttering 'oh no, it's *that* idiot again.'

Local newspapers or phone books are a good place to find out who sells what nearby. In our online age, the phone book has become a 'second class citizen', but it's amazing how many companies don't have much of a web presence; especially the 'old school' and long-established ones. The phone book is a treasure trove, don't dismiss it just yet.

Service and reliable delivery times are more important to me than saving a little money, but if you have time, it's definitely worth calling in at several places with your wish list and compare prices, especially for larger quantities. Judge your experience at each place, how did they handle your questions? Were they helpful etc? Juggle the prices they gave you with the way they made you feel; did they make you want to give them your business or did they make you feel like an idiot? Arguably, it's worth paying a little more for a friendly, reliable service at a place that looks after you well.

ONLINE RESOURCES

Having said all the above, the online market place gets bigger every year with the range of goods that shippable to your door increasing constantly. Definitely use them for smaller, easily shippable items where you'll make considerable savings and for when you can't find what you want locally. Free shipping is becoming common and even shipping larger items is becoming viable. Online stores can provide more choice, especially for things like...

- Special purpose fixings/fasteners, screws, nails, plugs, plasterboard fasteners, nuts & bolts, washers, rivets etc.

- Glues, sealants, and tapes etc.

- Ironmongery and hardware such as hinges, handles, brackets etc.

- Personal protection gear and clothing, safety glasses, gloves, coveralls, ear protection and safety boots etc.

- Spare parts for tools, home appliances, vehicles, and equipment.

- Specialist stuff or niche related (hobbies, sport, crafts etc).

- Photograph printing or storage (documenting the project for future reference).

- Tool catalogues for greatly increased range and variety.

- 'How to' books like this one! E-books or hard copies.

Find online stores by using relevant keywords on your favourite search engine or see appendices two for a list of places to start you off.

Of course, many people feel there's a moral issue with online stores and their impact on local businesses. It's the moral dilemma of our time I think; do you support local businesses, or find stuff cheaper online? That one is between you and your conscience. Arguably, it's not fair to use the local 'Mom & Pop' store for advice or research in person, only to go and purchase online because it's a little cheaper. Increasingly though, online stores are hosting forums etc. where you can ask questions about products.

Some online stores are simply an online extension of an existing bricks and mortar store. This gives you the best of both worlds, armchair browserability and easy online ordering, plus the reassurance of a high-street store should you need help. However, apart from a few *web only* special offers, it's unlikely the online version of a high-street store will save you as much as a dedicated online operation because of the operating costs of the real stores.

A double dilemma for some is buying stuff online from China. Buying from China was fine when it was the local store doing the importing and adding a profit, but with the increase of online portals into the Chinese market, individuals can buy a single item posted free to the door. I use Aliexpress.com for many small items with no problems so far. Everything is guaranteed should it fail to turn up, but you do need to plan ahead as delivery takes a few weeks to most places via containers in what is a pretty efficient postal service.

You need to be a little more 'product aware' buying from China because the quality varies from terrible to professional (remember some these guys are making the stuff in your high street...). As always, read the reviews and remember the price should indicate to you the quality to expect. If it's unfeasibly cheap don't expect great quality. In general, the good quality stuff costs about half what you'd expect to pay in your high street store.

Lastly in this section there is the possibility to find what you're looking for amongst your neighbours using local groups in social media. Simply choose your favourite flavour of social media and search for your hometown plus various suitable keywords. For example, searching for *items for sale + hometown* on Facebook.com. Simply apply to join the group, read the rules, and start searching for items for sale on your doorstep.

TRADE, RETAIL, AUCTIONS AND PRIVATE

Trade outlets or wholesalers sell to professional people who then go on to re-sell the goods to a third party, their customer or client via their services. Retail outlets are on the high street and sell to everyone. Auctions and private sales are where stuff ends up after the original owner doesn't want it anymore, meaning possible bargains for those who have the time to learn how it all works. Although increasingly online auctions are selling more and more new stuff too. Let's look at what you can expect from each one...

TRADE AND SPECIALIST SUPPLIERS

Trade rarely means trade only anymore (unfortunately for us tradesmen). You usually don't need to be a builder to buy from a builder's merchant for example, although it's wise to be slightly more informed about what you need before heading into some places. Some of the bigger trade establishments can be a little intimidating for non-professional people. Heck, I'm a professional and I'm intimidated going into a new and busy warehouse where everyone seems to know where everything is, and I don't know the system or any of the staff.

Occasionally though, you might come across a place that's strictly trade only and if you really want to buy from them (a particular kitchen supplier for example) ask if you can open an account as a self-builder. As a last resort, ask your friendly local tradesman to order it for you on his account. This obviously works better if you're going to be hiring him in to help you out at some point.

Stores aimed mostly at professionals are likely to be on the local industrial estate and are usually utilitarian in appearance, as they focus on stocks, fast service, and a comprehensive range, rather than fancy showrooms. You'll need to go elsewhere if you want cake and coffee with your two by fours... Although you might see the odd promotional bacon sandwich and coffee giveaway first thing in the morning.

If you do need help choosing what you need or advice before buying, you must visit stores at a quiet time of day (i.e. avoid the first and last hour and probably lunch times too) if you want a sympathetic ear. This is also a good time to find out how the system works.

Trade places employ efficient systems so they can handle large numbers of professional customers at once, often for large and complicated orders for complex materials, parts, and equipment. Trade customers usually know exactly what they want, and they tend to visit the store in concentrated periods such as, (yup, you guessed it), first thing in the morning, lunchtime, and last thing before closing.

Some places will have you go into the yard, pick up what you need and then a staff member will give you a 'ticket' to take into the shop to pay. Others are the opposite and you'll have to go into the shop first and get a 'ticket' to give to the guy out in the yard so he can get the stuff for you. Confusing huh?

Expect everyone around you to know where everything is and to know all of the staff (they come in most days don't forget). You'll have to be business-like and keep your head up and ask for help if you need it. If you're too meek and mild in here, staff will overlook you as they try to deal with that obnoxious big hairy builder's urgent order (Tip: they're all urgent...) Oh, and be careful not to get run over by a forklift truck, one place I use has 13 of them buzzing around like bees!

Trade and specialist suppliers also handle bigger orders for deliveries going to local building sites, often direct from the manufacturer's distribution centre. Do this in person, on the phone or via travelling representatives who will call on you at your 'site' (useful if your self-building a house etc). Quick and often free delivery is available on your order, especially if it's a reasonable size.

Another plus is that many builders' merchants can 'special order' things for you. If you've seen something you like in a magazine or on a website, ask at your local builder's merchant if they can get it for you. A good builder's merchant can get you almost anything, as they only stock a tiny percentage of the millions of things which are available. You might struggle if you only want one or two items, but still try, because some merchants combine orders from different customers and even other branches to meet minimum order levels from their suppliers.

Although most places still accept cash, usually trade establishments operate credit account systems to track what folks buy, billed at the end of the month. But accounts are great, because accounts mean discounts! Your level of discount might depend on your anticipated end of month spend or special deals you've negotiated with the staff. Indeed, it's best to open an account before you purchase anything. If they ask, just say you're a self-builder or you have a 'fixer upper' etc., and that's usually fine. Keep in mind that a credit check is likely, and sometimes you'll need to provide a couple of references from other people you buy from, just to prove you're not been naughty with credit in the past.

Trade places are a bit of a paradox when it comes to prices, stocking the reputable brands and high-quality materials that most professionals demand should mean high prices. But in practise, they sell large volumes (think whole housing estates rather than someone's garden wall) and prices for some things are considerably cheaper than in the average DIY store.

In general though, prices are a lottery in this aggressive and competitive market. Daily deals, special offers and loss leaders means there's no magic formula for knowing where the cheapest places are; legwork and comparing prices is the only way to root them out.

Without a doubt trade places are a smart place to buy, but keep an eye on their opening times, many open early and close early (especially on Saturdays) compared to their purely retail brethren. Oh, and avoid Saturdays at all costs, because that's when lots of 'non-trade' people go in asking lots of questions and it'll take an age for someone to help you...

RETAIL STORES

The 'big box' or DIY retail stores try to sell a little of everything and that can make your visits time consuming, especially if you're a little 'star struck' by the range. You'll probably find a wider selection of products on the shelf compared to a trade place but being able to special order stuff is unlikely. You'll also be able to buy smaller quantities of items than at most trade suppliers. A packet of ten screws for example, whereas in a trade place you might have to buy a box of

100 or 200. Predictably, the cost per screw increases considerably, but if you only need ten screws, you might save a little money.

Retail stores employ a variety of clever marketing techniques to draw you into the store and you'll find lots of special offers on commonly bought materials (called 'loss leaders'). Arguably though, the prices of other items (called 'add ons') are expensive when compared (quality for quality) to a builders' merchant.

Retail big box DIY stores are the place to go to if your local trade place doesn't have what you want, and you don't want to wait for an online store to deliver. They are also great for small quantities of the more unusual materials that you would have to buy in larger quantities from other more industrial places, such as aluminium sheet or small metal or plastic trims for example.

Retail stores are usually 'pick up' only, but they might deliver larger items direct from their warehouse to your home, and some stores offer trailers to borrow or hire to help you get your purchases home.

REAL WORLD AUCTIONS

Many towns have some kind of auction house where businesses and private individuals sell all the stuff don't need any more to the highest bidder, often at knockdown bargain prices. Some auctions are not for the uninitiated or timid, but they are getting better at dealing with the public and I guarantee you'll find auctions fascinating and see some proper 'characters'.

However, you must do your homework first and learn how the auction process works. Try going just to watch, it's extremely entertaining and allows you to absorb the way things work without any pressure to bid. Then you'll not look like a 'noob' and stick your hand up at an inappropriate time or buy a stuffed bear because you scratched an itch on your ear...

Some places have flea auctions selling stuff cleared from houses or by people looking to sell their household items quickly etc. Mixed boxes of household stuff can yield a few gems, tools etc. Ask at your local auction house if they hold 'small household auctions'. My local flea auction sells cheap bundles of timber off-cuts from local joinery shops, ideal for the hobby woodworker, plus lots of old tools, perfect for restoration.

Real bargains can be found at auction but be aware you'll likely bid against possibly the canniest and wiliest folks on the planet. The unbreakable rules...

1. You *must* know of the true value of stuff you're bidding on.

2. You *must* set yourself an *inflexible limit* based on No.1.

These are the *only* two rules. People get carried away (and to the cleaners) every day at auctions all over the world. Don't let it happen to you, do your research first and stick to your limit, no matter what. It's probably best to take someone with you, (at least the first few times), preferably someone who has the 'authority' to rein you in, should you momentarily 'lose your head' and start bidding on something you oughtn't...

ONLINE AUCTIONS

Increasingly, you'll find just about everything offered for sale via online auction sites like eBay, from both private people and companies, plus opportunities to buy internationally (increasingly from China so check delivery times). Coupled with a good delivery system, online auctions give you access to the biggest market place imaginable.

Be aware that online auction sites can become somewhat addictive and don't forget to add on the shipping or travel costs. Oh, and don't buy stuff you don't need just because it's a 'bargain'; remember it's only a bargain if you actually need the stuff!

You'll find the biggest savings of all among the huge amount of second hand or pre-owned stuff, where prices could be 50% of the new price or even less. The two rules we looked at in the real-world auction section above also apply here, maybe even more so, as it's so easy to sit on your sofa and go bid crazy. Research and strict limits are still very essential.

Don't forget to make room for the new stuff by selling all of your own unwanted stuff as well. Online auctions create a win-win situation with everyone getting what they want at a price they are happy with. Lovely.

LOCAL PRIVATE SALES

This is still an active market and you'll make real savings if you enjoy buying pre-owned or second-hand bargains. Start with the classifieds in the local newspapers, free newspapers, and the numerous specialist classifieds newspapers. It's also worth keeping an eye on supermarket and shop window notice boards. Some places even allow you to pin 'for sale' notices to old buildings, hoardings, telegraph poles and the like. Online classifieds are gradually taking over this marketplace with sites like Craigslist, Gumtree, and Loot etc.

There're also various websites where you can swap or exchange stuff for free, try freecycle.org or in the UK try ilovefreegle.org.

Private advertisers can be a good place to find small amounts of leftover building materials that folks want to get rid of very cheaply otherwise they'll have to pay to throw them away. Cheap and on your doorstep, it doesn't get any better than that.

Garage sales also exist in many places, although this varies from country to country. In New Zealand for example, Saturday morning is the time for mini garage sales after advertising it in the local newspaper. Early birds get the best deals with many starting at 7am! Quality varied, but with so many people emigrating to Australia, we found some real bargains. One variation on the garage sale is the 'car boot sale' in the UK, where folks gather in a local field or car park (notably on Sunday mornings), to sell their unwanted goods essentially from the back of their car. Increasingly these are attracting professional and part time traders, complete with fast food outlets to the detriment of the original concept.

By following the advice in this chapter, doing the local legwork and some proper research you'll always...

- Make informed, educated purchases.
- Avoid impulse buys.
- Avoid buying 'lemons' (products that underperform).
- Avoid buying stuff that doesn't meet your needs.
- Avoid overspending or paying inflated prices.
- Avoid overzealous salespersons taking advantage of you.
- Avoid buying stuff you don't actually need at all.

TIMBER

I'll include some advice on buying timber because it's the only 'once living' thing you'll buy, making it rather special and worthy of a few notes. It is also the one material fraught with production problems. Timber was once a living thing (obvious, but bear with me), and it takes time to realise it's not alive anymore and stop moving. This process of seasoning or drying can take months, which unfortunately doesn't quite fit into today's rapid production schedules or even in folk's DIY plans.

If you see a timber stack anything like the one in the next image, just nod politely, smiling as you say thank you and slowly back away. As soon as the assistant turns away, run like mad and head to another store. Seriously, you'll find nothing but pain buying timber from a place that keeps its timber in unruly stacks like this.

Store timber properly supported along its length with good air flow to avoid problems.

Tradesmen like me are ruthless when selecting timber to make sure we have the best possible material to start with, setting aside the rubbish and digging deep into the pile to get perfect pieces. Don't worry about leaving it untidy, the staff are used to it, and if they complain, throw it right back at them, with a complaint of your own, saying that if they did their job and the material was good quality, then you'd not need to waste your valuable time sorting it out into saleable stuff for them...

This next image is a pretty normal example showing some savvy person rejecting timber (piled on the left) by sorting through the stack to select good quality lengths to take away. You should definitely do the same...

The good stuff

The bad stuff

The timber on the left is still okay... if you're building a boat...

When you *sight down* a length of timber, bring one end up close to your face and look down one side, turn the piece through 90° and look again. You should clearly see any defects as the eye is a great 'instrument' for detecting curved things or anomalies.

Longer, smaller section timbers will naturally curve under their own weight, so sight down these whilst they're still lying on the rack to see their natural shape etc.

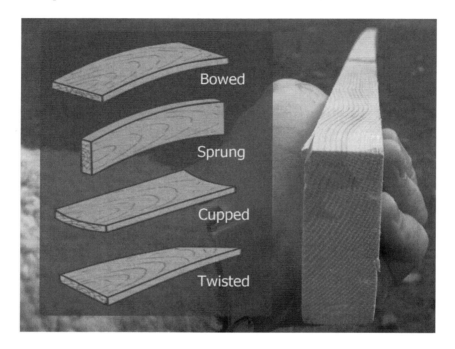

Bends are less troublesome than twists or cupping across the width. A slow curve in a timber (like in the previous image) is easy to straighten out on fixing, but twisted or cupped timber is difficult to flatten without splitting it.

There are all sorts of other things with funny names to watch out for when buying timber, like burl, splits, shakes, heart shakes, ring shakes, star shakes, twist, wane, wind (not the blowing kind!) not to mention insect and fungal damage or butt rot (eurgh!) and don't get me started on reaction wood (I'm just showing off now) okay, okay, okay, way toooo much information. In short then, just look at the timber making sure it's not too curved or cupped (see pics above) with clean, square edges, oh and no big splits. There, that's better isn't it? Sorry, I get a bit carried away...

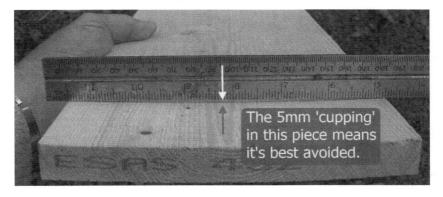

The 5mm 'cupping' in this piece means it's best avoided.

Because of this variation in quality, always select your own timber, even if you're having it delivered by the store. Because there's always the chance when you order it over the phone that some of this 'rejected' timber will find its way into your delivery. Of course, if you're a regular customer and the guys loading the truck know you, it shouldn't happen (because they know you'll come back and kick up a stink!) Simply arrange with the store to go down and select your timber beforehand and they'll put it aside ready to load onto the truck with the rest of your order. It's inevitable you'll end up with some bad timber occasionally but don't panic, simply set it aside and use it for your shorter lengths, where the defect will be less of a problem. You'll end up with little waste if you're careful and smart with your selection.

Once you get home, ideally store the timber where you're going to install it and in similar conditions (same humidity and temperature) to allow it to slowly acclimatise. Acclimatising timber can take from a few days right up to several weeks; it depends upon the original moisture content of the product and the conditions on the job. For example, if you keep your new timber in an unheated garage for two weeks and then use it in a room at 23°C, unsurprisingly, you'll likely have a problem with shrinkage. Keeping your timber in an unheated place isn't acclimatising, that's just storage!

Help it acclimatize by placing several supports under and in-between it and allow warm ambient air to circulate around it for a few days at least, or preferably a week or two before you start. You'll have less problems with shrinkage, twisting or cracking if you do. This is especially important with any flooring materials.

NOTES ON TIMBER TYPES, SPECIES & GRADING

There are two groups of timbers; Softwoods which come from evergreen, needle-leaved, cone-bearing coniferous trees, such as pine, cedar, and fir trees etc. Then there are the broad-leaved, deciduous hardwood trees which drop their leaves each autumn such as ash, beech, birch, mahogany, meranti, oak, sapele and teak trees etc.

The timber you use to build stuff grows on trees (I know, amazing, right?) and then machined into some common standard sizes and types. Three common types of timber you'll see in the store are...

- **Rough Sawn** square edged timber with a sawn finish straight from the sawmill, used for framing and roofing etc.

- **CLS** (Canadian Lumber Standard), the smooth round cornered timber used for building internal 'stud' walls or framing. Often lighter and kiln-dried for optimum use internally. Don't use this outside.

- **Planed Squared Edge** (PSE or its close cousin PAR, planed all round) smooth planed timber used for frames, trims, and finer work.

Sadly, the range of timber species easily found for sale has dwindled to a handful in recent years. Mostly white softwoods like pine for general construction with a couple of hardwoods, such as oak and mahogany for special, hard-wearing locations such as sills, thresholds, and floors etc. Most of the timber you'll see is softwood; (often all the white softwoods get lumped together and called *pine*, even if it's not strictly accurate...) this is not necessarily a bad thing, as softwoods are much easier to work with than hardwoods and lots cheaper to buy (so it's great for practising).

Timber mouldings; ideal for all those finishing touches, detail trims, cover strips, cabinetry and woodwork projects.

Timber is visually strength graded (and sometimes machine graded) at the mill to look for natural growth characteristics which might adversely affect strength, including knots or unusual grain slope, for example. For construction use C16 is the most common. The likely usage of the timber by size, will dictate is quality; timber suitable for floor joists for example will be a slightly higher grade, C24 usually. Higher grades such as C30 (and higher still) are available for especially highly stressed situations. If you're unsure what you need, just tell the guys in the store what you want the timber for and listen to their recommendation (in stores with trained or experienced staff).

The small trims and sections (often called mouldings) used to finish off many interior jobs will mostly be hardwoods, because such small sections are difficult to machine out of weaker softwoods (too many knots).

Typically, this includes dowels, cover strips, angles, beads, and quadrants etc. Be aware that small sized hardwood trims like these can be quite brittle and can easily split with careless nailing. If splitting occurs, you can drill clearance holes for nails or use very thin gauge nails or pins.

ODDS, ENDS AND OTHER USEFUL STUFF

Odds, ends and all manner of potentially useful things.

If you're smart, you'll start saving 'odds & ends'; i.e. stuff that might 'come in handy one day'*. This is stuff every handy person should have in 'stock' to enable you to find creative solutions on future projects. Save leftover materials and fasteners from your own projects, accept donations from other people (who aren't as smart as you) plus you can reclaim useful things from stuff you send for recycling. * Technical phrase, used by handy people all over the world...

Stack bigger stuff like timber on brackets in your shed, garage or even in loft spaces if the access is good. Save leftover materials in case you need to repair any damage in the future, especially stuff like floor coverings or ceramic tiles, wallpapers, etc.

To use this stuff, you need to be able to find it, so start a dedicated 'odds & ends' drawer. This magical drawer will miraculously rescue you when you're stuck half way through a job, long after the store has closed, and you miscalculated the number of fasteners you required, or you need to fabricate something or fix something temporarily. And guess what? The very thing you need might just be in your odds and ends drawer...

Simply nominate a large empty drawer or drawers if you are really getting serious and stock it with all those leftover fittings, fixings, fasteners plus little offcuts of this, that and the other. Wide and shallow works best for sorting through stuff, looking for inspiration. If the stuff gets too deep, it's difficult to sort though it easily and quickly. I separate metal, plastic, and fasteners into their own drawers (and yes, I've got the whole hoarding thing real bad...).

Your brain, amazingly; will remember in detail what you have in your odds and ends drawer; gently reminding you what you have 'in stock' to help you out next time you're in a pinch and need to find a solution to a problem.

To recap then...

SOME STUFF WORTH SAVING...

- Leftover timber off cuts or any clean timber from anything you've dismantled or taken down.

- Leftover fixings and fasteners, bolts, screws, nails etc.

- Leftover new materials, either for future repairs or for new projects.

- Fixtures, fittings, brackets, cables, and other useful materials stripped off anything going for recycling.

- Plastic sheeting for protecting stuff in storage, protecting floors during decorating or even in the garden to smother weeds etc,

- Large bits of cardboard are useful to protect floors or other work surfaces from damage when using tools etc.

- Fabric offcuts are useful to make small stuff or for the next pantomime or Halloween costumes plus of course rags for the workshop.

- Old sheets, curtains etc. are useful for covering down (dust sheets).

- Empty paint tins or glass jars make great nail pails or useful storage containers for small odds and ends.

- Metal stuff. Save a few pieces or sections of scrap metal to use when you need to fabricate something.

- Cracked plastic buckets are ideal buried up to their rim in the garden to hold any creeping invasive plants like bamboo. This stops them taking over the garden. Leaking buckets are still great for carrying tools or to put weeds in when weeding etc.

- Mobile phones and other tech stuff (even in a non-functioning state), are fun for young kids to play with.

- Don't save bent nails. They are not worth the straightening time, unless you're really into recycling and have the time...

- Unless funds are really tight don't save any 'less than perfect' screws you take out. This is not some change of heart regarding the environment, but simple effectiveness. If you try to use a damaged screw, you'll probably get into trouble when it's half way in. Not good.

THE DANGERS OF HOARDING

If you've got stuff tucked away with no hint of a project in mind (and it's been there for years), you might have a hoarding problem. It's okay to be an optimist but be sensible with saving stuff and don't save stuff that realistically, you'll *never* find a use for.

Remember, everything you decide to save brings responsibility, because you have to find somewhere to store it, you have to keep it safe, in good condition, and above all else, you must remember where it is. Your aim is to save stuff that might come in handy one day and maybe save you a little money, not to save everything until there is no space left to live.

One golden rule: only store stuff in proper designated storage spaces, i.e. not in your living space. Stuffing things all over the house is another indicator that you might have a hoarding problem. There's a million websites about decluttering your home. Get help!

What, you've spent it all? Oh, no, that's disastrous, because now it's time for...tools, tools, and even more tools!

Tools, Tools, and Even More Tools

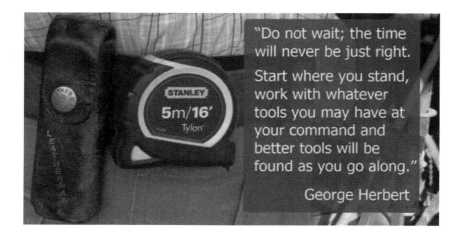

"Do not wait; the time will never be just right. Start where you stand, work with whatever tools you may have at your command and better tools will be found as you go along."

George Herbert

Don't panic about tools. You don't need to buy lots of them in one go, because your tool kit will grow with you over time as you tackle different jobs around your home. If you don't have any tools at all, or only own a single screwdriver, don't worry, you can fix a great deal of things around your home with just a screwdriver! When you find yourself with a spare hour (yeah, right!), have a wander round your local DIY store to find out what tools they have, pick them up to get a feel, read the blurb on the back and get an idea about cost.

If you already have a few tools of your own that's great, you have a head start, but you will need more; this *is* tools we're talking about, you can never have too many!

At the risk of sounding weird, I get a great deal of enjoyment out of some of my tools, notably the older, good quality ones, because they make producing good work much easier. Enjoying tools and what they can do for you is one of the cornerstones of being handy... But only if you keep the 'addiction' reasonable, Oh and avoid gadgets at all costs...

BIG BRANDS VS HOME BRANDS

Arguably, the old adage that 'only poor artisans blame their tools' is a load of old tosh because it's actually quite difficult to produce artisanal quality work with inferior or blunt tools. Good quality tools made by leading manufacturers will make you feel good every time you look at them (let alone use them), whereas poor quality 'home brand' tools will make you cry every time you pick them up. Fortunately, modern manufacturing techniques mean that buying good quality hand tools needn't break the bank.

Look for reputable manufacturers on the biggest displays in the most visible sections of the store; especially for tools with a blade (and that includes screwdrivers etc.). If funds are low, consider looking for good ones second hand; check carefully to make sure they're not worn out though. Oh, and please be careful where you buy second hand tools from. The theft of tradesmen's tools has reached epidemic proportions. And in my humble opinion, if you buy stolen tools, you're as bad as the thieves... (remember you're taking away a person's livelihood, the very food out of their children's mouths...).

As a professional, I need my tools to be tough and reliable. But even if you don't use yours quite so often, you should still buy good quality tools, (especially the one or two you'll use the most),

Avoid buying cheap, throwaway things because...

- Poor quality tools are often badly designed or unergonomic leading to awkward use, tiredness or even injury.

- Poor tools often perform poorly leading to damaged workpieces.

- Cheap tools utilise weaker materials, leading to shorter lifespans.

- Cheap tools arguably waste valuable resources in producing poor quality stuff in a non-sustainable way.

- Low cost tools encourage manufacturers to cut costs, often compromising the working conditions for employees.

- Throwaway stuff causes waste and recycling problems.

- Cheap tools encourage us to focus on price and not quality.

- You'll never experience the joy of owning a beautiful, leather handled, Estwing hammer...

Realistically, I understand your tool kit might be a little basic right now, and that's okay, they'll get you started. You'll soon learn which ones need replacing with something a bit better (once you have broken one or two...).

MINIMUM TOOL KIT

The following is a good basic tool kit, the ones you'll probably use the most, your everyday tool kit if you like. And even then, if you like, you can buy them as you need them to lessen the initial outlay...

HAND TOOLS

- A selection of different screwdrivers (slot, Pozidriv, Phillips, TORX).
- A claw hammer (16oz is great, or 20oz if you're a farmer...)
- A club or lump hammer (2.5 pounds or about 1kg is fine).
- A small wrecking or crow bar. The flat type are good.
- Cold chisels for masonry, 13mm (½"), 19mm (¾") straight chisels and a 75mm (3") bolster. Oh, and you'll need gloves for these...
- A set of wood chisels for, err... wood. 10mm ($^3/_8$"), 13mm (½"), 19mm (¾"), 25mm (1") will cover most jobs.
- A new hardpoint saw for timber.
- A hacksaw for cutting metal (junior or full size)
- A pair of pliers.
- A sharp craft knife.
- A small nail punch.
- A carpenter's square.
- A bunch of pencils.
- Oh, and something sturdy to store them all in. Minimum a big rubber bucket or a tool bag. Better is a tool chest on wheels...

Tool storage tip: get something with some spare space for future tool purchases and big enough so you're not struggling to find a particular tool because you've crammed the toolbox full to the top. You should also consider getting a few of those flexible plastic/rubber buckets which make cheap, effective 'day tool caddies'. I have one handy, so I don't need to take everything with me on smaller jobs around a big house and a second one to use for rubbish, packaging, offcuts etc.

They are also tough enough for mixing plasters and mortars in and are very easy to clean out afterwards, even if you 'forget' to do it on the day.

POWER TOOLS

There is lots you can do without power tools, but I must admit, an electric drill will be useful and if the budget runs to it, I would recommend you get two. A *mains powered SDS drill* which will drill holes in anything (wood, brick, blocks, and concrete). Plus, a mid-sized (14v +) *cordless drill driver* for smaller holes in wood and plastic etc and for using as a *drill driver* (driving in screws etc.). You're likely to fall in love with your cordless drill driver, so make sure you buy a pretty one (i.e. take note of the above issues with quality). I'd recommend getting a professional quality one, or you'll struggle for power and be charging the battery up every ten minutes.

Be wary of falling for the *bigger is better* trap (typically a 'man' thing) when it comes to cordless drills, because the weight of the bigger voltage drill is difficult to handle, especially for finer work or longer periods. Especially since battery technology improves year on year making even the smaller drills powerful enough for most jobs. I personally have a pair of very old Makita 9.6V drills plus a modern 14.4V one for heavier work.

Shiny combination tool chests that hold a dazzling array of different tools powered by universal batteries tempt many people. However, keep in mind that you'll burn through expensive batteries and no cordless tool can match its mains powered counterpart for performance and always-available power.

TOOL MAINTENANCE

Most tools require little maintenance and it's enough to keep them clean and dry. Many tools made from regular steel however, will go rusty at even a hint of moisture, so if they get wet, always dry them off before storing. Better still, once dry, squirt a bit of oil on a rag and wipe them over. Restore or revitalise any rusty tools with sandpaper, or wire wool and finish off with the oily rag or a squirt of WD40.

Always keep cutting tools super sharp and replace broken, damaged, or worn out tools before they can ruin your next project or hurt you. A large part of cutting-edge maintenance is not blunting them in the first place by look after them on the job and storing them in a way that protects their edges.

Power tools benefit from a blow through their air vents with an airline if they have been working in a dusty environment, you can buy compressed air in a can if you don't have access to an airline (or take it along to the garage next time you're blowing up a tyre). Keep an eye on power tool leads too as they fail regularly near the handle (see the fix in the *Repairing Stuff* chapter).

One tip to keep your best tools in good condition is to use them only for fine work. If you're doing rough work like trying to get paint out of an old slotted screw head, don't use your best screwdriver; use an old one instead. Cutting out an old window frame or ripping out an unwanted door set? Then you should use an old saw, then when you catch a nail or some masonry (and you will) it won't matter so much.

I call these tools my No. 2's (because they're crappy!) and watch out anyone I catch using my No.1 handsaw for rough work! Save an old screwdriver, a stiff scraper, and an old handsaw, plus a couple of old chisels for your 'rough tools'. Use these *No.2* tools when you know you're going to 'abuse' them, (hitting them with a hammer) during demolition or exploratory work etc.

If you use your best wood chisel to chop out an old window, you'd better allow plenty of time to re-sharpen it, because you're bound to hit a nail or screw etc. Re-sharpening a blunt chisel can take quite a few minutes to do well, but it can take an age to grind back a chipped edge because you hit a nail with it. Chisels with chipped edges are useless for nice work because the chips leave grooves in the workpiece...

HIRING 'EXPENSIVE TO BUY' TOOLS

Need a tool for a one-off job? An impossibly cheap power tool from the local DIY store might be suitable for a single project or very occasional use, but don't expect the best performance...

A sander costing the same as a dinner has 0.5mm orbits, but one costing a days wages will have 3.0mm orbits. Bigger orbits remove more material with less effort. The more powerful motor will also last almost indefinitely.

Instead of buying a cheap 'throwaway tool', consider hiring a professional quality tool. They're more powerful, quicker, more effective and you'll find it easier to achieve a high-quality finish.

Hiring tools saves capital investment and frees up storage space, plus you'll always have the latest tools and technology. It also gives you another person to ask for advice, especially since it's likely to be the first time you've needed that particular tool (don't worry, they are used to it!). Don't forget to ask for the safety literature and any 'how to' leaflets they might have.

MORE ADVANCED TOOL KIT

Acquire some of these over time when you need them for your particular projects and requirements. Buying online is cheapest usually but you don't get to try them first. Online in the UK you can try Screwfix, TooledUp, Machine Mart or Amazon.co.uk with B&Q and Homebase dominating offline. In the USA and rest of the world, start with Amazon.com to get an idea about prices etc. or look in a local 'big box' store near you.

Don't forget these are only a few suggestions, after all I've no idea what jobs you're planning to do. The list is alphabetical, no order of importance...

HAND TOOLS

Allen key set	Get a set that fold out like a pen-knife, or at least a set that stores easily.	
Bar 'quick' clamps	Used to be screw type 'G' clamps, but now are quick adjusting. Get a pair of 150mm (6″) or 300mm (12″) ones to start with.	
Carpenters square	Combination type for setting out and marking 90° and 45° angles prior to cutting.	
Centre punch	Centre punch makes starting holes in metal a cinch.	
Cold Chisels ¼″, ½″, ¾″ and 3″, 4″ bolsters	Used for chopping out masonry, (brick and blocks etc.) Cheap ones are fine although branded ones are not too expensive.	

Claw hammer	Don't go too heavy. I would start off with a 16oz one. 20oz if you are a big un'...	
Club hammer	Also, called 'lump' hammer in the UK. 2.5lb (appx 1.1kg) okay. The bigger 4lb (appx 1.8kg) is for heavy work and big un's.	
Craft knife or utility knife	Stanley knives are common Retractable blades best. Get lots and lots of spare blades and change them often.	
Drywall saw	A small 'pad saw' style handsaw for cutting small holes in drywall etc.	
File set	Flat, half round and round type are the most useful.	
Hacksaw	For cutting metal. Junior and regular size are useful. Get a spare blade or two, as they lose teeth and occasionally break.	
Hand saw or hardpoint saw	Cheap and cheerful hardpoint disposable saws are sharp and last well if not abused on nails and masonry.	
Hole marker (deep hole)	Very useful for marking fixing holes through the items, e.g. through a timber batten or shelf bracket. Sharpie or powder types, are both good.	

Magnifying glass	This might be my age but often you need to examine something really close up to see details or damage.	
Nail punch	For punching nails below the surface of the timber ready for filling. A set of different sizes is useful.	
Masons corner blocks	Used to hold a tight builders line in position on a wall. Plastic or wooden ones are available but it's very easy to make your own out of some 48mm × 48mm (2″ × 2″) wood.	
Monkey, pipe, Stilson wrench	Various names for the same type of wrench. Useful for lots of plumbing related tightening tasks. Compression pipe fittings, etc.	
Pincers	Occasionally great for getting a fixing out that's not protruding enough to use a claw hammer.	
Picks	Useful for all sorts of fiddly jobs from fishing out O rings to piggling paint out of a screw head. The curved one is great for removing a freshly laid tile which is in the wrong position.	
Plastic tubs	Thick flexible plastic and better than regular buckets for just about everything. Original ones from Gorilla. Very handy to store your working, or day-to-day tools in. Bigger the better.	

Pliers Side cutters Needle nose pliers	Handy for sorts of jobs and probably one of the first things on your shopping list. Pliers to hold stuff, needle nose for accessing fiddly stuff and side cutters for cutting wire etc.	
Sack Truck	As useful as another person to help you for many lifting and carrying jobs. From moving heavy raw materials to things like washing machines or fridge freezers. Can easily handle very heavy things (read 200kgs or more). Cheap too.	
Screwdriver set	Minimum will be the five common types: Pozidriv 1 and 2. Small, medium, and large slotted/ flat screwdrivers. Phillips 1 and 2 Plus, short or 'stubby' variations.	
Set of line pins and building line	Great for anywhere that needs a straight line. Setting out walls, laying bricks or landscaping etc. NB: Cheap pins bend easily.	
Socket set	Sizes from 5mm up to 24mm plus and imperial size equivalents. Ratchet drives is imperial, ⅜″ drive generally, with ¼″ for small sizes and ½″ for heavier work or even ¾″ drive for tractors, trains, and tanks etc...	

Special screwdriver bits	Set of small screwdriver bits in small or special drive styles. Common on electrical items.
Spirit levels	One small and a largish one, say 300mm and 1.2m (1' and 4'). 2m or 6' are great for door frames though.
T, star or TORX drives.	Star drive screw drivers. T20 very common on fridges and much more. Can be screw-driver style, fold out or indi-vidual.
Tape meas-ure	Worn on the belt at all times, along with a pencil stub behind your ear....... Buy one with a wide blade for easy measuring of longer lengths. Oh, and remember the end hook is supposed to move...
Tool belt with pockets and hanging points	If you're getting se-rious about all this... Choose one with the softest material for best comfort. Hammer loop is es-sential.
Torque wrench.	Helps get all your nuts and bolts the correct tightness. Essential for some jobs like tightening wheel nuts and cylinder head bolts etc. Somewhere in the 20-150f/lb. range is ideal. $^3/_8$ or ½ drives are common. Essential on vehicles.

Trolley, dolly, or cart	Useful for moving heavy or awkward objects around. Various sizes and wheel types.	
Trowels	Brick trowel, gauging trowel, pointing trowel and a 'bucket handle' (half-round type) jointing tool and possibly a plastering trowel if you're feeling very brave!	
Various sized scrapers	From 1" filler knives to a 3" heavy scraper, all are useful to have in the toolbox. Not just for scraping away old paint but a myriad of small levering tasks.	
Voltstick	A clever tool for finding live wires. Handy for finding simple failures like broken wires.	
Wire strippers	Better than pliers for stripping plastic sheathing from electrical wire. Changing plugs, wiring lamps etc. automatic type (pictured) easiest.	
Wood chisels	6mm (¼"), 10mm ($^3/_8$"), 13mm (½"), 19mm ($^3/_4$"), 25mm (1"), 32mm (1 ¼"). Oh, and something to sharpen them with... (Tormek machine is best, although a little costly).	

Wrecking bar or crowbar or prybar	For removing anything. Hexagon shaped ones are strong but the thin, flat type are great for getting into tight gaps.	

POWER TOOLS

You get what you pay for with power tools. Try to stick to the big brands. Such as Makita, Bosch, DeWalt, Black and Decker, Metabo, Dremel, Bostitch, Hitachi, Ryobi, Trend, Milwaukee, and Festool. There are many other niche manufacturers, especially in the USA.

NOTE: Bosch professional quality tools are blue (designed for years of daily use), but the cheaper DIY range are green. Both are good quality it is just that the pro range is more durable.

Combina-tion mitre saw	Perfect carpentry cutting, from skirting boards to fitting kitchens. Best to stick with the well-known brands for ease of use, quality of cuts and reliability.	
Drill driver/cord-less screw-driver	A necessity. Buy a decent quality bit holder and different screwdriver bits. Big drills are heavy to use. I like the 12v to 14v range...	
Mini grinder	Useful for cutting, grinding metal and brick/stone/mortar and wire brushing metal. 115mm is a common size.	

Jigsaw	Ideal for cutting many different materials. Great for curves in sheet materials, and for general woodworking duties. Use good quality fast cut blades. Cordless models are good.	
SDS drill (pneumatic type)	SDS type is the ONLY way to go. Drill bits have special mounting system and last ages and ages. Avoid 'hammer' only type drills with straight drill bits, they are next to useless and wear out drill bits in seconds.	
Set of drill bits	HSS set for wood, plastic, and metal (1mm to 10mm). Flat spade bits for wood, (6mm to 25mm). SDS set for masonry, or 6mm and 7mm sizes minimum.	

ADVANCED POWER TOOLS

Bench saw or larger table saw	For ripping down timber into whatever size you need. Cross cuts using a sled or guide in the slots. Either a portable bench saw (with legs) or a larger, full height table saw for the shed or workshop.	

Circular saw or plunge saw	Circular saws for general rip and cross cutting. Plunge saw with rails are a more expensive option, but are especially good when cutting sheet materials.	
Compressor	Useful for lots of jobs around the home from blowing up tyres to powering nail guns and staplers. Great for cleaning dust out of difficult to reach places too.	
Electric planer	From small 1mm per pass, up to professional 3mm+ per pass. Cheap ones are awful and best avoided.	
Nail guns	Small pinners for trims like architraves etc. up to huge framing nailers that can fire 90mm nails for the big stuff. Originally air powered, but now gas (Paslode), or even battery powered, (pictured).	
Pillar Drill	Essential tool for drilling accurate holes. Especially good for drilling metal. Depth stops great for drilling blind holes (holes that don't go all the way through). Needs a workbench or a stand to mount it to.	
Reciprocating saw	Useful for general rough cutting of materials, in the home or garden.	

Router	Handy for cutting grooves and profiling edges. Get a ½-inch drive if you intend to cut kitchen countertops with it, otherwise a ¼-inch one is light and useful.	

Right, now we need something to help hold everything together, and no, no, I don't mean a psychiatrist! Pull yourself together, I mean fixings and fasteners of course...

FIXINGS AND FASTENERS

Difficult to decide where to put this section as almost every aspect of DIY involves some kind of fixing or fastener. But since we already looked at tools such as screwdrivers and hammers in the previous chapter, I thought we should look at them sooner rather than later. Just remember the principles we'll go through here apply to all the other chapters from maintenance to assembly.

But first, what's the difference between fixings, fasteners, and hardware? Well, lots of folks use them interchangeably, but fixing describes the whole process (e.g. join the timbers together with a metal strap) and the fasteners (in this case) are the nails and the hardware is the metal strap.

The most important things to take away from this chapter is to learn the *correct fixing methods for the materials you're working with* and to always use *the correct type of fasteners for the task*. Not something 'near enough' just because you don't have exactly the right one in your toolbox...

In general then, before reaching for a fastener, ask yourself...

- Indoors or outdoors? Fasteners for outdoor use have much improved anti-corrosion coatings etc.

- What is the material you're fixing *through*; wood (e.g. a batten), metal (e.g. a bracket), cement fibre sheet, (e.g. wall boards in wet rooms), glass (e.g. a mirror), plastic (e.g. trim) etc.? Called the workpiece.

- What is the material you're fixing *into*; concrete, masonry, wood, metal, drywall etc.?

Sometimes called the substrate. There are many variations; timber to timber, metal to timber, timber to masonry, metal to masonry, metal to metal, drywall to timber or metal, etc. etc.

- Related to the material you're fixing; what type of head will hold the material the best? E.g. large, small, flat, countersunk, hidden, etc.

- Will the head of the fastener be visible or not, i.e. decorative?

- Weight; how heavy is the object you're fixing? Often classed as light, medium or heavy for many DIY jobs. This determines the gauge of the fastener; the heavier the load, the thicker the fastener you need.

- Related to weight; where is the load? Will it pull downwards (shear loads e.g. a big mirror) or outwards (pull out loads, e.g. a handrail).

- Also related to weight; how deep does the fastener need to go into the substrate to achieve suitable security?

All the above factors will help you to choose the right fastener for the material you're fastening, and fastening into, whether you're securing something to the wall, floor, or ceiling or just two pieces of something together. This is especially important when hanging heavy things like wall cabinets or fastening heavy things like storage racks to the floor or even heavy chandeliers from the ceiling. Let's go through a few different types of fasteners to help you choose the right type of fixing you need for any particular job... (forgive any rusty ones, they're from a real toolbox!)

SCREWS

Screws come in a myriad of different types, and in practise there is some overlap of uses for any particular screw. Screws are considered better for higher quality work or when you need to pull the workpieces together or up tight to a surface etc. I mostly use screws these days, which is a habit I got into working on commercial contracts (where noise is an issue). Plus, I think you have more control over the fixing process, and you end up with a better-quality job (no hammer 'half-moon' dents in the work surface or splitting from nails).

I know we already covered this in the *How Use a Screwdriver* section earlier, I'll repeat it here; the most important thing to remember when using screws is to use the correct size clearance holes and pilot holes to avoid splitting your workpieces. Sometimes you'll also need a countersunk hole if you want to be sure the screw head sinks into the surface (although on most framing type work in softwood, this is rarely necessary as the power of the screw thread is enough to pull the head well under the surface.). There are various 'self-piloting/self-drilling' screws around, but even these need care in thin pieces of timber or if close to an edge etc.

CHOOSING SCREW TYPE

The four things to think about are...

- Exposure to the weather or moisture.
- The type and thickness of the material or workpiece.
- The load the screw needs to carry or resist.
- If there are any special requirements specific to the job.
- The length of the screw and the shape of the head needed to satisfy the above three variables.

First one up is easy, indoors vs outdoors, or just ask yourself; will this screw ever get wet? If yes, look for the words *outdoor* or *galvanised* on the packaging. Normal screws suitable for protected work are mostly grey, shiny silver or yellow/gold coloured and have a tiny bit of rust protection (enough to cope with the natural moisture in the woods fibres etc.) but would soon rust and fail if used outdoors in an exposed location (2 or 3 years' max). Go for galvanised or stainless steel if there is even a small risk of dampness.

CHOOSING SCREW HEADS AND THREADS

Then you'll need to think about the material you're fixing and thus the type of screw head and screw thread you'll need. There are (of course!) many different types but the most common type for 'everyday' use is countersunk heads and these are suitable for most applications, especially where the screw head is not seen. These make up over 90% of my screw box and are fine for most work in timber etc. Slots are still quite common but becoming less so.

Occasionally you might want to leave a screw visible and then possibly a domed, raised head is more suitable, these are flat bottomed and often have a simple slot. No countersink hole is necessary for round head screws as the entire screw head sits on top of the workpiece. Often used for sheet materials like plastic sheet, mirrors, or plywood etc.

In addition to different heads, screws often have a range of different threads to suit different materials. Softer materials need large, coarse threads with plenty of grip, softwood, or particle board for example. Harder materials need finer and small threads, hardwoods, or metal for example.

Most common screw thread is a coarse twin thread suitable for general screwing into timber. Coarse threads drive in fast; a drywall screw for example has a long, coarse, and widely spaced, spiral of a thread making it very fast to insert in the soft drywall. In contrast, a self-tapping screw for metal, has short, fine, and closely spaced threads enabling it to cut threads in the much harder metal at a slow pace; plus, there'll be more threads to hold in the thin material once you're through.

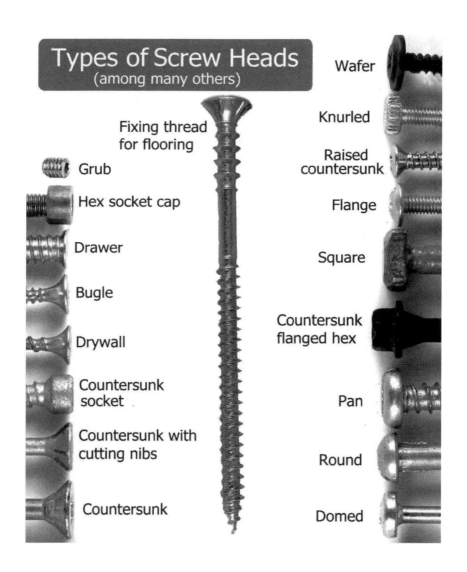

Types of Screw Heads
(among many others)

Fixing thread for flooring

Grub

Hex socket cap

Drawer

Bugle

Drywall

Countersunk socket

Countersunk with cutting nibs

Countersunk

Wafer

Knurled

Raised countersunk

Flange

Square

Countersunk flanged hex

Pan

Round

Domed

Some hi-tech screws have special threads designed to cut the timbers fibres rather than simply force them apart; this causes less splitting and may even do away with the need for clearance holes and pilot holes altogether. Timber decking screws are a good example. Other screws have a ribbed section (steady on!) in the middle designed to clear out the hole providing room for the thicker upper shank. Floorboard screws have a small set of threads which grab and hold the flooring material, greatly reducing the chance of squeaks in the finished floor (wouldn't that be nice?).

Next up is the load you want the screw to carry. Think about how the screw will handle the load. Is the load trying to pull the screw out of the wall (like a washing line anchor) and so needs greater length to achieve enough 'pull out' strength, or is the load mostly at 90° to the screw, (like holding up a wall cupboard) and so needs a thicker gauge? Often the load is dynamic, pulling in several directions (such as a hand grab or rail) which needs both long length and heavy gauge fasteners. Movement is another big issue; screws snap easily if repeatedly flexed. Anything that moves in use, placing strain on its joints, needs heavy gauge fasteners to avoid eventual failure. Phew, it's not exactly straight forward, is it?

CHOOSING A SCREW DRIVE SYSTEM

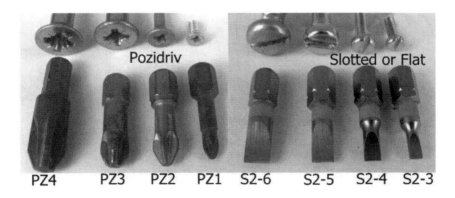

And then there are different drive systems too; lots of them unfortunately (strewth!). You might need a range of different tools, from simple straight, slotted screwdrivers right up to Allen keys and spline sets. Two common drives are Pozidriv and slotted or flat, pictured above...

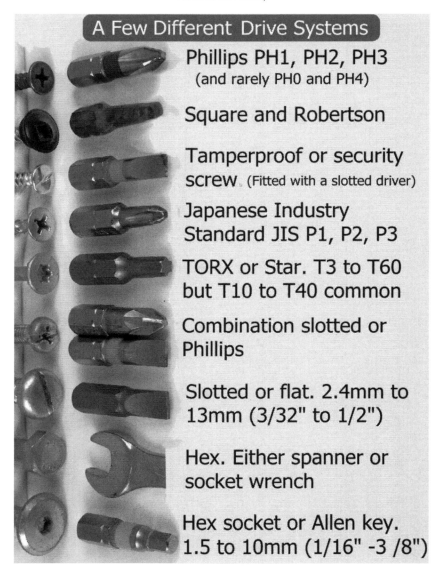

A Few Different Drive Systems

Phillips PH1, PH2, PH3
(and rarely PH0 and PH4)

Square and Robertson

Tamperproof or security
screw (Fitted with a slotted driver)

Japanese Industry
Standard JIS P1, P2, P3

TORX or Star. T3 to T60
but T10 to T40 common

Combination slotted or
Phillips

Slotted or flat. 2.4mm to
13mm (3/32" to 1/2")

Hex. Either spanner or
socket wrench

Hex socket or Allen key.
1.5 to 10mm (1/16" -3 /8")

If you find yourself struggling with screws, consider swapping drive system. The increasingly popular TORX drive screws are a little more expensive, but they hold much better and avoid cam out (the drive bit slipping out of the screw) and might be worth the investment for you, I know they are for me.

You'll need a T20 screwdriver anyway, as the T20 is a common size used on white goods like fridges for example (swapping doors over etc.). I find TORX is fast in use and offers superior performance.

These are 'T20' star drive screws, more expensive, but less risk of twisting out (cam out) due to their design and shape.

CHOOSING SCREW LENGTH

Sometimes screw length is automatically restricted because of the thickness of the timber you're fastening together. Screwing two pieces of 20mm (¾") stock together for instance, where you'd use 35mm (1 ¼") screws. However, when you're fixing to a frame or wall then aim for a screw length of approximately *two and a half to three times* the thickness of the material you're fixing (your workpiece). For example, to fix a 20mm (¾") thick timber batten to some framing, you'd use a 50mm to 60mm (2" to 2 ½") screw.

In addition, if you're screwing into the end grain of a piece of wood (down the grain) instead into the cross grain (90° to the grain) allow a little longer length because end grain doesn't hold a screw thread very well (when compared to cross grain) and be especially careful to drill good pilot holes as end grain splits easily, if the screw gets too tight.

CHOOSING SCREW GAUGE OR THICKNESS

The length of the screw gives good support against *pull out* forces but it's the gauge or thickness of the screw that really carries the weight and the expected load. A heavy *shear load* on a small gauge screw could simply snap the screw where the two materials meet. Fortunately, the solution is simple: Light loads = smaller gauges like 3, 4, 6 & 8's (2.5mm to 4.0mm) which are ideal for small lightweight stuff and lightly loaded things. Medium weight stuff; well, you'll need to use common sense here, but it's better to err on the side of caution and 'go large' as they say if you're not sure. Heavy loads = heavier gauges like 10, 12 & 14's (4.0mm to 6.5mm) which are ideal for bigger, heaver stuff or things expected to carry large loads. Incidentally, the size of the holes in most hardware (brackets etc.) indicates the gauge of the fasteners you should use, i.e. use the thickest gauge fasteners you can get into the holes.

Be aware that some lightweight items need strong fixings too. Although towel rails, safety grips and handrails for example don't weigh very much, you'll need to use *very sturdy* fixings on them to cope with the large, dynamic leverage or pull forces that folks exert on them. Door hinge screws also fall in to this category and short but very 'fat' or heavy gauge screws are common to cope with the repeated movement.

SPECIAL SCREWS

Of course, there are many different special purpose screws for hundreds of different applications. Some of these come with items you buy and might even be difficult to find in a local store (you'd need a specialist online supplier), so try not to lose them! Fortunately, most stores will stock a range of specialist screws to cover the most common projects like outdoor framing under timber decking, or terraces or hanging something heavy etc. Here are some common ones...

FRAME FIXINGS

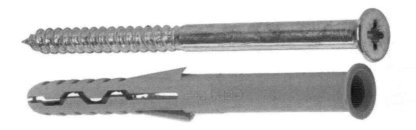

Specifically designed for window and door frames, although I love them for all sorts of bigger fastening jobs. You can of course use normal screws to fasten frames in place, but you'll find the job much easier using these dedicated frame fixings. With frame fixings, the screw and plug are the same length, so you never 'lose' the wall plug as you install both plug and screw from the front. Drill a hole through the workpiece using a wood bit (it's usually wood or plastic), then swap drill bits and drill the substrate (usually masonry). Blow or vacuum out the dust. Loosely insert the screw into the plug and push the whole thing all the way in. Sometimes I would put the plug in first and then the screw, brands vary. Tighten up the screw applying a lot of pressure towards the end. You might even need to have a spanner on the screwdriver, they are pretty big fasteners and do get tight. There are hammer versions which obviously just hammer in (although I prefer the screw in ones).

If you want the screw to end up flush with the frame, you'll need to tap the screw head before you start tightening and that will pull the plug into the surface a little. A small countersink in the frame helps here.

Doors and windows normally fit into slightly over sized openings, so you'll need plastic spacers/packers or shims of varying thickness to fill the gap and ensure the frame is perfectly plumb in all directions. A job made much easier on door frames if you have a 2m (6' or so) spirit level.

LAG SCREWS OR LAG BOLTS

Many things in construction are heavy or need to cope with large loads and a regular screw just isn't strong enough to cope. Enter the big boys, the lag screw or lag bolt...

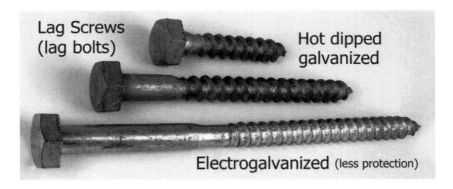

Difficult to describe lag screws, as they are somewhere in between screws and bolts (hence the fact they're often called lag bolts). Traditional lag screws are like a bolt only with a large screw thread at the end rather than fine threads and a nut. A large washer behind the head is still a good idea but be careful not to overtighten lag screws or you'll strip the relatively soft threads in the wood (the tightening force of a spanner greatly exceeds a screwdriver).

Lag screws are not known for their pull-out properties particularly, but more for their enormous shear strength due to the huge gauge. This makes them a first choice for things like heavy brackets etc.

You'll need to drill two holes to fit a lag screw, a clearance hole in your workpiece to clear the solid part of the shank and a pilot hole in the substrate, for the threaded part to screw into. Failure to drill pilot holes could easily result in splitting the timber because of the big diameter of the screw (unless the timbers are really massive (100mm or 4" thick or so).

One note though, there is an ever-increasing range of special construction screws now used in situations where lag screws used to rule. Which leads very nicely to...

CONSTRUCTION OR STRUCTURAL SCREWS

Arguably specialist in nature, this category of screw is growing all the time. You can buy very long timber connectors for fixing together large structural timbers (decking posts and joists for example).

Construction screws often have self-drilling tips plus deep, coarse and sharp threads to make driving them deep into big timbers easy. Big threads like this also hold extra securely, which is important on big joints.

Big hex drives are common on long screws as regular screw drives (Pozidriv etc.), would not be strong enough. There's also some rather nifty double threaded versions that need virtually no head because there are threads at the top and bottom of the fastener; available in tiny sizes for secret screwing of floorboards or large sizes for construction joints between big timbers.

Most of these big construction screws are usually outdoor grade as common use includes terraces, balconies, stairs, steps, framing etc. You'll also find screws which can drill their own hole in metal and then tap their own threads, perfect for corrugated roofing or cladding situations. Check the packaging for application recommendations and specifications.

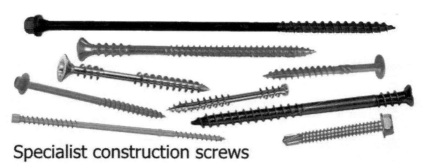

Specialist construction screws

MASONRY FIXINGS

In the old days, you'd chop out a mortar joint and hammer in a wooden wedge nice and tight, thus creating a wall plug to take a nail or screw. I even used to build 75mm (3″) squares of plywood into the mortar joints of my blockwork up the sides of internal door frames to give me great fixing points without resorting to drilling holes.

Nowadays there are screws that go directly into a drilled hole in masonry or concrete, but more conventionally you'll need some sort of expanding sleeve or wall plug to go into the wall to take your screw or bolt.

WALL PLUGS

Wall plugs hold in place by expanding in a radially outwards fashion. Simply put, when you put a screw into a plastic wall plug (or an old-fashioned wooden plug for that matter) it acts as a wedge, pushing the two halves of the plug apart and filling the hole very tightly. Friction then takes care of holding everything in place for all eternity; it's handy stuff friction... and best of all, it's absolutely free!

Most wall plugs are only 1 ¼" to 1 ½" (32 to 38mm) long and it's very important the whole length of the plug is in the actual substrate; brick, block, stone, concrete etc. (and not in the plaster). This is because the building blocks of the wall are very strong and can cope with the high forces created by the expanding plug (plaster, not so much...).

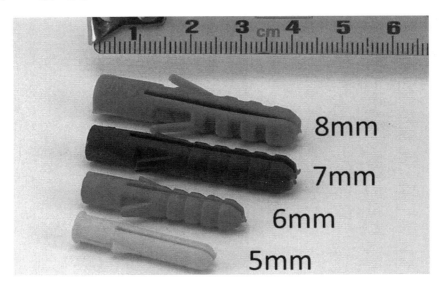

Don't worry too much if you drill the hole too deep, as the depth of the hole doesn't affect the wall plugs holding power (it grips radially outwards). Better a little too deep than not quite deep enough actually.

Most plaster on walls is between 13mm (½") to 19mm (¾") or so thick. So, doing the maths and taking the thickness of the plaster away from the length of the plug, you'll figure out that if you leave a wall plug flush with the plaster, not much of the plug is going into the brick/block/concrete where the strength is.

Plaster has little holding power and even the face of the brick cannot take much load without risking a 'fisheye' breakout when you put in the screw and apply the load.

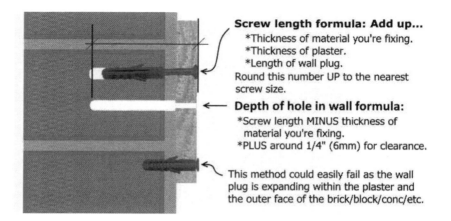

Screw length formula: Add up...
*Thickness of material you're fixing.
*Thickness of plaster.
*Length of wall plug.
Round this number UP to the nearest screw size.

Depth of hole in wall formula:
*Screw length MINUS thickness of material you're fixing.
*PLUS around 1/4" (6mm) for clearance.

This method could easily fail as the wall plug is expanding within the plaster and the outer face of the brick/block/conc/etc.

The wall plug is going to work best when at least its *whole length* is fully inside the walls main building blocks, thus relieving the plaster and the front face of the walling material from stress. Deep into the substrate is fine and will only increase the holding power. It's best if you don't drill all the way through though, (especially on any 'party' walls, as it does tend to annoy the neighbours for some reason...).

HOW TO INSTALL PLASTIC WALL PLUGS

- Mark out all your holes using a spirit level and/or tape measure. Try to avoid mortar joints if you can see them.

- Carefully drill each hole, starting off slowly (try with the hammer action off) until the drill bit forms a shallow hole (see image above to calculate depth), flick the hammer action back on and speed up to finish the hole. Draw the bit in and out, if it slows down (dust clogs).

- Vacuum out the dust or blow out the hole (use a length of tubing and watch your eyes) if you want to be 100% correct. Often omitted and you'll probably get away with it; unless the substrate is soft or crumbly, then it's essential...

- Push or tap your wall plugs into your holes, flush with the plaster (don't panic, you'll push the plug further in on a later step).

- Position your workpiece over the hole, put the screw through it and into the plug, twisting the screw a tiny bit by hand till it bites.

- Sometimes the above step is easier if you push the screw all the way through the item and then you'll easily get the pointy end of the screw into the plug, sliding the workpiece down the screw until it meets the wall.

- Using a small hammer tap the screw to push the plug through the plaster and into the wall itself and stop when the length of screw sticking out about equals the length of the wall plug.

- Tighten up the screw, try not to push hard for the first few turns, or you might push the plug in too deep (not good).

- Working this way ensures the plug is exactly the right depth into the wall and the screw will go all the way to the end of the wall plug when pulled up tight.

- Do not over tighten as this will strip the threads in the wall plug, stop when the screw is full up and tight. Don't force the screw to bury the head (unless the wood is soft), drill countersinks instead.

- Perfect. Rinse and repeat with the other screws.

- Kettle on, or head to the fridge depending on the time of day....

What to do when it doesn't work? Sometimes in poor or soft substrates like old crumbly bricks or blocks, the wall plug cannot exert enough pressure to create the friction necessary and the plug may rotate or just simply pull out. Probably because you didn't clean out the hole well enough, (dust can act like tiny ball bearings allowing the plug to move).

Also, drill bits tend to create oversized holes in soft substrates, especially when on the 'hammer' setting. See if you can drill the hole without the hammer action (but watch for excessive heat build-up on the bit tip). Alternatively, try drilling a hole 1mm (1/32 or so) smaller or undersize, which might hold the plug a little tighter. Try again with the screw.

If no luck with those methods, go back to the original size hole (just drill through the plug) and then use an adhesive as a crude, poor man's resin fixing (read more about this a little later). Essentially, you're going to glue the wall plug in place. Clean out the hole (important!), then using a 'no-nails' type tube adhesive, squirt a small amount as deep as you can get the nozzle into the hole. Push in the wall plug and use something blunt to push the plug into the adhesive and down to the right depth (a large nail or screw is good). Wipe away any adhesive that squeezes out of the hole (and don't put so much into the next one!). Wait 24 hours (I know, it's a pain, but what can you do!) and then try again with the screw. If that doesn't work, it's okay, you can blame me, I've got broad shoulders...

If you run out of wall plugs, improvise by using; matchsticks, cocktail sticks, thin slivers of wood, or as one reader of my website said, chopsticks! Tap as many as you can get into the hole and snap them off flush with the surface. It's an ideal tip for oversize holes. Don't laugh because this knowledge just might get you out of trouble one day, you know, like during the next big wall plug shortage...

HEAVY DUTY EXPANSION ANCHORS

Metal heavy duty expansion anchors transfer load to the substrate via friction in much the same way as the above wall plugs. Tightening the bolt or nut forces the bottom section of the anchor into a cone shape creating pressure and thus friction between the bolt's sleeve and the sides of the hole.

Heavy Duty Expanding Anchors

Expanding shield anchors

Throughbolts

Sleeve anchor

Use them in concrete (mostly), but at the lighter end of the range they are suitable for use in masonry as well. It's best to avoid mortar joints (in general actually), and especially the cross or vertical joints, as these may not be full or have the strength to resist the expansion force of the anchor. It's not uncommon on site (by less scrupulous bricklayers), to just 'tip' mortar onto the front edge of the brick in order to save time...

Anchor holes' range in diameter from 6mm (¼″) up to around 24mm (1″). Lengths range from 45mm (1 ¾″) or so up to 190mm (7 ½″) or so. Typically though, you're probably going to use an M10 (⅜″) or M12 (½″) anchor going into the substrate 75mm (3″) or so.

How deep you go, how close to the edge and what style of anchor you choose depends on the substrate. Hard substrates like concrete hold larger loads than say, brick and stone. It's probably best to avoid the heavier type of anchors in softer substrates like block work.

Anchors are either one or two part...

- Sleeve anchors are two part. A sleeve which goes into the substrate (like a plastic wall plug), followed by tightening a bolt and washer (through the workpiece) into the sleeve.

- Some sleeve type anchors incorporate a threaded bar, which then sticks out of the hole ready to slide the workpiece onto. Tighten up by adding a washer and nut.

- Popular now are through-bolts and sleeve anchors. Drill the hole though the workpiece and substrate in a single operation. Remove dust. Hammer in the anchor and tighten.

Some drive-in styles of anchors are made for concrete and will likely break anything else, so don't use them on masonry etc. As always read the packaging and look at the instructional videos all manufacturers have on their websites for help and tips on the best way to install their anchors.

Installation of expansion anchors is virtually identical to the plastic wall plugs mentioned above with one exception. You MUST clean out the hole after drilling. This is because the holes are much larger and therefore hold much more drilling dust which will interfere when you try to insert the anchor and tighten it up.

You need to get these anchors right first time, because if you get stuck half way in they are near impossible to remove.

RESIN ANCHORS

Resin anchors are an alternative anchoring system developed for high loads in difficult locations such as...

- Close to the edge of the substrate, where a conventional expansion anchor would likely crack the substrate.

- Softer materials, such as lightweight, ash or clinker blocks, certain soft or flaky stone, soft or crumbly bricks etc. where expansion anchors wouldn't be able to get a firm grip.

- Hollow substrates such as any brick with holes or frogs or blocks with voids etc.) where there is nothing for expansion anchors to push against to develop a friction grip.

- An alternative method when you need deep, very secure anchors, such as in rock etc. (think rope bridges, climbing anchors etc.).

Resin is ideal for all substrates though and gives absolutely immovable rock-solid anchors (groan, excuse the pun!). Basically, it's a threaded bar glued into the bottom of a hole and up top there's a washer and nut to hold the object down. For a neater look, use a mini angle grinder (or hacksaw) to cut the threaded bar off (flush with the top of the nut) after tightening, and cover with a plastic cap.

There are several resin systems. Some involve pushing a fragile capsule filled with resin to the bottom of a hole, followed by the threaded bar which breaks the capsule and mixes the resin components. More common is a two-part tube with a clever spiral nozzle which mixes the two-part resin as you squirt it directly into the hole, followed again by the threaded bar. In hollow or crumbly substrates insert a special plastic sleeve first which helps the resin stay in the right place and not run into the voids (there is nothing worse than being in the void...).

The holes are typically a few mm's (⅛″ or so) oversized to allow space for the resin. This means you'll need to support the threaded bars to keep them in the position you want (otherwise they will sag to the side or bottom of the hole, possibly at an angle (especially if on a vertical substrate). This is especially important if you're fastening multi hole brackets and the like. The best solution is to make a temporary support out of plywood (or thick cardboard in a pinch). Make a template of the holes and slide it over the bars, this will keep them in the right place and maintain the correct distance between the bars. If the bars are long, make two templates and put one at the top and one at the bottom, this keeps the bars centred and parallel to each other. Use a small magnetic spirit level to check bars for plumb or level depending on their location. You need to get resin anchors right first time, because they are impossible to remove without breaking open the wall.

HOLLOW WALL OR DRYWALL FIXINGS

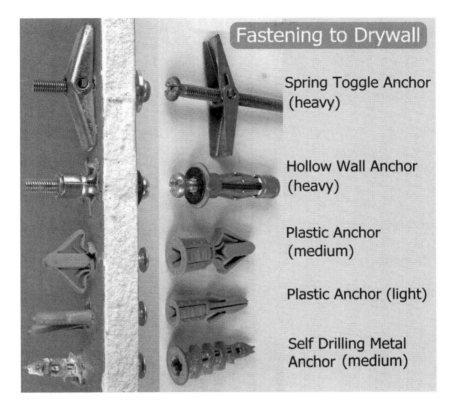

Fastening to Drywall

Spring Toggle Anchor (heavy)

Hollow Wall Anchor (heavy)

Plastic Anchor (medium)

Plastic Anchor (light)

Self Drilling Metal Anchor (medium)

Choosing the right fastener to hang stuff from drywall is all down to weight, as the fixing depth often remains the same i.e. the thickness of the drywall (or occasionally double thickness, for which fasteners are also available). Each class of fastener will handle a certain amount of weight before 'pulling out', with or without a chunk of drywall. You'll find the holding capacity of a drywall anchor clearly marked on the packaging.

If fastening something longer than 600mm (2′) to drywall, I'd recommend finding the timber framework behind the drywall and getting some longer regular screws into the timber for good measure (if at all possible). This is a good idea especially on long runs of wall cabinets or book shelves etc.

The hollow wall anchor (second down) in the previous image needs a cheap tool to 'set' or pull up the back side onto the drywall (it's possible to do it with a screwdriver but not easy). Also bear in mind you can't remove spring toggle fasteners without losing the spring toggle behind the drywall.

Alternatively, consider fastening timber rails or battens to the wall (screwing into the studs behind the drywall) and then fasten stuff to the rails. IKEA's new kitchen cabinets for example, now utilise a slim metal rail which you screw to the wall along its length and then the cabinets hang from the rail. This system gives maximum flexibility to find good fastening points.

Incidentally if you're building new stud walls and you know where heavy stuff is going to be in advance, add extra timber noggins between the vertical studs so you have a solid block of timber to fasten stuff too. I always build in 50mm × 200mm (2" × 8") blocks of timber (floor joist offcuts) at 900mm or 36" high (worktop height) and at 2m or 6' 8" high (top of kitchen cabinet height) which makes installing kitchen units a breeze because you can then just screw straight into the wall using regular wood screws.

New fasteners come out every year, getting cleverer by the minute, but here are some of the long-standing popular ones, the word inside the brackets denotes the type of load they are suitable for, but always double check the instructions on the packet...

NAILS

Nailing accurately without splitting or marking the timber requires practise, see the *How to Use a Hammer and Nails* section in the *Developing Practical Skills* chapter for the basics. Learning to hammer in nails is fun and it'll teach you a lot about hand-eye co-ordination. Just make sure you practise on some scrapwood first with a variety of different sized nails until you're happy. Oh, and do this before you nail something you want to actually keep in your house. Here's a selection of some of the nails I use regularly and the type of jobs or material they are suitable for...

CHOOSING NAIL TYPE

As with choosing screws, when choosing nails, there are a few things which will influence your choice...

- Exposure to the weather or moisture.
- The type and thickness of the material or workpiece.
- The load the nail needs to carry or resist.
- Any special requirements specific to the job.
- The length of the nail and the shape of the head needed to satisfy the above three variables.

Common Nails

Bright round wire nails. General framing and construction. Size 25mm to 150mm (1" to 6"). Common sizes 50mm, 75mm and 100mm (2", 3" and 4"). Various gauges.*

Lost head nails. Barrel type head is ideal for face work and is easy to punch below the surface. Size: 25mm to 100mm (1" to 4"). Common sizes 50mm and 65mm (2" and 2 1/2").*

Annular ring nail. Great for sheet materials. Size 40mm to 100mm (1 1/2" to 4"). Common sizes are 50mm, 65mm and 75mm (2", 2 1/2" and 3"). Difficult to remove.*

Galvanised clout nail. Small sizes have large heads ideal for roofing felt. Larger sizes make good general purpose nails for indoor and outdoor work. Size 13mm to 75mm (1/2" to 3"). Common sizes 20mm, 25mm 38mm and 50mm (3/4", 1", 1 1/2" and 2"). Also available in copper for fixing slates.

Oval wire nail. Ideal for finish carpentry as their shape means less likelihood of splitting. Small heads. Size 25mm to 100mm (1" to 4"). Common sizes 40mm 50mm and 65mm (1 1/2", 2" and 2 1/2").*

Square twist nail. Used on joist hangers and straps. Superior holding power and thick gauge. Size 30mm and 40mm (1 1/4" and 1 1/2"), both common.

Square cut or clasp nail. Stamped out of flat metal. Old style suitable for nailing floorboards or into light weight blocks. Large holding power. Size 50mm 65mm, 75mm and 100mm (2", 2 1/2", 3" and 4"). Common sizes are 65mm and 75mm (2 1/2" and 3").

Masonry nail. Very hard nail for nailing into hard substrates like brick and concrete (in theory). Sizes 25mm to 100mm (1" to 4"). Common sizes, no idea, I hate the blooming things and never use them...

Panel pins. Thin, narrow head nail perfect for fixing trims and thin panels. Sizes from 13mm to 40mm (1/2" to 1 1/2"). Common sizes are 25mm and 32mm (1" and 1 1/4").*

Galvanised staple. Used to hold wire and mesh. Size from 15mm to 40mm (5/8" to 1 1/2"). Common size 25mm (1").

Tacks. Carpet and upholstery use. Very sharp point and large head. Sizes from 10mm to 25mm (3/8" to 1"), all common.

*These nails are available galvanised for outdoor use.

Anything outdoors and exposed to the weather (or might be) needs hot dipped galvanised nails specifically rated for outdoor work. Regular or bright, plain steel nails have no corrosion protection and will fail if used outdoors in unprotected areas. Some jobs are outside but undercover, roofing work for example, and although roofing work is technically 'dry', I'd still recommend you use outdoor nails for their superior rustproofing and holding qualities (galvanised nails have a rough finish and hold well). Your local building control officer might even specify protected nails for roofing work too.

Some nails used indoors still get wet. For example, any nails under plaster (plaster's wet to start with don't forget), when you're nailing expanded metal lathing onto framework for example. Even painting unprotected nails with water-based paints can cause a problem with rust spotting through the paint finish. Light galvanised or coated nails is a better choice here.

Some different nail coatings then...

- Hot dip galvanized nails have a thick, often lumpy layer of zinc for heavy corrosion protection e.g. outdoors.

- Electro galvanized nails have a thin layer of zinc for light corrosion protection (sheradised, yellow zinc etc.).

- Vinyl coated nails are easy to drive in as the friction melts the vinyl. Once cooled, the vinyl sets and protects against corrosion, plus it makes the nails hard to remove.

Alternatively, you could choose a nail made from a non-ferrous metal which of course don't require coatings because they don't corrode under normal conditions. Look at aluminium, brass and copper; oh, and stainless steel, which is ferrous, but doesn't rust because of some clever skulduggery akin to alchemy in the foundry... Bit expensive though.

CHOOSING NAIL HEADS

The type of material, plus the load it's going to carry, dictates the shape of the nail head. Big loads mean decent sized heads (and long length and heavy gauge). Small loads mean tiny heads. Fragile material might need oversized heads to prevent tearing through, roofing felt nails for example.

Round bright wire nails with medium sized round flat heads are the most common for general framing and joinery. 50mm (2″), 75mm (3″) and 100mm (4″) are the most common sizes.

Lost head or finish nails (where the head is only minimally bigger than the gauge) are common for general finishing work where you don't want to see big ugly nail heads. Nail these in close to the surface and finish off by using a nail punch to punch the nail slightly below the surface (to protect the surface of your workpiece from your hammer). Common sizes are from 38mm (1 ½″) up to around 75mm (3″) or so.

Oval nails are in the middle and ideal for medium sized trims like architraves etc. Always orientate them with the long oval along the grain to minimise splitting. Oval nails can be a little tricky to punch below the surface due to their very narrow head.

Panel pins are small versions of the lost head nails suitable for small trims. From 12mm (½″) up to around 50mm (2″) or so in both bright steel and lightly galvanised or sheradised (which is just a fancy way of saying 'dry galvanised'), or even copper or stainless steel.

CHOOSING NAIL LENGTH

As with screw length mentioned earlier, choose your nail length based on the thickness of the timber you're fastening together. Nailing two pieces of 20mm (¾″) stock together for instance, where you'd use 35mm (1 ¼″) nails. Ideally though, aim for approximately *two and a half to three times* the thickness of the material you're fixing to. For example, to fix a 20mm (¾″) thick piece of timber to some framing, you'd use a 50mm to 60mm (2 to 2 ½″) nail.

One time you can ignore that ratio is when rough nailing purely for strength on non-face work. If access is good to both sides, then choose a nail that's 12mm (½″) longer than the combined timber thicknesses; drive the nail all the way through and hammer over the protrusion back onto the workpiece. This creates a 90° staple like effect, making the nail immovable.

If you can, avoid nailing into the end grain of a piece of timber (down the grain), because end grain doesn't hold nails very well. If unavoidable (and it often is), be especially careful not to split the timber. Drill small pilot holes if you need to (mostly on smaller timbers) and use longer and thinner gauge nails than normal if possible. Nailing up a 90° angle in framing using 50mm × 50mm (2″ by 2″) or 50mm × 100mm (2″ × 4″) timber using 100mm (4″) nails is common, but it will not be terribly strong on its own.

CHOOSING NAIL GAUGE OR THICKNESS

As with screws, the gauge or thickness of the nail depends on the weight of the item you're fastening, plus the expected load it's going to carry. Small lightweight stuff and lightly loaded things like trims etc. don't exert much pull on their fasteners so thin nails are fine. Once you start going up in timber size, the load or weight and pull on the fasteners increases exponentially. Medium weight things like fascia boards, or large skirting boards need nails in the middle of the gauge range. Save the heaviest, thicker gauges, for larger stuff like framing or fencing etc.

The gauge of a nail is often commensurate to its length as well; for example, in the store you'll not see very skinny and very long nails (they'd bend too easily) or very short and very heavy gauge nails. There are a couple of exceptions of course; tile lath nails are quite long and thin as the timber is soft and the nail goes in at 90° and twist nails for nailing joist hangers etc. are quite short and fat. But in general, there are not many different gauges per length of nail. Choose the gauge depending on your estimate of the loading on the fasteners for the job in mind. Light load, thinner gauge; heavy load, thicker gauge etc. Bigger is not always better because you might end up splitting the timber if the gauge is too heavy...

Related to length and gauge is the shape of the nails shank. Most regular nails are plain round in cross section, but you'll also see square nails and nails with twisted and even ribbed shanks. The purpose of ribbing and twisting shanks is to improve holding power and pull out strength.

SPECIAL NAILS

As we have seen above, many nails only have one job to do, from aluminium nails for concrete roofing tiles, to copper nails for roofing slate to plastic headed nails for plastic fascia boards; here are a few more...

MASONRY NAILS

You can hammer masonry nails straight into hard materials like concrete, brick, and block etc., well, at least that's the theory. In practise, I'd advise you in nearly every scenario to choose a different fastening method. Why? Well, masonry nails, as you can imagine, need tremendous hammer blows to get them to go into such hard substrates. If it goes wrong (and it will) you're looking at big dents in the material, or at worst a nail ricocheting all around the room like a bullet. Masonry nails are inherently dangerous due to their extreme tempering which makes them very hard. My apologies to anyone offended by this broad statement; but I don't think anyone just starting out on DIY projects should use them. Save masonry nails until you have a lot more practical knowledge about materials and hammering experience.

CUT NAILS

Cut or clasp nails, made by stamping them out of flat sheets of thick metal, are a bit of a throwback to earlier times. Being oblong in section and having blunt ends, plus a small 90° angle at the top, they have great holding power. Used to hold down floorboards in the old days, but now useful for nailing into light-weight blocks funnily enough (a real mixture or old and new tech!). Handy also to create that period look...

STAPLES

Seems the best section to include staples, since they are just nails curved into a U shape. Staples are excellent for holding fragile and otherwise difficult-to-fasten materials like metal or plastic mesh, wire strands, roofing membranes, polythene sheet or plain old fabrics.

Use a hand powered stapler to set small, light gauge, square topped regular staples (made from stamped and folded thin metal) to hold thin sheet material such as building paper, polythene, membranes, and roofing underlays etc. to timber. Although lightly galvanised, they are not suitable for exposure to the weather. Most often used to hold things in place temporarily whilst you employ a more robust fastener. A membrane behind timber cladding for example; staple the membrane to the framing and then the timber claddings fasteners hold it in place permanently.

Mid gauge staples most often fired from an air powered stapler have better protection against corrosion and are ideal to hold light gauge wire mesh in place; chicken wire for example. Most often they have slightly rounded tops, although wider versions may still have a small flat part on top. Longer staples are even strong enough to hold timber parts together such as thin lathing or bird boxes and the like. It's best to use divergent point staples when you need extra hold. Divergent point means the pointed legs twist as they enter the timber increasing their pull-out strength. Regular staples generally go straight in (look at the end of the staple legs, straight or pointed?)

Heavy gauge, round topped staples are ideal to hold wire; either single strands or heavyweight mesh such as chain link fencing. Heavy gauge staples are hot dipped galvanised and have the best protection against the elements.

CORRUGATED ROOFING NAILS

Made specially to hold down roofing sheets and they have enormous holding power. You can imagine the amount of lift a large roof must encounter during a storm. I've seen whole agricultural buildings try to lift and flex under severe wind load. Shallow pitched roofs act like aircraft wings or aerofoils and even gentle winds can create huge pressure loads.

Most roofing nail designs have a spiral or twisted design, causing them to enter the timber like a screw under the hammer. Usually very thick gauge nails, but pilot holes are not usually necessary as most roofing timbers are big enough to cope with the force. The nail head holds down a wide rubber washer which seals tight onto the roofing sheet. The sealing washer usually goes on the top of a corrugation on rigid roofing materials such as corrugated cement fibre, (whereas flexible roofing materials such as metal corrugated sheet, often use a screw in the bottom of the corrugation to prevent buckling). Roofing nails need to be tight enough to form a seal but not so tight you damage the often-fragile roofing material (incidentally, never walk on cement fibre roofs, especially older ones, always use a roof ladder).

CARPET TACKS

Tiny, needle sharp nails designed to fix carpet to wooden substrates. Largely superseded by carpet gripper, also known as gripper rod or tack strip.

Carpet gripper is a thin strip of plywood containing hundreds of angled nails which you either nail (wooden floors) or with an adhesive (solid floors) in place just inside the perimeter of the room. Most important is to angle the nails towards the wall. Stretch the carpet over the nails and press down.

Both carpet tacks and gripper are difficult to handle as they are extremely sharp, (seriously, they are evil things...). Take great care when using them and especially when removing old ones.

All good? Happy with your nailing skills? Oh, and yes, I realise this is a terrible place to introduce, erm... powered nail guns (I know, and you just spent ages practising with your hammer, right?). But don't worry, knowing how to use a hammer will still come in handy. Plus, the info about choosing the right nails for your project applies to both nail guns and hammers... (all this sounds like it's from a bad zombie movie, doesn't it?)

POWERED NAILERS

So, the powered nail gun. Once the preserve of only the most handsome of carpenters, is now available to everyone, even my 13-year-old daughter uses one, (under supervision). Originally powered by compressed air (for that fabulous 'psssh dunk' noise!), These days, if I do choose nails for a task, I'm likely to use air nailers because of their superior control and cleaner finish (no half-moon indents from miss hits with the hammer).

Mechanical nailers come in several forms now; with gas or battery powered nailers replacing the traditional compressed air. I'm sticking to my air nailers for now because it's what I'm used to (and it's what I already have), but the new generation of battery-powered nailers are ideal for DIY use as there are no airlines to get in the way or struggle with.

Nailers deliver nails decisively, accurately and with just enough force for the job. Just ensure you're using the right length and gauge (thickness) nails for the size timber you're nailing. Don't expect thin 18g trim nails to hold 50mm × 25mm (2"x1") battens and conversely don't use 75mm (3") clipped head nails to fix your architraves, because it won't look pretty...

Most mechanical nailers come with depth adjustment ranging from *just proud* to *buried deep* and you'll need to experiment with this because timber varies in density (even within the same piece!), which affects how deep the nail goes; (if you hit a knot for example).

As with all guns, what comes out, goes in a straight line which means powered nailers need to be at exactly the right angle to the workpiece for the nail to end up where it's going to do some good. Too shallow or too steep an angle leaves nails with little holding power. Larger framing nailers have spikes around their nose to allow you to jam the nose right where you want it and the spikes dig into the workpiece to hold the mailer steady whilst you pull the trigger. As a safety mechanism, you need to fully depress the nose before pulling the trigger to fire the nail.

Oh, and safety glasses are essential when using mechanical nailers, seriously, don't even think about it. I've seen and experienced nails coming out of the workpiece at crazy angles, and some that ricocheted around the room. Seriously, use safety glasses or goggles, every time.

Lastly, like all guns, it will occasionally jam, usually bending a nail. Always disconnect the power before unclipping the nose mechanism to clear the jam (pull out the battery, pull off the air hose etc.). Follow the manufacturers lubrication schedule to minimise jamming and extend tool life.

TIMBER CONNECTORS AND HARDWARE

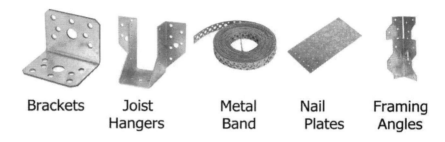

| Brackets | Joist Hangers | Metal Band | Nail Plates | Framing Angles |

Traditional joints such as the 'mortice and tenon' have fell by the wayside in regular domestic construction (although you'll still see them in oak framed buildings and barn conversions etc.) and nowadays big timber joints usually involve a selection of proprietary metal to timber connectors. There is one for just about every occasion and they're most commonly found supporting floor joists or in roofing applications. However, today the range is so big you could build almost anything with them, from a dog kennel to a timber framed house.

Timber connectors require nails (or occasionally screws) to fix them in place, but don't use your regular fasteners for this as they may be too weak. Instead, buy the special ones recommended by the manufacturers as they're much stronger (thick twist nails for example). Plus, you'll likely invalidate the connectors specs (and manufacturers guarantee) if you use plain galvanised clout nails for example, although you'll see plenty used in the real world on smaller building sites and for light loadings, you'll probably get away with it.

Always check the manufacturers installation specifications because some straps and hanger require you to nail every hole and some don't, it varies from strap to strap, depending on its use and location. Some have many holes just to give you a choice of fastening positions and some need every hole nailed to provide the required strength.

Sometimes there is a small tang or tack which you hammer in first to hold the hardware in position whilst you get your first nails in. Be wary of this moving you out of position though. Sometimes it's just easier to hold the thing and put your first nail in.

Metal banding is handy for general holding and reinforcing jobs such as bracing. Fasten it diagonally across timber walls and floors to create triangles, which as we know from our school days, is the strongest shape and ideal for bracing or strengthening structures.

Use heavier metal straps to join floor joists to walls, hold down wall plates/roofs or tying gable ends into roofs for example. Always ensure straps go across several timbers though, fastening to one isn't any good at all. Minimum of three and always add solid timber blocking in between or on top of the joists/rafters etc.

NUTS, BOLTS, MACHINE SCREWS, & WASHERS

There are enough different types of machine screws, nuts, and bolts to fill this book alone, so I'll stick to some of the more common ones. We'll look at the type of metal used, i.e. the strength; the type of heads, threads, and a bit about washers etc. We'll finish off with a few tips about bolting in timber and modifying bolts. Oh, and I know we looked at this earlier but remember, try to use a torque wrench to tighten all but the smallest fasteners...

Fortunately, most of the fasteners you'll come across are already a part of the item you're working on, so you don't need to worry about the bolt's specifications. It's only when you need to replace a fastener or if you're building something from scratch that you'll need to know a little more. Thankfully the range of fasteners in the local hardware store is only a miniscule percentage of the range available from a specialist engineering supplier. This means (unless you're building a rocket or maintaining your powerboat), the fasteners in your local store are suitable for projects in your home. The upper end of the bolt spectrum is more for specialist engineering locations such as aero, space or other high-performance arenas. The bolts on your kid's go-kart don't endure the same sort of stress, but then I don't know your kid...

General definitions then: a bolt is a threaded fastener which goes through two or more components and has a washer/nut on the end. A machine screw usually has no nut, instead it screws into threads cut in the last component of the assembly. Machine screws over 6mm (1/4"), change their name to *tap bolts* however. Clear? Well no, it's not really! Does a machine screw become a bolt if it has a nut (maybe!), and some bolts don't have nuts, so are they machine screws... (yes/no?).

It's complicated and no one agrees 100% about any of this. It's a bit like those daft statements... that all chickens are birds, but not all birds are chickens... Oh well, never mind. Let's look at some practical stuff we *can* understand, and we'll leave the bolt semantics to the engineers...

STRENGTH

The strength of a nut or bolt depends on the material it's made from (obvious, but bear with me); therefore, it's imperative you never replace one type of bolt with a different (read softer) one as it may be too weak to carry the load. Bolt classification varies so much from country to country and manufacturer to manufacturer it would mean several pages of mostly meaningless (for our purposes) tables and I don't see the point in that. Of course, you can always google the bolt marking system in your country if you want to learn the specifics. But adding a whole bunch of tables here, I think will just complicate matters, yes?

For now, let's just say that if the head of a bolt has no markings you can assume it's a general-purpose bolt suitable for most normal load situations (i.e. the majority of everyday machines and appliances). Conversely, if you're replacing a bolt which has markings on the head of the bolt, make sure the bolt you buy to replace it, has exactly the same markings (or a higher grade according to your research), especially if you're working on your Cessna...

To give you some general background; bolt ratings decide their typical use. A bolt going onto an aircraft for example, needs to be much higher grade i.e. stronger, than a bolt going onto a bicycle for example. And in fact, fasteners approved for aero use are manufactured in dedicated places (i.e. a different place to where they make regular bolts) to avoid the risk of non-aero quality fasteners getting mixed up and finding their way onto an aircraft.

Clean up the top of your bolt with a light wire brushing and look for any markings. Look for lines, numbers, or any other marks, either raised or stamped onto the top of the bolt head. Any marks are likely to refer to the mechanical properties of the material it's made from. Usually the more marks or the higher the number, the tougher the fastener is and the more load it can cope with before failing.

BOLT TYPES

Bolts consist of a head, a shank, and threads. Tap bolts have threads along their whole length, but regular hex bolts only have threads towards the end. The plain, non-threaded area on a regular hex bolt is the *grip length*. The grip length doesn't need threads because it's inside the component or components; only the protruding part of the shank has threads to receive the washer and nut (or to go into threads cut into the last component in the assembly).

Bolt heads vary in shape to suit a range of different applications. However, as above 99% of the time the bolts you come across will have a hexagonal (six) sided flat topped head to fit a spanner or socket and ratchet wrench. Some hex bolt heads have a flange on the bottom edge which negates the need for washers in some situations.

You measure a fasteners length by how deep it goes into the material. Measure a non-countersunk fastener from underneath the head to the end, i.e. just the shank length. Whereas you'd measure the overall length of a countersunk fastener, head included. For gauge, measure the diameter of the shank or the outside diameter of the threads.

Hex Bolts

Hex bolt with plain 'grip length' plus a plain washer and nut.

Fully threaded or tap bolt plus a plain washer and nut.

THREADS

No, not your clothes, these threads are what make your fasteners work. Threads or more correctly screw threads, have two forms; internal and external. Internal threads live inside a nut or component, and you can cut them yourself (if you want) with a tool called a tap (called tapping). External threads live on the outside of bolt shanks and you cut them with a die (called dying. Only kidding it's called threading; don't blame me, it's a funny language...).

As different countries developed their engineering capacity, several different screw threads emerged into common use and despite recent developments in standardization, some differences prevail. In addition, there are different sizes (pitch) from each manufacturer as well. And of course, nothing's interchangeable and yes, it's a pain in the derriere...

Thankfully though, the main types of threads you'll see are...

- ISO Metric*. Standard in Europe and common across the world. Sizes range from M1 through to around M36. Most common sizes range from M5 to M12. Most are coarse pitch by default, but there are fine pitches available for specialist applications.

- UTS Unified Thread Standard. Common in the USA and Canada. Available in coarse, fine, and extra fine...

- UNC (Unified National Coarse).

- UNF (Unified National Fine).

- UNEF (Unified National Extra Fine).

*(ISO comes from the Greek word isos meaning equal and is the global word for the International Organization for Standardization. In case you were wondering why it's ISO and not the acronym IOS. Just sayin')

Thread types vary from coarse threads, suitable for general work, up to really fine threads, suitable for screwing into a thin part or a high load application for example. Pitch is the measurement from the top of one thread to the top of the next and ranges from coarse to extra fine. Coarse threads resist stripping and cross threading better because the threads are bigger and easier to engage. They are also fast to install as they need less turns to drive home.

Fine threads have a larger contact area (because there are more threads) per length of screw, which means they hold better and are less likely to vibrate loose. However, fine threads are easy to install cross threaded due to the small starting angle and little distance between the threads. We looked at this in the *How to Use Spanners and Wrenches* in the *Developing Practical Skills* chapter.

The easiest way to figure your threads out, is to grab yourself a cheap thread gauge which you hold onto the thread in question; keep trying different ones until you hit one which fits snugly, then read off the type of thread on the side of the tool.

LEFT HAND THREADS

Most threads are right hand or normal, i.e. you turn them clockwise to tighten (remember 'righty tighty and leftie loosie'?). But on some rotary objects there is a risk of the rotational force undoing the fastener. In these instances, for the fastener to stay tight, the threads on the bolt must tighten the opposite way to the rotation of the object.

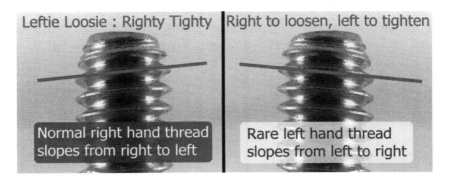

Leftie Loosie : Righty Tighty | Right to loosen, left to tighten

Normal right hand thread slopes from right to left | Rare left hand thread slopes from left to right

To achieve this, designers specify a left-hand threaded fastener which will tighten under the rotary load instead. You'll find left hand threads on bicycle pedals/cranks, drill chucks, circular saw blade arbours, some left-hand side wheel hubs and so on. If ever in a situation where a fastener appears to be unfeasibly tight and doesn't want to yield to your tool, take a look at the rotation of the object. If it is clockwise, there is a possibility that the fastener is a left-hand thread so check any threads you can see for orientation. If they slope from left to right, viewed sideways on then it's left handed...

MODIFYING FASTENERS

I'll include this here as it's the threads that pay the price if you get this wrong... If you're working on a bolt, to shorten one for example, you'll need to protect the threads during the process, as they damage easily. Never hold them directly in the jaws of a vice or grip them with a pair of pliers or grips etc. Buy some *soft jaws* for your vice (or make some out of two bits of wood) or try threading a couple of nuts onto the bolt, tighten them against each other, then you can hold the nuts tightly (steady now!) in the vice instead. This will protect the threads as you cut the bolt with your hacksaw or mini grinder. Oh, and anyway, you'll find it quite difficult to cut a bolt whilst holding it with a pair of pliers etc., a cheap bench top vice really is worth the investment. If you don't have a bench yet, you can bolt the vice to a length of timber plank.

After sawing the bolt, you'll find the end has a burr stopping you from threading on the nut. Using a fine-toothed file, create a small chamfer all around the newly cut end which should restore the startability (made up word) of the nut. Another way to ensure a clean end is to thread on the nut first, cut the bolt and then take the nut off. This should clean up the last thread, but it's still best to tidy up the end with a file.

One last thing about threads. Never hit them with a hammer. Ever. Tempting though it is to try and tap out a stubborn bolt, if you hit the end thread, you'll never get the nut back on again, *ever*. Always unscrew the nut until it's protecting the end of the bolt and then hit the nut. Oh, and it's best to use a soft faced hammer too. Hide and copper combination hammers are common. Copper being softer than steel, it should dent before causing any serious damage to the steel.

Cheap 'tap and die' sets are a bit weak for cutting brand new threads (unless you go real slow), but they are quite handy for tidying up damaged existing threads if you've been a little careless...

WASHERS AND SHAKE PROOF MECHANISMS

Washers have two closely connected jobs; first, a washer spreads the compression load exerted on the component by the action of tightening the nut or bolt. Second, washers make it easier to tighten the nut by reducing the friction between the underneath of the bolt head and the component. Without a washer, the rotating edge of the nut could score and dig into the workpiece. Instead the washer provides a kind of slip plane between the component and the nut making it easier to achieve the correct torque.

The harder the material, the smaller and thinner the washer needs to be. Conversely, soft stuff such as timber needs very big, thick washers, sometimes as much as 50mm (2") or so in diameter to avoid overly crushing the timbers fibres as you tighten them up.

Stuff that moves will vibrate, and vibration, in theory, can lead to a nut rotating, undoing it gradually over time. To combat this, you'd typically use either shake proof washers or shake proof nuts and/or a thread locking compound. On more serious stuff (safety related) you might also occasionally see things like castellated nuts which is a specially shaped nut which holds in place via a split pin through a hole drilled in the end of the bolt, or a twisted wire through holes in a series of bolts, holding them all together.

You can even add monitors on nuts or bolts; next time you're out, look at large truck wheel nuts, most have pointed fluorescent wheel nut indicators. If the points don't align, then something is coming undone... (i.e. not good).

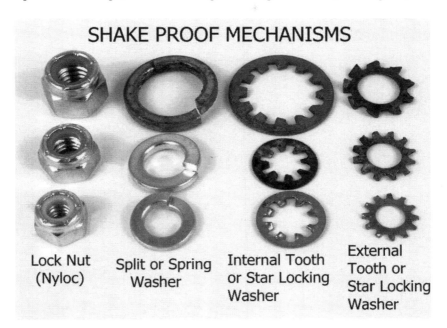

SHAKE PROOF MECHANISMS

| Lock Nut (Nyloc) | Split or Spring Washer | Internal Tooth or Star Locking Washer | External Tooth or Star Locking Washer |

SHAKE PROOF OR LOCK NUTS

Shake proof or lock nuts (NYLOC being the most common) have a little plastic insert right at the top of the nut (often blue) which grips the threads tightly. Be aware that shake-proof nuts will appear to stop once the bolt reaches the little plastic inserts in the top. If you have got that far you'll be fine, just keep going with a wrench and the bolts threads will cut or tap a new thread through the plastic. It's advisable to replace shake proof nuts with new ones every time they're removed (even though I know you won't!). Seriously, you *must* replace them on anything with a critical safety function (they are cheap). Ordinarily though, if you're working on your wheel barrow, it might not matter so much, but always use new ones on the Ferrari...

SHAKE PROOF WASHERS

To stop regular nuts shaking loose, use a special shake proof washer in conjunction with a plain or regular washer. Fitted in between the plain washer and the underside of the nut a shake proof washer digs into the metal on both sides, holding them in place. Shake proof washers come in lots of designs, some with twisted parts to dig into the metal (internal and external toothed or star washers) and others have a single split (split or spring washers). All these washers exert pressure in opposing directions to stop rotation of the fasteners parts once you've tightened them up.

THREAD LOCKING COMPOUND

Use a thread locking compound (Loctite being the most famous) when there is a risk of high vibration. The compound is essentially a glue (of varying strengths) which, on contact with clean metal fasteners and in the absence of air sets into a hard plastic. Because the compound fills the gaps between the threads it locks everything up and as a bonus helps prevent corrosion (no air or water you see?). Different manufacturers use different colours to denote different strengths and you'll most commonly see blue (medium strength) and red (higher strength).

Thread locking does make components more difficult to remove, as that is kind of the point. But not impossible; (some of the highest strength compounds might need heat to soften them). Generally, you'll still be able to undo nuts and bolts treated with Loctite using regular tools, they'll just be a bit tight to start off with, you might even need to 'shock' them loose with a good pull on the wrench to 'crack' the seal the compound makes with the metal.

Clean up the threads with a wire brush and wipe off with a rag. Add a small amount of the compound onto the threads before either inserting a bolt or stud into a component or a nut onto threads.

STARLOCK PUSH ON FASTENER

Don't confuse these with star shaped locking washers. Starlocks are retaining washers, push on washers, or just push nuts. Commonly used to hold small wheels on to shafts, like those found on prams, pushchairs, strollers, sack trucks and lawnmowers etc., or to stop a shaft from moving around or coming out once it's gone through a component.

They hold in place by spring loaded prongs; effectively one-way barbs which makes them tricky to remove.

Starlocks are considered single use and they are very cheap to buy so remove them by cutting the outer rim with side cutters and twisting them away. Replace with new ones. Alternatively, if you *must* save an original, the trick is to lever up the little prongs against the shaft itself to relieve their grip, one at a time. A pointed pick, a very small flat screwdriver or a tiny pair of needle nosed pliers will do the trick, work each prong up a little at a time going around and around them all. This should drive the starlock washer up, eventually freeing it.

Starlock Push On Fastener or Push Nut

Sometimes, if you lever up one or two of the prongs you can un-screw the washer like a nut to get it off. Don't lever the whole washer up around the outer rim, because that makes them dig in even more (unless the shaft is plastic, then the prongs will dig in and reverse direction allowing the starlock to come off at the expense of a little damage to the plastic shaft). Flatten down the prongs a little with a small hammer before re-fitting.

Some starlock washers have a cap or decorative dome which covers the prongs. Unless the dome cap pops off, you might just have to lever the whole thing off and hope for the best.

Removal usually damages starlocks, although if you're careful and take your time, you might get away with it, especially on something not particularly stressed like a toy pram etc. If you insist on re-using the old ones, tap the prongs back down a little with a small hammer before re-fitting as below. Don't risk re-use on your hot-rod though...

Install new starlocks by tapping them into place using a suitable sized hollow tube (ensure the prongs are sloping upwards). I find a suitably sized socket from a wrench/socket set works just fine. There are of course special tools for the job, although you'd probably have to order one online.

The dome styles often have a rim around the edge for fitting. If not try a piece of rubber or leather under the tube (to protect the thin dome). Don't tap the dome with a hammer (however tempting it is), you'll dent the dome, guaranteed. The ones in the next image I managed to push on with my big thumbs...

Dome style starlock washer to hold a sack truck wheel

BOLTING TIMBER

Of course, you'd expect to find nuts and bolts on mechanical things, but you'll also find them in buildings and even your furniture. Highly stressed stuff like chairs or tables for example, often utilize nuts and bolts (commonly hidden) to provide the high strength required to hold such relatively large loads (in relation to their size).

Bigger structural timbers, such as those in a roof, also utilise bolts to form structurally strong triangle shapes. You can buy special bolts which are ideal to hold big timbers together. Having large domed heads, timber bolts only need one tool as the head side looks after itself due to some clever spurs on the underside of the head. Some folks use regular coach bolts for bolting timber, but the small square on the underside of a coach bolts head should really go into a metal part (a farm gate hinge strap for example or a large metal washer with a square hole) to stop the bolt turning as you tighten the nut.

Nut & bolt with large washers and dogtooth timber connector

For general assembly of timbers not normally seen, (smaller roofs etc.) using threaded bar is a (cheaper) alternative to special timber bolts. Simply cut the threaded bar into the required lengths and assemble with washers and nuts both ends. However, bear in mind that threaded bar may not be as tensile/strong as regular coach bolts, so check with your structural engineer first if you're bolting really large or particularly stressed timbers. Use large washers to prevent the bolt head or nut pulling into the timber under load.

To improve all bolted joints in timber, use a dog tooth timber connector (see previous image) or even glue in between the timbers, to resist sliding forces, both methods add a huge amount of strength to the joint.

IMPROVISED & TEMPORARY FIXINGS & FASTENERS.

Sometimes you need to work with what you have to hand, because sometimes failures are totally random. You might not have access to your regular tools or materials and need to fix something temporarily to finish the job (or get home). Here are a few examples of stuff that's handy to keep in your toolbox, just in case...

- Wire. Often copper but also mild (binding wire for reinforcing bars and mesh etc.), galvanised (wire coat-hangers etc.) and stainless steel (anything where rust is an issue; marine, medical, agriculture environments etc.) plus aluminium (usually thicker diameter and easily bendable, fencing, etc.), all are common. Available as bare metal wire or with some sort of plastic sheathing or insulation. Electrical insulation is easy to strip off by running a knife along a short section at one end and then using pliers to pull the bare wire out of the side of the plastic or rubber coating. A bit of practise here works wonders.

- Plastic cable ties. Originally developed to hold cables in place in aircraft wings nowadays there are lots of different cable tie designs, from tiny ones up to ones strong enough to hold the biggest man (PlastiCuffs). Grab a cheap bag of mixed lengths next time you're in your local DIY store.

- Tape. Clear tape such as 'Sellotape' has it's uses, but electrical tape and reinforced duct tape are more useful. Tapes are often not much use in wet and cold environments though. Duct tape is brilliantly strong though and you should keep a roll handy in case of emergencies.

- String. A classic material, especially in the garden. Available in various different materials, some waterproof and strong such as Nylon (but watch your knots, some plastic strings can easily unravel)

- Monofilament fishing line. A brilliant material and near invisible which is useful for some projects. It's available in many sizes, from light line as fine as hair, right up to phenomenally strong and thick sea fishing lines capable of holding weights or 100kgs plus.

- Braided fishing lines. As above but made from multiple strands which means virtually no stretch and incredible breaking strength coupled with small diameter.

- Rope. Available from 2mm up to, well whatever really. Most practical size in the home is probably in the 6mm (1/4") to 13mm (1/2") range. Larger sizes are of course available. Plastic ropes are the most durable but natural fibre ropes look good, especially for craft or decorative purposes.

Usually temporarily after other fasteners have failed 'in the field' so to speak but some temporary fasteners such as plastic cable ties are capable of permanent work. As their name implies cable ties are designed to fix electrical cables in place but they are available in so many lengths and strengths (thicknesses etc.) that they are useful for lots of jobs in the home, garden or vehicle; temporary and permanent.

Been to IKEA lately? Oh goody, you'll like the next bit then...

ASSEMBLING & INSTALLING (FLAT PACKS ETC.)

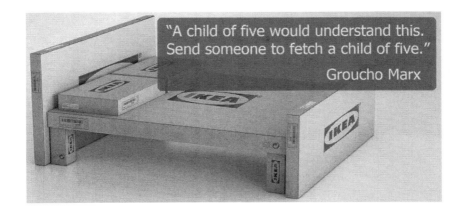

"A child of five would understand this. Send someone to fetch a child of five."

Groucho Marx

A little home assembly is pretty unavoidable these days, whether it's an infamous IKEA flat pack, or your new barbeque. This chapter will show you how to master the art of self-assembly, because properly assembled/fitted stuff lasts years longer than stuff thrown together without looking at the instructions.

Arguably, the manufacturer has done most of the hard work for you and self-assembly stuff is supposedly simple enough for 'anyone to do' by design... But I'll be honest, it does mean taking a moment sometimes and doing a little head scratching as you try to comprehend what the manufacturer means exactly. The ones to be especially careful with are the badly translated foreign instructions with dubious helpful pictures, you might need to spend a little time thinking it through before committing yourself. Flat pack assembly is an ideal starting point for you to start figuring out how things go together and to try out those new tools.

SOME IMPORTANT THINGS TO REMEMBER...

- Clear your working area of clutter *before* opening any boxes to create the best workspace possible (why struggle?) oh, and to avoid losing any of the small parts, (you'll need ALL of them!).

- Identify and familiarise yourself with each component as you remove it from its packaging (be observant!). Learn the terminology for each part as you check it off the packing list.

- Put all the small components into tubs, bowls or even an empty drawer (new kitchen?) so they don't get lost. Use separate containers for each package until you're more familiar with the parts.

- Read the instructions (yes really!) and keep them close for frequent reference during assembly. Afterwards, file them properly so you don't lose them, just in case, (well, you never know...).

- Check fasteners are in the right holes, lots of flatpack stuff is modular (used on multiple things) which means not all the holes will apply to your build. Holes look similar, so double check the instructions.

- Take care with alignment; double check parts are in the right place and pointing in the right direction.

- Take care with fasteners or fixings to avoid crossed threads. Always start and run them up by hand where possible. Applies to nuts going onto bolts and tap bolts going into threaded holes.

- Especially don't over tighten fasteners in chipboard, particleboard or MDF, as it's very easy to ruin the threads. Stop as soon as you hit the surface and it has pulled up with no gap.

A FEW WORDS ABOUT IKEA

Most folks love IKEA and can think of nothing better than a day spent shopping for wardrobes with a significant other and a couple of grumpy kids.......... Sorry, what, oh they don't? (What do you mean I'm weird...?)

Okay, okay, I'll admit it; some people don't like shopping at IKEA, even if it does come with meatballs and ice cream. Nevertheless, IKEA *is* a store full of modern, well-designed stuff, that's ready to go *and* affordable *and* you can easily replace something if you screw up... That's got be good, right?

IT'S *NOT* ROCKET SCIENCE

Problems with assembling flat pack stuff often leads to accusations that it's cheap and nasty. But in reality, most of it is well designed and it does have a long life *if* assembled properly, note that last word... *properly*!

If your idea of hell is a trip to IKEA, followed by the double hell of actually putting it all together, don't panic, it's psychological. Remember the first parts of this book; you *can* do it. This stuff is *designed* for *you* to assemble. For anyone who can pick up a screwdriver actually, and some bits don't even need the screwdriver! Don't let your past experiences or prejudices stop you from enjoying some of the best, low cost designs on the market.

Remember the basic principles we looked at earlier in the book... especially observation. Don't just switch off and say you can't be arsed or it's too difficult, because honestly, it's really not. And if you get stuck, don't forget you can always pick up the phone... (it's free, or you can even email them).

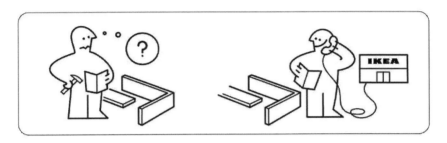

READ THE INSTRUCTIONS (NO SERIOUSLY, I REALLY MEAN IT)

It's understandable to dread assembling stuff if you're not familiar with the system, so get familiar by reading the instructions. Not reading instructions properly is the number one reason folks make mistakes. It's like there's a mental *troll* sitting in the brain saying, 'proper handy people don't need instructions' (it's a bit like not asking for directions when you're lost). But the truth is, you're wrong! Some professionals fit so many different things that reading instructions becomes a must and a perfect excuse for a coffee break.

So please, I implore you, grab yourself a coffee and *READ THE INSTRUCTIONS* from end to end before you start and then keep referring to them page by page during the build. I know, I know; it goes against all popular reasoning for a person to read the instructions first, instead of waiting until you get stuck. Nevertheless, reading instructions is essential, if you want to master the flat pack game and avoid an 'out of sequence assembly' which is like having an 'out of body experience', i.e. something to avoid at all costs...

I acknowledge that instructions often appear like an afterthought and are pretty poor sometimes, especially if the manufacturer's first language is not your native tongue. However, please persevere, sometimes you'll need to start the job and do it page by page before the instructions make sense. Or, try reading them out loud, it really does help sometimes. Plus, figuring it out and filling in the gaps is half the fun.

Pay particular attention. if something has a choice of 'hands', i.e. something can be on the left or right etc. Always look at the image at the top of the page, sometimes you need to jump forward to a particular page to assemble the thing exactly how you want it.

An often-ignored part of the instructions is the packing list of parts at the front. Use this list of parts to teach yourself the names (or reference numbers) of all the parts and fixings used in the build (and what they look like), because it will save you time during the actual assembly. Most importantly, it stops you using the wrong fastener. Getting the wrong fastener will either break something (if it's too long) or trip you up during a later part of the assembly (if it's too short). Good instructions (like IKEA) will show you what fastener *not to use* as well as the actual one to use (with reference numbers).

DRY RUNS

If you're not sure how something fits together or you don't quite understand the instructions, try what's called a dry run. Fit the parts together without glue or fasteners. Sometimes just holding the parts up allows the brain to figure it out in a way that it just can't see on paper. This really helps you to visualise what you're building and will help prevent mistakes. Once you confirm the parts fit together properly with no problems, go ahead for real. Dry runs are especially helpful if the assembly includes glue or sealant for example. It's horrible when you apply glue or silicone to everything and then realise that you've forgotten something, or it doesn't quite fit and you end up with rapidly setting gloop all over the place. Messy.

FITTING AND INSTALLING AFTER ASSEMBLY

Some things need fitting or installing after assembly. Wardrobes, cupboards, kitchen units, bookcases, shelves, and drawers for example. All the above will only perform well if you fit them properly. Use what you learned in the *Developing Practical Skills* chapter to help you fit things straight, level, plumb and square. Crooked or badly fitted stuff introduces stresses and strains causing poor performance, (drawers stick, doors catch, lids don't fit properly etc), plus it shortens the operating lifespan, i.e. it wears out quicker.

DISCREPANCIES IN THE FITTING AREA

In an ideal world, everything would be flat, level, plumb, square, and true, unfortunately, stuff built by the lowest bidder on a tight price and even tighter schedule, rarely meet that ideal.

Before you start, find out if there are any discrepancies where you're working. Knowing which way a floor or wall runs *out of true*, may give you an advantage later in the job. Usually, the older the house, the more *aware you need to be* about discrepancies, but new houses are not immune to errors either, so always check first.

Straightedges (or a long piece of straight timber or string line), spirit levels and a big square are your best friends here. Poke them everywhere and take note of anything they highlight, look for gaps, dips, hollows, bulges, big or small 90° angles, out of level, out of plumb etc.

Measure discrepancies and ensure there is enough adjustment in what you're working with to cope with how *out of true* the location is. Running out of adjustment backs you into a corner and there might not be an easy solution, in other words, you're stuck.

Each job is as unique as its discrepancies and once you've identified them, you'll need to really think them through and ask, "will this affect what I'm doing?". Think about how to get over the discrepancy and get the job to still look good. Maybe it's best to start in a particular place, a low point, or a high point, left or right or even in the middle! Maybe you need to add material to correct an area before fitting your new stuff (think extra plaster in a hollow area on a wall or a little 'self-levelling compound' in a dip on the floor). Maybe there is a way to hide the problem or cover it up (think trims, cover strips, end cover panels etc.). Maybe you need to remove material to correct a problem, an outward bump or curve in a wall where you want to put a new kitchen worktop for example (think, remove a little plaster).

It's a juggling act to find the lesser evil sometimes and of course there is always compromise. Read more in *the Making New Stuff* chapter.

MANOEUVRING AFTER ASSEMBLY

Sometimes you have no choice but to assemble something in one area (space constraints usually) and then move the finished article into its final place for fitting. Bear in mind that rough handling may seriously weaken the structure of many self-assembly things because they are just not designed to cope with those kinds of stresses. Two invaluable tools are the sack truck, which makes moving things easy, even heavy things like washing machines. Simply slide the thin blade underneath, tip the item back until the weight is balanced and wheel it wherever you need to go. The other tool is a wheeled trolley. These are flat boards with castors at each corner and come in various sizes. Simply lift the item onto the trolley and wheel into place. Ideal for heavy things like pianos and other things that are too heavy or big for sack trucks.

I used a sack truck to install my cast iron wood burning stove. A whopping 208kgs (458lb), on my own! And it wasn't even hard work. Pump the tyres up to the max pressure allowed for heavy stuff like this though. The cool thing about sack trucks is that you don't always need to hold the truck handles, you can hold the item instead which makes manoeuvring much easier. The truck seems to just 'stick' to the item under its own weight (get one and have a play, you'll not regret it).

Survived your visit to IKEA? Enjoyed your meatballs? Time for some 'Oh but I hate maintenance' then...

MAINTAINING STUFF

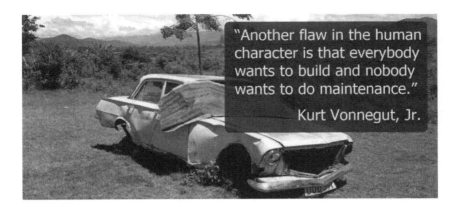

"Another flaw in the human character is that everybody wants to build and nobody wants to do maintenance."

Kurt Vonnegut, Jr.

I rather like the 'duffers' tool kit, which consists of a roll of tape and a can of WD40. The theory being; 'If something moves that shouldn't, you tape it up, and if something doesn't move, but should; you give it a squirt of WD40.' Although intended as a joke, when it comes to maintenance, it's actually pretty close to the truth. A little goes a long way in maintenance.

You might think routine maintenance is a bit boring, but routine maintenance (even if it's just to oil those squeaky hinges) will teach you lots of useful and practical things about stuff, including how to recognise when something's wrong.

Regular maintenance is important because it ensures your stuff functions as the manufacturer intended for the longest possible time. It's a fact that neglected stuff either wears out, breaks down, goes rotten or rusts away prematurely. You've already invested your hard-earned money, so spend a little time to keep it looking good and working well, thus protecting your investment as well as giving you years more use.

In addition, there's extra hassle if you don't maintain your stuff, because *Murphy's law* dictates it'll fail at some very inconvenient point; for example, your long-neglected lawnmower is more likely to cut out half way through cutting the lawn just before your big party than at any other time...

AN EXPENSIVE EXAMPLE

As a contractor, I once billed a client close to £5000 ($6200) to repair a leaky gutter. But wait, before you write me off as a 'rip off' builder, let me explain. The leaky gutter in question had been leaking for many decades with the guy who fitted it long gone. In fact, the gutter wasn't actually leaking, but rather so poorly positioned the water simply ran down the wall instead. Fast forward to today and this fine old English farmhouse now had a big problem, well three actually...

- Spalled brickwork because the frost had frozen the saturated bricks and crumbled away their surface.

- A rotten timber window frame because the water had run onto and eventually inside the vulnerable timber.

- Several floor joist ends rotted away because they were sitting in a constantly damp wall (old solid walled cottage remember).

All were time consuming and messy jobs, especially replacing the ends of timber joists built into the wall, since part of the floor and ceilings needed removing for access. Oh, and don't forget the re-positioning of the original offending guttering as well...

I hope you see that ignoring the maintenance on a house can get expensive and you're going to have even bigger problems if you ignore the maintenance on anything with moving parts. Especially machines with parts operating at high speed that need lubrication (engines, gearboxes etc). When these things fail, they can be *catastrophic non-repairable failures*, i.e. terminal, dead, 'time to go shopping for a new one' kind of failure. Sounds expensive to me.

WHAT NEEDS MAINTAINING?

It doesn't matter whether you're maintaining a vehicle (bike, scooter, motorbike, car, van, boat etc) or a wardrobe; the basic principle is the same. You carry out maintenance to *preserve conditions* and *counter wear and tear*.

Everything needs some sort of maintenance, from the window frames in your house to the chain on your bicycle. And as different as those two items are, so is the maintenance they need. One needs an occasional wash and wipe over with a cloth to remove contaminants, and the other, a thorough degreasing and a squirt or three of oil every now and then. I hope you can tell which goes with which...

The biggest enemy of your stuff is neglect, because neglect eventually turns into failure. Then simple maintenance no longer works and you're looking at repairs. Take your door locks for example, set aside some time once a year to maintain your locks. Wipe away any dirt or old lubricant (if applicable) and add a little of the right lubricant into the keyway. It's that easy. This simple and not terribly time-consuming effort could make your locks last a lifetime. Most folks don't do it and then wonder why their locks are stiff.

The trick to learning how to maintain something is to have a very basic understanding of how the components look and work. Don't worry, you don't need to know the science, just think about...

- Is this supposed to move, (yes/no or is it stiff/free)?

- How does it feel (the same or different)?

- What vulnerable parts do I need to protect from corrosion or wear?

- Is that supposed to happen (catch/rub/wear etc.)?

- What needs replacing regularly (parts, paint, etc.)?

THE FIVE ABSOLUTE BASICS OF MAINTENANCE

Let's use the above thoughts to create a basic regime to keep your stuff looking good and working well. Use one or more of the following five basic preventative maintenance tasks, depending on what you're maintaining...

- Keep stuff clean (dirt, grit, dust, and tired lube are bad).

- Lubricate vulnerable moving parts (lubricate and be free!)

- Make timely adjustments to stuff starting to wear (a few little tweaks go a long way to stave off failure).

- Replace service parts (service parts are designed to wear out over time to protect delicate or more expensive parts).

- Maintain finish integrity (rust, rot & oxidisation are bad).

Ignoring any of the above leads to little problems, which over time turn into bigger problems and eventually, complete failures or breakdowns. For example, if you fail to fix that leaky gutter, there's probably no immediate disastrous problem, but in a few years, you WILL have additional damage as well, maybe a rotten window or the saturated brickwork freezes and spalls or rots your floor joists. Keep on top of small maintenance jobs because they are easy and cost little; the longer the interval between maintenance checks the larger the final bill for repairs. Let's go over these five basic maintenance tasks...

CLEANING

I know, I know; you might think cleaning is repetitive and dull, but it is rewarding once you start. Cleaning away all that accumulated muck and revealing the gleaming surface underneath (especially on something you've rescued from the scrap heap) feels fantastic! You might even make it look brand new again. Not to mention the nice comments you'll get when people see it and comment 'Wow! That looks great!'

Keeping stuff clean isn't just about making stuff look pretty though (although it does), but more importantly, cleaning removes the grit and other contaminants held in the build-up of muck (lubricants especially attract and hold dust and grit). This gives your stuff a real reliability and longevity boost because tiny abrasive particles like grit increase friction, impede performance and cause components, surfaces and finishes to wear out prematurely. It's especially important to clean stuff before applying any new lubricants, otherwise you might push the aforementioned congealed contaminants and abrasives further into the working parts (not good).

Washing the car on Sunday for example, is not just to make it shiny; it serves a real practical purpose too. Because cleaning means getting up close and intimate with your stuff, you'll spot anything unusual or amiss very early on. You might notice a small, hardly visible malfunction; wear marks on a component or some tiny damage to a finish. For example, after washing your car (and before polishing it, and yes you need to do this, in the spring and just before winter), you'll be able to fill any stone chips you found in the paintwork whilst washing it (see how in the *Metal Maintenance* section later).

Cleaning is also the first thing to do with 'new to you' used things coming into your home to help determine their true condition and to evaluate what repairs or improvements need doing. At the very least, cleaning properly ensures it's fit to join your household by 'making it yours' and not harbouring any nasties, I mean, who wants other people's 'dirt' in their home?

Don't underestimate the 'feel good' factor of cleaning either. For example, I like old cars and I think there's truth in the maxim "the older it is, the cleaner you keep it". Remember how your home feels just before your mother in law comes to visit? (and don't you wish it could look like that all the time?!). Plus, you'll be less likely to throw things away, just because they're embarrassingly scruffy, (a win for the planet).

REGULAR CLEANING IS EFFECTIVE (AND EASIER)

Regular gentle cleaning of new things prevents excessive build-up of dirt and contaminants, so you never need to resort to more aggressive cleaning methods, which are hard work, take longer, and cost more.

But if you have old stuff that's been a little neglected you might need the big guns like powerful chemicals. The up side is, you'll get mind bogglingly satisfying results from such deep cleaning because dirt and grime builds up unnoticeably slowly over time. A deep clean might just reveal to the once hidden beauty of the item in question. I've lost count of the times I see folks cleaning something up with the intention to sell it on, only to fall in love with it all over again. My mother used to complain bitterly that their cars were never so clean and shiny as the week before my father planned to sell them...

Build your cleaning into a routine (remember I polish my car each spring and just before winter?). Nominate a time of week, month, or year etc., depending on what you're cleaning and stick to it.

After just one years use, this jigsaw needs cleaning to remove potentially damaging sawdust.

Pay particular attention to anything you own with vents or fans etc. because dust and shavings naturally get pulled into them, causing clogging and eventual overheating. Once a year I clean all mine with a quick blast of compressed air or even a tickle with a paintbrush and the vacuum cleaner. Aim through any vent slots or other openings, especially around any motors. Use the tyre airline at the garage or buy a can of compressed air from an electronics shop if you don't have access to a small compressor.

Remember that WD40 makes a mini high-pressure cleaner too. Use the thin tube to blast out old lube, grit etc on a bicycle part for example, wipe off and then re-lubricate with the recommended light machine oil.

Even if you are good and have planned routine cleaning, the following cleaning jobs need doing *on the spot* or as soon as you notice them...

- Wipe clean dirty outer casings, exteriors, and surfaces after use to prevent dirt becoming ingrained.

- Blow clear clogged ventilation grills and other cooling vents to keep them clean and clear (prevents overheating).

- Clean away any grit to prevent premature wear of mechanical components or surface damage.

- Clean anything that gets greasy before it gets the chance to attract grit and other contaminants.

- Wash fabrics often. Dust and grot wears out fabrics prematurely, sweat is particularly corrosive (yuck!).

USING CHEMICALS

Hard work used to be the preferred method of cleaning, but today, there are many different chemicals to do much of the scrubbing for you. Bearing in mind the desired end result you want, study the *applications,* or *uses* on the packaging of the product to ensure it's suitable for your project (you can really damage stuff if you get this wrong). You can always double check with store staff if you need something, especially symbols, explained in more detail. The store might also have additional technical sheets, especially related to using the product safely (many strong cleaning chemicals will burn skin and eyes).

Although the blurb on some packets might claim the product is a simple spray on and rinse off process, this is rarely the case and a good soak does wonders with nearly every cleaner, reducing 'elbow grease' dramatically. Spraying on a cleaner and then immediately attacking it with a brush wastes effort and chemical. Agitate the chemical well into the gunk with a brush for best penetration, repeating several times for even better results. Don't forget, old toothbrushes are great for cleaning small or intricate stuff.

The exceptions to the above are the more powerful or acid-based cleaners, which *are* time sensitive. Reading the manufacturer's instructions is very important or they may remove more than you bargained for. *Always* protect your eyes and any exposed skin when using powerful acid cleaners.

LUBRICANTS

We can't talk about maintenance without talking about lubrication, the mainstay of keeping things going. But lubricants do much more than you think, let's go through some of the benefits...

- Friction and wear: If moving parts were to touch each other, friction would quickly wear them out. Lubricants keep moving components separate (even if it's microscopically) and prevent wear to individual parts by reducing or eliminating friction.

  Be aware that some components have self-lubricating parts (due to special materials), and yet others are sealed for life, so check the manufacturer's information first.

- Cooling: Friction also builds heat as you know, and lubricants soak up this heat carrying it away from vulnerable components. The oil in an engine is a great example, it's not there just to lubricate, it acts as a coolant too.

- Cleaning: lubricant attracts debris such as particles from the surroundings and microscopic particles created by wear This debris degrades the lubricants quality and is why lubricants need replacing from time to time. Engine oil turns from a golden honey colour to black goop for example.

  Before replacing lubricant, first, you'll need to remove any existing lubrication (i.e. drain old engine oil or use a degreaser to remove old lube). Also, any lubricant filters (think engine oil filter), need replacing, thus removing any contaminants they contain.

- Corrosion: lubricants are great at preventing corrosion by excluding air and water from the oxidising reaction.

- Sealing: lubricants help seal against air and water finding their way into places where they'd cause damage. Smearing petroleum jelly (Vaseline) onto a hosepipe O ring for example, not only helps facilitate repeated coupling and uncoupling, it will protect the seal making leaks less troublesome. Lubrication also helps seal gas or air tight fittings.

- Power: lubricants are incompressible, making them ideal to transfer power via hydraulic action. Telescopic rams on construction equipment or the fluid inside a vehicles automatic gear box etc.

In practise, lubricants can do other things too... You can free stuck or seized things with several soakings of a penetrating lubricant like WD40, which is an oil-based lubricant and water dispersal agent (although any penetrating type, thin oil should do the trick). Don't forget to give them plenty of time though. Some people even soak stuff like chains, cycle parts, padlocks, vehicle parts etc. in a lubricant (like diesel/paraffin/kerosene/etc.) overnight to free everything up (wear gloves and ventilate though), before wiping off and adding a suitable lubricant.

COMMON LUBRICANTS

Visually check any lubrication points or moving parts to identify what type of lubricant is already there (consult the original maintenance documents if possible or search online). Choose the same or similar specification (grade) lubricant for best results. Generally, slower moving things need thick lubricant like grease and faster moving things need thinner and high-performance lubricants (for their stickiness and stability under extreme conditions).

Be vigilant for any signs of stiffness, creaking or squeaking from any moving component, a sure sign the lubrication has dried out completely. Any seized component, (e.g. moving parts that don't) needs attention immediately or you risk other components breaking because of the extra stress the non-moving part adds. Here are a few of the most common lubricants...

WD40

WD-40 is the *40th* attempt to make a *Water Displacement* chemical and is very useful for lots of jobs. WD-40 has five basic properties:

- **Cleans**. WD-40 helps to dissolve dirt, grime, and grease. It also dissolves adhesives, allowing removal of labels etc.
- **Displaces moisture**. Use WD40 to get rid of damp in electrical systems to eliminate moisture-related short circuits.
- **Penetrates**. WD-40 loosens rust-to-metal bonds and frees stuck, frozen, or rusted metal parts.
- **Lubricates**. WD-40 is a light lubricant suitable for moving parts.
- **Protects**. WD-40 protects metal surfaces against rust with its corrosion-resistant ingredients

LIGHT MACHINE OIL

Light machine oil is a thin, almost transparent oil, that has many uses around the home and garden, lubricating tools, hinges, nuts & bolts, firearms, bicycles, wheels, fans and sewing machines (remember the saying "running like a sewing machine"? Light machine oil is responsible. It's highly refined and very thin, it gets into tiny spaces ensuring free movement. It's so thin you'll need a rag when using it; apply a drop or two, work the mechanism and then wipe away any excess dripping down. Repeat as necessary. 3-in-one is one of the most famous brands.

ENGINE OIL

Engine oil is a heavier, often golden coloured lubricant available in many grades to suit different operating conditions. Although primarily for inside engines, engine oil makes a good all-round lubricant for many moving parts and is handy to have in the workshop in a little pump action oil can. Available in two broad types, organic or mineral and the more modern synthetic oils. Oil is measured by its viscosity when cold (w means winter) and when hot, hence the two numbers on the packaging e.g. 20w50. The 20 in this case wouldn't be very good for a cold engine in a cold climate, it's too thick and could impede starting and cold running. 5w40 would be better. The second number is the viscosity of the oil in a hot engine and needs to be higher to allow for the thinning that oil undergoes when heated.

However, used engine oil is a dangerous chemical cocktail and needs recycling safely, although some old timers swear by it painted onto rough metal stuff to stop corrosion. That may be useful if you own a tractor which lives in a field, but don't try it underneath a sports car which lives on your drive...

COPPER GREASE

Copper grease is a thick, very sticky, shiny copper coloured (unsurprisingly!) lubricant. Apply it to bolt threads when reassembling components as it prevents future corrosion and seizing (making future maintenance easier). Sometimes known as *anti-seize compound*. Also commonly used sparingly on the back and edges of vehicle brake pad back plates to reduce squealing. Copper grease copes well with high temperatures and sticks well to moving parts.

GREASE (LITHIUM USUALLY)

Grease is a thick (often yellow looking) lubricant to protect against wear of moving parts on machines. Often called high melting point grease.

Grease is made from oil mixed with special soap, which makes it very sticky. It's ideal for fast moving components like bearings, but also for slow moving components like, levers on machines, rotating parts, slides, and contact points like door latches etc. Apply grease directly to the parts, operate a few times to work it right in and wipe away any excess.

Grease Nipple (UK) or Zerk Fitting (USA)

Pump new grease into bearings via the spring loaded ball bearing at the tip

In addition, you might see grease nipples on some machines. Grease nipples (Zerk or Alemite fitting in the USA) allow you to easily push new grease directly into a bearing etc., using a special, (but cheap to buy), grease gun. Simply wipe the nipple and the nozzle on the gun clean, push the nozzle onto the grease nipple and pump (check the machines instructions for how many strokes) or until it oozes out of the bearing or vent hole.

DRY LUBRICANTS

Lots of smaller moving parts still need lubrication, but would be susceptible to gumming up over time, due to the accumulation of dust and debris sticking to wet lubricants. Things like lock cylinders for example. Your key needs to go in and out of a lock without getting all greasy every time. Enter dry lubricants. Old school (and still pretty good) is graphite (yup, the same stuff they make pencils out of) which is super slippery and ideal for inside dry mechanicals. Don't add graphite to anything previously greased though or you'll make a nasty black paste (thoroughly clean it with a degreaser or solvent and let it dry before switching to a dry lubricant).

Modern dry lubricants are a little more complicated than pencils though. Look out for the word MOLY (short for Molybdenum disulfide). PTFE (short for polytetrafluorethylene) or for brand names like Teflon, a slippery material you'll already know about from non-stick pans.

There is one last dry lubricant (for humans!) that you might have forgotten about, a surprising one maybe, and that's talcum powder. As anyone who has ever danced on a floor dusted with the stuff or sprinkled it inside rubber trousers will attest. Oops, giving too much away there...

SPECIALIST LUBRICANT

You'll find all sorts of special lubricants in this bunch, maybe even one or two that you'd not thought of as lubricants...

- **Silicone based** lube for rubber seals, O rings, washers etc.

- High temperature lubricant for hot environments (it doesn't thin or run in high heat applications).

- **Cold temperature** lubricants for cold environments (it doesn't thicken and go stiff in conditions of extreme cold).

- **Long life** lubricant for difficult to access components or where you need a long service life.

- **Food grade** lubricants; designated safe to use on food processing machinery.

- **Edible oils**. Stops food sticking to surfaces during the cooking process itself, (think cooking oils etc.) as well as actually a foodstuff in itself (think olive oil etc.).

- **Skin safe** lubricants which don't harm sensitive skin or other areas; think lip balms, hand creams, sunscreen and other erm, let's just say... more intimate, personal lubricants, (I say, steady on!).

DEGREASER

I'll add a note here about degreasers as you'll need to use one before reapplying a lubricant. We use degreasers all the time in the home from washing the dishes to cleaning dead flies off car bumpers. These light detergent-based degreasers are fine for general cleaning of lightly soiled surfaces or parts; but there are more industrial degreasers out there, designed to shift even the most stubborn grease or old lubricant. Often solvent based for spraying onto greasy surfaces or in liquid form for dipping smaller parts into. Follow the instructions carefully as some are powerful enough to damage surrounding finishes.

Some of the solvents you have lying around (like petrol, alcohol, various spirits, lighter fluid etc.) are also brilliant for removing grease, but they are very flammable and dangerous, so you really shouldn't use them; but if you must, ensure you have good ventilation and be careful not to spill any. Be particularly careful how you dispose of any rags etc., as they too are now flammable. Oh, and if you do screw up and burn your garage down, remember I did tell you not to use them...

MAKING TIMELY ADJUSTMENTS

The song says, 'nothing stays the same' and this goes for most of the stuff in your life too. Little by little, friction wears away microscopic amounts of material. Eventually this causes stuff to require small adjustments to maintain a proper fit. Even if you properly maintain your stuff, moving parts will still wear down and although lubrication slows the process down considerably, eventually some adjustments are necessary to maintain ideal operation.

Usually you'll need to adjust something for one of two reasons; when something becomes either too loose or too tight. Sometimes this happens together; a loose cabinet hinge for example might make the door rub its neighbour. Unintentional physical contact nearly always causes excessive wear and tear on at least one of the parts affected.

Periodically, or better still, 'as-you-notice', examine moving parts closely and try to determine which parts should move freely, (like the cabinet hinge pin for example) and what should be tight (like the screws holding the hinge for example). Again, it only takes a few seconds to look at the hinge, turn the screw to pull the door back into line and it's fixed (experiment with the screw, you'll soon see which way it goes to move the door).

LOOSE STUFF

Anything that's loose causes wear in two ways. First, slack parts cause impact damage within themselves as they move around. A loose fastener for example moves around into opposite ends of its hole under load, causing the hole to become elongated. Over time, this movement compounds, further elongating or damaging the hole until one day the whole thing will tear out of the now much enlarged hole. For example, the screws holding up the handrail on your stairs will last indefinitely when they're tight. However, when loose they allow the handrail to move around, eventually tearing those screws right out of the wall. This damages and enlarges the holes making it impossible to re-tighten the screws. Second, loose fasteners or worn parts increase the range of movement of each part, often allowing parts to collide with other parts. Loose screws in a door hinge allows the door to hit the frame or worse the other door, bad news if it's a pair of glass doors on a bathroom cabinet or shower cubicle for example.

Checking bolts and other fixings for tightness periodically, stops vibration shaking something completely loose (petrol lawnmowers are famous for this). In essence, it's back to the RELEARN method, i.e. look, feel, and listen for loose stuff as you go. Be aware enough to notice excess movement in your everyday stuff and either make a note of it for when you have more time or better still, adjust or tighten it on the spot, (get someone to buy you a Leatherman tool for Christmas...). It takes just a few seconds to adjust or tighten a loose screw or fitting etc. for example, so don't ignore them!

However, be careful not to over tighten stuff, especially if it's something which repeatedly comes loose. If something repeatedly becomes lose you need to find out why. Look for vibration, catching or rubbing that might be causing stress on the fasteners or look at the way you use the item (i.e. are you abusing it!) Alternatively, if it's a nut and bolt type fastener, try adding a *shake proof washer* or try swapping the nut for a *shake-proof* one, (remember those from the *Fixings and Fasteners* chapter?)

It's easier improve a fastener or to come back and give something an extra turn to nip it up than to fix a stripped thread. If you routinely over tighten fasteners and fixings, (making them difficult to undo), you're just building in difficulties to trip you up during future maintenance. Remember that torque wrench I keep bangin' on about? Yup, that one...

STUFF THAT'S TOO TIGHT

Anything that's tight or a poor fit vastly increases friction and that means you often need to use excessive force to operate the item. Repeatedly forcing something that's too tight can stress the whole construction, eventually leading to seizure or failure. Stuff that's catching or rubbing also wears out much faster.

Maintaining intended gaps between moving parts is vital for long life. If something is tight or catching, find out why by examining closely how it works. Look, listen and feel for catching parts, wear marks are often visible as rub marks in the finish. Try to determine if it needs lubrication, or if there is debris in the workings (e.g. dirt in tracks) or if fasteners or hardware have loosened or sagged, or even if there is extra material in the way, for example, doors and/or frames swollen from moisture etc.

For example, a door repeatedly pulled or even kicked to close or open it, will eventually become weak at its joints because of the stress caused by excessive twisting. This will eventually damage the frame too, removing paint or even loosening the frames fasteners. Fortunately, to tighten some screws, adjust a hinge, or plane a little off a door is not too difficult, just look at the gaps between the door and frame to find where it's tight and remove material where the paint shows wear marks until you have even gaps again. You want at least the thickness of a coin all the way around. Make sure the seals are not causing trouble as well (they often dislodge).

Fix tight stuff by either cleaning, lubricating, tweaking adjusters, tightening fasteners, or removing excess material to increase clearance and ensure proper operation. Make sure the problem is not a symptom of another underlying problem though. Going back to the door example, if an outside door starts catching for example, is it swelling because of water getting into it through damaged paint or a leaky gutter or poor drainage or excessive splash back from high ground levels or is it loose fasteners, a loose frame etc.

REPLACING SERVICE PARTS

Some things are simply not possible to maintain by just looking after them because they contain parts specifically designed to wear out. It might seem a nuisance, but most service items are there to protect the more expensive parts, thus actually saving you money. Therefore, ignoring or failing to replace service parts makes no financial sense at all. An oil filter and fresh oil for example costs peanuts when compared to repairing an engine damaged by an ineffective oil filter clogged with contaminated old oil.

All manufacturers publish instructions regarding maintenance and service intervals for consumable parts. Check your manuals or search online for specific service details for your stuff. Be aware also that not keeping to a manufacturer's maintenance schedule can invalidate any guarantee you might have in the first few years.

Of course, manufacturers will disagree, but you can extend the life of *some* service parts by dismantling and cleaning them. Especially on older, less valuable machines. For example, remove and blow air filters through with an airline to clean out dust and debris at least once on some machines (note I said 'some' here, please don't try this on your classic Ferrari!).

In general, neglecting the replacement of service parts will have an adverse effect on the efficiency and performance of a machine. For example, the aforementioned clogged up air filter, will have been causing excessive fuel consumption as the engine would struggle to maintain the correct air to fuel ratio needed for maximum efficiency and performance. Similarly, a clogged dust filter on your vacuum cleaner will make the motor work harder and run hot, shortening its life.

TYPICAL SERVICE ITEMS

- **Oil filters or screens**; replaceable paper or cartridge types or clean metal screen types).

- **Air filters or screens**; replaceable paper types or wash out the oiled foam types, add new oil and squeeze out the excess).

- **Fuel filters**; replace at specific timed intervals.

- **Lubricants**; remove and replace (oil, grease, gearbox oil, transmission fluid, differential gear oil, etc).

- **Bearings**; some minimally worn bearings might last a little longer if cleaned out and repacked with grease. Once noisy though, it's generally a remove and replace job.

- **Fluids**; drain and replace (brake fluid, coolants, hydraulic fluid, etc.). Air conditioning fluid/ gas needs specialist equipment to replenish as it's dangerous stuff, for you and the environment.

- **Brake systems**; brake pads, brake disks, cylinder seals, remove and replace when worn out.

- **Belts and other drive mechanisms**; usually replaced at specific intervals or when broken on non-critical stuff.

- **Seals**; O rings, gaskets etc. replace at specific intervals to prevent failures or leaks in use.

- **Drive**; clutches and other drive plates. Replace when friction material wears away and drive starts to slip and or motion is lost.

- **Bushes**; rubber or plastic isolation parts which cushion parts from one another under load. Replace when movement is excessive.

- **Electrical**; high voltage items need replacement at set intervals due to electrode wear. Includes brushes in motors, spark plugs in engines. Low voltage items such as batteries, replace when ineffective.

- **Tyres**; the tread or surface material wears away and once the built-in wear bars (solid bands or rubber which cross the tread) become visible, the tyre needs replacing.

MAINTAINING DIFFERENT MATERIALS

Let's look at some basic maintenance you can do on just a few of the materials you'll find around your home.

Some (but not all) materials have a surface finish or coating to prevent deeper damage from the elements or to protect it from contaminants. Other materials, like masonry for example, don't have a coating as such, but still need protecting by taking some simple preventative measures, mostly related to keeping them as dry as possible... Remember, water is a pain in the derriere, and not just to tennis and cricket players...

The surface of any material is under attack all the time from a wide variety of factors... here are some of the 'enemies'...

- **Water**; including moisture present in air (×2 because it's that bad).

- **Air**; e.g. oxygen and water mean rust on steel and iron.

- **Sun**; ultraviolet radiation causes UV degradation. Also causes thermal instability by expanding coatings and base materials (oh, and sunburn; ouch).

- **Heat**; accelerates many chemical reactions between elements.

- **Cold**; especially below freezing temps. Causes thermal instability by shrinking coatings and base materials.

- **Chemical**; salts, acid rain, oils or sweat from your skin.

- **Friction**; physical movement; accelerates wear and tear.

- **Careless use;** causes damage such as scratches, chips & dents.

Once unprotected, (even if only by a tiny bit) most things outside eventually rot, corrode, erode, degrade, or discolour, even so called 'no maintenance' plastic. To guard against this damage, always keep any finishes and coatings 100% intact to protect the underlying material. Plus, it's important to re-apply finishes before the original finish fails completely and starts flaking away or you'll have much more work to do.

All materials react differently to exposure to the elements...

- **Timber** will rot or attract bacteria or bugs which feed on it. Damp wood is a bug magnet (just ask any bug)! Dry wood lasts centuries.

- **Masonry** goes soft and crumbly or spalls.

- **Ferrous metal** containing iron rusts or oxidises extensively because iron oxide is not protective.

- **Non-ferrous metal** such as aluminium, copper, brass, lead, tin, zinc etc. don't rust, but can corrode, discolour, oxidise, or react to other metals. Some oxides are protective, e.g. the green coating on copper.

- **Metal alloys corrode**; e.g. brass, bronze, pewter or stainless steel also don't rust, but can, discolour, oxidise, or react to other metals. Some of these oxides can be protective.

- **Plastic discolours**, degrades, or goes brittle, sometimes this only affects the surface.

- **Rubber goes hard**, perishes and splits.

- **Fabrics can rot**, disintegrate, go stiff or tear easily. Think tents, covers, coats, etc.

Most of the above materials have some kind of protective finish that needs maintenance or topping up periodically. Let's take a look at the specific things you can do to a few different materials...

PROPER PREPARATION

I'll put this here, before we look at specific materials as the principles are similar whether you're maintaining a wall, woodwork, or a metal gutter. Preparation is critical, just slapping on new stuff simply won't protect the material, even if it looks good initially. Generally...

- Scrape away any old flaky layers of old paint.

- Clean paintwork with a 'house cleaner' detergent, with a mould killer element if there are green of black spores on the paintwork.

  A bucket of cleaner and another of clean water and a couple of sponges work well indoors. Wipe over with one sponge and detergent and 'rinse' with the other sponge and clean water. Outdoors, careful use of a pressure washer to pump cleaner onto the paintwork works well (don't go too close). Scrub with a small brush on a long handle and afterwards rinse everything away being careful with the angle you use (avoid getting water behind anything), mimic how the rain would hit the surface to be safe. Allow plenty of time for everything to dry.

- Sand down the surface, removing any 'shine' to provide a rock-solid base (called 'key') for new coatings.

- Use a suitable primer on any bare areas, maybe even two coats. Lightly sand with a fine sandpaper to flatten again.

- The final sanding grade should be 120/180 grit (or finer) otherwise the scratch marks may show through the final finish.

- Apply the finish coats flowing the manufacturer's instructions (usually two for best durability).

- Lightly sand in between coats with fine sandpaper and work in a super clean environment for time consuming, but glass smooth results.

Cleaning, scraping and sanding before painting prevents your hard work looking like this after a relatively short time.

If you can't identify the existing finish, you should ask your paint supplier for advice because some finishes are not compatible with each other. Try to take in a sample if possible, remove a small opening window frame or a small drawer front for example.

The world of paint is getting complicated. Gone are the old days of water-based paint for the wall and oil for woodwork. There is a water-based paint for all situations nowadays. Oil is still the most durable in my opinion, but the long drying times and high odour is a problem many folks won't tolerate any more. I haven't used oil-based paints in a client's house for years. Oil is still popular for external works though. Be careful to follow the manufacturers recommendations, especially for thinning as many don't allow it, chemically.

Be aware that there are a few timber species that are naturally rot resistant like cedar, chestnut, white oak, douglas fir, larch, redwood, or cypress and you'll see these used without further protection.

A note about any sealants you find between differing neighbouring materials. Flexible sealants are critical to stop water penetrating gaps because the material behind any sealant you find is often poorly protected against damp. Door and window frames for example may only have a coat of primer on the parts of the frame you can't see. Water that gets past these sealants and into the nooks & crannies around the frame/timber can hang around, eventually causing decay. Check each year to make sure your sealant hasn't dried out leaving gaps. Silicone sealant is a popular (but poor) choice here, but paintable 'mastic,' or other non-setting type is preferable. You *cannot* paint silicone, which makes future decorating difficult.

Now you're a prep expert, you'll need the *Renewing Paint and Other Finishes* which you'll find in the *Improving Stuff* chapter since you might be painting a new thing, not necessarily maintaining an old one...

TIMBER MAINTENANCE

Internal conditions are usually too dry for timber used internally on door, skirting boards, architraves, and trims etc to decay. Maintenance is limited to redecorating when the originals become dirty or out of date. However, it's worth checking regularly any timber in bathrooms or close to external doors, washbasins, showers, washing machines and dishwashers etc for early signs that any surrounding trims are getting damp because of a problem with the finish or indeed from leaks from any of the above appliances etc.

Some internal timber finishes require specific cleaning and polishing with dedicated chemicals, French polishing on fine furniture for example.

Most other timber comes bare and unprotected, with the exception of timber designed to live outside permanently like fencing or decking products (which are pressure impregnated with a green or brown preservative). Most of the timber inside your house stays in this bare state and needs no further protection (unless you suspect a pest problem like woodworm). Examples would be; floor joists, stud walls, roof timbers and floorboards. When you see bare timber in your home (in the attic for example), it's worth looking out for signs of new insect activity, especially in the spring and summer. Look out for small holes and 'frass' (it looks a bit like sawdust). Also, look for any white stains, which could indicate a water leak, especially around any valley (sloping upwards between two different parts of the roof), gully (flat junctions between two roof sections), chimneys or other abutments. Be especially vigilant looking for evidence of insects if you find any damp timber in your home. Most wood boring insects don't like dry conditions, but they go absolutely gaga for slightly damp timber... it's heaven to them.

Protect all exposed timber outside, such as window frames, door frames and timber trims with several coats of paint or other timber preservative such as varnish, timber stain, wax, oil, or other chemical preservative. You should expect to re-apply most types of finishes at set intervals to maintain protection against decay. Re-application intervals range from a few years in locations exposed to wind and rain or near the coast, to a decade or more in sheltered locations.

Check in the springtime once the weather warms up, look for...

- **Flaking, lifting, or peeling**; caused by several things, poor preparation prior to painting, or just weather and time.

- **Crazing and cracking**, (paint surface looks like alligator or crocodile skin). Could be because of poor preparation prior to painting, mismatched paint types, or an adverse reaction to older paint (i.e. hard oil paint over softer water-based paints), or just too many layers of paint because of extreme old age.

- **Blistering or bubbles**; could be poor preparation again (are you starting to see a pattern with this? Hint, the majority of paint problems are caused by poor preparation... just sayin'), but also trapped moisture or solvent in between coats or even because the paint was applied in the sunshine and the outer layer dried too quick.

- **Chalking**; where aging paint, usually in exposed spots dries to a dusty surface over time.

- **Mildew or mould**; usually in damp areas that don't get a lot of sunshine. Needs cleaning with a cleaner formulated to combat the spores. Spray on with a pump-up garden sprayer and leave to soak and usually rinse off with water. But read the instructions first!

MASONRY MAINTENANCE

Masonry is durable stuff... if it's able to dry out easily after getting wet or frozen. Long periods spent wet and/or frozen will quickly cause damage. The absolute best way to protect all types of masonry is to keep it as dry as possible;

it's as simple as that. Sounds unlikely I know, it's a wall; *but*, preventing *any* wall getting excessively wet will prolong its life considerably.

Minimise unnecessary water from soaking into your masonry by making sure everything is doing its job and there is only one way to do this, yup, you've got to watch it, live, in action... when it's pouring down with rain, the harder the better. No good waiting until it stops, all the interesting stuff is over by then. Next time it pours down with rain, 'suit up', don your sou'wester or grab an umbrella and go and take a slow walk around your property (ignore the strange looks from the neighbours!) and watch to see where all that water is going, you'll learn lots, or nothing. Both is good; well, one isn't really, as it does mean you have a problem, but looking at it on the bright side, at least you now know what the problem is...

Start at the top and ensure the roof is doing its job and *all* the water is running off the roof and into the guttering properly and that the gutter isn't overflowing. Check it doesn't dribble back from the roof edge, missing the gutter completely and run down the wall.

Check the amount of 'splash back' (water that bounces up onto the wall from hard paved surfaces). Ideally the ground level is (at least) 150mm (6″) down from your Damp Proof Course (DPC). Make sure any paving at the base of walls drains away from the wall too and doesn't puddle next to the wall. It's a great idea to have a 300mm (12″) loose gravel 'buffer' between any hard paving and the wall (or a small soil border with ground cover type plants) as this also stops rainwater bouncing up the wall. It still needs to be at least 150mm (6″) down from your DPC though.

You'll find the DPC around the base of your house, usually underneath the bottom of the door frames. On older homes this may consist of (one to three) courses of especially hard bricks like blue bricks or red engineering bricks, with or without a thin layer of lead sheet on top. On more modern homes, it's an impermeable layer of bituminous felt or plastic etc. You might be able to see the plastic or felt damp proof course as a thin black line in the horizontal mortar joint at the same level as the bottom of the doorframes. If not, it's probably just behind the surface of the mortar joint.

Any freestanding garden walls need effective cappings (on top) incorporating a means of stopping the water from running down onto the face of the wall. This is usually a groove cut or cast into the underside of concrete copings (called a drip) or nibs on projecting tiles bedded underneath hard bricks etc. The drip allows water to fall away from the face of the wall. Try watching the water running off the capping of the wall when it's raining hard. Ideally, the top part of a wall should have a damp-proof course underneath the capping material as well, but many tradesmen fear that vandals will easily disturb the capping, so it's unusual to find one.

A word about sealing your masonry to keep water out. Hmm, some folks love it and others will tell you it'll sound the death knell for your poor wall. Personally, I think it will end badly if the wall has underlying damp issues. If water is getting into the wall, it must find a way out and if you seal the surface.... yup, it's going to cause damage somewhere as the moisture fights to find a way out.

However, if you've a wall that's rained on whatever you do, or a chimney getting a beating every time it rains, then by all means go for a breathable silicone treatment, with one caveat. Do it at the end of the summer after a long, long period of dry weather to ensure the brickwork is bone dry to start with. To stop water getting into the wall, consider covering it up for a while (with an air gap to allow evaporation) before treating it. Always follow the instructions as products vary and find one that's breathable for best results.

In addition to protecting your masonry from water, you'll need to check it annually for movement damage. Large cracks can be serious if caused by *subsidence* which is movement associated with damage from nearby large trees or leaking drains. Minor *settlement* cracking is less serious if caused by the 'normal' settling in of a house over time. There are several situations which can lead to movement and subsequent cracking. Look out for...

- **Zig zag cracks**. These follow the joints, running across your walls, usually low down. Either 'live' or active and moving; or old and stable. Monitor to determine by using 'tell tales' fixed across the cracks (google it!). Log your readings over time.

- **Shear cracks**. Straight cracks running up through the bricks and joints; they are always serious. Might indicate a design fault or movement needing attention. Imagine the stress it takes to break fully bedded bricks in mortar. Not good...

- **Large trees**. Close to walls: These suck up lots of water drying out the ground, shrinking it. The amount of water varies with the seasons causing the soil to shrink and swell, pushing against the masonry. Roots also eventually grow big enough to push against walls and into gaps or cracks where they act like a jack.

- **Tree stumps**. Close to walls. Large trees take up a lot of water, if removed, the water that once went into the tree causes the soil to swell and 'heave' up, pushing against the masonry.

I know, the two scenarios, above right? Catch 22 huh! Deciding whether to leave a tree or take it out depends on any evident damage caused, go with the lesser evil.

- **Leaking drains**. Could be leaking for years before anyone notices. A leak washes soil into the drain and away, undermining nearby hardstanding or walls. Look for sunken areas of garden or paving or leaning or sagging walls.

- **Rainwater systems**. Leaking rainwater systems saturate and destabilise the soil around the base of walls. Make sure your rainwater is going where it's supposed to.

- **Distortion.** Look out for difficulty in opening window or doors. This might indicate wall movement (or just old/ poor joinery).

- **Efflorescence**. Look for white deposits on the wall, often just above ground level and up to about 1m (3') high. These are soluble salts left behind when water evaporates from a damp wall. Brush them off and carry out further investigation to rectify the cause of the damp.

Some masonry outdoors ends up covered in render (sometimes called stucco). Render is plastering outside basically. This maybe by design from the outset or applied as an attempt to tidy up (read cover-up) a wall in poor condition (with spalled bricks etc.). Covering poor walls with render rarely works because the source of damp damaging the bricks in the first place, if not rectified, will carry on, eventually blowing the render off the wall as well.

Check render annually...

- **Salt**. As with bare masonry, look for wavy lines of white salty marks or deposits on the first metre (3') from the ground. Often means water is in the wall and evaporating out through the render, leaving the soluble salts behind.

- **Hollow areas**. Gently tap with a piece of wood and listen for hollow areas where the render has separated slightly from the wall. Hollow sounding areas are a sign water is behind the render and freezing/ expanding.

- **Bulges and bumps**. Look for actual bulges and bumps which are another sign water is behind the render and freezing (thus swelling and causing the bumps).

- **Edges**. Look at the edges, corners, bottom etc. where there might be metal trims going rusty and blowing off the render.

- **DPC**. Look around the bottom edge if it's near the ground, does it cover the damp proof course? Render should NEVER cross the damp proof course as it would allow damp to run straight up the wall.

- **Cracking**. Look for hairline cracks or spalled areas which will be letting in penetrating water, making the wall wet inside. Fill any cracks with outdoor flexible filler and re-paint.

- **Spalling**. Look for crumbly, or missing areas which are letting in penetrating water, making the wall wet inside. Chop away damage and re-render, (see *Render Repairs* in the *Repairing Stuff* chapter).

- **Paint**. Check any paint coverings for integrity and durability.

- **Coverings**. Check any texturing for integrity (Tyrolean, roughcast or pebbledash etc.) Poor quality stuff literally falls off when lightly touched with a paint scraper etc. Replace coating as necessary.

One last comment regarding walls, as attractive as it can look on certain properties, it's probably best to avoid growing creeping plants up your walls. Although creepers are unlikely to damage the brickwork itself, they can certainly damage doors, windows, guttering and your roof. If you insist on creepers, make sure you cut them back annually at least 300mm (12″) from all the above-mentioned areas, especially at the roofline. You could also consider growing them up a trellis instead of directly on the wall.

Oh, and p.s. *genuine* rising damp is less common than you think. Help old walls by restoring them to their original breathable condition (i.e. no cement!) and managing the water at the top and the bottom of the wall and you might just find you don't have a rising damp problem after all...

PLASTER MAINTENANCE

Maintain internal plaster by wiping it free of marks as they happen and re-painting every few years after washing down and filling any dents or scrapes etc. with a decorator's filler and a quick sand flat. High traffic areas like hallways and entrances might need decorating every 3 years and low traffic areas like spare bedrooms every 10 or even 15 years.

ROOF MAINTENANCE

Roofs are generally maintenance free, anything you need to do to a roof is really a repair, so we'll come to that later. That said you should check the roof regularly and clear away anything you find growing on the roof such as moss, weeds, or even small trees (believe me, especially in valleys, chimney back gutters, central gutters etc.).

On a nice day, grab or borrow a pair of binoculars and head out to a spot where you can see most of the roof. If you have access to a ladder and understand you should have someone stood on the bottom of it and somewhere to tie off the top to, then by all means go up to gutter level and take a closer look. Either way, check for the following...

- Missing ridge tiles (the ones right on the top or apex).
- Missing, cracked, askew or loose tiles.
- Missing mortar or tiles at the edges of the roof.
- Missing or disturbed flashings around chimneys, windows, skylights, pipes, or anything else penetrating the roof.
- Missing or disturbed flashings at abutments, parapet walls or adjacent properties etc.
- Cracked or damaged valleys or central gutters or troughs.

Any damage you see or find needs immediate repair, even if you don't yet see any sign inside of water getting inside the house. Roofs are amazing in their capacity to soak up water in the timbers, insulation etc. before it leaks into the room below. The longer you leave it, the more repairs you'll have to do. It's much better to replace a slipped tile or two than to replace rotten rafter feet and the wall plate, I do both regularly and I know which I prefer...

PIPE MAINTENANCE

You'll need to isolate and/or insulate any water pipes exposed to the cold in the winter time (think, outside taps in the garden).

Don't forget the 'other' pipes going out of the house, usually underground. Predictably these pipes carry all sorts of horrible stuff. Sticky stuff, greasy stuff, and stuff they shouldn't be carrying at all, (think plastic, shaving gear, non-biodegradable stuff and even dead pets etc. Oh, and latex stuff, you know what I mean? Yup, don't put those in the toilet either).

Two totally *unbreakable* golden rules. Only stuff you have eaten plus toilet paper in the toilet and never put oils or grease in the sink.

In sinks, oil and grease solidify when they hit the cold pipe further down and will build up over time. Wipe greasy pans with kitchen paper and store used cooking oils responsibly, i.e. in an old 5L plastic container and periodically recycle it (google 'fatbergs' to really freak yourself out).

Toilets block easily when stuff snags up at joints, bends, or poorly constructed parts of the system etc. Even something small will attract other stuff like tissue paper building up and up until the pipe blocks completely and water backs up the pipe.

The blocking process can happen over several days as pipes in the ground have a considerable capacity. Once a toilet starts to fill up, it's time to grab a special toilet plunger. Place the plunger in the bowl and pump up and down, this pushes the water and air in the trap back and forth and may dislodge a small obstruction... maybe, but probably not.

More likely you'll need to head out into the yard and check your access points (inspection chambers or IC in the UK, formerly manholes). If the first one is full of, erm, water (hint, it won't just be water...) head down to the next access point and so on. Repeat until you are at an access point which is empty. If they are all full between you and the main sewer in the street, then the blockage is in the last section of pipe between your last access point and the main sewer (or in the main sewer itself, canvas neighbours to see if they have a problem. Blocked main sewers are the local authority's responsibility).

To clear a blocked drain, scrape around the edges of the covers over the access points with an old knife or trowel. Remove any screws (if any). If there are 'key' holes, go and buy a cheap set of drain keys, insert, turn 90° and heave. Otherwise, using a couple of prying implements (small pry bars, old flat screwdrivers, thick scrapers etc), gently work around the edge and lever the cover up. If really stuck, try tapping with a rubber mallet as well as getting progressively more aggressive with your levering. Never use a metal hammer, because cast iron covers are brittle and easily broken and steel ones dent. Scrape out and wire brush any rusty frame grooves and the edges of the cover. Put grease in the frame groove to make this easy next time.

Right, now you're ready to go 'drain diving'. Put old waterproofs on and duct tape the tops of some rubber gloves to the jacket and grab a set of drain rods (cheap, especially when compared to calling out a plumber). Pop the screw attachment on and place the rod in the pipe 'upstream' towards the full IC. Keep screwing rods on until you hit the blockage. Twist the screw into the blockage and push/pull. You'll feel the blockage clear and hear the rumble of water coming from 'upstream', (hint: time to bug out!). Let the build-up of sewage flow away and clear.

Always use drain rods carefully and *always be slowly turning the rods clockwise* as you push them in and draw them out. NEVER go anticlockwise *ever*, or you'll 'unscrew' a section and lose rods in the drain (then you're in even more trouble).

Once you've cleared the main blockage run a hose pipe down the drain (from the first access point) or flush the loo several times to help clear any remaining debris and to keep the debris moving until it's in the main sewer. A bucket or three of screaming hot, soapy water down the toilet won't do any harm either... Oh, you might need a hot shower too, at this point...

You'll only need to do the above once, before you learn your lesson to never put stuff into drains that have no business being there...

Lastly the guttering needs checking (and yes, I know a gutter is only a 'half' pipe!). Empty it of leaves and other debris which builds up over the year. After the autumn, once all the leaves have dropped is as good a time as any to do this, even if it is a little cold by then. Working safely from a ladder, scrape and brush the debris into a bucket. It is usually difficult (in the UK at least) as the roof tiles get in the way.

During your annual 'pouring with rain' inspection, check along the length of the gutter run and especially the end opposite the downpipe to ensure it's not spilling over the top of the gutter (especially at the back where it's difficult to spot) during heavy rain.

Check the downpipes for blockages (check especially any bends, top or bottom) which cause the pipe to fill up and leak from joints above the blockage. If there are no blockages but the down pipe still leaks, check the pipe for splits and that the joints are the right way around; i.e. male part into female part etc. I know, I know I dislike the crude terms too, but it's accurate. Oh, and don't google it either, (shudders), if you want to learn more, check out this page... en.wikipedia.org/wiki/Gender_of_connectors_and_fasteners.

SILICONES AND CAULK MAINTENANCE

Hmm, maintenance might be a misnomer here, because maintenance usually means replacement. Still, you're here now, so we may as well take a look!

These tips apply pretty much to anything in a tube with a nozzle...

- Do all your preparation work first because you cannot sandpaper caulks or sealants in any way.

- Primer (if applicable, caulks mostly). Caulk sits better on a painted or primed surface (because it stops moisture from the caulk soaking into the substrate, thus it slows drying out and there's less shrinkage).

- Only buy good quality stuff, cheap ones shrink like heck-a-doodle.

- Treat yourself to a 'heavy duty' caulk gun, because they are 10 times better than the cheap ones and good gun doesn't cost the earth.

- Cut the long nozzle at around 45 degrees close to the tip.

- Grab a permanent marker and draw a line back from the nozzle tip on the longest side. This helps to correctly orientate the tip when you can't quite see properly.

- For silicone sealant, run a rubber-based tool over the bead at an angle. This takes off any excess and leaves a nice shape bead.

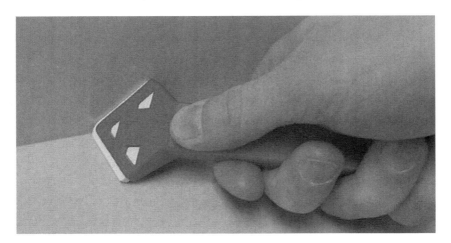

I now use the expensive 'Cramer Fugi' silicone tools, but I've also had good results with the one in the previous image.

● Don't push too hard on the tool though. Because it's generally difficult to get a truly flat bead like the left-hand side bead in the next picture, (but that is the strongest). The one in the middle is what you get
mostly.

Bead Profiles for Silicone Sealant

Most volume of
sealant at edges.

Okay volume of
sealant at edges

Thin volume of
sealant at edges, (it can peel away).

For best results,
always use a
rubber smoothing
tool if possible.

BEST   OKAY   WORST

● For decorator's acrylic caulk; wet a finger (or thumb) with a damp rag
and smooth out the line of caulk, pressing it back to where you want it.
Usually as small as possible.

Use the damp rag to tidy up any excess caulk from places you don't want it.
Fold the rag over if you've got sealant on it, to avoid getting sealant everywhere.
Rinse out the rag every few runs.

● Wipe any excess sealant on your finger onto the top of the gun (to save
your trousers/rag etc.), and just cut it off occasionally.

 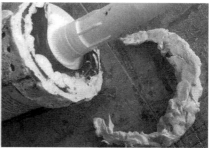

Always wait before painting paintable caulks. Overnight is best (even if it
says 1 hour on the tube!). Remember you can't paint regular silicone...

METAL MAINTENANCE

All bare metals react when exposed to the environment. Metals such as aluminium and stainless steel create a microscopic protective oxide layer which effectively stops further corrosion (lucky them) making it not strictly necessary to paint them. Other metals such as steel and iron are not so lucky and corrode extensively in the right conditions, namely in the presence of water and air. Areas of bare steel or iron will start to rust in a few hours or even quicker in ideal conditions.

Other factors such as salt (from the road or in the sea air) or acid rain, act as accelerators, worsening corrosion. One last factor to be aware of in the presence of salty air/water, is adverse reactions between different metals (such as stainless steel and aluminium) called *galvanic reaction or corrosion*. In plain language, this is an electrical reaction (not dissimilar to what goes on inside a battery) and causes severe corrosion; as anyone who owns an old Land Rover knows (they have aluminium bodies and steel chassis). Check any paint, coatings, sealants, or tapes keeping apart different metals and replace them if showing signs of failing.

Maintaining metal finishes falls into two parts; preventing contaminants damaging the coating and repairing any physical damage that occurs.

First then, finishes and coatings on most ferrous metal, (iron and steel stuff that rusts) living outside are under constant attack from potentially harmful contaminants, which damage the surface over time. In broadly alphabetical order, contaminants range from acid rain, ash and soot, bird droppings, building dust like cement or plaster, fingerprints, grit, rail dust (microscopic metal particles created by decay, vehicles, industry, oh and trains, hence the term), spilled fuel, splattered bugs, tar, tree sap, all the way to water, which leaves behind 'hard to shift' deposits when it dries out. Even the ultra violet rays found in lovely sunshine will damage some coatings believe it or not. The paint on older, red, and yellow cars is particularly vulnerable to serious fading caused by ultra violet rays if not regularly protected by polish. Even silly things, like writing "clean me" in gritty road dust on a friend's car will introduce microscopic scratches and mark the finish.

Fortunately, as mentioned earlier in this chapter, the answer is tediously simple. You must clean contaminants off your metal finishes more-or-less as they happen. Bird droppings for example are chemically nasty, but the real problem (found by vehicle cleaning experts Autoglym) is the way paint expands and contracts in the sunshine. Anything sitting on the paint as the sun warms and softens the layers, risks becoming microscopically embedded into the coating as it cools. You can imagine, paint has a pretty tough job as it is, trying to stay attached to a piece of thermally dynamic metal. Here in Norway for example, the temperature ranges from minus 30°C to plus 30°C, that's a whopping 60°C of expansion and contraction the paint has to cope with, without coming unstuck, (which I think is amazing) ...

Fortunately, there is a silver lining to cleaning your metalwork finishes... it is an ideal time to spot the second problem; *damage* to coatings.

Keep a constant eye open for physical damage when cleaning. Don't ignore any small damage to finishes because the corrosion process on steel for example is so very fast. Look out for...

- **Small chips**, often small but deep 'holes' caused by flying debris like stones. Repair with a tiny drop of matching paint on the very tip of a cocktail stick or toothpick. The paint flows into the chip and flattens out almost perfectly; brushes, even tiny ones tend to just smear the paint all over the place. Use nail polish in a pinch.

- **Scratches**, repair with a like-for-like propriety product or cover with something that repels water to keep out the elements. On less visually important stuff, silicone or bitumen products are common or wax polish in a pinch.

- **Dents** on their own are not too troublesome if they are shallow, but often dents crease the metal and creases are likely to 'crack' finishes, lifting the coating from the metal, letting in the elements with predicable results. Scrape away loose stuff and refinish.

- **Flaking, lifting, or peeling finishes**; caused by several things, poor preparation prior to painting, stressed or excess movement of the metal or a result of weather and time. Scrape, sand and refinish.

- **Crazing and cracking**, (paint surface looks like alligator or crocodile skin). Could be because of poor preparation prior to painting, mismatched paint types, or an adverse reaction to older paint (i.e. hard paint over softer paint), the metal could be too thermally active hot/cold, or too many layers of paint and/or extreme old age. Scrape, sand and refinish.

- **Blistering or bubbles**, could be poor preparation again (are you starting to see a pattern with this? Hint, 65% of paint problems are down to poor preparation... just sayin'), but it could also be moisture or solvent trapped in between coats or even because the paint was applied in the sunshine and the outer layer dried too quick. Scrape, sand down and refinish.

- **Chalking**, where aging paint, usually in exposed spots dries to a dusty surface over time. Sand and refinish.

- **Mould**, usually in damp areas that don't get a lot of sunshine. Needs thorough cleaning with a cleaner formulated to combat the spores. Spray on with a pump-up garden sprayer and leave to soak and usually rinsing off with water. Read the instructions first! Then sand down and refinish.

- **Faded coatings**, can become micro porous and lose its ability to protect letting in contaminants like water etc. Protect faded paint temporarily with a lot of polish. Otherwise, sand down and refinish.

- **Rough paint**, paint on vehicles will 'collect' lots of tiny metal particles called rail dust (all vehicles produce tiny metal dust particles in use, originally from train wheels/tracks etc., hence the term). Thrown up off the road they embed themselves into the paints surface. Rub your hand over the paint surface to feel them. Wash, and gently rub a well lubricated 'clay bar' over the paint to remove them. Re-apply waxes and polish as the surface will be totally clean/bare.

Repair any small damage with a suitable matching product straight away. Aim to prevent minor damage like scratches or chips in paint or other coatings from getting any worse. Because get worse they definitely will, 100% guaranteed. Water will creep into every little crevice and start its deadly work.

Re-coat any areas showing signs of weather or wear. You can buy all kinds of paint for metal; from small touch-up bottles incorporating a tiny brush up to paint suitable for spraying. Head for your local car parts supplier and DIY paint stores for more info.

It's essential you maintain any finish before the existing protection degrades or starts to fail. Once the paint starts to show the metal beneath, its game over and the only answer is to get right back to a sound surface and re-apply the coating. Arguably then, this is not maintenance but a repair.

It's possible to stabilise neglected and rusty metal with special rust stabilising chemicals from your local motoring supplies store. You can even paint straight onto rust (if it's clean, dry, scraped and properly wire brushed first) with paints such as Hammerite, which is available in a smooth or dimpled (hammered) finish. Search online for 'hammered paint' to find this kind of paint near you.

Protect inaccessible areas using a wax-based compound via a spray or pump lance. Simply thread the lance into holes, gaps, behind panels etc and spray the wax liberally in all directions as you draw it out. The wax will creep into crevices and can 'self-repair' minor damage from stones and scratches etc. Waxoyle is a well-known brand in Europe, search for "corrosion protection products" to find something similar in your area or visit an auto supplies store. Cheap endoscopes are available to plug into your laptop, making it easy to check inside hidden areas (e.g. inside structural members under vehicles).

Arguably, you can use anything that repels water for rough protection on less critical things like lawn mowers and so on. Things like silicone sealant, waxes, polish, waterproof tapes, waterproof glues, or adhesives and even oil or grease. However, don't do this if you intend to paint the item in the future, as paint adhesion will be a problem; use a rust stabilising primer instead.

You can polish some metals with wax based or special polymers to provide extra protection, but in fact, you're protecting the life of the metals protective layer, i.e. the paint! However, this mostly applies to vehicles, for some reason, folks never want to polish their metal drainpipes, gates, lampposts etc. even though it would prolong the life of their coatings...

RUST AS A FINISH

Some heavy items of metal don't need additional protection and function quite happily with a layer of corrosion (rust or iron oxide). This doesn't cause a problem because the items are so very thick or solid that corrosion is too slow to cause loss of function during their expected lifespan (brake callipers and some suspension parts on vehicles for example.)

Rust is also becoming an acceptable 'finish', mostly on street furniture and art, where by design, the metal is thick enough to avoid structural weakening by corrosion over time.

Unprotected non-ferrous metals (stuff like gold, silver, copper, and aluminium) don't rust like steel, but can tarnish and discolour when exposed to the air. Use a special, mildly abrasive metal polish to clean and maintain a shiny finish. The abrasive action removes tarnish, sulphates, and oxides, at the same time protecting against further tarnishing by excluding air and moisture. You can restore brass, chrome, aluminium, gold, silver etc., from a very tarnished condition repeatedly. Be wary of plated items (microscopic layer of valuable metal over a cheap base metal) though as over polishing with abrasive polish can rub completely through the thin plating if you go bananas.

Sometimes though, the development of a patina is desirable. Copper used as a roofing material for example; often left to develop a characteristic blue-green tint. Note, it can take many years in some locations for the thin layer of copper sulphate to develop. There are chemicals to accelerate the process towards green, as well as waxes or oils to prevent it, keeping the shiny copper look, (you pays your money and you makes your choice ...).

PLASTIC MAINTENANCE

Most everyday plastics only need an occasional wipe over with a damp cloth or mild detergent to remove potential contaminants. As with wood and metal, removing potentially corrosive things like bird faeces or potentially acidic chemicals in soot or carbon is a good idea. Plus, the surface of most types of plastic is relatively soft and easily scratched by abrasive dust and grit.

Some types of plastic discolour when exposed to the suns UV rays over time and may eventually become brittle or show signs of surface degradation. It's possible to slow down this damage by regularly using a proprietary plastic protector, which will clean, restore any faded colour, and protect against further discolouration. Most plastic living outside would need regular application to maintain protection and looks; although to be honest most people don't bother because they believe plastic to be maintenance free.

For example, some of the black plastics used on vehicle trims and bumpers etc eventually turn grey over time. Using a proprietary plastic restorer like 'Back to Black' (or similar) will restore the original colour fairly successfully and regular application will build up a protective layer.

RUBBER MAINTENANCE

Once considered an old-fashioned weak and friable material, with the addition of many different elements, rubber has morphed into a modern, high performing, hi-tech composite material. Adding synthetic compounds, fillers, reinforcing strands of metal, cloth, or fibre, has made it stronger, better at handling temperature extremes and much more durable. For example, drive-belts containing strong threads or fabrics to help limit stretch and resist breaking strains, now last for many thousands of hours with minimal wear. Tyres also contain miles of reinforcing fabric and steel wires or bands.

However, age comes to us all, and exposure to sunlight, extreme heat or cold, chemicals, friction and excessive stretching or compression eventually causes rubber stuff to perish or fail, either slowly or catastrophically. Perished rubber looks 'dried out' and shows crazing on the surface. Perished rubber can keep going for a while, but as you can't tell how deep the perishing goes, you should replace anything severely perished as soon as possible to prevent serious failures. This especially applies to tyres on vehicles, although arguably, you don't need to panic about your wheelbarrow!

Because rubber leads such a demanding life it's difficult to protect, but there is one thing we can do to help, we can try to shield it from the worst of the elements. For example, UV rays will damage tyres (especially those not regularly used), turning them grey as the 'carbon black' UV stabiliser gets older and less effective. Seriously consider covering up tyres on stuff you only use occasionally like trailers, motorhomes, RV's, boat trailers, classic cars, and the like, to keep sunshine off the rubber, they'll last longer if you do.

Using your tyres also helps protective waxes built into the tyre; migrate to the surface, protecting them from things like the naturally occurring Ozone in the air, (a great excuse to take out your toys, i.e. "I'm just maintaining the tyres dear; I'll be back in a couple of hours...").

There are various rubber conditioners you can use to top up this built-in protection and slow down deterioration. Spray or wipe the conditioner on tyres, window seals, door seals and weather seals etc. Rubber conditioners have been somewhat controversial of late, so look for brands that specifically state they include UV protection. These should be available from your local motor supplies store.

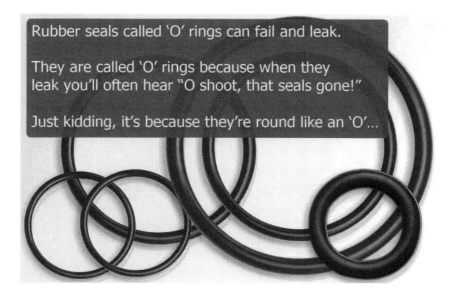

Rubber O rings are round seals (although they can be square, rectangular, or oval etc.), to stop liquids (or air) from leaking. They either go inside a pipe in a groove (e.g. pipe joints) or outside a pipe in a groove (e.g. quick fit hosepipe connectors)

These rubber rings harden over time, cracking or even splitting into several pieces causing dripping or full-blown leaks. Check annually and make sure they are properly lubricated, this helps maintain a good seal and protects the rubber O ring itself.

To improve an older, neglected O ring, gently remove it and clean with hot, soapy water. Wipe out any old lubricant from the groove it sits in, re-lubricate the seal, and pop it back. I don't like metal O ring picks (I worry about scratching the groove, causing a leak), preferring instead to use a plastic spudger (no, seriously they are a thing...) or any softer material really, and slide it underneath the ring and to the side to pop up a section, whilst holding the back side to stop it rotating.

Remove bigger external O rings by wiping it dry and 'pinching' it together to lift a section up slightly and then roll it off. The tiniest O rings are difficult to remove without damaging them, so either just wipe them clean and re-lubricate them in situ or replace them with new ones (they are cheap).

Lubricating O rings helps protect them from damage by abrasion, pinching, or cutting. It also helps to seat the O ring properly and makes them last longer. Dry O rings that move in use, stretch in one place, and compress in others, which is bad for the rubber and the seal it's trying to keep. How often you do this depends on usage and environment. Lubricate the O rings on your hosepipe connectors once a year, but the camera case you use for deep-sea photography, well, I guess you'll already know how often you need to do that (i.e. quite often, maybe even every time you use it).

Opinions vary on what to use to lubricate O rings, with some controversy around the use of 'PET' or petroleum jelly (Vaseline etc). Most O rings, especially automotive ones are 'petrochemically safe' these days. Personally, I think PET is better than no lubricant at all 99% of the time, but if you're worried, simply use a dedicated O ring lubricant, especially if you're working on the space shuttle or deep-sea submersibles etc...

Obviously, rubber is also rather famous for stretching, sometimes too much. Once stretched beyond its design limits rubber will eventually snap. Drive belts for example can stretch and lose tension, resulting in them slipping (listen for it squealing usually) and even coming off altogether.

The rubber belt driving engine ancillaries being a classic example. Although often called a 'fan belt' this composite rubber belt rarely drives a cooling fan anymore (most engines have temperature controlled electric fans now), but rubber belts do drive lots of other vital components like power steering, water pump, air conditioning pump (if applicable), and the alternator which provides electrical power.

Most belts are good for the first few years but after this initial period, about once a year check all drive belts for tension and especially look for any micro splits or perishing, especially check the backside on ribbed belts.

As a very rough 'field guide', a drivebelt is correctly tensioned if you can twist them in the middle of the longest run through 90° or so. Otherwise, measure the deflection of the belt on its longest run (see the previous image) and compare it to the manufacturer's specifications, or use a special drive belt tension-measuring tool.

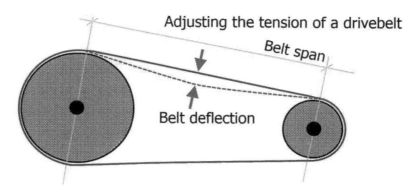

Adjusting the tension of a drivebelt

Belt span

Belt deflection

FABRIC MAINTENANCE

We all maintain fabrics every week... on washday. Okay, so we mostly wash our clothes to make them smell nice, but washing fabrics also maintains them by removing dust, grit, and dirt. These tiny particles are abrasive and if you add in the friction caused by movement (assuming you don't live on the sofa!), you have ideal conditions for excess wear and tear. Fabric worn next to the skin also of course soaks up sweat, which is mildly corrosive to many natural fibres, (yuck a doodle...).

Waterproof fabrics are a little more complicated as there are several different types. Maintenance varies from reapplying an oil or wax to spraying with a water repelling chemical and some you simply wash in a washing machine on a special setting. Read the manufacturers label to find out what type of fabric it is; always follow any aftercare instructions and contact them if you can't read the label anymore, as getting this wrong can remove the fabrics waterproofing properties completely.

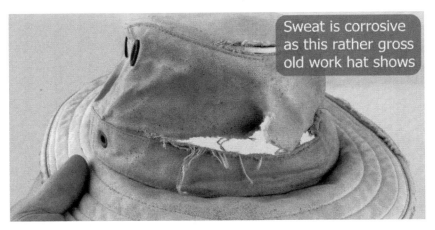

Sweat is corrosive as this rather gross old work hat shows

MAINTENANCE SCHEDULES

Many people, especially when on a budget, adopt a 'don't fix what isn't broken' approach to things (and that's fine for your toaster). However, when it comes to vehicles or checking your gutters etc., there's sense in sticking to a proper maintenance schedule. Because if you do, you'll avoid breakdowns and failures. If that's not enough, remember this; when it comes to selling something on, well maintained stuff (with receipts or records to prove it) sells quicker and for a higher price. Plus, prospective future purchasers of your stuff might easily walk away if they suspect there has been any neglect, (there are plenty more out there after all).

Consider drawing up your own maintenance schedule to record what you've done and what needs doing next. It doesn't have to be anything fancy; start with a simple list of jobs and when you aim to carry them out; either weekly, monthly, or annually, whatever fits your lifestyle.

Something popular with my well-heeled clients is to have several maintenance 'wish' lists; one for stuff they want to do this year, then another two lists with stuff they want to do within say five years and lastly a list for things they might want to do, but without a particular time frame (time and money permitting). All three are 'live' lists which you can amend continually.

How much you do and how often, depends on your location and each particular task or job (oh, and availability of time and cash of course!). However, as a general minimum, check your stuff before winter and then again in the spring. That way you avoid working when it's really cold and miserable plus you'll repair any small damage before the harsh winter weather sets in. Checking and doing a few maintenance spruce ups again in the spring also makes your stuff look good ready for the summer season (and doesn't waste valuable sunshine!).

Also, don't be a 'slave' to a schedule if the conditions don't warrant it. Maintaining something just because it is X years since you last maintained it, doesn't consider the current condition or 'need'. Regular checks will help you decide if it needs maintenance as planned in year X, or whether the recent harsh conditions means it needs redoing sooner, or the opposite; if recent mild conditions mean it can wait a little longer. Just-in-time maintenance is cost effective because it prevents neglect and gets the most out of your stuff.

If you have an older home, you could start by looking online for a great document from the conservation folks in Dublin called 'Maintenance: A Guide to the Repair of Older Buildings' just search ISBN 0-7557-7537-6 and look for the www.dublincity.ie domain to grab your free copy. Or see appendices two for online access to my Home Maintenance Guide.

UNSCHEDULED MAINTENANCE

Some things don't need a schedule because you do them on-the-spot or as you notice them. See the two-minute-rule in the *Working Efficiently and Being Productive* section in the *Developing Practical Skills* chapter. Some examples of unscheduled maintenance...

- Loose stuff; e.g. a screw in a hinge on a cabinet door.

- Damage to vulnerable coatings; e.g. a stone chip on paint.

- Dry or stiff stuff needing lubrication; e.g. door hinge etc.

- New and unusual sounds need investigating immediately.

- Leaks of any kind, of any liquid, need immediate attention.

- Unusual smells need investigating immediately.

- Unusual vibration; if it feels different, it needs investigating right away.

VEHICLE MAINTENANCE

I'll not go into too much detail here as the topic can fill books on its own, but I'll just tell you that although machines and vehicles are complex, most regular maintenance tasks are usually quite easy. Sure, occasionally you might need a special tool, but most are not particularly expensive to purchase, and most are easy enough to learn how to use via the instructions or YouTube.

You'll also need some easily found, specific technical information related to your vehicle (intervals between services etc., specifications for different fluids, tightness, or torque settings for fasteners etc.). This you can often find in the owner's handbook which comes with all machines or find an independent one from someone like Haynes*. Libraries often have manuals for the most popular vehicles and there are lots available second hand online if you don't mind the odd oily fingerprint. These types of manuals and handbooks offer easy to follow maintenance information specific for your vehicle (this is the one-time step-by-step info is a good idea, as each car is essentially identical). *Haynes.co.uk in the UK or Haynes.com internationally.

In addition to the manuals, there is a lot of video content online related to servicing (and repairing) vehicles; maybe because vehicle mechanics are more technically minded than most and like making videos?

Incidentally, whilst you're in the motor store you might also be able to get advice from their usually enthusiast staff (don't try this when they're busy though). Asking them to recommend a good product for a particular task is an easy way to break the ice.

If you own a vehicle you plan to keep a while, it's a good idea to find and join the owners club or forum for your vehicle. This is simply the best way to find solid maintenance information given freely from fellow fans of the marque. Search online for the vehicles name +owners club or +forum to start with. These guys often put lots of effort into posting about their own experiences along with lots of solutions for common problems on the forum.

I know searching forums is time consuming due to their size, but if you get the keywords right, you'll find really specific information. Don't let the information flow one-way either, if you fix something, post a quick note on the forum to help others. You're more likely to receive help yourself if you help others and earn some kudos. And definitely don't be the guy who signs up today and immediately begs for help, this makes you appear a more than a little rude. Don't be a 'taker', sign up and join in before you need to ask for help yourself. Even if it's just to say 'Hi, looking forward to joining in.' or to leave appreciative comments on other threads etc.

As always, the trick with vehicle maintenance is to study the parts in conjunction with reading through the steps FIRST. Repeatedly if necessary, until you're confident you understand at least how to begin the procedure. Also, make sure you have everything you need before you start (unless you have access to another car). There is nothing more annoying than partially dismantling something and then having to put them all back again to drive to the local motor store to pick up something you forgot...

And be prepared to get frustrated from time to time working on vehicles. Out of all the stuff I work on, fixing vehicles is the most likely one to annoy me. Either a component is very difficult to access, leading to skinned knuckles or worse; or something has corroded beyond reason and is proving very difficult to work on because it's seized solid. Imagine the two together, yup, it happens. All the time.

Sometimes you need to remove a lot of other things which are in the way to just see the darn thing which has broken; time consuming, tedious and there is always the risk of damaging something that was perfectly fine before you had to go in with the big hammers.

All I can say is, allow plenty of time, and make yourself as comfortable as possible. Use an old thin mattress to lay on and even something to support your head if you're underneath. Get the vehicle as high off the ground as you safely can and I really do mean safely, people die underneath falling cars all the time... Invest in a good, high lift jack and strong axle stands to support the weight after you've jacked it up. Never work under a vehicle on a jack alone, death or serious injury beckons if you do.

Learn about rust and understand what causes it, it's the main Achilles heel on vehicles, it affects nearly everything. Buy a good anti-rust product by the gallon and don't be mean with it, spray it everywhere you can underneath, as we looked at before, rust often starts from the inside out, so get the stuff inside all those awkward to reach places.

Most folks running older vehicles adopt a 'if it's not broke, don't fix it' mentality and to be honest that's fine. Except when it comes to fluids. Even on the rattiest runabout, change the oil often, and that applies to all the other liquids too; gearbox, steering, cooling, brake, and AC coolant to name a few. Keep moving parts greased and stop stone-chips from spreading with any water repelling stuff you have to hand.

So, you've been a good egg and maintained your stuff religiously, but something went and broke anyway, life huh? Read on...

REPAIRING STUFF

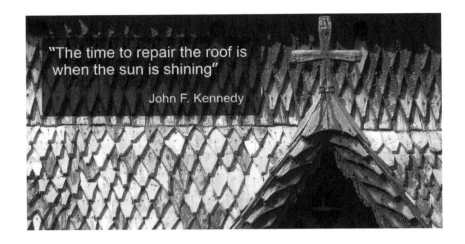

"The time to repair the roof is when the sun is shining"

John F. Kennedy

Being able to repair stuff is one of the most useful aspects of being handy, because it's so convenient. No waiting for 'a man' to come and fix it or taking stuff to the repair shop and waiting weeks to get it back. And even better, no going to the store to buy replacements. Sometimes things break down or fail in the simplest way (even complex things) and the repair only takes a few minutes. Sometimes repairs are more complicated, requiring new tools and new skills, but either way, this chapter will guide you through the process of looking at broken stuff and get you itching to reach for your tools.

Plus, when it comes to broken things, my theory is; 'there is nothing to lose by having a look'. Big ticket stuff like vehicles excepted, most things these days are likely to be beyond 'economic repair' because the cost of hiring a professional often exceeds the cost of buying a new replacement. Therefore, if *you don't fix it*, it's going into landfill. So, there you go, *nothing to lose* and possibly, *everything to gain*. Even if you can't fix it, the experience is great practise and will teach you something small but useful, ready for next time.

Realistically though I'll be honest, *you won't be able to fix everything* because, (as we've looked at earlier), some things are just not designed with repairs in mind. Plus, some complex machines would need specialist diagnostic equipment to even find what part has failed. And then there's stuff that's just plain worn out, kaput, game over, beyond repair...

You might also encounter mechanical things which have carefully designed lifespans, especially at the lower end of the market. This 'planned obsolescence', is a practise I find morally dubious, but that's big business for you. Therefore, when 'budget' (read *throwaway*) stuff fails, it's usually catastrophic in nature, rendering the item little more than scrap (but don't forget to strip any useful bits off it first: cables, plugs, metal, fixings, or fittings etc.).

One last point before we get started; guarantees. Return items still within their guarantee period to the store, as attempting repairs yourself will invalidate your guarantee. Also, always ensure you fill in and return the manufacturers registration card on new stuff to prevent potential problems with repairs under guarantee later.

Remember that in addition to the standard '6, 12, 18 or 24 months' guarantee you get from the outset, you have legal rights or statutory rights too. Things must be (so called): 'fit for purpose', for a *reasonable* period. For example, your expensive new lawnmower might come with a 12-month guarantee, but if it fell apart after 13 months, you could easily argue 13 months is not a 'reasonable' lifespan for a lawnmower. Always consider contacting the manufacturer before attempting your own repairs to see if your statutory rights are still in play. For example, you're covered in England for up to 6 years (on some goods) if you've properly maintained the item as per the manufacturer's recommendations, (and it's free from obvious signs of abuse). Google terms like 'consumer rights' or 'statutory rights' to learn more about consumer laws where you live.

Thankfully, modern manufacturing means most things are reliable and problems within the guarantee period are relatively rare, hence the large profits made though 'shop purchased breakdown insurance'. Most of the stuff we might want to repair will be older things, stuff that's still useful but probably beyond professional economic repair.

BUT I WANT A SHINY NEW ONE!

Well, of course you do! We all like new and shiny stuff; it makes us feel good to surround ourselves with nice things. But first, I want you to try and repair your broken-down stuff, to give it a chance to last as long as possible (plus if you repair it you could always sell it on and put the cash towards the new one), just a thought...

THINK ABOUT THE ENVIRONMENT

Oh no, not that old story again you might say, but there is a point. If everyone were to live as we do in the 'developed' world (fridges, freezers, dishwashers, washing machines, coffee machines, TV's, computers, cars, electric toothbrushes, (and God forbid), a spiralizer, etc. etc.) the planet would simply not be able to provide all the raw materials needed to make them all (sorry for the rant, but I lived in Africa for a few years, and learned a lot about the 'necessities' of life...). We need to make the most of the things we purchase by making them last as long as possible, for the good of all, capisce?

IT'S BROKEN, WHERE DO I START?

A list of all possible failures across all things, would look like a pile of phone books, so where do you start when something goes wrong? Well, some things are obvious repairs; what I mean is, when a pane of glass breaks, it obviously needs replacing; or you notice a missing screw, you know to replace it etc. easy peasy. But what to do when the problem isn't obvious...

To 'deconstruct' the problem and diagnose what went wrong you need to go back in time, (no Marty McFly not like that...); Try to think back to a time before the problem, or when did you first notice something was amiss? What was the exact first thing that you noticed?

...hmm, this is where it gets tricky. Diagnosis is always a big challenge, especially with electrical or mechanical things. You're going to need to do a little sleuthing, a bit of detective work...

So, grab your magnifying glass (seriously) and let's go through the four steps to try and figure out what to do. It looks like a long list of questions which is clumsy on paper I know, but as a mental process, don't worry, it's a script you'll run through in a sub-conscious flash whenever you're looking at something with a problem. Got your magnifying glass? Then let's go...

FOUR STEPS BEFORE REACHING FOR THE TOOLS

STEP 1: RECOGNISING & EVALUATING WHAT HAPPENED

Think back in time about *exactly* what happened, remember the *RELEARN* method, use all your senses and memories... dig deep, it takes time to remember those little signs hovering around the edges of your consciousness... work down the list... anything ring any bells?

IN GENERAL

- Don't forget to look for the obvious. It might not be immediately apparent, check for fuel, power, etc. because overlooking the obvious happens regularly, (a lot more than you'd think ...)

- Something changed; (became tight or loose, a new situation, a new or different noise, different circumstances, i.e. it got wet, it dried out, overheated, frozen, etc. etc.)

- Something broke, or came apart, or is missing.

- It started after (insert XYZ event) happened (dropped, got wet, etc.).

- You had noticed a definite problem, but you ignored it, (because you hoped it'd go away, didn't you?).

- It worked fine last time you used it, but now it doesn't.

- It just stopped while you were using it, with no warning.

- It made horrible noises before it stopped.

- It made a specific noise, (bang, groan, knock, pop, scrape, screech, snap, squeal, squawk, tap etc. etc.).

- Something is missing, (a part, a fastener, lubrication etc.).

- It made a funny smell (what did it smell like?)

- Smoke came out of it (which part?).

- It felt funny just before it stopped (vibration etc)

- Something came off (drivebelt, lever etc).

- Now you think about it, there was something odd the last time...

- Or maybe you've had a 'funny feeling' about it for a while.

- It's so tired and worn out, you can't believe it still worked at all...

STEP 2: ASSESSING WHETHER TO FIX IT

Follow up by asking yourself these questions...

- How attached are you to the item, is there any sentimental value?

- How old is the item, roughly?

- What would the normal expected lifespan be? E.g. (laptop = 3 to 4 years, washing machine = 8 years or so, TV = 10 years or so, car = 15 years or so, etc).

- Is it something that's commonly professionally repaired (washing machines for example), or is it an item generally thrown away after failure, such as a toaster or a hair dryer etc.?

- Roughly, what do you think it would cost to get it repaired professionally; is it easy to find out?

- How easy is it to find spare parts to fix it yourself? (Search for the part number or machine serial number online).

- How much will spare parts cost, including shipping etc?

- How long is the spare part delivery time and is there a pressing need to get it fixed quickly? (washing machine being the classic one!)

- How much would it cost to buy a new replacement today?

STEP 3: WHAT TOOLS WOULD I NEED TO FIX IT?

- Do you have tools to open it up or dismantle it to fit the new parts?

- Do you know anyone who might be willing to lend you the tools? (Friends, neighbours, colleagues etc.).

- If you need to buy new tools, how much do they cost, and will they be useful in the future on other projects?

STEP 4: THE CASE FOR THROWING IT AWAY

- Are the repair costs getting anywhere close to the cost of a new replacement? Anything even half way needs serious thought.

- Are newer versions more efficient, giving potential money savings in the future? Replacement justification?

- Were you considering an upgrade anyway?

- Sometimes repairs are just not worth it, unless there is love in there somewhere...

MAKING A DIAGNOSIS

Okay, you've taken a moment to run through the above four steps and you might already have a conclusion or two or found something obvious. At best, you already understand what's wrong and confirmed it's viable to consider repairs (either yourself or by hiring in a specialist). At worst, you've confirmed it's broken beyond economical repair and it's time to upcycle/recycle/scrap it with a clear conscience (plus, it gave you diagnostic experience).

Remember also, stuff rarely happens in isolation. People talk about stuff going wrong all the time and go looking for answers online, often posting solutions of their own. Do some research online for anything relevant to your experience, because folks love to rant about stuff that's gone wrong... If it's something that's manufactured by the million, it's statistically improbable your problem is unique. Of course, if you stuffed a parrot into your toaster, then all bets are off!

Keeping in mind step one above, try to determine what might have gone wrong from what you saw/heard/smelt/felt at the time. Here's a random selection of possibilities, I've seen them all...

- Sudden stop on electrical stuff could be a tripped breaker or a blown fuse (in the home or in a vehicle)

  Think why though? Unplug or switch off everything and see if the breaker stays on. Switch items on one-by-one and see which item blows the fuse or trips the breaker (easy).

- A sudden or intermittent fault could mean corrosion on a connector causing it to lose its conductivity. Remove the connector and clean with fine sandpaper (easy repair). Consider protecting the connection to prevent water getting in and corroding it again (petroleum jelly etc.).

- Intermittent operation or on-and-off operation (when the cable or item moves?) could mean a broken wire in a cable. Replace the cable.

- Sudden stop on an engine could be electrical (might need specialist diagnostic equipment to find item) diagnosis often tricky, repair is usually an easy part replacement.

- A stuttering stop could be fuel related, check any filters, pumps, etc. (easy repair once located).

- Sluggish operation could mean dirt or corrosion slowing things down. Affects potentially anything that moves; even motors clog up with carbon. Dismantle and clean. Use air and re-lubricate if applicable (potentially easy repair).

- Snapping, twanging, or rapid slapping noise in a machine could mean a damaged drivebelt. Replace the belt (easy repair).

- Smoke or bad smells could mean the electrical components burning out or bearings overheating (hmm, repairs depend on the item and quality of the machine).

- Vibrations from a machine could mean damaged driveshafts or bearings. Replacement is often the only option (could be expensive).

- Grinding noises could mean busted gears or bearings breaking up. Replacement is the only option (getting expensive).

ADD IN ANY CIRCUMSTANTIAL EVIDENCE

If someone else used something of yours that subsequently fails, remember that you'll never get the 'full' story. You'll need to tease out the details to find out what *exactly* happened. Just keep talking; the truth tends to come out gradually, especially if there's any degree of wrongdoing, especially with children, big and small! Mostly the 'wrongdoing' is through ignorance, and let's be honest here, if you don't own an item, it's not very likely you're very skilled in using said item either, is it?

I CAN'T FIND ANYTHING WRONG!

Are you absolutely sure? Make sure you don't jump to conclusions or make assumptions. Take another look. Nope, not with that confused look on your face, you're looking but not seeing! Now try again and *really* look at it and think! Still nothing? ...Okay, it happens. Not everything fails in an obvious way. You've looked at everything and nothing seems out of place. You've wiggled, pulled, and prodded but still you can't replicate the problem or find anything obvious outside. Depending on the item of course, you might need to do all of the above again... after going...inside... gulp...

But before you go diving inside something, it's time to grab a cup of coffee and take a minute and gather your resources. Here are some bullet points from the *Developing Your Handy Ability* chapter to refresh your memory...

- Check any original brochures, instructions, diagrams that you kept for trouble shooting tips.

- Search online for your numbers (serial, model etc.) and look for results on forums etc., looking for people ~~talking~~ complaining about the same problem with their own stuff.

- Manufacturer's websites help lines or technical departments. If you haven't already, dig out and read the brochures, leaflets, diagrams, and instructions that came with the item and find their telephone number or dig it out online.

- Read up. Try the library for repair manuals; in the UK, most libraries have car repair manuals for example.

Ask people you know or a friendly and approachable local professional (of course you'll pay for their time).

I'll mention one last diagnostic technique here as it's common, even amongst professional repair guys (arguably standard for some professional repairs...), and that is 'substitution with a known good part'. I know you're not likely to have spare parts handy for many things. Nevertheless, it's worth keeping in mind for things you might have several of; problems with bulbs, fuses, batteries, and other small electrical items for example. Simply remove the part you suspect is causing the problem and replace it with one you know to be working okay. Replacing the little starter unit from a flickering fluorescent light is a classic example here.

GOING INSIDE

Since I don't know whether you'll be working on a toaster, tractor, or a kid's toy, let's go over a few generalities to get you thinking about how stuff goes together and what to look out for once 'inside.'

IT SAYS, 'NO USER SERVICEABLE PARTS INSIDE'...

Oh great, so it's over before we even started? Probably not, the 'no user serviceable parts inside' is the most improbable phrase ever so don't panic just yet. What they're really trying to say is "hands off buddy, we'd really prefer it if you go and buy a new one!" But often you *can* dismantle these parts and at least have a look. Don't worry about 'breaking' it, it's broken already remember. Oftentimes you'll find single use fixings, such as bend over lugs, plastic welds, glue, or rivets etc. It's often possible to carefully break these open and see if there's anything obviously wrong inside.

Reassembly might require a little creativity though; sometimes you may get away with using the original fold down lugs or tabs. Other times you need to recreate fixings using glues (superglue, hot glue guns, silicone sealant, general-purpose adhesives etc.) new rivets or... dare I even write it... duct tape and cable ties on more agricultural items etc., (duct tape and cable ties are made in heaven, I kid you not...)

Sometimes of course, 'no user serviceable parts' means just that; and you might not be able to do anything useful inside, but by now you should know my theory; i.e., it can't hurt to have a little look now, can it?

FANCY FIXINGS

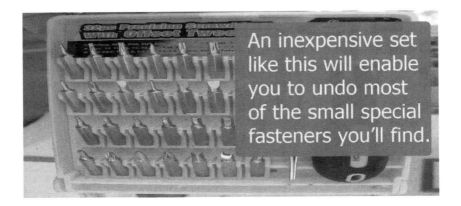

An inexpensive set like this will enable you to undo most of the small special fasteners you'll find.

I'll drop this in here (don't you just love cut and paste...) in case what you're looking at isn't screwed together with common fasteners like slot or 'cross' type screws. Some manufacturers don't want you fiddling around inside their products for a variety of reasons, (they say to protect you from invalidating the guarantee) but mostly it's because they don't want you to see how crappy the insides of their products are, or they want you to buy new ones. To discourage you they may use special shaped fixings, from triangular drive to pin centred star drives. The only option if you want to get past these, is to grab a set of special screwdriver 'bits', the type that slot into the end of a screwdriver like tool. Fortunately, they're very cheap...

I'll include a word about *rivets* here too, although not a particularly 'fancy' fastener, some folks think they're 'undoable'. Rivets are quite easy to remove by lightly drilling into the dimple in the middle using a 6mm (or so) HSS drill bit (metal bit). The head of the rivet will come free and you can push the rest of the rivet through. Replacement rivets are cheap and easily installed with a special 'rivet gun', (also cheap).

HOW TO GET IT APART BY LOOKING AT IT...

No, young Jedi, not like that! Old school like this... If the item is small, clear an area on the workbench (or the kitchen table if you're not fussy...) because this stops small parts getting lost amongst any clutter. Put something down to protect the work surface (and delicate items,) like a short length of leftover lining paper or any other pale coloured paper; backside of wallpaper, paper table protector etc., or even a sheet of A4 for small stuff. Old bed sheets or pillowcases are also good because stuff doesn't roll around on them (I use old sheets from when the kids were babies). Use newspaper in a pinch, but you'll find small black screws tricky to see, unless that's just me getting old...

Larger stuff or 'fixed in place stuff' needs preparing to make working comfortable. For example, working under the sink on a leaking pipe is much easier if you completely empty the cupboard. Never struggle on top of loads of junk because you think you'll save a few minutes, you won't. Any kind of crawling around in tight spaces needs good access and if you're underneath something, grab something soft to lay on.

It's also a pretty good idea to grab a container or two for putting small parts into as you dismantle. Because I promise you, anything you drop on the floor disappears like magic. Honestly, you'll waste eons of time looking for them, so always use some sort of container. Those ice cream tubs are so useful, aren't they? Yummy.

Make sure you have plenty of room to lay things out logically when dismantling stuff. Ideally mirror the place they came from i.e. working from left to right etc. This really helps to prevent the biggest drag of all time, the 'out of sequence re-assembly'. Imagine, you get it all back together and yet there is a single bolt left on the bench. Argh! Then you're forced to take it all apart again, put the bolt where it's supposed to go and then rebuild it all. Tedious, time consuming and worst of all, it'll make you feel stupid.

Really take care during the dismantling phase and the reassembly will go smoothly, I promise. Treat the dismantling phase as 'reverse instructions' to show you how to put it back together again! Plus, you have the old parts to use as a reference for fitting any new parts. Always take notes and *always, always, take lots of photos* because they are a great guide and often save the day when you're stuck.

You can even press screws/bolts/etc through a piece of cardboard with notes next to each one, which is invaluable on jobs with many fasteners. You could even draw a sketch outline of the part and push the fasteners through in their respective places; taping any small parts to the sketch. Some folks like refitting each bolt back into its respective hole after removing a part. This prevents bolts from getting lost or mixed up (esp. good for bolts of differing lengths). These tips are particularly useful if you're removing something and it will be some time before you'll get back to it because you're waiting for spare parts to arrive or you have other commitments. However, before you can remove any fasteners, you need to find them first...

Get up close and look for evidence of fasteners. Remember the lessons in the *Developing Practical Knowledge* chapter and look for anything that even hints at being a fixing point. It helps if you hum while you do this, or maybe a couple of hmm's or ooh's, or if it's really tricky, try a sharp intake of breath...

Screws are the most obvious, (don't forget to check deep wells or even under labels or rubber feet). Look for gaps, seams, clips, tiny slots in casting seams or worst of all, nothing (which usually means some sort of adhesive). Not everything is obvious or clear, there may be hidden stuff or multiple types of fixings; in fact, more often than not, this is the case.

Opening glued or welded together stuff is a little destructive. Gently working through the material along the joins or seams with a craft knife, fine toothed wood saw or hacksaw. You could try using a red-hot knife to cut thinner plastic. Hold a thin, sharp blade in the flame of a blowtorch for a minute and then work quickly along the join. Watch the fumes, they'll be dangerous.

On symmetrical casings, round or rotary stuff that could in theory go back together in a different place mark across any joints with a marker pen (or scratch across the join with a sharp implement or even a metal file on heavy or dirty things) before you take it apart. On re-assembly, line up the marks and hey presto, it's back together in exactly the same place.

THINGS TO WATCH FOR GOING INSIDE PLASTIC STUFF

Although plastic casings are usually strong in themselves, they may have little hidden tags and clips that hold some parts together which will easily snap if forced. Many plastic items consist of plastic mouldings in two halves like a clamshell, simply held together with screws. Remove the screws and the two parts lift apart. Sometimes though, it's screws at one end and then snap fixings or clips at the other end. You might also find clips or lugs that need sliding or turning slightly before lifting away. The screw part is obvious, but if there are clips etc., they might not be. When separating the casing, knowing where to lever the casing and with how much force to release any clips etc. only comes with trial and error (or bitter experience). Many clips need pushing inwards slightly to release a tiny hook type mechanism.

Start close to where you removed any screws, or if there are slots or indentations. Gently push and pull to see what moves and what is solid. Try carefully inserting an opening tool (see next pic) or a thin blade from a small paint scraper or filling knife into the seam between the parts and lever slightly. A kitchen knife will do in a pinch (don't tell the other half and at least wipe it before putting it back the drawer!).

For now, the best advice when separating plastic parts is to go as gently as you can, keep stopping to look really closely, using a magnifying glass and a torch if needed (seriously, you'd it's amazing how useful these are, and not just for old codgers like me). Sometimes you'll get lucky and the clips will spring apart sometimes you won't, (hey, I'm just being honest!). Never use a screwdriver for levering, unless it's a heavy casing and you can clearly see space for one. Screwdrivers are likely to damage the delicate edges of most casings. Remember, go gently my friend; snapping plastic is a horrible sound...

Once you've removed the fasteners and unclipped the clips and the two parts have initially separated, stop. The side with the fasteners is usually the side you lift away first but be very carefully as you lift it. Keep looking underneath and checking you're not dragging anything out of the lower part, especially wiring, switches, linkages, springs etc.

THINGS TO WATCH FOR GOING INSIDE METAL STUFF

Metal stuff is usually more predictable and not so easily damaged. Fasteners tend to be obvious, bigger, and likely to be of the nut and bolt or screw variety. Although likely to be tight, with the right tools, metal stuff is easy to unfasten (unless they are rusty!).

A few notes about metal stuff...

- Metal is heavy (duh!): You need to support yourself, the tool, and the item properly whilst you undo fixings.

- Fasteners: Undoing tight ones, (that suddenly 'let go') causes more cuts and scrapes than anything else, so brace yourself and hold the wrench in a position where you can control it with both hands if possible. Oh, and watch the wrench position to avoid the wrench slipping off the nut (rounding off the corners in the process).

- Rusty fasteners: Re-read the *Force* section of the *Developing Practical Skills* chapter for more details. In short, soak with a penetrating fluid first (like WD40); tapping with a small hammer to 'break' any rust seal, apply extra leverage and as a last resort, try carefully heating up metal components with a small heat source like a blowtorch if it's safe to do so (no flammable items nearby).

- Captive nuts: These hide in inaccessible areas and often rust. Prevent the captive nut breaking free as it makes removing the bolt near impossible (without resorting to cutting). Use plenty of penetrating fluid and if any bolt gets tight whilst undoing, try going back and forth, as you undo the bolt. For example, undo the bolt ¾ of a turn and then re-tighten ½ a turn. This method clears any obstruction on the thread and prevents bolts seizing or snapping. It's slow but preferable to a sheared captive nut or snapped bolt believe me!

- Left hand threads: Found on rotary stuff like drill shafts or motor spindles. If you find you can't 'undo' a nut, look at the threads sticking out and check them against a regular bolt; are the threads running 'the other way'? If so, reverse the direction to undo. I know, it messes with your head, but they do exist, and they *will* catch you out!

- Overtightening: Be careful when re-assembling metal stuff. You need to stop tightening way before reaching the point where you might 'strip the threads', (often less than you think), especially when tightening into aluminium. (hint: use your new torque wrench!).

BRUTE FORCE AND IGNORANCE

Sometimes stuff just does not play nicely, and you need to resort to brute force or be more heavy-handed than you'd like to get stuff apart. The problem is the ignorance part...

If you know how something goes together and it's just stuck (like a car wheel after removing the nuts) then it's safe to use a heavier force. It's when you're unsure how something fastens together that you can get into trouble, maybe you missed a fixing or maybe there are hidden lugs or catches somewhere and your excess force ends up snapping them.

Be especially careful with cast iron, it's pretty tough as it's usually a thick casting, but it is brittle and will always crack rather than bend if you hit it hard enough, remember to use a soft faced hammer...

Sometimes though, you'll reach an impasse and simply can't move forward because the said item simply won't budge. Then you either stop and seek help from a third party or accept there's a risk you might break the item by going forward. Remember it might be scrap anyway if you don't get it open and find out what's gone wrong. Obviously, this doesn't mean go crazy and yank it apart, you still need to be careful, just keep applying force past where you feel comfortable until something gives. Sometimes you'll be lucky, and the item will pop off without damage, other times, not so much...

WORKING OUT THE LOGIC

So, eventually you're inside and it looks scarily complicated...... but that's fine, it's normal. It'll be all right. Relax, take a deep breath, just remember to go slowly and carefully, and be observant. This is where you learn what really makes stuff work. Let's take a look at the inside this cordless power drill for example...

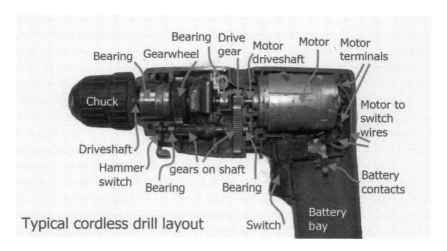

Typical cordless drill layout

Take a moment to look at all the parts logically and try to figure out how things move or work inside here. Look at what the various parts are and what they do in relation to each other. Start with big stuff like the motor; then see if you can follow how the power drives each gear towards the end driveshaft.

Briefly, the power from the battery goes through the contacts into the motor terminals making the motor spin the small gear which turns the large gear and rotates the small shaft. The small gear on the other end of the small shaft then turns the large gearwheel on the main driveshaft and thus the drill chuck rotates. Obviously, the above cordless drill example won't apply if you're working on a wardrobe, but generally, the principle of observation is similar whatever you're looking at. You're trying to follow how stuff operates from start to finish.

Especially look at any moving parts you can see, (motors, linkages, levers, hinges, driveshafts, gears etc. etc.). Try to follow how the power travels through the machine, converting into action and how it gets to the 'other side' to carry out its function. Part A drives part B and so on. Which parts move and how does that affect other parts?

Driving parts are usually a complex system of shafts, gears and levers that transfer the rotary motion of the motor to a specific movement related to the machine.

Most machines convert one kind of energy into another; remember your science lessons at school? Some different examples...

- A manual lawnmower converts a push movement into a rotary movement via gears.

- A jigsaw converts the rotary action of a motor into the up and down movement of the blade.

- A heater forces electricity through thin wires causing them to heat up and glow orange, producing heat.

- Electricity illuminates a bulb by forcing itself through wires so thin, that it causes them to become white hot.

- A spring stores movement energy, ready to release when needed.

- A compressor turns the rotary action of a motor driven piston into air stored under pressure via a one-way valve.

- A computer stores up problems, releasing them when it's calculated to be the most inconvenient time for you... (joking...maybe?)

It's not necessary to understand the full complexity of what you're looking at, but if you can follow roughly what's supposed to happen, you're more likely to notice anything obviously amiss. Stuff such as snapped or broken things, missing stuff, things away from their proper location, or stuff that looks out of place or even just something that intuitively feels wrong.

Look also for any control parts like, switches, valves, dials, sliders, regulators, computer chips, green printed circuit boards, etc. and, where are they? Anything with a wire or pipe going to it is a potential source of problems. Sometimes the smallest of things can stop something large working, especially sensors and valves.

This logical way of looking at something unknown, to broadly work out how stuff looks, moves, and works, is fundamental to being handy.

Remember that exploded diagram that you filed away when you bought the item? Now's the time to dig it out or search online for one.

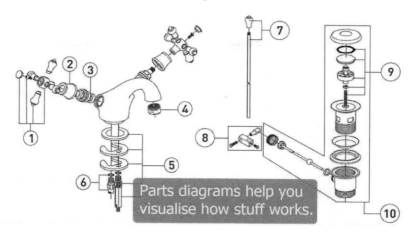

Parts diagrams help you visualise how stuff works.

If you can visualise very roughly how something works, this helps you draw conclusions about how it failed, you have a starting point to diagnose what might have gone wrong and thus how you might fix it.

Oh, and NEVER even think about switching anything on whilst partially dismantled to see what happens, not even low voltage cordless tools, bits will fly all over the place and make you cry...

Let's look at some of the things that can happen inside stuff...

MECHANICAL STUFF

- Linkages can break, bend, or come off their mounting points when retaining clips or mechanisms break.

- Control cables or rods can stretch, snap, or come unsecured at their ends and lose tension.

- Gears can jump, strip their teeth, or rotate freely on their shafts (when the key shears off). Distorted keys are a sure sign of overloading. Keys are usually square or rectangular in cross section but be aware there are such things as offset keys... it's complicated!

- Screws or bolts etc. come undone, strip their threads, or shear off.

- Things seize solid from either rust or lack of lubrication.

- Bearings can break up and fail, (very, very common), sometimes spectacularly.

Sometimes you might have a combination of any of the above, because as one component starts to wear out, it puts excessive load onto connected parts, eventually wearing them out too. Lack of lubrication is a classic; without lubrication, things become stiffer and stiffer until the parts start bending as they try to move. This continual micro flexing, loading, and unloading, causes microscopic damage in the metal (metal fatigue) which grow in size over time until the metal eventually snaps. All for a few drops of oil...

FOREIGN BODIES

No, the CIA hasn't been in your house whilst you were at work; I mean unwanted things inside your stuff that's *definitely* not supposed to be there. Remember the sticky liquids in TV remote controls and mice inside engine bays and so on I mentioned earlier?

Foreign bodies like grit for example, cause havoc with rubber seals or washers, often causing them to leak. Grit also loves to stick to oils, greases, and other lubrication, making a wonderfully abrasive compound, wearing your stuff out in a flash.

Warm or moving things attract dust and other debris and it really builds up over time, especially on fan blades and inside computers etc. Saw dust and building dust is unavoidable for many electrical tools, as the fan pulls in the airborne dust that's inevitably around.

This fan will work much more efficiently without the sawdust!

In addition, some foreign bodies are an 'inside job', when something vibrates loose or breaks, falls inside and jams up the works for example. Look for empty holes or broken linkages etc.

ELECTRONIC STUFF

Obviously, electricity is dangerous so you must ALWAYS unplug anything running on mains voltage electricity before working on it. In addition, wait a few minutes after using the item to allow parts to cool down and for any capacitors (which can hold powerful charges) to dissipate their charge.

Incidentally, a word about capacitors. Lots of common household appliances, such as amplifiers, TV's, some fluorescent tube lamp fittings, microwave ovens, camera flash assemblies, radios, battery chargers etc. have capacitors inside them. Capacitors hold a charge of electricity to help smooth and stabilise power flows through certain circuits. Some capacitors hold onto this charge for some time. Most small capacitors will drain their power quickly. However, some large capacitors can in theory hold their charge for much longer, sometimes days or even weeks.

Capacitors often look like little batteries, and that's because in a way they are, since they do store up electricity. Also, look for anything with a + or a – sign (positive and negative), as they are a sure indicator that power is around, possibly in the form of a capacitor.

If you want to work on a circuit containing a capacitor, it's best to discharge it first. You can buy special resistors and tools for this, but most small capacitors will discharge through a small household bulb and a pair of wires. Be careful to not touch anything else to the capacitor terminals or you might get a direct short, a bang, a flash, hot flying debris and smoke (usually in that order!). I don't recommend directly shorting out a capacitor using a screwdriver, as its unduly cruel to the screwdriver, and the resulting flash/bang will make you jump, and you might hurt yourself...

In addition, you *must* take precautions to prevent static electricity damaging any sensitive electrical parts, (especially computer parts). Read this: en.wikipedia.org/wiki/Antistatic_wrist_strap. Buying a cheap wrist strap to 'ground' yourself is much cheaper than 'losing' a component because of an electrostatic discharge (ESD). Anything with a circuit board is vulnerable; simply clip the strap to the metal case of the machine. Damage to components can occur at voltages well below what you can feel (as a crackly spark) and can it take months before problems manifest themselves.

Some folks leave the component plugged in (to a grounded outlet) and tape the switch in the off position and then touch the bare metal in the case. This will discharge any static, but the thought of having the machine plugged in to a live socket still bothers me. Better to grab a single insulated wire and pop a plug on one end (be 100% sure the wire goes cleanly to the ground or earth pin *very important* and not the live or neutral which will kill you) and the other to a small crocodile clip. Plug in and attach the crocodile clip to the bare metal case and this will carry away any static when you touch the casing.

There are many different types of electrical things, but the internals are often similar; delicate green printed circuit boards covered with unfathomable components (electronic wizardry that tells stuff what to do, called PCB's), lots of spaghetti like wire, some sort of switch plus maybe a motor etc. etc.

WIRING

Wires, wires, and more wires, oh there always so many wires. Wires carry current or power to components for conversion into different forms of energy (movement, heat, light etc.). A wire may be a single core (solid) or made up of many smaller ones twisted together (stranded). Mostly wires have plastic insulation or sometimes rubber sheathing. Different colours identify the wires purpose (live, negative, switch etc.) for an overview about common wiring colours used: http://en.wikipedia.org/wiki/Electrical_wiring (especially since the present confusing system is changing to harmonise colours).

Cable or flex is where you have multiple wires running together inside an outer plastic or rubber 'jacket', typically consisting of a live, a neutral and an earth or ground wire (twin and earth). Inside electrical items you will find single wires in many different colours along with wire tapes (multiple wires in a flat band) and plugs for individual components.

Wires cause problems in several ways...

- Overheating (indicating a problem component) causing blackening/burning of the plastic/rubber insulation.

- Wire insulation becomes hard and brittle with age and/or after mild overheating (e.g. putting a 100W bulb into a 40W rated light fitting).

- Loose wires at the connection point, causing arcing, blackening of contacts or intermittent 'on/off' problems.

- A broken wire at a stressed point (repeatedly bent or stretched). A full stop or intermittent on/off problems (e.g. power tool lead).

- Corrosion on connectors if the item has ever been damp.

- Wires occasionally come adrift completely.

A cheap voltstick will detect live wires and is your last line of defence to protect yourself against electric shocks.

A voltstick is a nifty little tool that detects live cables. It also finds breaks in live cables by sliding the tool along until the light goes out, indicating the location of a break. Always check your voltstick is working by touching it to a nearby live point (a switch or power socket front should work).

As always when working inside any electrical system, you must isolate the part you're working on. Unplugging electrical items or switching off the power in your fuse box. You should isolate the breaker/fuse labelled for the circuits you're working on, then double check you've isolated the right circuit by touching your (tested to be working) voltstick to the part you're working on.

Incidentally, whilst we're talking about wires and overheating...

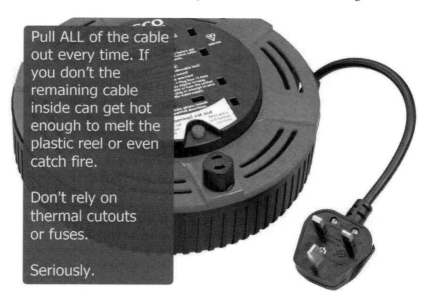

Pull ALL of the cable out every time. If you don't the remaining cable inside can get hot enough to melt the plastic reel or even catch fire.

Don't rely on thermal cutouts or fuses.

Seriously.

PRINTED CIRCUIT BOARDS (PCB'S)

Individual failed components on a PCB need special diagnostic equipment (and the knowledge to understand it!) to find. However, that doesn't stop you looking for anything obvious like blackened or melted components. Check online to see if the failed component is available and/ or an 'easy' replacement to fix. Usually though, the quickest and cheapest repair is to replace the whole PCB. Most boards have plug and socket wiring connections, so carefully pinch and wiggle to disconnect or unplug them and remove any screws holding the board in place. Gently lift out the old PCB and place the new board in its place and re-affix. Carefully locate the wiring plugs over the sockets on the board and firmly push back in.

Sometimes the components are fine, but their connections fail when the solder (the silvery stuff melted around the component pins in the board) 'dries out' and cracks, resulting in arcing. This has happened to stuff in my home twice this year already... (a hob extract fan controller and an under cabinet multi lamp fitting). But this is good news as it's an easy fix.

Look for tiny black sooty deposits or missing solder that looks like 'rings' around component pins. Fix this cheaply by replacing the solder. Gently wipe the soot away with a cloth and dab the pin with a blob of flux (this chemically cleans the new solder joint). Then touch a hot soldering iron to the pin on one side and hold soldering wire to the other. In a second or two (no longer) the solder will 'run'. Lift off the heat immediately or you'll damage the component. Dried out solder joints are a common problem with high load components like control unit PCBs on washing machines.

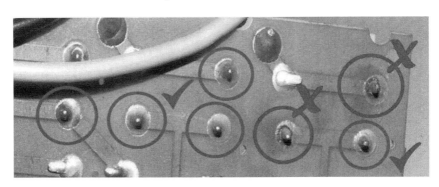

REPAIRING AND REASSEMBLY

Okay, so you've taken it apart, had a look at a few different things and found a problem. It looks like a particular part has failed or broken and you want to make the repair...

REPAIRING INDIVIDUAL BROKEN PARTS

If the problem is mechanical, i.e. something has snapped, cracked, or broken into pieces and the part does a relatively low-stressed job it might be possible to join them back together.

Most folks first thought is to reach for the glue and that's fine for low stressed components. Just make sure it's the specific adhesive for the material you're joining together (i.e. it's critical you read the instructions on usage, especially for plastic types). Things repaired with adhesive often end up a little weaker than the original which is a problem if the item needs to carry any kind of significant or important load.

If you think glue alone might not be strong enough, sometimes it's possible to support glued joints, (if there is room and it's not too aesthetically important) by reinforcing them with additional material. This extra material acts like a brace or splint and increases the surface area of the adhesive or physical fasteners you can use.

Metal is of course weldable (by you or your local engineering shop), but only if the part doesn't take a critical load. Metal undergoes fundamental changes when it stretches to breaking point and snaps. Welding it back together further complicates matters. This would leave highly stressed parts vulnerable to further breaks. Replace anything with a safety function with a whole new part to be safe.

Impromptu repairs: In the field once, (on dirt roads), a broken plastic valence underneath the truck was flapping so much on the rough road, I feared the whole thing would tear off. So, I took a couple of plastic store cards (credit card size) and 'sandwiched' the crack, drilling holes through the plastic and 'stitched' the whole thing together using lots of cable ties, bingo, no more flapping (and I never did get around to a 'permanent' repair!).

Finding a way to re-connect broken parts (temporarily or permanently) often involves some lateral thinking and improvisation...

- Adhesives (regular glues, 'super' glues, epoxy, hot glue etc.), sealants like silicone (it is a fair adhesive). It's important to use the correct one for material you're working with.

- Thin or thick wire, cable ties, string, rope, or other physical restraints work well for temporary or rough repairs in the field and of course, duct tape fixes anything...

- Nails and screws work best on broken timber items (add adhesive for a better repair though). Screws hold well in some plastics too.

- Repair or penny washers are larger than usual washers handy for enlarged or damaged holes. Use in place of the regular washer where a fastener has 'torn' out.

- Flat metal plates, flat angles, metal banding with holes, brackets etc. work well to reinforce thin materials. Screw or bolt in place via the holes, although adhesive works and it's even possible to 'stitch' repair plates in place using wire or cable ties, depending on the item and the broken part.

- Flat plastic plates, angles, brackets etc. work well to repair broken plastic stuff. Glue in place or 'stitch' plates in place using screws, wire, or cable ties etc. (like the plastic valence mentioned above).

- Sometimes it takes a combination of any of the above...

And finally, take your time. Any repair that needs any kind of adhesive runs a real risk of failing again if you put it back into use too soon. Even so called 'fast-setting' adhesives benefit from a longer curing time, 24 hours if possible. I know, I know, most things fail whilst in use and so you need it repaired right now, but unfortunately, it doesn't work that way. Rushing a repair back into service is a sure-fire way to screw up the item permanently, because it's much more difficult to glue something up a second time. Things never go together as well the second time because the first lot of glue is in the way etc.

REPLACING INDIVIDUAL PARTS

If a broken part is a single piece that's simply shaped, it's possible to clone or copy the part to make a new one out of material you might have lying around (remember the materials you saved from old junk before it went in the recycle bin?). Use the original part as a template; draw around it and drill any holes you need first, before you cut it out (it's easier and safer to hold larger things whilst drilling).

In addition to replacing whole parts, sometimes it's necessary to replace a part of a part, i.e. if there is a hole. Find a suitable, similar material and cut out a repair patch larger than the hole. Fix it in place over the hole using a suitable glue, screws, nuts & bolts, rivets, wire, cable ties etc. etc. I once repaired a hole in an exhaust silencer with metal from an opened-out tin of beans, some pop rivets, and a tube of exhaust paste (we were on holiday in the mountains...).

If the part is a complex shape or contains several components etc. you need a new part; then you have one choice to make, whether to go for an OEM part or an aftermarket, (pattern or copy) part...

ORIGINAL EQUIPMENT MANUFACTURER (OEM)

Supplied by the original manufacturers of the item (or by third party specialists brought in by them) and is the costliest option. For your money though, you will get a part guaranteed to fit and to be of the same or better quality than the part you're replacing, you might also get some good fitting advice from the experienced folks at the suppliers who know all about their products inside and out.

Keep in mind that many manufacturers streamline their manufacturing process by buying in parts from specialist suppliers. Therefore, it's possible for a part to be 'original' but stamped with a different name. These specialists are the 'Original Equipment Manufacturer' or OEMs and these parts will be the same or sometimes better (because of improvements in design and progress over time) than the original ones on your machine.

Vehicles for example, may have the braking system manufactured by Lockheed or Brembo, the lighting and engine management equipment manufactured by Lucas, the glass by Pilkington, the gearbox by Getrag, the tyres by Dunlop and so on. Your computer will also have parts from several different OEMs inside; a chip from Intel, or a hard drive from Western Digital for example. This works well because it allows each manufacturer to concentrate on their core business, focussing on their particular USP (unique selling point) and not having to reinvent the wheel (excuse the pun) when someone else already does it better. e.g. I once replaced a worn out NSK (English/Japanese) bearing in a Bosch (German) alternator on a Saab (Swedish) car...

PATTERN OR AFTERMARKET PARTS

Original parts are expensive and on older machines, you might need to find more cost-effective parts to carry out repairs. Plus, many manufacturers only make parts for a certain amount of years after the product ceases production. This is where pattern or aftermarket parts enter the market, usually at a significant discount. However, the quality of some pattern parts does cause fitting problems because of differences in manufacturing tolerances (OEMs are usually higher). Very occasionally, you might have to modify a pattern part slightly to make it fit (filing out a hole for better alignment or clearance for example). Modern manufacturing techniques does mean they're improving every year though.

Again, sticking with vehicles for example, typically, your local motor factor will sell mostly pattern or aftermarket parts and you'd need to go to the vehicles dealership to find original parts.

FITTING REPLACEMENT PARTS

Once you have the replacement part, offer it up to see how it looks using the old part as a reference and of course after reading any instructions supplied, especially exploded parts diagrams. The new part should look the same and turning the part around until it matches the orientation of the original will highlight if there are any differences. Contact the part supplier if something looks awry.

Check any numbers stamped or written on both parts. Again, exploded parts diagrams and parts lists will help here...

To replace a part, you must first remove the original. Obvious huh, but it's amazing how many folks don't pay enough attention when removing the original part. Don't forget the RELEARN method here, look at everything closely, take photos, make notes etc.

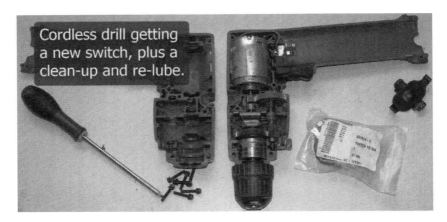

Cordless drill getting a new switch, plus a clean-up and re-lube.

As I mentioned before, it's critical to treat removing the original part as a reverse practise run to show you how to fit the new part, it's the best info you'll ever get. Also, remember the working practises we looked at in the earlier chapters to avoid losing fasteners or crossing threads etc.

When you think you're finished, stop a moment, and mentally go through what you just did, here are a few things to think about...

- Do you (God forbid) have any leftover fasteners?
- Did you double check all the fasteners for tightness?
- Did you test the strength of the repair, by flexing or pulling it etc.?
- Did you try turning or moving the item by hand, before turning on the power to ensure it moves freely? (if applicable).
- And lastly, are you really sure you remembered everything!?
- Okay, time to put the repair to the test and try it out...

HOORAY, IT WORKS, YOU FIXED IT!

Well done you! Time for a well-deserved coffee break or even a beer if it's that time of day...

OH SHOOT, IT'S STILL BUSTED

What can I say? I'm sorry; it happens. Sometimes even with the best of knowledge and intentions, some stuff simply refuses play ball. Sometimes you just can't see why something failed without specialist diagnostic equipment. Or it's one of the increasingly common things with a finite life span. Console yourself with the fact that some stuff just isn't designed to be fixed. And lastly sometimes stuff is just plain worn out and realistically, you never had a chance from the start.

Regretfully then, there comes a time to call it a day, and gracefully admit defeat. However, Auguste Rodin once said, *'Nothing is a waste of time if you use the experience wisely'.* Make failure motivate, not discourage you, because you've gained valuable dismantling experience, plus you now understand a little more about how that particular thing works. Everyone has moments like this; sometimes it's just not sensible to spend any more time trying to repair something. Put it down to experience and get on with something else.

RECOVER ANYTHING USEFUL

All that's left now is to remove and recover any potentially useful things. Cables and plugs, fittings like brackets, handles, hinges, wheels, nuts and bolts or other fasteners. It's even worth saving any usable metal, plastic, or other materials. Fill up your 'bits and bobs' drawer with invaluable stuff to be useful on another repairs and projects.

EXAMPLE: REPAIRING A BROKEN POWER LEAD

Oh, go on then, just this once I'll relent on the 'step-by-step' thing, because my editor says you will want a practical example here!

Repairing a power lead is a good example as it's half repair and half replacement. Power tools fail with monotonous regularity where the cable constantly flexes close to the handle. Eventually the wires break up causing either intermittent operation or a short circuit (with corresponding loud bang and flash of sparks!). If the outer flex/sheathing also breaks open (common), exposing any damaged inner copper cores an electric shock is a real risk. Repair the flex when it first shows signs of damage, usually in the form of intermittent power (turns on/off as you move the item around).

We know from moving the cable around and watching the tool switching on and off as the cable moves and connects/ disconnect the power that one or more of the wires inside the cable have succumbed to metal fatigue and broken.

We can't join the two parts of the wire together again because it's a mess of blackened half melted copper and ruined insulation.

So, we need to replace the broken wire. But wait, you don't need to replace the whole cable, it's just the bit at the end that's broken, right? The remainder of the cable is good, so let's just remove the damaged part at the end and re-wire the 'new' good end of the cable back into the machine (see, half repair half replacement!).

To do that we've got to go inside (it's okay, we looked at that already above, let's go through it again and practise it...). Many power tools have a plastic casing split down the middle like a clamshell. It's usually possible to follow the joints and identify the different sections. Some tools also have front and/or back sections that need removing first before you can part the casing down the middle. Some better-quality tools designed for easy servicing have removable panels for service items like the electric motor brushes that may hide additional fasteners.

The side of the tool with the fasteners is usually the side you carefully lift away first, (once the fasteners are all undone, removed and safely stored to one side). Very carefully lift away the top part, looking and checking you're not dragging anything out of the lower part, especially wiring/linkages/switches/springs etc.

STEP-BY-STEP TO SHOW THE PROCESS

Don't panic if your tool looks completely different though, the whole point of this book is to show you how to figure out the differences yourself. i.e. I show you the fundamentals and then you can work out the details, remember?

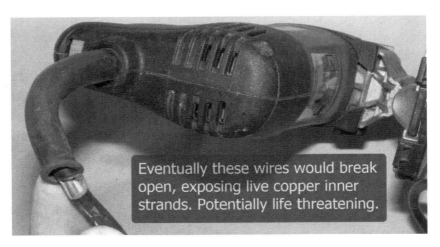

Eventually these wires would break open, exposing live copper inner strands. Potentially life threatening.

First, carefully remove the screws in the top part of the casing and put them somewhere safe, a bowl or plastic container is great. Make a note where any special ones go on a notepad. Alternatively tape them to a rough sketch of the tool in your note pad or push them through a sketch on a piece of cardboard to show their location.

Screws can be very tight on power tools, apply lots of downward pressure to prevent slipping and damaging the screw head.

Then carefully prise the casing open, easing it up a little at a time evenly all the way around with something thin and flexible. I love old kitchen knives but don't use the Sunday best ones, or at least don't get caught...

An old kitchen knife or thin scraper is ideal for gently easing apart the tool casing halves.

Don't force it, if it doesn't come easily, you might have missed a fastener. Go back and make sure you've got them all out. Once the casing starts to come apart a little bit, stop and make sure you're not going to pull out any components in the top half of the casing when you separate them. It's common for stressed items like switches to sit in secure grooves, slots, or indentations (to stop them moving about in repeated use), sometimes they stay in the bottom part and sometimes they want to stay in the top part; keep an eye out for them so that you don't pull out any wires or linkages.

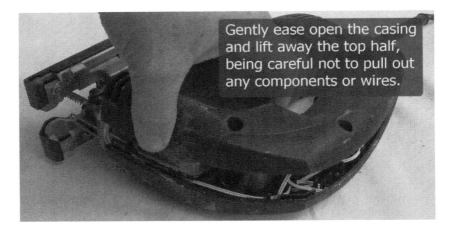

Gently ease open the casing and lift away the top half, being careful not to pull out any components or wires.

Once apart you must take note of which wire goes where, so you can put everything back properly, a photograph works great (apologies as I know this is black and white in the book!). Never, and I mean never, try to remember where the wires go, you *will* forget once you take the old ones out, I promise you. Plus, it only takes a few seconds to take a photo or make a note of where each colour goes. Then remove the cable clamp (plastic 'bridge' with a pair of screws) and follow where each of the wires go.

Take a reference photo like this, to ensure everything goes back in exactly the same place.

Loosen (or remove) the screws from their terminals and carefully lift out the wires. Luckily this tool uses screws. Some tools use solder so briefly touch a hot soldering iron to the terminal to soften the solder and pull out the wire.

Try to disturb as little as possible, there's often tiny components waiting to spring out!

After cutting the damaged section off (around 100mm or 4"), copy the existing cable for length and lightly run a craft knife around the outer insulation, being very careful not to 'nick' or cut the wires inside (you only need to go part way into the outer insulation). Then bend the cable back and forth a little to break the outer insulation fully, it will then slide off easily.

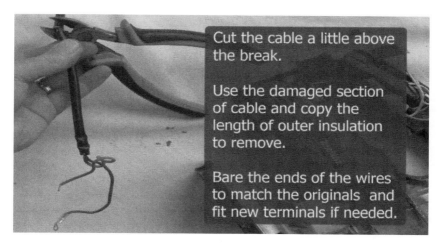

Cut the cable a little above the break.

Use the damaged section of cable and copy the length of outer insulation to remove.

Bare the ends of the wires to match the originals and fit new terminals if needed.

Bare the ends of the inner strands, twist them together with pliers to minimise fraying and re-fit them as per your notes/photograph, tuck everything back into its proper place and refit the cable clamp not forgetting the rubber protective boot (you'll forget the first time probably!).

If you want, make new solid ends to your twisted inner wires by touching a hot soldering iron to them and adding a touch of solder. Solid ends mean no stray strands of wire and they tighten up lovely.

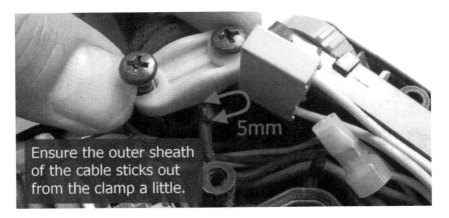

5mm

Ensure the outer sheath of the cable sticks out from the clamp a little.

Re-fit the casing in reverse order, being careful not to trap anything. Check the casing joint between the two halves afterwards for gaps. A gap, or if the casing needs pressure to close, means something inside hasn't seated properly or you've trapped a cable etc. Once happy that everything is back where it belongs and the casings fits together snuggly, replace the screws, following any notes you made, and gently tighten. Fully tighten the screws and check the tool operates normally.

REPAIRING DIFFERENT MATERIALS

All good? Okay, now let's look at some repair techniques and tips for a few of the materials you'll find around your home. Some of this overlaps with the examples given above, but repetition is good practise remember...

TIMBER REPAIRS

Timber breaks, it even disappears completely sometimes, i.e. it rots! You can repair some broken timber with glues or mechanical fasteners but in some cases, it's easier to replace the whole part. When timber rots you'll either cut out the bad section and splice in new timber or replace the whole length depending on where it is and whether it's carrying a high load.

There are three main ways to repair broken timber items, glue, mechanical fixings and fasteners or replacement of the whole section. In most cases glue is the most obvious, especially to repair 'dry joints' which is a glued joint broken apart by stress. A chair leg being the classic example. Try to scrape the residue of old glue away to create a tiny space for the new glue to go. Use a knife blade or wood chisel held at 90° to the wood and scrape along the grain, front to back, which will peel off just enough glue to be able to re-glue the joint together again. Blow away the dust before applying a little glue to all faces and pushing the parts back together again. Use clamps, stretched duct tape for awkward shaped things, or the tourniquet clamp (pictured below) to hold the joint until set. Wipe away the glue as soon as you've clamped as it's difficult to remove once its fully set, a damp rag works well for normal 'white' wood glues.

Make your own powerful tourniquet clamps using some cord and a stick.

Simply tie the cord around and thread the stick through and wind it up, wedging the stick once tight (sometimes called a 'Spanish windlass').

Always use a suitable glue for the environment in which the repaired timber will live and read the instructions on your glue to determine its suitability for the job. There are glues for; indoors, outdoors, cold weather, waterproof, gap filling, UV resistant, animal glues, two-part resin glues, marine proof, and fast drying to name a few. Remember also that glue needs contact with the actual wood fibres, so remove any paint etc. in the way using a scraper or chisel as I mentioned above.

For broken timber, remember that it takes a lot of built up stress to snap a piece of timber, which tears up the grain around the break terribly. The trick when repairing these breaks with glue, is to fit the components together dry first, using a clamp if necessary, to try and push all the torn and twisted grain back into shape. Pull out any small splintering preventing the pieces coming together for an exact fit. These broken 'joints' often go back together like interlocked fingers so it's crucial you spend some time making sure everything goes back in the right place before applying glue. There is nothing worse than assembling something all covered in glue only to find that it will not go together or align properly. You end up covered in the stuff and that will make you grumpy, so always try it first.

Then apply your glue, usually sparingly, following any instructions on the packet, and clamp together until it's dry, (a few minutes up to 24 hours depending on the glue).

Mechanical repairs to timber consists of nails, screws, nuts, and bolts or even metal plates. Use these where timber parts have come apart or adrift; nails for lose trims etc. Screws for holding two pieces of timber together in more stressed locations or on things that move. Use lag screws or nuts and bolts to repair larger timbers or structural beams etc. Fixing up an old tree house? Then use these big fasteners and not thin screws or nails which don't resist movement very well and will eventually snap if flexed a few times under wind and children type loads.

Use metal brackets, hangers, banding, plates, and angles etc. nailed or screwed over or around broken sections of timber to reinforce them. All shapes and sizes are available, see the *Timber Connectors or Hardware* section in the *Fixings, Fasteners, and Hardware Chapter* for more info.

DINGS, DENTS, SCRATCHES, AND GOUGES

If the timber is bare or oiled (or you can sand away any hard finishes) you can lift out shallow dents by placing a damp cloth over the damage and rubbing a hot iron over the damage. Wait a minute in between rubs to give the fibres time to swell. Repeat as necessary. The hot steam swells the fibres, lifting them up. Sand and refinish as required. This method is also worth a try on scratches too, it won't hide any cut fibres, but it will lift any compressed ones making the damage smaller and therefore less visible.

Once you've lifted the fibres as much as you can, you'll need to visit your local paint store who'll be your new best friend and sell you some 'magic' wax type sticks, perfect for hiding scratches and small imperfections etc. There are various colours (even white to repair dings in melamine/cabinets etc.), and you might need to mix two together to get the exact match. Simply work the warmed coloured wax into the mark and scrape off any excess with a flat blade. A rag dipped in a spirit will tidy up the edges if it smeared a little. I've even seen children's wax crayons or even shoe polish used to good effect, hiding small imperfections, ideal for after those 'parents are away parties' (whistles innocently...).

Any timber with big gouges etc. or a hard painted/ lacquered finish is a more complex repair as the above methods won't work. Your only recourse is to fill the area with a suitable wood filler (colour matched on lacquered finishes), let it dry, sand it flat and re-apply the finish to the piece. For non-paint finishes like wood stain etc., check the filler is 'stainable', i.e. it will take up the colour you're applying. Some fillers don't take up colour very well, if at all and are for use under solid paint colours.

VULNERABLE TIMBER

Because your timber was once a living thing, it can't wait to complete its natural cycle, i.e. go rotten. However, conditions need to be just right for timber to decay; e.g. moisture and air (warmth will speed up the process too). Any timber getting close to or above 20% moisture content is at risk of rot...

- Any timber close to the ground is vulnerable (fencing, outdoor screens, timber cladding, wooden furniture etc.).

- Any timber in contact with masonry affected by damp (penetrating rain or water rising from the ground) is at risk (floor joists, roof timbers, water leaks etc.).

- Timber with defective protective coatings won't last long either, (usually stuff almost out of sight), fascia boards, window and doorframe bottoms are classic examples and worth checking regularly for soft spots with a firm press of the thumb.

- Any timber close to potential sources of water, external doors, cabinets under washbasins, trims around sinks, showers, baths, toilets, washing machines, dishwashers etc.

In non-structural stuff, it's often possible to replace just the rotten or broken sections of timber...

- Remove anything in the way like glass or hardware.

- Just above the rot, saw upwards at 45° from front to back as this creates a larger area for the glue; makes it easier to use screws or nails to fasten in the new piece, plus it makes for a weatherproof joint between the old and new timber (if outside).

- Remove the rotten wood and clean up.

- ◖▸ Copy the parts you removed or measure out and cut a new piece of timber. Try it for size and adjustment with the saw/plane/chisel until it fits well.

- ◖▸ Apply a coat or two of primer or wood preservative to the new piece and onto the cut areas of the item you're repairing.

- ◖▸ Preferably glue (or screw or nail) the new piece carefully into place and clamp or duct tape up until the glue sets.

- ◖▸ Replace anything you removed to affect the repair and any coatings.

If you have the time and patience, it's rare for timber stuff to be beyond repair. In addition, the material cost of repairing the rotten bottom of a window frame for example, is peanuts when compared to the replacement cost of the whole window. Repairing this way is time consuming though, hence most professionals recommending complete replacement because it's cheaper to quickly replace a window (for example) rather than spend a day or even two, repairing the old one.

On structural timber, such as a rotten floor joist for example, it's best to replace the whole piece if possible, although you can sometimes replace rotten timber with new and then and then add new timber either side to reinforce the joint (you're close to needing a structural engineer here though).

Remember also from the maintenance chapter that damp timber will also attract insects who'd like nothing better than to chomp up your home.

Don't forget also to find out and fix what caused the problem in the first place. It would be crazy to spend a couple of days repairing a rotten window and then ignore the leaking gutter that caused its eventual demise (remember my leaking gutter story earlier?).

MASONRY REPAIRS

You don't generally hear the word masonry in everyday language (unless you're into rolling up your trousers in dim temples, full of apron wearing, dark suited men...), but it's a great word to collect together all the different ways there are to build walls. I'll use the word from here on for clarity, but the principles are quite similar for stone or brick or block or clay, lime-based mortars or cement-based mortars etc.

Masonry usually 'fails' in two main ways; movement, i.e. settling of part or all of the wall, or erosion, (either of the mortar joints and/or spalling of the material face). Both failures are more prevalent in older walls. Newer cavity walls (brick or stone outer leaf & block inner leaf) sit on deeper concrete strip footings where movement is less likely, and the durable cement-based mortars probably don't need re-pointing (yet). Thus, I'll concentrate on older walls here. However, if you do have cracked/frost damaged/ settled bricks in a modern cement mortar-based wall, the principles are similar.

Generally then, walls built between the fifteenth century and the Second World War walls (in the UK at least) used a lime based mortar (softer mortar, easily scraped out with a screwdriver or even a fingernail) and are usually solid (i.e. one brick thick/ two half bricks thick, (or more on larger structures), with no air gap or cavity). Even the youngest of these walls are getting on for 100 years old now and many will need repairs, especially if maintenance has been lacking over the decades. Some may also have been in appropriately repaired with cement-based products before the true horrors of using cement on old walls were fully realised. Some common problems then...

SUBSIDENCE AND SETTLEMENT

Earlier, footing courses (wide, stepped brickwork), built straight onto the soil in a trench, were 'not quite deep enough' to prevent movement. Nowadays a rigid layer of concrete (footings) laid deep into good weight bearing subsoil, (averagely around 1m deep) means *subsidence* or even minor *settlement* is less of an issue with modern homes.

An older, 'softer' built house, (for want of a better description), is moving all the time (don't panic!); settling into the ground under its own weight and moving with the soils seasonal shifting. But don't worry, it's perfectly normal, as are a few hairline cracks here and there in the mortar joints (learn to live with them if they are not causing a problem). Most cracks are not too much of a worry, especially if they are old and stable. However, if they are allowing rain to penetrate, (creating dampness inside), you should rake the mortar joints out and re-point them (learn how a bit later on in this chapter).

Serious movement causing large cracks or shear cracks heads into territory called subsidence, which strikes fear into the most hardened of hearts and for good reason. It's advisable to borrow the eye of a structural engineer to ensure you've got all the factors covered here, because the underlying cause could be a complicated combination of factors.

First, monitor any large cracks using the *tell tales* we looked at earlier in *Maintaining Masonry,* to see if the movement is 'live' and ongoing, i.e. getting worse. This may take 12 months (to go through all seasons).

Any 'shear' cracks running in straight lines through the bricks and joints are always serious and need repairing. The solution is to replace all the cracked bricks, effectively 'stitching' the wall back together.

But first you need to fix the underlying problem, it could be...

- Trees. If walls fall within their "zone of influence" i.e. if a tree is too big and close to the wall it may cause problems. Either by ground movement because of water movement or physical problems from roots.

- Drains, laid poorly or otherwise damaged will leak, pulling away soil and washing it away from under your walls.

- Leaking water pipes, washing away soil from nearby walls.

- Flood damage causes the ground to swell and then shrink destabilising the ground around your home.

- Bad construction, poor design, poor foundations, unskilled builders, or weak material choice, (dodgy builders are not a new problem!).

If a foundation under a wall has lost support, the repair is to underpin the foundation. Typically, you'd dig down underneath the wall/foundation in sections and 'underpin' the original foundations with concrete or if extending downwards (to create a basement etc.), you'd pour a new *concrete strip footing* and then build a wall up to the old brick footings. It's becoming common to add a new floor underneath a house this way (popular in big cities where land is expensive and space is at a premium).

Underpinning is difficult, cramped, dirty and knuckle skinning work for sure. I have a friend who does this full time and his mini-truck is full of spades, shovels, pick axes, rakes etc. all with short handles (because there's not much space to dig), he used to say he bought the truck and tools off a gnome!

Be aware also that genuine subsidence is something your home insurance may pay for, but it comes with a downside, it may affect your ability to obtain insurance in the future and even our ability to sell the property (future purchasers may find it difficult to obtain a mortgage).

Complete large repairs to a sagging wall in sequential bays. i.e. dig out and concrete bays of the same number at the same time; both bay 1's to start with followed by the bay 2's etc.

You'll need to devise a method of linking each bay together, usually by driving short steel reinforcing rods into the sides of each hole so that the bars end up half in the bay you're working on and then you'll find the other half sticking out of the concrete when you dig out the adjacent bays. The plan view below shows you a typical underpinning plan...

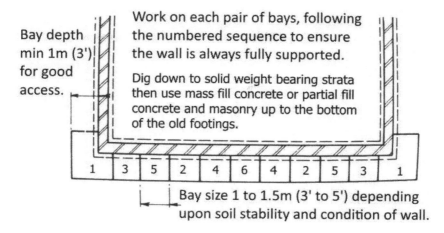

Bay depth min 1m (3') for good access.

Work on each pair of bays, following the numbered sequence to ensure the wall is always fully supported.

Dig down to solid weight bearing strata then use mass fill concrete or partial fill concrete and masonry up to the bottom of the old footings.

| 1 | 3 | 5 | 2 | 4 | 6 | 4 | 2 | 5 | 3 | 1 |

Bay size 1 to 1.5m (3' to 5') depending upon soil stability and condition of wall.

...and this next image shows the cross section or side view through the new foundations showing a typical bay excavation...

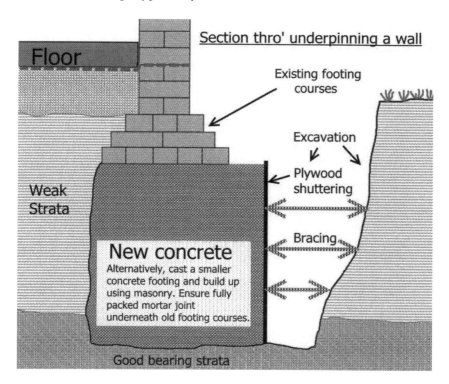

Section thro' underpinning a wall

Floor

Existing footing courses

Excavation

Plywood shuttering

Weak Strata

New concrete
Alternatively, cast a smaller concrete footing and build up using masonry. Ensure fully packed mortar joint underneath old footing courses.

Bracing

Good bearing strata

EROSION OF LIME MORTAR JOINTS

Lime mortar joints are sacrificial by design, i.e. any moisture trapped in the wall should evaporate from the joint, so don't panic if your mortar joints are eroding, they're supposed to. Many people really worry about this, but it's much better for the wall for moisture to evaporate from the joints, as this protects the bricks which are much more difficult to replace or repair.

Generally, re-pointing your mortar joints in a matching mortar can wait until the joints have eroded at least 13mm (1/2″) and *not* a moment before; the only exception being if a particularly exposed wall is letting water penetrate through to the inside, causing damp issues. Re-pointing using lime mortar is a perfect DIY proposition, despite the fear lime mortar evokes amongst even professional tradesman. Working slow and carefully suits lime mortar (due to its long setting time) making it a perfect project for you.

There's plenty of free advice about lime mortar out there, much of it from local authorities or conservation organisations (see the resources section in appendices 1). Alternatively, if you have a specific query, you can call the very helpful guys at SPAB (Society for the Protection of Ancient Buildings) who are total hero's regarding lime mortar, they are probably all devilishly handsome too, so give them a call... On historically valuable brickwork you might want to get a sample of the mortar tested, then design a mortar which exactly matches the existing stuff (as far as you can).

Remember to *never, ever* use a cement-based mortar to repair a wall built using lime-mortar, because it forces moisture inside the wall to evaporate from the brick itself, which then freezes etc. often causing spalling of the brick face, especially the edges...

Any yes, I know the wall will look great to start with and might even look great for years, decades even, but over long periods of time, the hard pointing will damage the edges of the soft bricks due to the movement going on in the softer lime mortar in the wall (rant over!).

To re-point typical mortar joints...

- Only carry out these repairs in warm, clement weather.

- Rake out any loose mortar with a narrow, sharp implement until the joint is typically almost twice as deep as it is tall. 19mm (¾″) is common on average joints. Ensure your raking out leaves nice clean, square back corners and is a minimum of 13mm (½″) deep.

  (Usually if you need to use a grinding wheel to cut the mortar out, you should ask yourself "why am I re-pointing this?").

  The exception to the above is if the wall's been 'repaired' with cement mortar. Carefully cut in the middle of the mortar joint using a thin cutting blade (not the thick grinding blades). Gently chip out the cement mortar using a thin bolster or plugging chisel along with a small hammer or mallet. Avoiding damage to the delicate brick edges needs care so take your time.

- Wash the joints out with water, starting at the top of the area, this leaves the joints nicely damp. Don't go crazy and totally saturate the wall, nicely damp is the aim. A fancy head for your hosepipe works well, use a fine setting which delivers less water, i.e. not 'soaker'.

- Mix up your special mortar mix, alternatively a common lime mortar mix 1:2 ½ lime and sieved sharp sand (particle size from dust up to around a third of the average mortar joint height, e.g. 0.1mm to 3mm). Measure your ratios (1:2 ½) it MUST be accurate, no guessing with a shovel, the mix will always be too weak...

- Make sure your mortar is not 'sloppy'. 'Too wet' mortar will be difficult to get into the joints without staining the brick face. Re-pointing mortar is a much drier mix than bricklaying mortar for example.

- Dampen joints again with a fine mist from a sprayer/pipe if it's dry.

- Push the well mixed lime mortar into the joints using a narrow 'finger' trowel. Push and pack it right into the back of the joint and fill up to the front of the bricks. Scrape off flush with the brick face.

- Wait for the mortar to set quite firm (a few hours normally) and then 'tap, tap, tap' the face of each joint with the stiff bristles of a 'churn' brush. This compacts the joint and leaves a rustic finish to the joint face. Finish off with a light brush over with a soft bristled brush.

- Cover down with hessian or fleece and a polythene layer. Keep damp for at least a week, misting daily if warm.

That's it, re-pointing old walls; nothing frightening at all. Now you can go and do it for your neighbour down the road and earn a small fortune...

REPLACING SPALLED OR DAMAGED BRICKS

Spalling is when the surface of the brick crumbles away, usually in highly exposed locations subject to lots of water and/or freezing temps. As we looked at above, hard cement mortar re-pointing also causes spalling because moisture evaporating from bricks eventually damages them. Replace spalled bricks as soon as possible to prevent water getting further into the wall and causing damp problems on the plasterwork inside the house.

Fortunately, it's relatively easy to chip out the old lime mortar surrounding each brick (using a plugging chisel and hammer); if your mortar is harder than average though, consider first drilling a series of holes close together around the brick using a thin masonry bit in your drill. I often use a thin cutting disc in a grinder to cut the joints, because I find it relieves pressure on the brick's edges and I'm less likely to chip bricks when removing the mortar. However, be aware it takes a lot of control (read skill) to use a grinder without catching the bricks here and there (therefore it's frowned upon to use grinders on historic brickwork for that very reason). Once the mortar is mostly all out the brick will wiggle free, (not on its own, don't panic, it's not going to jump up and run away...), just work at it, back and forth till it's free.

Alternatively, if you're not going to re-use the same brick, break it up with a club hammer and cold chisel or small bolster. Ensure you're always chopping in towards the middle of the brick and never, and I mean *never*, lever (or even touch) the chisel against the edges of the surrounding bricks to try and lever a piece out, *you will chip them...* 100% guaranteed. Some folks hit the brick directly with the hammer a few times to 'break it up', this does work, if you're an accurate shot and sure you're going to hit the right brick...

Unfortunately though, even with the best will in the world, occasionally a brick surrounding the bricks you're removing will chip by accident. Just remove that one as well, it's no biggie usually...

Once everything is out, clean, scrape and chop away all traces of old mortar (and I mean all!) and damp down the hole with a garden sprayer. Sometimes you can turn the existing bricks around (if they're still solid and the rear face is a good match) and re-bed it using a suitable matching lime mortar (the 1:2 ½ lime and sieved sharp sand is okay for this too). Alternatively replace with a matching brick. Finish off the mortar joints the same way as you did with the re-pointing above, including the protection and keeping damp for a week or so.

Damage removed, cleaned out and ready for damping down prior to re-building.

Complete larger areas of damage in one go, up to one metre wide is self-supporting in areas of walling (like the previous image), but if there are additional factors, such as a corner or underneath a window etc. add additional support using adjustable steel props etc. for the duration of the repair.

Cut bricks with a hammer and bolster chisel; practise on a sand bag for best results (and never on a hard surface like concrete, it'll make the break unpredictable). Once you're more skilled with old bricks you'll find they cut easily with a special brick hammer, or even the edge of your trowel if you're a bit of an animal! Shape special cuts with a scutch hammer (a hammer with replaceable toothed and straight blades perfect for chipping small amounts of brick away). You can also cut bricks with a large grinder (but it's difficult to hold the brick securely and safely) or even hire a wet cutting table mounted saw.

One very important last thing; ensure the last or top joint is completely full of mortar. It's my pet hate to see just the front edge filled in. Yes, I know it's difficult and time consuming to push little bits of mortar all the way to the back and pack the joint solidly, but really, if you don't, the replaced bricks will not hold the weight above, quite literally...

Use a finger trowel slightly thinner than the joint (I custom make my own by cutting down cheap pointing trowels), push the mortar onto the top of the brick and then to the right, packing it tight, all the way to the back, repeat until the whole joint is full. Hint: it takes a while and lots, and lots of finger trowels full of mortar to do properly.

RENDER REPAIRS

A common wall finish is a flat or textured coating broadly called 'render' (or stucco). These can be 'self-coloured', painted or even have small stones embedded into the coating. Tap the render gently to check for good adhesion to the wall. Any loose or flaking areas need repairing after rectifying what caused the failure in the first place, (usually water and/or frost getting behind the render). Avoid using steel trims to form new edges or corners in render repairs as they'll eventually rust (even the galvanised ones), blowing off the render. Use the more expensive stainless-steel trims or better still, render up to a temporary shuttering, (a piece of flat timber) instead, doing one side at a time (this costs nothing and there's no metal to go rusty...).

Repair by applying two coats of mortar; (or more if the wall is not flat). Don't make the mix too strong (too many folks do). For the first or coat, I like a 1:1:5 ratio (100% accurately gauged in a small bucket) consisting of one cement: one builders lime: and five plastering sand (bit coarser than bricklaying sand) and a 1:1:6 for the second, finish coat (one extra sand), when rendering on cement based walls. For lime-built walls ditch the cement and mix one-part lime to 2 ½ parts well graded sharp sand for good results. You'll get advice from your local sand supplier/ builders' merchant about which sand is best for rendering in your area (you might have to use soft building sand mixed with a little sharp sand if there is no specific plastering sand).

Many folks like to use special rendering additives to the mortar mix as they make the mix more workable, slow down the setting time and add waterproofing qualities. Personally, I think they are a good idea used correctly in troublesome damp spots, but used incorrectly they could cause more problems than they solve since they don't allow the wall to 'breathe'...

A brief overview on how to repair a patch of blown render...

- Gently chop back to sound render using a small bolster and a hammer, irregular repair shapes are technically fine, if not aesthetically brilliant. You'll likely do more damage hacking off good render to make the repair 'square'. You can make shallow cuts with a mini grinder to help, but don't go into the bricks.

- Ensure the wall is free of loose mortar or dust and rake any loose mortar out of the joints.

- Damp the wall down before rendering it. The wall should 'look' wet but not be running with water.

- 'Dub' out any deep hollow spots. Your first full coat of mortar needs to be a uniform thickness to aid even drying (thick and thin areas dry at different rates and can lift away from the wall).

- Apply the first coat of mortar onto the wall, starting at the bottom and aim for around 10mm (⅜″) thick mortar. Apply a square meter or so each time, then...

- Use a plasterer's straight edge or straight piece of timber to 'rule' the excess off. Drag both ways across the mortar. Work from one 'square' onto and across the new one to flatten out the mortar as you work across the wall.

- The above straight edge will highlight any low spots, fill them in with a little more mortar and rule it off again; repeat as many times as necessary to get the mortar flat and even.

- Once the mortar has hardened up a little, rub a plasterer's 'float' over the surface in a circular motion. This rubs off micro high spots and fills any micro low spots.

- If the mortar drags under the float, it's still too wet. If it skids over the surface, it's too dry (flick some water on it and work like heck. Oh, and next time keep a better eye on the setting up time...).

- Once this first coat has started to harden off (time varies on weather, temperature and humidity, some hours generally), gently scratch the surface to provide a key for the next coat. You can use a special 'comb' type pronged scratcher or make one from stiff wire or popping 3 or 4 thin nails through a float (devils float). Gently create wavy lines in the surface of the mortar or go at 45° both ways to create a diamond shaped pattern. Not too deep and never through to the wall. Adjust the 'scratcher' to ensure all the scratches are the same depth.

- Allow the scratch coat to dry out a little. Generally overnight, it depends on the thickness of the render, plus of course on the weather, temperature, and humidity again. Don't worry about any light shrinkage or cracking and don't try to 'correct' them, (no need).

- Slow is good when allowing the scratch coat to dry out. Keep humidity high and draughts out.

- It's ready when you can't dent the surface with your thumb. The surface should still be slightly damp and usually only needs a fine spray of water from a garden sprayer before applying the second coat. If too dry keep wetting it until the surface stays damp looking.

- Knock up your mortar and trowel it on around 6mm (1/4″) to 10mm (⅜″) or so on top of the first coat, spreading and flattening it out a little as you apply it. Once you have completed a small area, (say a square yard or metre) use a plasterer's aluminium feather edge board and run it over your newly plastered area both ways (up and down and side to side) to 'rule it' flat again.

- Use any existing surrounding areas of render as a guide for your new mortar. If the patch is small with old render either side, you're lucky. Use a suitably long straight edge to rule the area off (maybe with a side to side sawing motion) making sure you keep the ends of the straight-edge on the old render as a guide. Repeat to fill in any low spots.

- Once this second coat has started to harden off (time varies on temperature and humidity, a few hours generally) this second coat needs finishing off. This is the process of working in a circular motion using a wooden float gently pressing and rubbing at the same time. This will work up a little softness in the surface, removing mortar from remaining high spots and rubbing it into the low spots. You may need to add little 'gobs' of mortar here and there as you notice little circles in the surface pointing out especially low spots. Splash a little water onto the surface if it's dry in places (but not too much).

- Usually the top or anywhere catching the breeze will be ready slightly before the centre, but again, the wet stuff will let you know as the float drags and digs in the stuff that's too wet and skates over too dry areas.

- Finish off the surface with a damp sponge or a final swirly finish straight from the float for more texture.

The above is to repair straight, flat render; add textured finishes like Tyrolean once it's dried, except pebble dashing where you gently hurl small stones directly into the wet mortar. If you don't like the patchy look of spot repairs, then use a good quality masonry paint to even up the colour, you can even get it grey/ mortar coloured if you want it to look natural...

ROOF REPAIRS

The first inkling most folks get that their roof needs repairing is when it lets rainwater into the house during a particularly nasty storm. It's not surprising that folks neglect their roof; it's up there, largely out of sight and often out of mind. But you of course will be checking yours annually, yes?

How you carry out repairs depends on how old the existing roof coverings are and the material it's made from. Any roof without an underlay (if you can see the tiles from inside the attic space) would benefit greatly by replacing the whole thing. If you're carrying out repairs every year, it sounds like the roof needs replacing. Don't end up replacing the roof one tile at a time over the years, spending as much time and money on repairs as it would cost to just replace the whole thing in one go. An added benefit is the opportunity to upgrade the insulation during roof replacement (over 250mm or 10″ is best).

I don't need to tell you that the main problem repairing or replacing a roof covering isn't the covering itself, you'll learn that part easily. No, it's just that the roof covering is, well; on the roof (duh!), but there is the problem right there, access, or rather, the lack of it.

Ladders are fine to replace a slipped tile on the first half meter or couple of feet, but after that you'll need a roof crawler ladder to get higher up. These are hard to get into position on the roof as you are standing on the top of a ladder yourself. It's imperative you tie the ladder you're standing on to a secure point (and possibly even to hook a leg through the ladder and over a rung to stabilise yourself). Once you've hooked the crawler over the ridge, tie the foot of the crawler to the ladder. If there isn't anything to tie the ladder to, drill a hole in the wall or eaves timberwork and install a proper eye. Much cheaper than a stay in hospital...

Even properly secured, working from a crawler requires a huge amount of confidence at height, and is arguably still inherently dangerous. Fall arrest gear and a harness is difficult to employ as there is little to secure them to, although I've seen a rope thrown over the roof from the opposite side and used to secure a fall arrest kit, but still, it's risky.

Scaffolding is a much better option for anything more than a few slipped tiles or a dislodged flashing and indeed might be required under health and safety law in some circumstances and countries.

ROOF COVERINGS

You'll need to find exact replacements to repair missing material from your roof. This may prove problematical on older roofs; most likely you'll need to find a reclamation yard near you. Some common roofing types you'll see are...

- Concrete tiles, flat plain tiles, pan tiles or double pan styles.
- Clay tiles, pan tiles, half round or flat plain tiles.
- Slate. Often thin, flat oblongs of numerous different sizes.
- Flat roofs. Built up felt, asphalt, fibreglass, rubber sheet, etc.
- Plastic. Corrugated or flat twin or triple wall (usually on conservatories or car ports etc.).

And some not quite so common ones...

- Shingles. Felt or timber.
- Metal sheet. Copper, Lead (think churches), plastic coated steel etc.
- Metal sheets pressed to mimic large squares of pan tiles.
- Corrugated roofs. Metal or cement fibre etc.
- Thatch, reed, or straw.

Replace a concrete or plain tile, by pushing up the row above a little. If the tiles have nails holding them in place, use door stops or wooden wedges to hold up surrounding tiles slightly instead. Wiggle out any broken pieces and pop the new one in. Pull down the row above or remove the wedges. Jiggle (technical term!) all the tiles around the new one to ensure everything seats properly and lays flat. You'll need a small trowel to lift up the tiles enough to get your fingers underneath. A pair of gloves is handy unless you've hands like a gorilla and don't need to worry about snagging anyone's stockings...

Slates are more complicated as they are triple layered with hidden fasteners to keep out rain. You'll need a special tool called a *slate rip* to remove the remaining part of the tile (they usually break across the nail holes) plus the old nails. Slide up underneath the broken tile and hook the nails each side. A sharp pull downwards will pull out or cut off the nails. Once the old bit of tile and nails are out, using a heavy gauge stainless steel or copper wire strip, form a tight bend in the end and nail it into the lath between the two underlying slates. Form a second small hook on the bottom, about level with the bottom of the neighbouring slates (you'll need to do this with a pair of pliers; if you can do it by hand the wire probably isn't strong enough...). Slide the new slate into place over the wire and wiggle it back down into the small hook. Sometimes it's difficult to get the new tile all the way in, so slide the slate rip up first, at an angle, and then slide the slate on top of it, the rip will guide the slate up and onto the top lath. Avoid using copper strips or even worse, lead strips for this, snow and time will open them out, which obviously allows the replacement slate to slide out again (I see this an awful lot!).

In general, use aluminium nails for fastening roof tiles as they are much softer than steel nails, this avoids cracking the tile on the last couple of hits. It's traditional to use copper nails for slate though. You don't need to hammer them in really tight (you'll still risk cracking the tile, leading it to fail after a short time), just lightly up to the tile is usually sufficient.

RIDGE TILES

Ridge tiles are most prone to blowing off during storms if the holding mortar is too weak (phenomenally common) or very old. Traditionally, strong mortar holds ridge tiles in place. Replace new ones by bedding them in a stiff (sloppy mortar will slump) mortar mix consisting of 1:1:2, cement/sharp sand/soft sand. Place broken bits of tile underneath the gaps in between ridge tiles to support the mortar used to point up the joints. There is little point in 'pointing up' over old mortar, if you can lift the ridge tile off by hand, do so, clean it up and re-bed it instead. If you can't lift the tile off by hand, then leave them alone and go fishing instead.

The modern trend is heading towards dry fixing methods (nails, clips, and wires) so expect to see mortar disappear for good on roofs in the future.

FLASHINGS

A major source of roof leaks stem from misplaced or poor flashings around anything protruding through or abutting the roof covering. If not properly secured into a brickwork joint, the wind, sun, and frost will, over time, pull the lead or metal pieces out of the joint. Push and dress the metalwork back into place using lead dressing tools or a small piece of timber and a light hammer. Tap the small folded down tab into the brick joint and ensure its firmly in place on top of the brick edge below. Hold in place with clips and point up the brickwork joint using a special tubed joint sealant. Traditionally, we used to do this with small rolls of lead hammered into the joint and then point up the joint with a stiff mortar (not officially recommended nowadays).

VALLEYS AND TROUGHS

Traditionally you'd form a valley out of short sections of lead sheet dressed onto a timber underlay with small angled fillets of timber either side to form a barrier to stop water running through and into the roof. Plastic or glass reinforced plastic is also a common material for valleys.

Flat troughs (or gutters) in between pairs of sloped roofs usually have small steps every metre (3' or so) to form drips and prevent large areas of lead.

Lead and plastic are both thermally unstable, i.e. they expand and contract a lot when they are hot or cold; this can cause cracks in pieces which are too large to cope with the build-up of stress.

Weld cracks in plastic (see plastic section later on) or use a proprietary sealant either directly over the crack or to stick a patch over it.

It is possible to weld cracks in lead sheet, but to be honest, cracked lead most likely means it's improperly installed. Either the lengths of lead are too long, or the gauge is too thin or held too securely (nailed in too many places). Any of the above means it will probably crack again, possibly somewhere else. Plus, it's quite a difficult skill to learn and would entail a lot of practise and an expensive specialised burning tool to melt the lead sticks. Use sealant as a short-term crack repair in emergencies (to protect the roof timbers), until a proper and permanent repair is possible (usually complete replacement).

A better but more time-consuming repair is to remove the tiles either side of the valley and replace the lead sheet. To give lead sheet room to move, nail only the head or top of short lengths of lead (never any longer than 1.5m or 4' 6") working up from the bottom of the valley. One long strip of lead will eventually crack and leak (even if you think having no joints is a good idea...).

Lead comes in different thicknesses depending on the location and use. The bigger the area, the thicker the sheet. Learn how to install lead properly, google "Calder: Guide to Good Lead Work' and download their free guide.

Chances are that old valleys and troughs have been leaking for a while which means the supporting timber underneath and the sheathing (felt in the old days) will need attention as well (I've never done one that didn't). Probably time to consider the condition of the roof as a whole...

Sometimes so-called spot repairs, especially on a small roof seem to take as long as replacing the whole roof. This is because ripping everything off and starting afresh is easy, quick work; whereas repairs need careful, time consuming dismantling and re-assembly to do well without causing further damage to the fragile surrounding roof. Roof crawlers are a classic example. One broken tile to replace, but how many more will you break whilst walking up the roof on the crawler...? (Sh*t happens on old roofs, trust me...!).

PIPE REPAIRS

Repair broken, frost damaged or nailed water pipes by replacing the damaged sections. Frozen pipes will split open when they thaw (or occasionally it will just push open the fittings). Cut damaged sections out with a rotary pipe cutter and insert new sections and pairs of new fittings, compression, or plastic push fit usually. Making room to get new fitting in means finding some wiggle room to get the ends of the pipes into the fitting. Unclip what you can to create some slack or carefully bend the pipes outward (or up or down) just enough to get the fittings on (mark the pipes so you know they are in far enough). Double check everything is fully home and tight before switching on the water (it's easy to forget to tighten up something). Insulate the pipe to prevent a repeat occurrence if the pipe froze.

Plastic waste pipes rarely give any trouble, but repairs are similar to water pipe. Cut out the damage with a saw (any) and tidy up the cut ends with a file before inserting a new section of pipe and fittings, (use lubrication).

To find damaged underground drain pipes look closely at the ground along any drain runs, (from grates to access points and in between access points for example) because when drains leak, often material surrounding the pipe washes away down the drains. This erosion eventually causes depressions in the ground or subsidence under walls and hard standing areas etc., clear giveaways there's a problem below the surface.

Oh, and leaking drains always leads to... Trees. Roots just love leaking drains and roots will seek them out like crazy. Wrapping themselves around and into any gaps or cracks like an octopus. All those lovely nutrients flowing right on by make for happy plants... Left long enough they'll fill the pipe.

Roots of all kinds just love leaking drains, it's all those juicy nutrients...

Alternatively, hire a drain camera to see exactly what is going on underground. Cameras are locatable from the surface, so you always know exactly where they are, (handy if you see any damage via the camera). If the damage is deep underground or in an inaccessible location, consider hiring in a specialist who may be able to insert a sleeve and repair the drain from inside, without digging it up. Not a cheap prospect, but probably much cheaper than a complete dig up.

It's possible to make a homemade drain camera using a cheap USB endoscope camera fastened to a set of drain rods and a laptop (tape the camera in the middle of the screw attachment). You'll not know exactly where the damage is apart from the length of rods you have underground and the image won't always be the right way up on the screen. Still, it's kinda fun to try, (and the cameras are cheap).

Shallow pipe damage less than say 1m (3′ or so) deep, is easy enough to dig up. Put down some polythene sheet and dig down to find the pipe. Go easy when you feel it and excavate around and underneath the pipe to expose the leaking section and create some elbow room or working space. Cut out leaking/broken section using a mini grinder with a suitable blade for the material (or use an old wood saw if it's plastic). Remove any burs on the cut pipe ends and add a small chamfer (with the grinder or a hand file), aim for around half the pipe wall thickness.

Underground plastic drain pipes showing their chamfered ends

Courtesy of Hunter Plastics

Push two lubricated *slip collars* or rubber pipe connectors all the way on over the cut ends. Cut a piece of new pipe to fit tightly into the gap between the collars/joints and chamfer the cut ends. Smear a little more pipe lubricant on the pipe ends and wiggle it into the gap. Push, rotate and slide each collar/joint onto the new section of pipe until the new collar/joint is half way over each cut. It helps if you mark the pipe about 60mm (2 ½") back from the ends, then you'll know when you've centred the slip collars.

Surround the repaired pipe preferably with pea gravel, or in a pinch with the soft 'as dug out' material. Once the pipe's covered, backfill the hole to the top, compacting as you go with your boots, leaving it a little high as the 'backfill' will settle a little in time.

DRYWALL REPAIRS

Drywall is comparatively soft and easily dented or scratched. Fortunately, it's just as easily repaired using a 'decorators' filler. Apply the filler in thin layers and trowel/press flat with a paint scraper or drywall knife (spreader/trowel). Once dried, you might notice the filler has shrunk back a little below the surface (annoying and time consuming but pretty common). If so, wrap some 120-grit sandpaper around a sanding block and sand the whole area of filler flat to get rid of any high spots or ridges, then apply a little more filler trowelling it flat once again. If you put loads of filler on the first time, it might not have shrunk back below the surface, but you might have quite a bit of sanding to do, which can damage the surrounding board if you're not careful.

Premixed fillers are easy in theory, but you'll get better results and save money using the powdered fillers you mix with water (as the professionals do). Aim for a stiff porridge consistency somewhat thicker than toothpaste and brush any loose dust away before filling.

Repair small holes or larger damage in drywall by replacing the damaged area completely. NOTE: Use only proper drywall screws, as ordinary ones will rust through the paintwork due to moisture in the joint compound.

Be careful that there are no wires or pipes hiding behind the drywall first, (look for outlets nearby etc.), then...

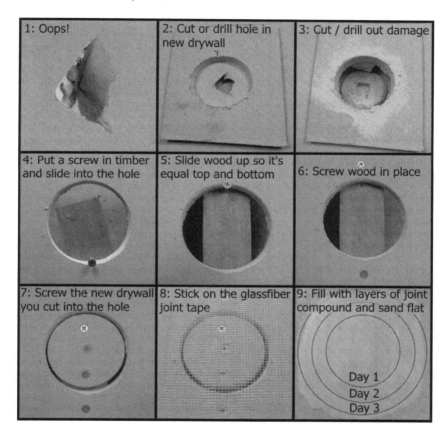

1. If the filler slumps in the hole then the hole is too big for filler, use the following method instead...

2. Cut out a new piece of drywall big enough to cover the damage with a drywall saw or a large core drill.

3. Use the new repair piece of drywall as a template to mark and cut out the damage in the wall.

4. Pop a screw into some scrap timber lath (50mm × 25mm or 2″ × 1″) and thread it into the hole.

5. Slide the lath up until it's equal top and bottom.

6. Screw the lath in place. Bigger holes need several laths, or you can fix lath around the edges of the hole instead.

7. Pop the new piece of drywall board you first cut out as a template, into the hole and screw it to the lath.

8. Apply drywall mesh (or bed some drywall tape) over the joints.

9. Apply drywall 'mud' or joint compound over the joints, pushing it through the mesh tape and into the gaps. Fill the screw heads too. The next day spread a very thin layer of drywall compound over the whole repair, preferably with a wide drywall trowel, spreading it out a little both sides finishing to a feather edge.

   The following day sandpaper the whole area using 120 grit until the repair is virtually invisible. Apply more filler over a slightly wider area if necessary or in low spots and sand again the following day.

   For larger repairs you can follow the drywall installation instructions in the Making New Stuff Chapter a little later on.

METAL REPAIRS

I'll stick to light metal repairs here because impact damage (tearing, bending, or denting) or corrosion, rarely affects heavy or solid metal objects because of their large mass. Thin metal however is very fragile, as anyone leaving their car in a crowded supermarket carpark knows only too well.

How you repair damage to metal depends on its location and anticipated stress under load. Some repairs need to be invisible such as repairs to the visible topside of vehicles, the underside of vehicles, not so much. Loading also matters, for example, you can repair light duty things like a metal mudguard on your bicycle any old how you want, but the structural parts of your bicycle frame, nope, that needs a structural repair, usually welding. Welding remains the best way to repair broken metal but it's difficult on really thin metal, (we'll come back to welding a little later).

On lightly loaded, non-aesthetically important things, like your lawn mower or something in the garden for example, you could repair or patch broken parts by screwing, riveting or even gluing (liquid metal or metal epoxy) metal plates over the break. Heavier parts need nuts, bolts, and washers. Normally you'd need at least two fasteners either side of the break to stop the repair plate twisting under load.

Cut and shape a plate to cover the break and glue into position holding everything firmly until the glue sets. Clamps or weights work well, awkward shapes hold well under a homemade sand bag etc. For physical fasteners align the broken parts back together and hold securely, position the repair plate evenly over the break and drill through both parts. It's often best to drill the repair plate on a block of wood first and us it as a template to drill the holes though the item, either side of the repair. Consider combining both glue and physical fasteners...

CUTTING METAL

We got ahead of ourselves in the last paragraph didn't we, talking about cutting repair plates before we'd looked at how to cut metal! You can go 'old school' and use a hacksaw and hand file, which is not as hard work as it sounds for smaller jobs. A faster, more tricky method is to use special cutting discs (1mm to 3mm thick) in a mini-grinder (eye protection and gloves are essential). The new 1mm cutting disks are particularly good as they remove little material, but they are quite unforgiving and require a steady hand due to their thin construction. Clean up your cuts and grind away excess metal using thicker grinding discs (5mm+ thick). Don't use a grinding disc for cutting (it's too thick) and never, ever use a thin cutting disc for grinding (it will shatter and it's doing 10,000RPM...). Metal cutting jigsaw blades are also available but personally I find them noisy and crude, not to mention a little bit scary...

Some non-ferrous metal like aluminium clog up regular metal cutting equipment, so you're better off cutting them with blades specially made for the purpose. Always follow the instructions that come with any blades, especially if they recommend using a cutting fluid or coolant.

Be aware that cut edges in metal are wickedly sharp and very unforgiving. Again, gloves are virtually compulsory when handling metal. Cutting metal always produces a burr on the back side. Easily 'de-burr' them by running a file across them a few times at an angle.

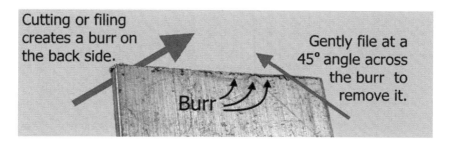

Cutting or filing creates a burr on the back side.

Burr

Gently file at a 45° angle across the burr to remove it.

WELDING METAL

Breaks on anything remotely structural needs welding to repair, effectively forming one piece again. Consider welding in some reinforcement whilst you're at it, because if it's broken once, it's likely to break again in the same place. Add plates, ridges, right angles etc. to bolster the area (if possible). However, do not try to repair truly stressed, structural metal such as steering components on vehicles for example; the loads they carry are too extreme to chance a repair holding, replace them instead.

I'll be honest, welding isn't for the faint hearted; but it is quite possible for the average person to learn how to do it well enough to make some small repairs or fabrications. Remember that old Daimler I bought when I was 19? Built in the motoring heyday of the 1970's, (irony) so inevitably, my cheap, second hand MIG welder was my (chronically unreliable and frustrating), best friend for quite a while... At least I had an excuse to go to the pub occasionally to replace my CO^2 bottle!

These days I love the opportunity to get the welder out, I don't know about you, but there is something exciting, dramatic and gung-ho about fusing metal together by melting it, and the noise it makes... pure magic! I mean, you can go blind if you look directly at a weld for goodness sake, this is clearly seriously heroic stuff...

For DIY, there are two common types of welding, electric arc (stick welders) using replaceable welding rods (good for thick metal) and electric MIG welders using a replaceable reel of wire and a bottled shielding gas such as argon or CO^2 (MIG is easier all round, especially for thinner metals.) MIG welders are now commonplace, affordable and you'll be pretty good after a few hours' practise (there are literally loads of 'how to' videos on youtube.com to learn the technique). You'll probably never be able to weld 'pretty', but to repair a broken spade for example, you'll get by. Stick to steel as well, because realistically, welding other metals such as aluminium and cast iron is arguably highly specialised.

A third, less common method is to use a 'gas welding' set, which can cut and shape metal as well as welding it using a filler rod. Arguably though, this is pretty specialised because it's many times harder to do well compared to 'point and press' electric welders.

Half of learning to weld is understanding and mastering your machine and the other half is understanding the weld bead and the heat it pumps into the metal. Master the machine by practising on scrap with a variety of settings (make notes on the actual settings you have success with for each metal thickness). Recognising a good weld will come naturally after playing about with your machine.

Excess heat is the enemy and will distort your workpiece, so mostly you'll need to weld in small increments to avoid the metal building up too much heat and warping. Tack weld (spots) to start with and follow up with leapfrogging small seam welds on opposing ends of the piece, to allow maximum cooling time in between welds.

As a general rule, if the metal is less than three millimetres thick, leaving a small space between the two parts is a good idea. The gap should be about the thickness of the metal. If the metal is more than three millimetres thick, bevel both top corners to an angle of 45º, otherwise the weld will sit on top and not penetrate very well. Thicker metal (over 6mm or ¼" or so) often needs several 'passes' to build up the required amount of weld bead.

BRAZING

And lastly, although not welding in the strictest sense, you can join metal items together by brazing, where you melt a special metal filler rod into the joint. Brazing isn't welding per se, as it does not melt the workpieces and the filler rod has a lower melting point than the workpieces too. The workpieces need to be a very close fit as the filler metal is drawn into the gap between close-fitting parts by capillary action. You'll use a cleaning flux first and the whole process is very similar to soldering two copper pipes together.

Heat the filler metal until it melts and flows over the base metal (called wetting) and as it cools it joins the workpieces together. You can even joint different metals together with brazing. Old school method but still worthy.

DENTS AND BENDS IN METAL

Metal is an elastic material, but we don't tend to see it that way. Mostly because once bent or dented, most metals tend to stay that way, (great news for auto repair shops!). This means you'll need to use significant force to persuade the metal to go back to its former shape. This creates complications when there is serious damage to sheet metal because the metal stretches as it absorbs impact (see, I told you metal was elastic!). This 'extra' metal has nowhere to go when you try to force the metal back into the shape you want. Severely dented metal is further complicated because a crease twice reinforces sheet metal; physically (think corrugated iron roofing) and atomically (bending metal will *work harden* it, up to a point).

Pros in auto body shops straighten out damaged metal using special panel beating hammers and a supporting form (called a *dolly*) on the backside. Classic car pros are good enough to leave the metal almost good enough to paint after using their straight and curved dollies, but relax, no one is going to mind if you use a little auto body filler to smooth over any imperfections before painting and in fact, most folks do.

You can also use a *dent puller* or *slide hammer* to pull out dents. This tool hooks through a small hole made in the centre of the dent (or a hook tack welded on) and then a heavy section slides upwards against a stop, literally pulling the dent out (picture a kind of reverse hammer). After using the slide hammer for the big stuff, dress the holes and mini dents flat with the above-mentioned panel beating hammer and dolly before filling and re-painting.

We've already agreed that metal bends easily, and that's handy... if you want to bend it. Bend small pieces in a metalworker's vice using a hammer, preferably a soft faced one (hide or copper). Larger sheets need a tool called a *bending brake* (I know, but it's not me making them up!) or a *sheet metal folder*. Small bending brakes are little more than a pair of hinged angle irons with long handles and cost little, but they are perfect for creating neat, straight angles in your work-pieces.

CORROSION IN METAL

Different metals corrode in different ways with non-ferrous metals like gold and silver only tarnishing slightly which is arguably a maintenance issue. Whereas ferrous metals like steel can rust right through, destroying cars and battleships alike. Because corrosion in steel is such a serious problem it's best treated like a disease, i.e. you must cut all the rot or rust away, right back to bright shiny metal.

Corrosion usually starts because a coating fails or wasn't there to begin with. On sheet metal, corrosion can start, (often unnoticed) on the backside or inside of stuff and work its way through the metal until you notice it on the surface bubbling through nice paintwork. Alternatively, on neglected metal, a small amount of damage to the coating on the surface lets in water and allows corrosion to spread underneath the coating surrounding the tiny damage, (stone chips on vehicles are a great example).

Often by the time you notice corrosion the metal is probably more corroded than you think. Poking and scraping at the affected area with a small screwdriver will reveal the true extent of the corrosion. Don't worry about making it worse (it's already bad) so don't be miserly; it's much easier to fix a larger patch into good metal than a small patch into rusty metal.

When repairing sheet metal, be careful not to create future problems. i.e. don't leave surfaces unprotected inside your repairs. If it's not possible to paint onto the surfaces inside, then use a sprayable wax or oil designed to creep into nooks and crannies to protect them. Use seam sealers between components or weldable primers if you're serious about repairing metal. Always think long term, ask yourself, how did it fail this time and how could this fail in the future? Ask yourself, what can I do to prevent this corrosion?

One of the best ways to prevent future corrosion is to ensure you've got it all this time. Prepare metal thoroughly before repairing and re-painting. If you have access to it locally and can afford it, consider using an abrasive blasting service as this removes every single trace of corrosion. Otherwise it's donkey work for you. Grinders with flap wheels, drill mounted abrasive wheels, sanders, and wire brushes (manual or powered) are just a few ways of removing corrosion. As already mentioned, if possible, cut out the corrosion and let in new metal for the very best repairs.

Corrosion on heavy items always starts on the surface and works its way in, but thankfully the mass of metal involved means it rarely causes a structural failure (think *RSJs* and heavy castings).

PLASTIC REPAIRS

Plastic is everywhere because it's incredibly versatile, plus it's cheap to manufacture in any shape imaginable, (you can even print with the blooming stuff). It is very strong in comparison to its weight, but; if you're going to break something, it's more than likely going to be plastic, isn't it?

Most plastics fracture because of abuse, impact or because stress overcomes the design parameters. Plastics either snap into two pieces or fail spectacularly, virtually exploding actually. Repairing plastics depends on the type of failure (snapped or exploded), the amount of distortion at the fracture site and your access to a suitable method or adhesive to re-assemble the pieces.

I'll be honest here, repairing plastic is tricky and the more stressed and the smaller the piece, the less likely it is you'll succeed. Big, simple, low stressed stuff on the other hand often repairs beautifully, so read on.

To start with there are two basic groups of plastic (with lots of different types within each group), and nowadays almost all of them are weldable or there is an adhesive out there which will bond to it (it hasn't always been this way, some used to be impossible to fix). The two broad groups are thermoplastics and thermosets...

THERMOPLASTICS

You can heat thermoplastics and reshape them whilst they are 'plastic', i.e. soft and mouldable. Once cooled they should stay in shape. Very hot water or a hairdryer can be hot enough to re-shape some plastics. Be careful with heat and plastics though, some are scarily flammable and will emit ferocious burning, spitting globules and literally lethal smoke...

There are too many to list them all, but here are some common ones...

Name	Properties	Main uses
ABS (Acrylonitrile butadiene styrene)	Resists most corrosive chemicals. Good against physical impacts. Easy to machine and has a low melting temperature.	Automotive parts like dashboards or wheel covers etc., toys, LEGO, kayaks canoes, helmets etc.
Acrylic (Polymethyl methacrylate)	Stiff and hard but can be brittle and easily scratched, durable, good electrical insulator. Easy to get a good surface finish.	Signs, storage box covers, canopies and windows, car light covers, hand basins and bath tubs etc.
HDPE (High density polyethylene/ polythene)	Hard, stiff, easily sterilisable.	Plastic bottles, tubing, and household equipment kayaks, canoes etc.
LDPE (Low density polyethylene/ polythene)	Tough, flexible, fairly soft, resists most chemicals, insulates against electricity well.	Toys, packaging including most bottles, packaging film and plastic carrier bags etc.
Nylon (Polyamide)	Cream in colour, tough and hard, self-lubricating. Resists wear, and most chemicals.	Bearings, gear wheels, casings for power tools, and clothing etc.
Polypropylene	Light, tough and hard, but easily scratched. Resists most chemicals, flexible and resists work fatigue.	Medical equipment, lab equipment, hinges for containers, seats, string, rope, and kitchen equipment. And 95% of late model car bumpers
Polystyrene	Very light, hard, stiff and resists water penetration well. Can be brittle.	Toys, especially model kits, packaging, boxes, and containers etc.

THERMOSETS

Thermosets are generally stronger than thermoplastics and better for high-temperature applications. However, they are more brittle and you can only heat and shape them once. Some common ones...

Name	Properties	Main uses
Epoxy resin	Good electrical insulator, hard, needs reinforcing to avoid being brittle, resists most chemicals.	Casting and laminating, good for adhesives and bonds to other materials well.
Melamine formaldehyde	Stiff, hard, strong, resists some chemicals.	Laminates for work surfaces and cabinets, electrical insulation, and tableware etc.
Polyester resin	Stiff, hard, brittle unless laminated, good electrical insulator, resists most chemicals.	Casting and lamination, bonding to other materials well.
Urea formaldehyde	Stiff, hard, strong, brittle, good electrical insulator	Electrical fittings, handles and control knobs and adhesives etc.

Before you can do a thing, you'll need to identify what type of plastic you have as this dictates how you repair it. Fortunately, it's fairly easy to identify plastic parts from classification marks stamped into them (used for recycling purposes). Check these marks against the chart below to identify the type of plastic you have.

Bear in mind that some things you think are plastic might be fibreglass or GRP (glass reinforced plastic) or even carbon fibre.

1 PETE	PET or PETE (Polyethylene Terephthalate) Clothing fibers, bottles and containers for foods, thermoforming in manufacturing, and to make engineering resin
2 HDPE	HDPE (Polyethylene) Plastic bottles, corrosion-resistant piping, geomembranes, and plastic lumber.
3 PVC	PVC (Polyvinyl Chloride) Rigid pipes, profiles, bottles, non-food packaging & credit cards. Flexible pipes, cable insulation, imitation leather, signage, LP's and inflatables
4 LDPE	LDPE (Low Density Polyethylene) trays, containers, work surfaces, snap-on lids, six pack rings, cartons, computer packaging etc. playground slides and plastic wraps
5 PP	PP (Polypropylene) Piping, medical & labs, kettles, living hinges, non-woven clothing (nappies), carpets, rugs & mats, roofing, moulding, sheets &stickers
6 PS	PS (Polystyrene), Rigid: lab containers. expanded: insulation materials, packaging, trays, plates, bowls and fish boxes, as rigid panels
7 O	O (Other. Acrylics, ABS, PLA, Nylon, PC, PLA) Baby bottles, sippy cups, water bottles, water containers, juice and ketchup containers, eye glass lenses, epoxy resins, dental sealants, discs, lab equipment, gears, snowboards, car parts, phones, computers and power tools.

I know, No.7 right? Not very useful, especially as it includes some very common plastics like ABS and acrylics. You'll need to google the actual name of the plastic if you can find it stamped anywhere, try trade names etc. too, as many plastics are known by their trade name rather than their chemical name, e.g. Bakelite (the first plastic), Mylar, Nalgene, Nylon, Perspex, Plexiglass, Teflon, Zytel to name a few off the top of my head...

Identifying the type of plastic is crucial as using the wrong method or the wrong glue means the repair probably won't work, it might even destroy (melt) the plastic. Always test your proposed method on the back of the workpiece or a similar scrap piece first. Especially double check the 'application instructions' on glue packaging to ensure it's suitable for your type of plastic.

Okay, so you've identified the type of plastic you want to repair and now it's time to explore using your favourite search engine to find out what will work to repair it. Repairs broadly fall into one of four methods, (keeping in mind that sometimes a combination might be advisable to claw back some of the original strength inevitably lost due to the breakage) ...

- Welding with heat.

- Solvent welding.

- Adhesives or sealants.

- Mechanical (cable ties, nuts and bolts, rivets, screws, wire, etc.).

There is an amazing array of tools from old soldering irons to laser beams and ultrasonics for welding plastics. Generally you can't conventionally weld thermosets without a special plastic welder, as they will simply burn, (creating deadly fumes). However, it is possible to 'weld' them by heating them up and adding an additional plastic rod, in a process similar to brazing metal.

CUTTING PLASTIC

You might need to cut up some old plastic to create plastic filler rods on bigger welding jobs or to tidy up something before repairing it. Regular wood-working tools work well on most types of plastic to cut, saw, drill, file, and sand. However, plastic dust (as with any kind of dust really) is not a good thing to have inside you, so always wear masks when creating dust from plastics. Only use high speed power tools with extreme care, because holding the workpiece firmly enough to prevent snatching is difficult.

Be careful when sawing plastic because if the saw catches it will easily break or shatter the plastic. Large course teeth are bad and small teeth are good. A metal hacksaw is useful in most cases. Another technique on thin plastic sheets, is to repeatedly score the plastic with a sharp blade such as a sturdy craft knife. It may take several slow, steady runs through the same score, but you'll easily get half way through and then you flip it over and cut in the crease to finish off. Make sure you always keep your fingers behind the blade in case you slip.

WELDING USING HEAT

There are two ways to apply heat to plastic; using friction or a hot air/ hot metal device. Friction is a simple method whereby you spin a thin, stiff plastic rod at high speed and push it against the two parts you want to repair. Use the same type of plastic rod as the parts you're repairing. Pop the plastic rod into a Dremel type tool with a short length protruding. Tape the parts together and hold the workpiece firmly; run the tip of the plastic rod at high speed into the joint. Friction builds and melts the three parts of the weld (the plastic rod and either side of the joint). It's crude and messy looking but can make a strong bond if you can spin the rod fast enough and get enough pressure on without it skidding away.

Alternatively, (and I think an easier method) is to use a modified soldering iron (they are cheap). Grind the tip into a squared off chisel shape (use a file or grinding wheel) which makes it easier to manipulate the molten plastic. Some soldering irons come with a range of interchangeable tips so look out for one of those. You can of course buy inexpensive dedicated plastic welding kits which often come with a handy range of different plastic filler rods for melting directly into cracks etc.

NOTE: very important to mention here are fumes. Heating and melting plastic has the potential to create VERY dangerous gases. Don't heat the plastic so much that it smokes (that's too hot) but you're bound to create some fumes, so it's vitally important you do this in a well-ventilated space. Trust your nose, if you smell burning plastic you are already inhaling fumes and *you **must get out***. Stop what you're doing and rearrange the ventilation, take it outside, blow a portable fan across the workpiece, rearrange your working position to the side or whatever. You *must not* breath in plastic fumes; they are *seriously dangerous*, okay? Can I trust you? Yes? Right then, here's a typical repair procedure for a small crack in polypropylene or polyethylene etc. using a soldering iron with a flat tip...

- Consider duct taping the pieces together on the opposite side to which you're working on, especially if it's an awkward shape.

- Fully support the workpieces to stop them coming apart or flexing apart as you weld.

- Working on the back or 'not seen' side if you can. Briefly touch the hot tip of the 'iron' to the crack in a few spots to create tack or spot welds to hold the pieces in place.

- Run the hot tip down a short section of the crack, to melt a groove almost through to the front and then push over the softened semi-molten plastic back into the groove you just made from alternating sides whilst the plastic is still soft and pliable.

- Go back over the bit you just welded to flatten it out and tidy it up.

- ▸ Repeat at another place along the crack. Alternate places to stop too much heat building up in one spot. Think leap frog etc.

- ▸ An alternative method is to pulse the hot tip in and out of the plastic in a kind-of-stitching motion to fix the crack.

- ▸ If required, go back and smooth over the rough bits with the flat part of the iron or hold the iron on the inside of a small spoon and use the curved back of the spoon to flatten your weld.

- ▸ Alternatively, heat up a flexible knife or scraper with a blowtorch until it's hot and use it to smooth out lumps and bumps.

- ▸ Avoid getting the plastic too hot, you want to melt it, not burn it (if it's smoking, it's too hot).

- ▸ Again, always work on small sections and keep moving; alternately work on one end and then the other to keep things cool.

On larger or thicker material, you'll need to burn deeper into the plastic and possibly add some extra plastic filler to make a good repair. You can buy plastic welding filler rods or make your own by cutting thin strips or rods from the same type of plastic. So far, I've seen folks use cable or zip ties, strimmer cord (usually nylon), yogurt pots (often polystyrene) and various bottles (polyethylene). I've even gently carved little shavings of plastic from webs or unseen edges etc. inside the same piece I'm repairing to work into the weld.

One last method of heat welding is to use the craft type, hot melt glue guns to repair cracks. The little metal tip which protrudes from the gun gets very hot, push it slowly along the crack allowing it to melt the plastic whilst pumping a small amount of the hot glue stick into the weld and pressing everything together (more hands needed?). Hot glue sticks are a complex mixture of plastics making them suitable for lots of low stress applications. You can even mould new plastic items or parts using a hot glue gun, it's essentially an easy way to melt plastic you see...

WELDING USING SOLVENTS AND GLUES

Builders merchants sell solvent welding materials consisting of a cleaner and a solvent paste for PVC pipe installation (common in plumbing). They are phenomenally effective if you follow the instructions: However, if you don't work quickly enough, you'll end up stuck in the wrong place, quite literally. Because once your solvent adhesive grabs or sticks, it's permanently stuck at a molecular level, i.e. game over for movement.

A crude homemade solvent welding technique involves dissolving some small offcuts of your plastic in the correct solvent for your type of plastic. 100% acetone (among other solvents like methyl ethyl ketone/ MEK or dichloromethane/ DCM) work on many plastics, testing first is advisable. Snip small pieces of plastic and dissolve them in a small amount of your chosen solvent to make a thick plastic goop. Stir this well and use a small amount in between your broken parts and more on top to reinforce your weld. Be careful what you use to spread on your solvent-y goop, in case that melts too. Cleanliness is extremely important for this method to work. Wipe down everything with a good degreaser/cleaner.

Most plastic glues are actually a form of solvent weld really, hence dumping them together in this section...

- Always double check the 'application instructions' on packaging to ensure it's suitable for your plastic.

- Always clean all mating surfaces well to remove grease.

- Always try a dry run to make sure the parts fit together well without any gaps.

- Small amounts are usually enough for the weld between the broken parts to work. Use up extra by adding reinforcement across the joint (it broke once remember...).

- Wait until the new join sets fully, be patient!

- On fancy work where you'll see the repaired crack, grind down the excess plastic, and use a filler before painting.

MECHANICAL FASTENERS

One last method is to use mechanical fasteners like screws and rivets. Plastic takes a screw thread quite well and drills very easily. Drilling holes and fastening parts together using cable ties or wire is effective for rough and basic repairs on non-aesthetic stuff. Mechanical stuff makes for good reinforcement to back up a welded or glued repair, in much the same way as glue and pins in woodwork. Which leads wonderfully to...

REINFORCING REPAIRS

Using mechanical reinforcement or additional material on the rear of broken sections as reinforcement is a good idea if there is room (and it's not seen), especially on something poorly designed which breaks often, or stuff folks often abuse, (read motorcycle plastic!). Stick or weld extra material across the repair.

Use extra plastic pieces, or thin metal or even short pieces of wire melted across the joint as reinforcement. I use paperclips as the rounded ends prevent pull-out (straight wire can pull out). Even better is the thin aluminium mesh from the auto store (used as a backer for filling holes in car bodywork). Simply put strips of the mesh over the crack and heat it with the soldering iron until it pushes into the plastic, smooth over the plastic oozing through the mesh and you've got a solid reinforcement.

RUBBER REPAIRS

With age and exposure rubber perishes, splits, tears, snaps, or turns into a gooey mush, which generally means it's not repairable. In addition, rubber goes hard and loses its main attribute, flexibility.

Once rubber is no longer flexible, it will either break up or in the case of rubber seals, become totally compressed. Once rubber loses its flexibility, it's lost its 'superpower' and won't seal against metal or plastic, causing leaks. Tap or faucet washers fail this way and although sometimes you can turn them over and get a little while longer out of them, they're so cheap it's hardly worth the trouble. Leaking O rings are also 'repaired' by replacement; fortunately, they only cost a few pennies too.

If the rubber is in good condition though, repair tears and holes using a special patch or plug and an adhesive often called *rubber cement*. We've all glued rubber together as kids, remember all those bicycle punctures? Yes? Well, that's how it's done.

Abrade the area around the damage with some fine sandpaper removing the smooth finish and blow away the dust. Apply the rubber cement to an area fractionally bigger than the patch and allow it to go tacky (a few minutes usually). Once tacky press the patch firmly over the damage, working over the area with your fingers to expel any air bubbles. To stop any excess adhesive surrounding the repair sticking to anything, rub chalk onto sandpaper, tip the dust onto the repair and rub it into the excess adhesive.

Incidentally, if you don't have any patches, make your own by cutting a suitably sized repair piece from any similar rubber. Got a shredded inner tube? Keep it and use it to make improvised patches (or you can cut a spiral shaped cut around it to make long rubber straps...)

Wait a few minutes before putting the rubber back into use. TIP: use this time to investigate what caused the damage. It'd be a shame to put the rubber back into use and damage it again. Use a small fluffy rag and wipe it around the area the rubber is in contact with (around the inside of a tyre for example), hopefully it will snag on or find any sharp or foreign object.

Other rubber sheet used to make roofing systems; rubber inflatable boats etc., also use similar kits to repair damage. You'll need to contact the manufacturer and get hold of a suitable repair kit.

Oh, and never just assume there is only one piece of damage... Seems impossible to get two holes simultaneously I know, but still...

Some things are a composite of rubber and metal. These two components separate over time, sometimes unnoticeably. Vehicle engine or suspension mountings are good examples. Try removing the load on composite mountings and see if the metal and rubber parts separate, leaving a small gap. Jack up a vehicle and examine any composite mountings for example, any gap between the metal and rubber part of a mounting means the bond has failed. It might be possible to inject a suitable rubber to metal adhesive into the gap using a syringe (if you have good access to clean up and get the adhesive in). But in most situations though, it's probably not worth the work, (metal and rubber are difficult bedfellows) and usually they are in a very stressed environment. Replacing the part is probably easier and quicker in the long run.

FABRICS REPAIRS

We all know how to repair regular fabrics which is of course to use a needle and thread. However, it's rarely possible to sew together the two sides of tear in fabric without making a raised ridge that looks bad. Consider instead repairing without stitching by using 'iron on' adhesive reinforcing patches placed on the inside of the damaged area, holding everything in place. Alternatively, use decorative patches to go on the outside of any damage, covering it up, (kids knee patch style).

Head over to places like craftster.org, etsy.com or pinterest.com for lots of inspiration from the crafting crowd on how to make repaired fabrics look cool again using ingenious methods you'd probably never have thought of.

If you tear something valuable, it's possible to remove the thread using a cheap, special unpicker along the seams and remove the whole panel. Use the removed piece as a pattern to mark out a new section. Cut out the new panel and either sew or get a seamstress or tailor to sew it back in for you.

Seam ripper or stitch unpicker

Sometimes you can turn a piece over; worn out shirt collars for example. Unpick the seam and turn the collar over and re-stich the collar in place, hey presto, a new shirt in 10 mins, (and yes, I do this, and yes, I have a beard, and yes, I wear out shirt collars at an alarming rate...).

Repairing waterproof fabrics might depend on getting information from the manufacturers; there may be special patches and adhesives. Try your local outdoors shop for solutions or search online for "waterproof repair patches" + "insert name of fabric".

Us the smallest diameter needles you can find to stitch anything to a waterproof fabric and use a 'seam sealer' afterwards to fill the needle holes. Try also to find a nylon thread (and not cotton) as it resists mildew better and doesn't rot like cotton will.

GLASS REPAIRS

Nope. Sorry, can't do it, you need a new piece. Here's how...

- Apply duct tape in strips across the cracks in the glass to hold it in place whilst you remove it.

- Carefully remove whatever is holding the glass in place; likely to be linseed oil putty on old single pane windows (use an old wood chisel), or wooden or plastic beads on more modern windows (wiggle a thin blade into the gap and lever up).

- Lever out or break out the glass wearing goggles and thick leather gloves. Be careful, broken glass is evil stuff...

- Clean up the reveal where the glass sat. It needs to be spotless or you could break the new glass when you push it in.

- Get the glazier to cut the new glass (or make up the new double-glazed unit) for you. Seriously, life is too short and glass cutting is a pain to learn. Don't forget to allow 5mm clearance for fitting (or measure the old one and copy that).

- Buy the correct sealing system for your glass. Ranges from new linseed oil putty (wait for a warm day) or a putty-on-a-roll system, or a rubber self-adhesive seal etc. Ask at the glass supplier.

- Seal any bare areas of wood using shellac or knotting (it dries quickly. Paint (or prime them at least) any new wooden beads.

- Apply the sealing system to the inside back, vertical face of the glass rebate and push the glass into it, evenly and quite hard. You might need to push up the bottom of the glass slightly on plastic packers to centre the glass (never lever the glass with a screwdriver etc.).

- Apply the exterior sealing system, pushing hard onto the glass to get a good seal. Finish off putty with a smooth trowelling motion using a clean putty knife etc.

- Remove any excess sealant using a fine scraper or putty knife (not applicable for rubber seals etc.).

Now you've repaired the broken handle on that sledgehammer which has been languishing at the back of the shed for a while, let's go and knock something down; are you ready?

Easy tiger!

DISMANTLING & DEMOLISHING STUFF

Some things are nearly ready to fall down by themselves...

O h, yes, we all like a bit of dismantling and demolition, don't we? Ripping out old fashioned or tatty, worn out stuff is the first real indication that new and exciting stuff is happening. Moreover, it gets rid of all your pent-up frustration... providing you follow these tips and avoid skinning your knuckles or damaging something you want to keep. But first, a little caveat, before you leap into this for real, can I ask you to jump to the end of this book and read the *Health and Safety* chapter? It's okay; go on, I'll wait......

..... back so soon? I hope you didn't skip anything; this chapter is where you're most likely to lose some skin... (or worse). Now I've frightened you, let's go through some general principles to think about when dismantling or demolishing something...

UNDERSTANDING THE RISK

Risk is inherent in many things we do, but dismantling or demolishing stuff carries especially high risks of personal injury or unintentional damage to property. This is because stuff is rarely taken down the same way it's erected, i.e. one piece at a time and slowly. Most dismantling and demolition jobs happen in a fraction of the original build time because folks get excited and rational thought often goes out the window with the rubbish. This means an awful lot of material coming down and out in a short space of time. Large amounts of fast-moving materials are more difficult to control, making accidents more likely.

The risk of an accident also increases because unexpected things happen and most of this stuff is heavy or sharp. In addition to the risk getting hurt, if you get this wrong, you risk damaging your stuff or even weakening the very fabric of your house. For example, when creating a big opening in a wall, (you must support the surrounding structure). Expect the unexpected; the nice chaps who built your home might not be such nice chaps after all; especially if they tried to save a few bucks by bending or ignoring the rules...

Less dramatic risks are the small injuries, (cuts, bumps, and scrapes), which are common when working with tools and heavy or awkward materials. Be especially careful when...

- Handling or moving heavy or large material.

- Working off the ground, even low-level falls hurt...

- Working with or on machines (appliances, vehicles etc.).

- Using unfamiliar tools or equipment.

- Clearing up and removing rubbish, junk, or spoil.

- Removing or dismantling... well, anything at all really.

MINIMISING THE RISK

If you're in any doubt about anything related to the structure of your home, give your local authorities building control office a call (it's their job to help and what you pay your taxes for). You might need to satisfy local building regulations anyway, (you may even need calculations from an engineer or architect), so call or visit your friendly BCO (Building Control Officer) early for advice, they'll be happy to help, and their advice is free (in the UK at least).

It's vital during the planning stage of any job that you identify the critical things in your structure and things that are not, (before you start knocking things down!). A wall upstairs in your house for example, might be a non-load-bearing timber stud and drywall construction, which you can remove without adding any structural support. Whereas the brick wall between your lounge and dining room for example, might have a wall on top of it or the first-floor joists. This makes removal more complex because you'll need to support the structure during the work and add some structural members to carry the intended loads afterwards; then it's probably time to call in your architect or a structural engineer.

If the wall has nothing at all sitting on top of it, it's non-supporting and removable, in theory. Personally, I'd still recommend you seek advice from the local building regulations office to confirm it. Remember, even if a wall appears to be non-structural with nothing sitting on top of it, the wall may still be providing a stiffening, supporting role in the structure which of course you'll weaken if you bash a big hole in it.

Walls which do have something sitting on top of them, either another wall, floor joists or other structural things like roof timbers etc., definitely need support during any demolition work.

Other structural parts of your house include the floor joists and the roof structure. You can usually remove and replace rotten floor joists 'one at a time' without any danger and the same with rafters and ceiling joists. However, there are important timbers in your roof, such as purlins, bearers, ridge, hips, posts and so on, that you *must not* remove without supporting the load they are carrying. Don't forget, snow and wind add incredible loads to a roof.

Never remove structural timbers during any alterations, without consulting your friendly structural engineer to determine what support you need to use during removal, and afterwards to support the load. And remember, just because they're in your way in the attic (and you can't see the point of them or what they do), it doesn't mean they're not providing a vital supporting role in your house...

Thankfully though, you can safely remove many non-structural things in your house, for example...

- The kitchen or bathroom (with a little knowledge about how to isolate your wiring and plumbing systems).

- Non-load-bearing stud walls (timber and drywall).

- Internal or external doors and their frames (be wary for missing lintels above frames in old houses).

- Window frames or their sashes, lights, or casements (be wary for missing lintels above windows in old houses).

- Flooring; chipboard, plywood, parquet, or T & G (tongue and groove) floorboards (be careful not to fall through, especially if there is a ceiling below!).

- Flooring finishes such as carpet, linoleum, tiles etc.

- Ceilings; either timber, drywall or lath and plaster types.

- Plaster finishes, cement, lime plasters or drywall etc.

- Any wooden trims like skirting boards, architraves, cover strips, quadrants, or other small wooden trims etc.

- Electrical items or circuits, after isolating and making bare ends safe (local regulations may vary, check first).

- Plumbing, pipes, or appliances. Isolate water supplies, drain pipes where necessary and *always* seal any open pipes to stop debris getting inside them and causing a problem later on.

The last part of minimising risk is to protect the things you want to keep. It's very simple; if you want to keep it, you must protect it...

- Protect the floor; thoroughly clean first (to remove any grit) then use plywood, hardboard, old carpet, polythene sheeting or dustsheets in descending order of protection.

- Use a length of scrap timber to protect a surface you want to keep, especially when using pry bars or crowbars to remove trims etc. on plastered finishes.

- Be especially careful near drywall, it's quite soft and extremely soft if not skimmed with plaster.

- Duct tape (or pin) thin pieces of scrap timber to doorframes or jambs, especially if using wheelbarrows.

- Cover up with dustsheets anything you don't want covered in dust (duh!) and use a polythene layer for seriously dusty jobs like working with old lath and plaster. Fine dust goes through woven dustsheets, (I learned this the hard way...).

- Isolate any water and power in the working area. Also, have some buckets and towels handy, if working with any pipes that may still have water in them.

COMMUNICATE THE PLAN

One last thing, you might be doing this kind of work with a friend or two and if so don't forget to communicate! I've seen stuff go badly wrong on multi-person tasks because each person didn't have a clear idea what was going to happen. It's been my experience that five people will have five different opinions on how to do the job, with the most dominant person leading the way and everyone else trotting behind. However, it doesn't necessarily follow that the most dominant person is the most knowledgeable about the best way forward. It's your job; you're in charge, you choose, it's not a democracy!

To avoid everyone pulling in different directions, be a 'task leader' (or appoint one) and explain exactly what's going to happen. Each person must understand what's expected of them and what's going to happen. Encourage everybody to 'speak up' if they don't understand or are having a problem (can't manage the weight etc.). It's NOT macho to grin and bear pain, A & E wards are full of folks like that.

Treat any difficult or heavy jobs the same way a pilot pre-flights his aircraft, i.e. get green lights across the board before doing anything. When carrying something heavy for example, have the task leader go through the plan and get each member involved to shout up 'okay' in turn, followed by asking if everyone's ready and get a 'yup' from everyone. Then on the count of three, count down the lift etc. Oh, and when lifting, its 'one, two' and lift *on* 'three'...

But better yet, avoid the heavy stuff all together and hire machines to do it for you. I spent years manhandling heavy beams before I 'discovered' manual lifting machines. They deliver direct to your house, they fit through a standard doorway, wind up and down from the floor to the ceiling like a mini fork lift truck and can handle anything you throw at them. Jobs that used to need six men now only need two. From oak beams to steel RSJs, all are now easy and more to the point here, safer to handle. You make a better job too because you have much more time to place the item (instead of 'heave and shift') I believe they call it working smart. And that leads very nicely to...

BRUTE FORCE AND IGNORANCE

Using brute force is a very popular method when dismantling and demolishing stuff and I'll be honest, it is effective, not to mention lots of fun! However, brute force AND ignorance damages stuff you want to keep. This means extra work or expense for you, and that's a very bad thing, especially if you're trying to make money...

The laws of physics insist that almost everything is a potential store of energy. For example, imagine a length of timber, screwed, or nailed into place and you're using a pry or crowbar to remove it (because you're not re-using it and it's quicker). The bar applies lots of pressure behind the timber until it overcomes the holding force of the screws or nails. What happens to all that force once the fasteners give way? Yup, the timber suddenly springs out in a millisecond hitting anything in the way; something like you. Always start at one end and lever along the length using just enough force each time, don't start in the middle and use so much force that the whole thing springs off the wall in one go. Better still, remove as many fasteners as you can find before trying to tug the thing apart because this gives you more control of the dismantling process (brute strength is unpredictable).

Using pry or crowbars makes supporting some items difficult, as it's often not easy to lever the pry bar and hold the item at the same time. Even a simple wall cupboard in the kitchen has *potential energy* stored up waiting to turn into *kinetic energy* as gravity causes it to plummet to the ground when you lever out the last fastener! Whilst we are usually thankful for gravity stopping us flying off into space, it can be a problem when dismantling stuff because it means we need to support everything before removing the mechanical fixings or breaking any adhesive.

Always be aware of the weight and size of stuff you're dismantling. Making sure to either support it, so you can lower it safely, or have a clear area for it to fall into without damaging anything, (including you!). Support stuff by using anything you have to hand, from leftover timber wedged underneath to getting a friend to help hold stuff whilst you take out the last few fasteners.

DIRE CONSEQUENCES

Don't fix one problem and cause another. Men are particularly good at this; i.e. so focused on the job in hand they're plonking tools down on unprotected worktops or tables etc. Protect surfaces by making some 600mm × 900mm (2′ × 3′) surface protectors out of carpet offcuts; then you can put your tools down knowing you're not going to damage anything. A friend of mine gets his by asking at the local carpet store for old sample pieces. These lovely felt backed 600mm (2′) squares with bound edges spread out on work surfaces really emphasises his care and professionalism.

Don't be ignorant about what's likely to happen because of your hasty actions. I'm not saying you can't go bananas, but always consider what *could* go wrong. Be careful, think about what you're doing and make sure you've protected any stuff you don't want damaged.

Also, never put anything really heavy straight on the floor because you'll have a devil of a job to pick it up again. Always throw a few pieces of old timber on the floor first and put anything heavy on the timber. That way you have a gap underneath which makes picking it up a whole lot easier. Fork lift truck drivers do this all the time obviously, otherwise they would never get their forks underneath the object, be like a fork lift truck driver...

REMOVING DIFFERENT MATERIALS

There's not room for everything obviously, so let's just go through some of the more common materials you're likely to want to rip out...

MASONRY

Let's start with masonry, and not just because it's my personal 'specialist subject', but because it's the heaviest thing you're likely to tackle and the one most likely to hurt you if you get it wrong.

Living requirements gradually change over the decades, placing new demands on our houses, such as inside bathrooms etc., (anyone under age 50 or so won't remember this, but toilets used to be in the garden, I know... right?!). Any old house still sporting its original layout will need at least some of its walls removed or altered to create more a more open layout or to house a new bathroom or kitchen etc. Smaller modern houses often need a wall or two removed or altered to gain access to a new extension or conservatory etc.

In the UK, masonry walls are usually of two different types, solid walls up to the 1940's when cavity walls with two independent leaves (or skins) either side of a cavity became the norm, (tied together with metal or plastic wall ties across the now insulated cavity). Solid walls are usually brick or stone, and cavity walls are usually brick or stone on the outer leaf and usually blocks (concrete, lightweight, breeze, ash, cinder etc.), on the inner leaf (early houses may be brick inside and out). I'll use the word bricks from now on for clarity, but you can read block, or stone as the techniques are similar.

As mentioned in the *Repairing Masonry* section in the *Repairing Stuff* chapter earlier, brickwork due to its interlocking nature tends to be self-supporting over small openings, up to around a metre or so (40″), making removing masonry to create a new regular size doorway conveniently easy. Bigger openings need skyhooks, prayers, and good insurance cover... Or you can install some support... (err, highly recommended in case you were wondering).

SUPPORTING MASONRY FOR BIGGER REMOVALS

Masonry is heavy stuff obviously, and we're talking about the actual fabric of your house here, which means you need to take it seriously to avoid hurting yourself or your house. I'll be honest and say that breaking out and removing masonry isn't for the meek-and-mild, because it is hard work and a little bit brutal in practise, plus there's a fair to middling chance of skinned knuckles... However, masonry does have a couple of qualities that will help you out; it is largely stable and predictable. This means you only need to learn a few techniques and you'll be able to overcome the solidity of masonry and literally have it crumbling at your feet.

First and most importantly, you'll need to find out if the wall you want to remove is supporting anything else. Read the *Learning About Your Home* section back in the *Developing Practical Skills* chapter and learn how to 'read' your house, to figure out what goes where and how it all fits together.

If floor joists and other timbers go into the brickwork above your proposed opening, support them using adjustable steel props (Acrow for example) hired from your local builder's merchant or tool hire centre. Place stout timber bearers underneath and on top of a series of said steel props. Use blankets to protect floors and ceilings. This supports the floor joists which then supports the brickwork sitting on top of them (providing they are well mortared in and the masonry above is good).

However, if your joists are in the adjoining wall and your wall simply goes up through the ceiling to the first floor, support is more complicated. The traditional way to support brickwork above this kind of proposed opening is to insert temporary beams called 'needles' through the wall and onto adjustable steel props. The props then transfer the load to a solid base, usually onto more timber bearers sitting onto a concrete floor.

Strongboy Masonry Support

Remove a mortar joint above the opening using a SDS drill or hammer and chisel.
Tap Strongboy into empty joint.
Support with a steel prop.

A more common method today is to use a proprietary system; the simplest being 'StrongBoy' (often available to hire or buy from a local tool hire depot or of course you can buy direct from the manufacturers).

These are special metal 'heads' that sit on top of adjustable steel props and into a slot cut into the mortar joint just above the brickwork you want to remove. StrongBoys support the brickwork above whilst you remove the brickwork underneath. Make sure the 'blade' is long enough to support the whole width on wider cavity walls. You'll probably need to remove part of the ceiling and upper floor to fit them just above where the new beam will sit (but that is good, because good access and visibility makes for easy and safer work).

There are also other systems available such as the Brick Brace Safety System, which converts the masonry above the proposed opening into a temporary pre-stressed lintel. Or the 'No More Props' system which fits into a shallow slot cut into a mortar joint above the proposed new opening. Contact your local tool hire companies to see what's available near you.

REMOVING MASONRY

Be aware though; even though you might have properly supported any load above, you're still in a potentially precarious situation, so it pays to be very mindful in your working methods, get the hole cut out and the new support in as soon as possible, and be ever vigilant for anything amiss. You see something move that shouldn't, you get out pronto! Have a clear code phrase if you're working with others and make sure everyone knows it, you hear that phrase, you know to get the heck out, like your life depended on it, (because it might...). We use: OUT, OUT, OUT! which is self-explanatory and yes, it's in capitals, because we'd be shouting if we ever needed to use this! Oh, and wear gloves or you're going to skin your knuckles for sure.

Now for the hard part, or not; because it depends you see. Generally, masonry is either very easy to remove, or very hard, depending on how old it is and what type of mortar it's built with. The old lime mortar in pre-WWII homes we talked about earlier is very easy to chop out with a *plugging chisel* and *club hammer,* but cement-based mortar in newer properties is much harder to demolish by hand and hiring a small electrically powered breaker is advisable.

You might note that I've switched from 'demolish' to 'remove' here, and that's because it's rare you'll get to 'demolish' anything by swinging a blooming great big sledge hammer like you see in the movies; because if you did, you could end up bringing half the house down. Masonry is weak in tension remember, so hitting it hard sideways is a bad idea and will damage the wall over a large area or even dislodge your supports. Especially on cavity walls where each leaf is actually quite thin and fragile. Solid, one brick thick walls are quite tough though, and will absorb more abuse without destabilising.

Usually, (after doing any of the supportive work mentioned above, if required) a controlled method of brick removal is best. Start at the top (or one or two courses down), remove your first brick, which incidentally, is *always* the hardest one to get out! I described in detail how to get the first one out in the *Replacing Spalled or Damaged Bricks* section in the *Repairing Stuff* chapter, so I won't go through it again here.

Once you have the first one out, remove the bricks either side of it, continuing until you hit the outer edges of the new opening. Once I have three bricks out, I like to pop the middle one back in place with a pair of wooden wedges hammered in tight over the top. This helps hold the brickwork above steady whilst I'm removing the rest of that 'difficult to remove' first full course, but then I am a bit of a belt and braces kind of guy, (but no mishaps either in over 30 years, so go figure...).

Getting the first course out is always going to be hard work because it's under load, it's compressed if you like with the weight of the wall above. It's fine to break up the actual bricks on this course if you want, keep going along, brick-by-brick, breaking them out piece by piece.

Try to direct the force of your blows along or down the wall (if you can) instead of across it (it's weak that way remember). You can use more force directing your blows along or down the wall (without damaging the wall itself) because of the support from the other bricks behind it. Whereas hitting across the brick wobbles the whole wall because there is only air behind it. Plus, any brick you hit hard crossways is liable to break with parts of it flying across the room at high speed.

Once you've got your first course out, this greatly facilitates the removal of more masonry, working down the wall one complete course at a time. Take advantage of the load free situation now by directing your chisel into the bed joint underneath the brick, again working along the wall. Usually this pops the brick right off in one piece (not so much on well stuck cement mortar) and sometimes placing your chisel into the cross joint also works to pop off the brick, especially in soft mortar.

One final method is to use a crowbar or wrecking bar as a long lever in any empty joints, either the empty back half of a poorly filled cross joint or in between the two halves of a one brick thick wall. For extra gentle force use two opposing crowbars/ wrecking bars, pulling one and pushing the other to pop off the bricks.

Once you have enough space, I like to get the new supporting beam into place (steel, box, concrete etc.) ASAP, packed tightly up to the brickwork above, before taking out the rest of the wall below. I like to pack the top of my beams with solid mortar, but I know many prefer to use little itty-bitty bits of slate etc. I get the new support beams in quickly, mostly for peace of mind, because the sooner I've fully supported the wall above the better (IMHO). Leaving large, old, heavy, walls sitting on props for any length of time would keep me awake at night, because you just never know 100% of the walls history or if any stresses have built up in the wall over the years.

I also love to sit new beam-ends on cast-in-situ concrete padstones made by shuttering up around the wall underneath the beam ends and filling up the boxes with concrete. If the job calls for it, I'll even drill the ends of the steel and drop a couple of bolts through the steel into the concrete... (belt and braces re-member!). Some folks use strong bricks or concrete blocks to build up padstones though, follow what your engineer recommends for your job. Leave the tempo-rary supports in place for three days or so to allow any mortar or concrete to harden off enough to hold the new load.

When it comes to the sides of the new opening, you need to either saw or chop the bricks off cleanly. Sawing with an electric or petrol driven saw gives a brilliant cut and finish, but it's only really suitable on the outside skin of a house or on total rebuilds as it makes a heck of a lot of dust (check what your local tool hire store has in stock though, saws are getting better all the time). In most cases, you'll be able to chop the bricks using a hammer and bolster; simply tap alter-nately the front, top and the backside if you have access (moderately gently and repeatedly) until the brick breaks away (cleanly... ish). Mark an accurate plumb line either side of your new opening before starting and don't forget to allow a little extra width to either fit/pack the new doorframe or for the new plaster-work in plain openings. For smaller jobs consider using your SDS power drill to drill a series of holes close together along your cut line etc. (two or three holes per brick). The brick is very likely to break through the holes, enabling you to better control the breaking point.

Remember that bricks laid in lime mortar are very desirable as they clean up easily for reuse or you can sell them on and make a good profit. Whereas, it's quite difficult to remove mortar from bricks laid in cement-based mortar (9 times out of 10). They are usually only good for further breaking up and using as rubble or hardcore on landscaping jobs in the garden or landfill.

A note about chimneys: Although I don't know why, folks are always re-moving chimneys and regardless of what your neighbour or the bloke in the pub says, chimneys are *always* structural and any remaining sections *always* need supporting, unless you are taking whole thing down, through the roof and right up to the chimney pot, i.e. everything! I couldn't sleep at night if I thought you were going to take the chimney breast out in your bedroom and leave the rest of the stack hanging in the attic space... (preferably you'll need a steel beam under it, or custom-made steel brackets if it's a small one (google gallows brackets for more info).

REMOVING CONCRETE

Oh, what fun you're going to have! Concrete is, as you know pretty tough stuff and guess what, it's tough to remove as well, so no surprise there. But there are some tricks you can use to make the job easier. First, enrol at your local gym and hit the weights. Second (only kidding). Nope, muscles will help you, but technique; now there's a heavy hitter.

You see, concrete *is* incredibly strong (bear with me) ... but *only in compression*. In *tension*, not so much. The secret is to attack the concrete at its weakest point and that's at the edges, where it's in tension and not supported very well. Hitting it at the edge applies the force across the slab, putting the top in tension. You're not trying to crush it (where it's strong), you're trying to snap it, (where it's weak). If you can lever the slab up a little using a large bar, (even a tiny bit) you'll create lots more tension in the slab and find it even easier! Hitting concrete in the middle will never break it., i.e. because it's surrounded (and supported) on all sides by more concrete. The hammer will bounce off.

First up, a word about shrapnel (and no, you don't need to head for your bunker!). You're applying huge forces when you hit concrete with a sledgehammer and part of the surface shatters into lots of small pieces, some of which will fly out in all directions. So, save your shorts for the beer after you've finished and wear sturdy trousers for this job. Oh, and don't forget to prop sheets of plywood up against anything breakable. You know, like doors and windows. Don't say I didn't warn you...

The best place to start is in a corner or an edge as second best. If you're inside a room you might need to start with a club hammer and a chisel (and gloves/goggles), because there is not enough room to swing the big hammer. Once you have a broken edge started, keep moving, don't hit same place twice, it'll just chip, work along an imaginary line with your sledgehammer, a little bit back (say 100mm to 150mm or 4″ to 6″) from the freshly broken edge and aim to break off small sections. Never wander further into the slab hoping to break off a bigger chunk, always keep close to that broken edge.

Try to stand on the slab itself and not on the rubble you've broken off already. I know it's not always possible and sometimes it does feel like it breaks easier working towards the non-broken part of the slab, breaking the slab down and towards you; just watch your footing or better still, move each piece of broken concrete out of the way as you go. Try both ways and see what works best. Each slab behaves differently under the hammer depending on its quality. Ironically, sometimes soft concrete is harder to remove than hard stuff, because soft concrete absorbs some of the blow, whereas hard stuff is brittle and snaps.

Once you've hit the concrete a few times and you have a small section that's broken away a little, you still have some work to do to get it out. Further hits with the hammer might help, but try a long pry bar in the new cracks as well, and use it to lever away sections of concrete. Pry bars work amazingly well because the remaining slab is a very good point to lever against as it's immovable. Using bars like this applies a huge force against the little piece you're trying to shift, to great effect.

If the hammer is not breaking the concrete, go closer to the edge i.e. to take smaller pieces. If it's still not breaking, then it's likely you'll need a concrete breaker. Electric ones are the easiest for concrete up to 100mm (4″) or so, but if you're going much above 100mm (4″) then you'll need a compressor driven breaker (large, heavy, and noisy).

Occasionally you might find steel reinforcement embedded in the concrete. Be careful with this, it's easy to hurt yourself as its springy stuff. Use an electric angle grinder with a cutting disc and cut it away regularly (you still have your goggles and gloves on, right?). Watch that the sparks from the grinder don't hit any glass because they can be hot enough to embed themselves. I once ruined the rear windscreen on my old Daimler cutting rusty metal out of the floor, lesson learned the hard way.

REMOVING STUD WALLS

Most folks just use brute force to remove the drywall itself as it's not terribly strong. But if you want to be more methodical, or you're removing a small or specific area; locate the fasteners and remove them first. To find the fasteners you'll need to find the timber inside the wall. Look for studs spaced at various centres (distance centre to centre between studs). Common spacing is 600mm (24″) but 400mm (16″) is also very common and you'll also see 450mm (18″) and even 500mm (20″). Sometimes the spacing's are all over the place, depending on the age of the wall, its size, the location of the wall and the general competence or mood of the carpenter on the day he built it. Personally, I usually work left to right so the last spacing on the right will be an odd size (unless the wall length fits multiples of the stud spacing I'm using). But a left handed or Arab carpenter might do the exact opposite...

Proper 'stud detectors' are available, but you can also use a small handheld electrician's metal/volt detector to find them (set to find metal). You can also try wrapping a small, powerful earth magnet in tissue or thin cloth, suspended from a string, hold the string and magnet on the wall, moving it back and forth where you suspect there are screws/nails (you'll feel a slight 'pull' as it passes any metal). On true drywall (not plastered) you might see the tiny depressions over the fasteners (because most fillers shrink slightly) by shining a torch across the painted surface. Logically, finding the fasteners tells you where the timber studs are...

Use a pointed bradawl or similar, to scrape out the plaster or filler over the fasteners and then remove them. Once the fasteners are out, cut a small hole (to get your fingers in) and pull out the drywall, joint tape breaks easily.

Once the drywall cladding is out of the way, either knock the bottom of the studs along the wall until the nails are free, then twist out the tops. Alternatively, saw through the stud down at an angle (square cuts will jam and be difficult to remove) and lever out the top and bottom pieces (this method works well when removing window and door frames too). Then remove the head plate (nailed or screwed into the ceiling joists or noggins) and the sole plate (nailed or screwed into the floor.). Hopefully you'll find the ceiling and flooring were in place prior to building the stud wall, making it easy to make good any damage. If you find a difference in floor or ceiling levels, you're in for some creative correction work to find a workable levelling up solution.

REMOVING PIPES AND WIRES

The law is pretty tight these days about what you, the homeowner can do with your own electrical and even water systems; but this varies from country to country, so I'd be silly to try and cover everything here. I don't agree with a lot of the restrictions, as I believe a well read and competent homeowner can carry out small alterations to as good, if not better standard than some qualified folks I've seen. But the law is the law, so I must recommend you hire a qualified person for anything which might contravene the law in your area (or at least don't get caught, because I'll deny everything if they ask me and this book is set to self-destruct if you quote anything from it...).

But you might want to remove a few things ready for some improvements which shouldn't get you into trouble. Both pipes and wires carry seriously dangerous or potentially property damaging stuff. Gas, water, heating oil, waste water, sewage, and electricity are just a few things you don't want to mess with. The No.1 rule is: don't touch anything that's carrying something, without removing the 'something' first. Mostly applies to water pipes, gas pipes, heating oil pipes, oh and don't forget the wires (just because you can't see electricity, doesn't mean it's not there, waiting patiently to kill you!).

STOPCOCKS (TO ISOLATE WATER PIPES)

As mentioned before, often found in really stupid locations such as underneath kitchen sinks or deep into airing cupboards and even sometimes underground out in the yard. And because they live in the dark and rarely used, they are far from easy to close when you really need them (fully close and 7/8ths open yours once a year as a preventative measure from now on okay?).

Stopcocks or water valves stick because folks open them fully and then leave them there. Over time, a valve stuck hard in the fully open stop is very difficult to persuade to move again. The correct way is to open them fully and then close them half a turn or so. This enables a little 'wiggle' room for the valve when it slowly becomes stuck again. If I know I'm going to open an old valve, I'll use a penetrating lube the day before, (WD40 or such like).

If your stopcock is stuck, use a lubricant first and leave it awhile, then try tapping gently around the valve with a timber stick (never anything metal...) at the same time as trying to 'rock' the valve back and forth (oh, and don't forget to pray...). Some valve designs have a gland nut (behind the wheel where the stem goes into the valve), which you can loosen slightly to relieve pressure on the seal/washer etc. (prepare for some small weeping/leaking when the valve finally moves). Use extra leverage like wrenches on the valve at your peril, you might get away with it or it could go horribly wrong...

WATER PIPES

Have I mentioned isolating the water supply first? What, only half a dozen times? Cool, hopefully you'll know how to do it now, yes? Here are some of the different kinds of pipe you might see...

- Lead pipe (seriously, I still see this occasionally), Lead is an easy one to figure out, see it, remove it. All of it. Replace with new stuff or it might eventually send you bananas, allegedly...

- Black iron. Still common and you'll need large wrenches to dismantle it. BSP British Standard Pipe in the UK and NPT in the USA. Parallel threaded fittings compress a rubber seal/washer or O ring; whereas tapered male threads have a sealing compound or material (PTFE tape or hemp and plumbers jointing compound) wrapped around the threads before tightening.

- Copper pipe. Installed several different ways...

  Solid, non-dismantlable soldered fittings. Use a rotary pipe cutter to remove any pipe you want to modify or re-use. A hacksaw is fine to remove anything you're recycling.

  Brass compression fittings with threaded nuts. Undo them with a pair of wrenches, hold one onto the body of the fitting (holding it tight to prevent movement) and the other (facing the opposite way) to turn the nut (spanners also work if you have them this big). The pipe will have a small 'olive' or ring tightly gripped close to the end of the pipe, cut this off with a junior hacksaw to recover the nut (without nicking the pipe). You can buy olives separately and re-use the main fitting and nuts.

  Push-fit fittings (brass or plastic). Various designs, some have a retaining ring you push, some need a special little tool to push back the retaining ring and some have screw off nuts similar to the compression fittings above.

  Note: as mentioned above, never re-use a pipe you've sawn off with a hacksaw in push-fit fittings, it's too rough. Always use a rotary pipe cutter which leaves neat, slightly rounded pipe ends which won't damage the O rings inside the fittings.

- Plastic pipe. Usually installed using push fit fittings with O rings although occasionally with compression fittings as above. Most plastic pipe systems need small metal inserts in the pipe ends to stop the pipe crushing as it goes into the fitting.

WASTE PIPES

Unfortunately, there is no way to switch off a waste pipe as they are empty when not in use. So, make sure that nothing is going to go into the pipe once you have dismantled part of the system. You wouldn't believe how many tradesmen I've seen emptying water into a sink that they have just removed the trap from... plus you really don't want anyone to flush a toilet upstairs whilst you're dismantling a pipe downstairs... Use duct tape to tape down the toilet lid (and other access points) and use a marker pen to write *do not use* in big letters on the duct tape, you'll be glad you did...

If your pipe fittings (joints, bends etc.) have large(ish) rims where the pipe enters, then it's a push fit design. These have a big rubber seal, not unlike an O ring (in fact, small diameter waste pipes are just big O rings) this seal grabs the pipe tightly. The fitting lubricant dries out over the years and you'll needs to twist and pull quite hard to dismantle them after a few years (especially the 110mm or 4″ underground or vent pipes).

If the pipes fittings are slim looking, then it's been solvent welded together and you can't dismantle these. Saw out what you don't want using an old wood saw or a hacksaw.

Be aware that any traps will be full of water and any pipes not laid to a perfect fall will probably have dirty water sitting in them as well. I often throw dry sand into toilets before moving them to soak it all up.

ELECTRICAL WIRING

I think I've already mentioned isolating the electricity supply first? Yes? Okay, 'nuff said. Your second line of defence is the voltstick we looked at in the *Repairing Stuff* chapter, if you didn't buy one then, definitely buy one now.

Alternatively, just switch off the entire electricity supply using the main breaker in the fuse box. I say this because not everything is logical, especially on an older house where stuff might extend into another 'zone', making the descriptions on each breaker unreliable. Never trust a breaker description; remember the golden, never to be broken rule "isolate and test before touching". It's possible an electrical shock won't kill you, but then again, it you're taking a 50:50 chance, (so; do you feel lucky, punk?). In addition, even if you do survive, you're likely to suffer a whole plethora of other nasty side effects from burns to neurological problems. Still tempted? Then read up 'electric shock' on Wikipedia, that should relieve you once and for all of the temptation to take risks with live wires...

So, you've isolated and taped down the right breaker (or the whole system) and you've tested the wires you want to remove. First step is to label everything you remove. Wrap white electrical tape (or masking tape in a pinch) around the cable and back onto itself, creating a tag. Write on it where you're disconnecting the cable from. Take a photo of the wires in situ if you intend to replace anything later (although re-connecting might take you outside what you can legally do yourself...)

Next, remove any covers, switch fronts, power socket fronts etc. and using a proper electrical screwdriver, undo the individual wires. Make the bare ends safe by popping them individually into separate terminal blocks, or preferably separate Wago style terminal blocks.

If you cut cables to remove whole sections (still 'label the cable', coo, that rhymes!) and bear mind cutting cables may trip the whole fuse box (if you've only isolated the part of the system you're working on). This happens because breakers only kill the live side of the circuit or system. When you cut a cable, you unintentionally connect the neutral wire to the earth wire via your metal cutters. Because neutral wires connect together throughout the system, the sensitive breaker will read a small voltage from elsewhere and most likely trip the breaker, even though the power is technically 'off' in the circuit.

Incidentally, to refresh your school physics, electricity works by sending a current from a live 'bus' bar in the fuse box through a breaker (or fuse) down the live or hot wire to an appliance. The current returns down the neutral back to the fuse box. A third wire is the earth or ground wire which under normal circumstances carries no current. The earth wire connects literally to the earth which has an infinite capacity to absorb current. If a fault develops and earthed metal components of the system become live, the earth wire exists to carry away any current and dump it safely into the ground until the breaker (which monitors the earth wire for current) trips out the live wire, thus breaking the faulty circuit (it takes milliseconds normally).

Unfortunately, electrical standards vary a lot between different places so I can't go into specifics here, but here are some different circuits anyway...

- Radial, where a live or hot wire runs from the fuse box directly to the appliance (especially common for high load stuff like cookers or water heaters etc.) and the neutral runs back to the fuse box. Most often in a single cable containing three wires, live, neutral and earth (hence often called twin + earth). Various sizes depending on the loading; e.g. lighting, power outlets, cookers, heaters, or AC etc. Typically, 2.5mm, 4mm, 6mm and 10mm cable etc.

- Ring circuits where a cable (twin + earth) jumps from outlet to outlet and then back to the fuse box (e.g. power outlets in the UK). Typically, 2.5mm cable).

- Lighting circuits where a smaller cross section cable runs from light fitting to light fitting in zones or even whole floors (typically 1.0mm or 1.5mm cable).

- Zone circuits where power goes into a zone (room or area) and around from outlet to outlet (combined power and lights).

- Two-way (or more) circuits to switch an outlet (e.g. a lamp in a corridor or stairwell) from multiple locations. Cable contains an extra core (three core + earth).

- Network cables to provide internet and phone services (CAT 5e or CAT 6 etc.). Incidentally, don't run these together with power cables as it can cause interference.

- Small misc cables such as security alarm cables or old telephone cables or doorbell cables etc.

- Earth circuit (green and yellow) running from metal pipework around the property to the fuse board and from the fuse board to a long earth rod hammered deep into the ground outdoors.

- Armoured cable circuits. Anything outdoors and in the ground typically needs extra protection. Usually, heavy steel reinforcement and thick plastic sheathing. Typically used from the fuse box to the garage, workshop, or even larger sheds.

- Commercial or conduit wiring. Typically, industrial premises (including offices) use easily accessible open trays or covered conduits to run wiring. Usually individual wires instead of cable (twin + earth etc.). Lots of additional colours in use too.

If you need to cut a cable (after isolating it of course) to remove part of a circuit, you can make the end temporarily safe as per the next image or better still, put a junction box on the end, or terminate the bare wires properly inside WAGO or 'sugar cube' style terminal blocks. Never mix colours of course...

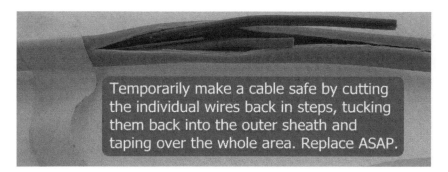

Temporarily make a cable safe by cutting the individual wires back in steps, tucking them back into the outer sheath and taping over the whole area. Replace ASAP.

WHAT SHALL I DO WITH ALL THE STUFF?

Obviously, it depends what you're taking out or dismantling, but many things might be useful on future projects, either your own or someone else's. But in brief, remove the stuff, clean it up and make it safe (take nails out etc.) and then either...

- Store the material for use on your own future projects, e.g. fit old kitchen cabinets into the garage/workshop.

- Sell it to someone else via classifieds, notice boards, auction or even a placard outside your home.

- Give it away (friend, neighbour, or classifieds). Remember if you give it away, you don't have to dispose of it yourself, so this does have a very real time and monetary value.

- Upcycle some of it into art or find a completely different use for it; three old doors hinged together to make a folding screen, or an old ceramic sink into a garden planter (or a working outdoor sink) etc.

- Dispose of it via a waste disposal company using a builder's skip, container, or bin; they usually separate it back at their yard and recycle where possible.

- Take it to a local town or municipal recycling centre. Make life easy by keeping different materials separate, as you usually need to put them into different containers at the centre.

- Throw it away into landfill (absolutely the last resort).

I always reclaim clean and intact stuff, e.g. good timber, bricks etc. However, for the broken, dirty, obsolete stuff...hmm. You must evaluate how much work it takes to make something good enough to either store yourself, give away or sell, in relation to its actual worth. For example, it's not worth saving a piece of timber, if it's going to take ages to take all the nails out of it and scrape thick paint off it etc. However, timber studs from inside a wall which only have a couple of nails at each end might easily be worth keeping for future projects or bundling up with others to sell or give away.

Right, that's the wall out and you've given the old kitchen units to the neighbour for his workshop; are you ready to make some improvements?

IMPROVING STUFF

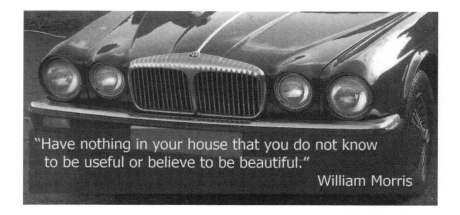

"Have nothing in your house that you do not know to be useful or believe to be beautiful."

William Morris

Refurbish, remodel, renovate, regenerate, rehabilitate, rejuvenate, renewal, restore (and that's only the ones that begin with 'R'!), plus a few like upgrade, home improvement and modernise are all words you might hear when folks are talking about fixing up their homes. All of them are subtly different in their exact meaning, but really, they all mean one thing; *changing your stuff to make it better suit you and your needs*, in other words *to improve it*.

Making improvements in and around your home really is the umbrella under which all your DIY skills will gather. You'll probably use something from *all* the chapters in this book. You might be assembling stuff, demolishing stuff, installing stuff, or even making stuff from scratch. Everything from restoring your bargain antique fair furniture find to ripping down that wall and popping in a bigger, fancier kitchen.

Now this chapter naturally overlaps with several others in the book; I mean; is re-decorating a bedroom maintenance or an improvement? Arguably both! So, bear with me and forgive me if I wander into repairs or maintenance along the way (or repeat myself... again).

Where do you start when you want to improve something in your home? Broadly, you need to think about three things...

- Evaluate what you have now and note exactly how it fails your current or expected future needs.

- Decide exactly what look/feel/function you want to achieve and how it should be once it's finished.

- What exactly do you need to achieve that end? i.e. the DIY 'big five' materials, skills, tools, time, and cash of course.

Let's look at each of these in a little more depth...

EVALUATING WHAT YOU HAVE

It's very likely some stuff in your home is bugging you and you're not even aware why. We all do things a certain way because of the constraints imposed on us by the layout and fixtures already in place. Reaching up to put that large pan on the top of the cupboards three times a week? Why? Do you need more under counter storage space? Fed up with kids dumping coats and bags on the floor when they come home or leaving wet clothes all over? Maybe you need more cloakroom space or a utility room to hang up wet sports gear or better yet, to create a dedicated 'mud' room (if you're a little bit 'posh'). Still struggling to mow the grass on that awkward slope in the garden because it's always been there? Maybe you could build a wall to level it out or reshape it completely etc. etc.

Make notes about everyday things which repeatedly annoy or irritate you. These will help you evaluate why your stuff fails you; for example, the light switches are all different heights in a long corridor we have (which really niggles me) so it's gone on the list to swap out the plates and level up the heights next time we re-decorate.

Use these notes to help you decide what it is you really need, because removing everyday niggles improves practicality and makes for more harmonious relationships with your stuff (you might even be less grumpy with your other half...). When planning your needs, you'll have the opportunity to improve how things look, in addition to improving practicality and function. Nice bonus.

You're probably subconsciously improving your home all the time, even if it's just deciding that a grubby area in your hallway really needs bringing up to date with some new flooring, trims, and paint.

Mentally you've already...

- Noticed the grubby walls and chipped trims.

- Realised the paint is beyond fixing with a thorough cleaning.

- Remembered there's none of that paint colour left over.

- Decided a change of colour would brighten the hallway.

- Remembered you need new paint roller sleeves/ brushes.
- Realised you'd been ignoring how frayed the carpet is.
- Thought about what sort of new flooring you want.
- Thought about which long weekend you could do it.
- Thought about when you could pick up the materials.
- Remembered the wall needs cleaning to remove dirt, grease, and other contaminants etc. before painting.
- Remember reading that two coats make a better job.
- Remembered to ask Google whether you paint the walls or trims first (trims, in my opinion...)
- Remembered to ask Google how to fit laminate flooring.

Wow. And that's what you did just walking through the hallway as you leave the house each day...

Don't forget the rest of the house at this point too. Preferably, you should draw up rough yearly plans for projects you'd like to do over the next five years or so. Integrate your plans to avoid decorating the lounge the year before you decide you want to open-up a nearby wall, spoiling the work you've already done. Some of my clients have annual, five and even ten-year plans for their houses (I know, most of them are a little bit posh too...).

If you're new to a place, definitely take some time to 'live' for a while before you try figure out what works and what doesn't with the space. It's very tempting to make sweeping changes in a new house, but this is costly if after a couple of years, you wished you'd gone for something a little different.

Consider...

- How do you use the different spaces day to day? e.g. where do you eat, hang out, relax, store stuff, washing requirements etc.
- How does your use of space change in the evenings or at the weekends? Flop on the sofa for a movie and pizza or beers you're your mates in the garden etc.?
- How does your space fit all of your entertaining needs?
- Are you using all the area you have, or are there 'dead' areas that are underutilized or even places you never use?

- What about your storage needs, is there enough? Stupid question, there is never enough.

- Are you storing stuff you never use? (Recycle, give away or sell it!).

- Do you struggle or get frustrated with anything? If so, think about why and what you'd need to fix the problem.

- What are your furniture needs? Breakfast, daytime, night time, evenings, entertaining, inside, outside etc.

- Are there enough power outlets and are they in the right places? (err, never!).

- Is there enough lighting? Think about mood, placement, and different situations (cleaning, reading, guests etc.).

- Is your space practical? How do you handle rubbish, laundry or firewood, workshop space, is there an 'out of sight' working place in the garden etc. for all your practical or working stuff?

- How do your needs change throughout the seasons?

- Do you have enough outside space, storage, parking, etc?

- The garden? Oh, there's always more to do in the garden!

Dig deep with your plans (they are free!) but be realistic. Don't make grand plans for your garden if (in reality) you know you'll only have time to sit out there on the odd warm evening in the late summer. Consider instead having low maintenance areas, rather than gently winding paths though elaborate flower-beds and water features.

If you're planning improvements to other stuff like furniture or vehicles etc., you can still think about the condition they're in now and how you want them to look when you're finished. For example, do you want to restore that old veneered chest of drawers to make it look 'as new' or do you want to modernise it with a coat of paint and new handles or just clean it and leave it 'shabby chic' etc?

DECIDING WHAT YOU WANT

Just going to the store tells you we're a pretty individual (read weird!) bunch of folks, with products, colours, styles, and ideas ranging from the *'who would ever buy that?'* Right up to the *'that's insane, I love it,'* with a thousand variations in between.

The media, our upbringing and our peers influence us when it comes to making decisions about what we want in our homes, but don't let that stop you expressing your personality. Sure, you might need to think carefully before painting your doors and windows purple, but if your plans aren't going to hurt or offend anyone and it doesn't break any rules, knock yourself out! Arguably though, it's sensible to consider the long-term effects of any improvements you do; or at least ensure they're reversible or adaptable to something else if needs change. Respect that not everyone will appreciate your efforts, especially if your taste wanders into territory some might consider bizarre.

You can't do too much research finding out what your options are. Especially as you'll probably have to live with the end result for some time, decades even for kitchens, bathrooms, and landscaping etc.

WHAT DO YOU NEED?

The usual; cash, good looks, and a winning personality? No, not really, but you do need the DIY 'big five' which are materials, skills, tools, time, and cash. Plus of course the plan you made after reading the *Preparation and Planning* chapter earlier. You did make a proper plan, didn't you? Can't be bothered? Okay that's your choice, but here is the minimum you should do....

- Write up what you want to achieve.

- Make a list of things to buy, materials, tools etc. and where from.

- Confirm any outside help you've hired (if applicable).

- Brush up on any new skills and techniques you need to learn.

- Make a list of tasks; really break the job down step by step, including a brief note on how long you expect each one to take.

- Draw up a time schedule, when to start, how long each part will take and thus how long you expect the whole job to take etc.

IMPROVING YOUR HOME

If you don't include maintenance as improving your home, improvements generally fall into two broad categories, structural and cosmetic. Structural stuff is when you're working on the actual fabric of the house, removing walls, or adding extensions etc., and cosmetic is everything else, stuff like decorating or even replacing your old kitchen.

GETTING ADVICE

It's unlikely you've thought of all possible solutions, so get advice or inspiration from others. This varies from looking at Pinterest.com for inspiration on a theme for your lounge, to contacting a local architect for inventive solutions on how to get a new staircase up to that playroom you want in the attic.

Whilst cosmetic stuff is solely your domain, structural stuff nearly always means getting advice from outside (architect, structural engineer, or builder etc.) and obtaining approval from your local authority before you begin any work.

Getting approval is a good thing however, as it ensures what you want to do makes sense and is structurally sound. It'll also give you a blueprint to follow with specifications and advice. I've always found the building control dept. of local authorities to be extremely helpful, as long as you're trying to do a good job and treat them politely and with respect. Getting the proper approvals will also protect you from future legal problems if you want to sell the house. Remember, the local authority is not your enemy and treated properly, could turn out to be a useful ally...

You might also need approval from the authority for a project in the garden, especially if it involves any boundaries with neighbours. Boundary disputes are big business for lawyers and I'm always amazed at the lack of communication between folks who live *next door* to each other, for goodness sake! Always check first with the authority AND your neighbours before erecting your local tribute to the Great Wall of China.

GETTING APPROVAL

It's common in lots of places to have a two-tiered system for controlling building projects. One that covers the agreement in principle to go ahead with your project (Planning Permission in the UK) and another to handle the actual technical or structural details of your project (Building Regulations in the UK) to ensure what you build is safe and abides by local laws or standards.

PLANNING PERMISSION

You'll need planning permission for larger jobs (like extensions above a certain size) or for any work likely to have an impact on your neighbours. Planning laws exist to encourage development in line with local authority objectives and to stop people building anything that's unreasonable, offensive, or unfair to people living nearby.

People usually make a big fuss about 'overly restrictive' planning systems, but to be honest I've always found them sensible. If the authority denies permission for your project, there's normally a good reason; e.g. the proposed project negatively affects someone else's property in a significant way. Remember that not everyone views your project the way you do; they may have reasonable objections based on wider implications (and there may be issues you don't know about). Don't forget that if a local planning department approves something for you; it's difficult to refuse others who might want to do a similar thing. Over time, this may alter the whole character of an area (remember satellite dishes and solar panels...?)

It's the responsibility of urban planners in the local planning department to shape an area for the good of the community as a whole. The local authority really *wants to see* development and isn't just being mean if it refuses your plans. Development is a good thing because it indicates investment and commitment to the area. Overall, planners want to work *with you,* but of course, your plans must make everyone happy, including those closest to you. And forget the stories about corruption, I find it difficult to believe how this happens in today's more transparent committees with the ever-hungry media watching every move. An individual or a few individuals going against the flow would surely stick out and warrant increased scrutiny, but maybe I'm lucky to live in a relatively fair country, or am I just being naïve ...?

If you are proposing to build something and you think might need permission, don't be frightened to ask your local authority for advice. It's what they're there for. They'll also send you any appropriate forms to complete, along with details about the inevitable fees to pay.

Most authorities these days have streamlined the decision process using all manner of online tools. Mostly this means answering a succession of questions, mining down to the end result of: [1] your proposal is allowable under permitted development rights or [2] you need to apply for planning permission.

PERMITTED DEVELOPMENT

You might not need planning permission as many local authorities automatically grant permission for common smaller projects and cosmetic stuff. These *permitted development rights* apply if your project conforms to a set of widely published clear rules.

Permitted development approval systems prevent folks overrunning the local planning authority with applications for common small projects (where they'd grant permission anyway). However, if you live in a conservation area or in a place of historical interest, you'll face stricter restrictions. On historically valuable properties, you may not have any permitted development rights at all. It's always best to check with your local authority in any restricted area before starting anything. Find the local authority website for your area and search in the planning department for *permitted development rights* or search online to get an idea of what's allowed where you live.

One last point on planning permission, check your property deeds or paperwork for any *restrictive covenants* related to carrying out work on your home. You may need permission from the original builder (for example) before carrying out your project. Although this may appear to be a paperwork formality, failing to do it may cause delays and incur additional costs when lawyers acting for any future prospective purchaser find out...

For example: I bought a pair of tiny houses with the intention of combining them into one regular sized one. Planning permission check: not required. Building regulations check: only new doorways between the two properties needed inspecting. Great, went ahead and all went well. Come to sell the finished property and the sellers legal beagles asked for the permission paperwork from the original construction company (bear in mind the houses were 35 years old). Turns out there was a restrictive covenant requiring homeowners to notify the original builders of any intended work for the first 99 years. Since there was no system in place to notify the original company, I had to pay for an 'indemnity insurance', which must be a wonderful revenue earner with negligible risk for the insurance company. All good in the end but I could have saved myself some hassle by reading the small print. It is not widely known, but you can often get covenants modified or removed for a relatively small fee, especially if they are old and arguably irrelevant or obsolete because the situation or conditions have changed.

BUILDING REGULATIONS

Laws governing the technical aspect of buildings exist to ensure what you're planning to do is safe and conforms to modern best practise for your type of project. With any project including a structural element like foundations or removing walls, or a safety element such as electricity or gas installations or an environmental impact like energy usage, you have a duty to ensure you carry on in a manner unlikely to endanger either yourself or future owners of your property.

Even if your project is a small one that doesn't need a specific planning permission approval, most often you'll still need to obtain building regulations approval to ensure your work is safe and does its best to help the environment.

Even if you don't need an actual inspection, your work still needs to comply to common best practise standards relevant to the rules of the day.

Small, like-for-like repairs usually don't need building regulation approval, however most bigger projects such as extending a building or erecting a new one, obviously require building regulation approval. What's less understood is that nowadays the following smaller jobs, such as replacements or alterations for example; need building regulation approval (in the UK at least): For example, if you...

- Replace your fuse box or connected electrics.
- Change your pipework to install a new bathroom.
- Alter any electrical wiring in a bathroom.
- Install an air-conditioning system.
- Install new windows and doors.
- Replace roof coverings on pitched or flat roofs.
- Fit or replace a heating system.
- Modify or extend a heating system.

Don't be shy, contact your local authority before you begin and ask for advice; get them to send you the forms requesting building regulations approval whilst you're at it (unless your authority has gone totally online for applications...). You'll have to prove your proposal complies with the regulations by submitting the forms and any detailed specifications you have about your proposed project. Any structural elements need calculations, (usually from a structural engineer), to prove the work will conform to current rules. Once approved, this indicates your proposed work is safe and conforms to the current best building practises. After you've completed the work and had it inspected, you'll get a certificate confirming it meets the regulations.

Now for some weird aspects of the complex building regulations: some work is exempt from the regulations such as: buildings not frequented by people, greenhouses, some agricultural buildings, temporary buildings, and some small detached buildings and even some small extensions such as conservatories, porches, or car ports... Although electrical regs. (part P) and insulation (part L) do apply to some of the above... And for the final kicker, even if your project is exempt from all building regulations, you might still require planning permission. Like I said, you are going to have to spend some time reading your local authorities published docs and most likely end up giving them a call to confirm your status.

KEEP GOOD RECORDS

Always keep records on file for any bigger home improvements, especially stuff like extensions, new kitchens or bathrooms, new heating systems or any structural work, inside or out. It might be important one day to know exactly when you removed the chimney or when you fitted the new hot water tank. Store everything from receipts to guarantees and even your own notes about the job. Any official paperwork related to permissions etc., from the local authority obviously gets pride of place in this file. Everything will be interesting and useful to you and any future owners.

IMPROVING YOUR GARDEN

TV shows about improving your outdoor or garden space are as popular as home makeover shows because you have a lot of latitude and freedom when it comes to improving your garden. This expansion of possibilities is largely due to the huge and ever-increasing amount of resources available from garden centres these days. Gone are the days of a grass lawn with narrow borders around the edges. Enter decking (thanks Mr Alan Titchmarsh, you made me a lot of money!) or a hundred shades of patio, as well as a warehouse full of different materials to use and furniture to sit on to enjoy the results of your labour. And not forgetting the plants; now from every corner of the globe, many specially chosen to cope with the weather conditions where you live.

The first step is, as usual, to get to know what you already have in your garden and how it works. You'll need to think about...

SOFT STUFF...

- Which direction does the sun come from?
- Note the shade and full sun areas as they change throughout the day on a rough sketch of your garden.
- Note any dry or damp areas on your rough sketch too.
- Note any 'frost pockets' or cold spots in the winter time.
- What soil do you have, acid, alkaline, sandy, loamy, clay, rubble, rocky etc? Cheap testing kits are available or search online for "soil testing"; the BBC gardening and RHS are great for advice.

- Are there any special factors that affect your garden, wind, sea air, high rainfall, low rainfall, heavy snow etc?

- The above points will help you choose suitable plants for each area. All plant labels have symbols to indicate what conditions they like to grow well.

- Garden use; how do you use the space? Do you sit out relaxing a lot? Or do you like to be busy in the garden working with plants etc? Or, do you just enjoy looking at it out of the window because you're busy? Design a planting scheme that fits your lifestyle.

- How much time do you have for maintenance & upkeep?

- Do you go away often? Choose plants that can cope with dry conditions unless you have accommodating neighbours or can afford to install complex automatic watering systems.

- As a shortcut, what are neighbours growing? Copy planting schemes when it's clear they are thriving. Ask for small cuttings to get free plants if your neighbours are friendly. Steal them when they are on holiday if they are not... (just kidding...).

- Google 'seed swaps' or 'seed exchanges' in your area to get cheap or free seeds close to home (and to meet interesting people).

HARD STUFF...

- What are your parking space requirements, and will they change when any children get older etc?

- Do you hang washing outside to dry? A line or a carousel?

- Do you entertain in the garden or cook outside regularly?

- What seating requirements do you need?

- How much hard standing area do you need in relation to the soft-planted areas? Do you need landscaped pathways to access all areas?

- What storage space do you need for garden tools, lawn mowers and other gardening paraphernalia etc?

- Do you need a greenhouse or cold frames or space for planted cuttings or seedbeds etc.?

- Do you have space for a small vegetable garden, (or large if you're fortunate)? You should, you really, really should you know, you'll love the end results...

- What storage do you need for any outdoor pursuits like bicycles, skis, sports equipment, and sledges etc?

- What other storage space do you need for stuff like trailers, caravans, or if you're lucky, a motorbike or a boat etc.

- Incorporate a small area screened from the general garden at the side of or behind a well-positioned potting shed for example. Use it for your compost heap (in the sun if possible), spare bamboo canes, wheelbarrows, water barrel, new cuttings, etc.

- And for those of us in colder climes, you'll need to think about snow; or more specifically, where to put it!

As you can see there's a lot of practical stuff to design around when improving the average garden, it's not just about looking pretty. Fortunately, there are lots of websites and books around to help you with the specifics, but remember one thing, *stuff grows*! Try to *future proof* your garden as much as you can. Remember what you want now might not be appropriate as you grow older. That cactus garden you desperately love might not be so hot with little kids running amok in the garden. Or those fast-growing bushes you wanted to kick things off quickly, might turn into a curse in a couple of decades, just when you want to be taking it easy in the garden. Elaborate planting schemes in a garden will turn into a near full time job once established. It's best to aim for a careful balance between high and low maintenance stuff, if you're to enjoy your garden and not see it as a chore in the future.

IMPROVING OTHER STUFF

Maybe you already have a project sitting in your shed, or finally you can afford that old car you always fancied. No matter the project, there's no doubt improving stuff for fun is, well, erm, fun obviously... It's also a great hobby; a good way to relax; it's a way to show off your creative passion and it's a great way of getting good stuff cheaply. What's not to like?

And it's a good thing that improving stuff is fun, because sadly, making improvements to many objects makes no financial sense, i.e. the finished item is worth less than your costs to restore it. Hence, it's usually a labour of love, since you might never get your money back. But thankfully there is more to life than the bottom line (did you know hobbies can help you live longer?). Labours of love consistently produce works of such beauty you could call them art. The internet is awash with the amazing things folks have done to a plethora of inanimate objects. From the mundane to the outrageous, from the cute to the downright funny. All your projects are worthy of the time you invest in them for the satisfaction alone, not to mention the awe and envy among your friends and family of your creative handiness! For inspiration and ideas, Google combinations of your items name with keywords like 'makeover', 're-model', 'before and after', 'design ideas' and 'project' etc.

But first, you need to consider your projects end point; how you want it to look or what you want it to do when you're finished. Generally, there are two options: restoration (part or full) or modernisation. Actually, there's also a third option becoming popular; you can simply use it as it is, they call it shabby chic... Oh, and a fourth option where you upcycle or re-purpose stuff into something completely different... I'd better stop here (there's more), but you catch my drift, improving stuff is a pretty big field...

And all ~~two, three,~~ four options start off with, yup, you guessed it.... *cleaning*... But we already looked at this in detail in the *Cleaning Stuff* section in the *Maintaining Stuff* chapter, so you can relax. Phew.

RESTORING

Proper and full restoration is a serious undertaking and whilst it's possible to make most things look 'as new', it'll take serious resources; e.g. time and maybe even all your money... Oh, and you'll need space, maybe lots of it and for a long time (read years) for projects like vehicles etc. It took me over 6 years, on and off to finish my Daimler Two Door car...

For some things, completely dismantling them is the best way to go. Vehicles for example, often need stripping out to gain access to areas needing repair before repainting and then replacing any worn parts as you rebuild. At this level of restoration, you'll probably need to remove finishes back to bare surfaces (see *Physical Removal of Finishes* coming up in a couple of pages). Even a piece of furniture will be much easier to work on if you first remove any doors, drawers, handles, hinges, and anything else remotely easy to remove.

Head down to the local auction or second-hand shop and look for sound but scruffy furniture bargains. Or you might have inherited some classic furniture from your grandparent's you can't bear to throw away, but it doesn't 'fit' you or your home in its current state. Or of course you might have been really bad at maintaining your stuff and now it's looking decidedly shabby and not in a cool, 'shabby chic' kind of way. Improve them cheaply by cleaning and re-applying new finishes. Hmm, is that improvements or maintenance, I've strayed again, haven't I?

Being able to tidy up older stuff is a real money saver because lots of old stuff has little value and sometimes no value at all, i.e. they can't give it away. Now I'm obviously not talking about that Louis XIV carved walnut chaise longue here, but rather the overlooked stuff from a decade or three ago. My work often takes me to local refuse and recycling centres, and I see amazing stuff folks have thrown away. Don't worry I am not suggesting you become a 'bin monkey' scavenging around in the local dump (although you'd find some great stuff). No, try searching for very cheap projects amongst stuff people don't want any more in local classifieds, local flea markets, online classifieds or increasingly, online auctions like eBay. My local 'eBay' website even has a treasure trove of a 'give away' section. Most online auction sites allow you to set up notifications or alerts using your keywords... simple.

MODERNISING

Of course, sometimes cleaning and painting isn't enough, you want to drag something kicking and screaming into your life, and for that you need, modernisation.

Instead of buying something new or simply restoring something old, look for different and innovative ways to modernise old stuff you find or already have. It requires a little imagination or research but by being a little creative, you'll end up with some very cheap and unique furniture. Websites like pinterest.com are invaluable for inspiration, in fact it will blow you away how creative some folks are.

A few simple modernisations will bring stuff up to date by altering finishes and hardware to make it fit into a more modern environment. A 1960's dark oak kitchen I worked on for example, had antique style handles, wavy edged top and bottom trims and a very dark walnut stain. I cut the all the wavy edges off the trims to square them off, found some simple, silver handles and painted the whole lot white and wow, those 50 years just dropped away...

Fashion influences most areas of our lives, with some things sticking around and some that fizzle out almost instantly (thankfully!). The fact you might want to modernize something means fashion has already influenced you, however little you acknowledge it...

Just think carefully before committing to any permanent changes though, and don't make impulse decisions. Changing something in your home isn't like buying a new shirt; you can't just stick it in the back of the wardrobe and not wear it. Obviously, this is especially important with anything that would take a lot of work to reverse. Sure, you could try to remove the paint from the natural pine balustrade and spindles you painted at the weekend, but it will be a huge task and will never look as good as it did before you started.

Consider instead sticking with evergreen designs and styles that never really go out of fashion. I'm sure avocado bathroom suites will come back into fashion again one day (hopefully long after I'm dead and gone, once per lifetime is quite enough thankyou...), but classy stuff and good practical designs last a long time *because* they are classy and a good design, i.e. the exact opposite of daft fads and fashions centred around cosmetics.

Okay, so you've got some classics you want to work your magic on. Changing a few details can be very effective in bringing them up to date. Some things to think about....

- Change the colour or introduce a different finish.

- Remove an unwanted finish and go naked or bare.

- Introduce a finish to a previously bare piece.

- Cover up things you don't like the look of. Use timber panels, trims, fabric, plastic, metal, grills, screens etc. Hinge a painting over an ugly seldom used access panel, James Bond style...

- Add a flat board to make raised panels flat and add mitred trims to flat things you want to look like raised panels (fashion huh?).

- Change hardware like handles, hinges, brackets etc.

- Change the lighting in, on or around the piece (a surprisingly effective and often overlooked technique).

- Modify or remove unwanted parts. E.g. remove any doors and go open plan, or hang up fabrics instead of doors etc.

- Add complementary pieces, isolation can be a terrible thing. Consider a theme, pairs, or sets of items.

- Match colours and styles. Look for threads (colour, style, texture etc.) to tie and connect different pieces together.

- Work on layouts and rearrangements. Moving stuff around makes a big difference sometimes.

- Look for problems. Then think about what would 'fix' the problem? Visual, storage, flow, and use etc.

PHYSICAL REMOVAL OF FINISHES

Since I mentioned it above a couple of times let's look at removing finishes. But first, even if you're completely replacing the finish, don't think you can skip the cleaning part altogether because grease, grime and muck clogs sandpaper rendering it useless. Sanding can also push contaminants deeper into some surfaces, causing problems later with adhesion or shine of your new finishes (I know, great news huh?).

If your existing finish is peeling away or extensively damaged, you'll need to remove all the layers back to the bare surface. Painting on top of partially peeling or crazed paint or poorly prepared rust for example, will guarantee you have problems later, (even if it might look good to start with).

Removing a finish down to the bare surface is a big and often messy job so to save time, consider contracting out the removal of old finishes. Abrasive blasting (originally 'sand blasting', but it's likely to be a different media today, such as plastic, glass or even walnut shell...), is brilliant for old painted and rusty metal items; before repairing damage and re-finishing.

I even 'sand' blast reclaimed oak beams, removing every scrap of paint, rot, and woodworm damage. It leaves an amazing, beautifully contoured surface the colour of honey; my clients go bananas and love them, (ka-ching!).

Another way to remove paint on regular wooden things (doors etc.) is to get a local furniture restorer to dip them in a powerful alkaline caustic solution; it leaves a wonderful looking aged wood patina. Ask the company to check over the thing you want dipping to see if there is anything incompatible with their solution, some small items (especially if stuck with old style animal glue) can become unstuck during the process. Ask if they have a hot dipping tank, because hot dipping means immersing the door for a much shorter time, reducing the risk of damage to joints, warping etc. Cold dipping is more suitable for metal items.

You can remove finishes in various ways at home depending on the material, its surface complexity, and the tools available to you. Some common ways are...

- Sandpaper by hand to flatten and smooth rough parts. This also removes gloss and glaze to provide a key, ready for new paint.

- Use an electric sander, as above but quicker. Flat sheet types are easy and gentle to use but the rotating belt sanders will remove much more material. Small, detail or 'delta' type sanders are useful on small projects or intricate parts on larger ones.

- Various scrapers, flat types, and ones with a blade 90° to the surface. Will remove huge amounts of peeling and poorly adhering paint but can be hard work due to downward pressure needed.

- Chemical paint strippers are powerful. Apply and leave to soak before scraping away. Consider lightly scoring the surface of very thick paint with a pointed implement to allow the solution to soak further in. You'll probably need to scrape and apply the solution several times. Good for anything with complicated details, although cleaning away the sticky residue is time consuming and fiddly.

I repeat though, that sound surfaces won't need completely removing before re-finishing. A thorough clean, followed by a light sanding to provide a *key* for the new finish is usually sufficient. Just remember to use a good degreasing agent if there is any grease around (think kitchen areas etc.).

MAKING NECESSARY REPAIRS

Now it's clean and prepared for re-finishing, check it over carefully and see if you need to do any repairs before reaching for the paint etc. Of course, this depends what you're working on, but if you're lucky, repairs might just consist of using a suitable filler to fill any imperfections on the surface before re-applying the new finish.

Take this opportunity to replace worn out items or parts showing slight wear that might fail soon. It's easier to replace stuff now (to be on the safe side) than in a years' time when the piece is already in use and you're busy with other projects. This is especially important with mechanicals, it's obviously daft to put worn components back into a freshly painted machine...

The first thing you should check, are any moving parts for excess movement; drawer runners, hinges, latches etc. on furniture for example. On furniture check all joints for tightness, punching in any protruding nails etc or injecting in a suitable glue and clamping up any loose joints. Don't forget to wipe away any glue that squeezes out after you've tightened the clamp with a damp cloth and do it a couple of times, folding the cloth over or into itself to avoid spreading the glue all over.

Second, check for things that are too tight and binding or rubbing etc. Adjust to realign and ensure good clearances between moving parts. On worn things, sometimes you can use shims to help hold things apart. For example, use metal washers, plastic strips, wooden strips etc. to pack something out where needed (common behind hinges etc.).

The last thing to decide for some types of furniture is whether to replace any fabrics and stuffing. Quite a difficult job to do well, but not impossible. Many local colleges even have short courses on upholstery, where you can work on your own projects, which might be worth a look if you're keen.

RENEWING PAINT AND OTHER FINISHES

High up on your DIY list of things to do is probably renewing a finish such as paint. But the old adage of "if you can pee, you can paint" does a disservice to painters everywhere. To start with, painting involves learning a lot about a whole bunch of different chemicals (from water based to oil based and some fancy hybrids in between) and how they relate to a whole bunch of different materials (from plaster and wood to metal and plastic) and another whole bunch of different conditions (from an old chair in a dry, shady spare room to a lounger on a salty aired, wind lashed balcony which also sees full sun in the summer); see, not so easy after all huh? And then of course is the actual act of putting those fancy chemicals onto your stuff in a nice manner, from your ceilings, walls, floors and trims to furniture or craft projects. Oh, and no brush marks, dry edges or runs, please.

Always replace or repair existing finishes with *like for like* materials. Some types of paints and varnishes etc. mix okay, but some will lead to adhesion and crazing problems if applied on top of an incompatible finish. Shops selling paint are very well informed about what finishes are suitable for different projects, you just need to ask; honestly, they're used to it (it's the easiest way to learn about the different types of paints). If in doubt, just don't mix different finish types i.e. don't put water-based stuff on top of oil-based stuff etc., (or at least not without seriously flatting down with sandpaper and applying a proper 'adhesion promoting' primer or undercoat...).

There are various ways to apply finishes; from the humble paintbrush, paint pads and rollers, all the way to air powered sprayguns or even airless sprayguns. All methods have their own merits, depending on what you're finishing, how complex a shape it is, how big it is and how often you'll be doing this kind of work. Brushes and sprayguns work for most things, rollers are great for applying material quickly and evenly and airless spraying works great with most thinner finishes and even wood preservatives.

As with most things, the secret to a great finish is in the preparation. I know you've heard this before, but it really, really is true; skimp on the preparation at your peril. Areas for painting need to be clean, smooth and dust free because paint hides absolutely nothing. In fact, paint usually exaggerates the tiniest of imperfections, especially in certain light conditions.

Here's what I've learned watching professional painters for 30 years (and no small amount of hands on experience). In no particular order...

- Try to work in a clear space. If you can't empty the room (best), then pile everything in the middle (and cover it down) to get at least 1m (3') of working space, (preferably more) next to the surface to paint.

- Don't work in awkward positions, and ensure you have good access to the paint, don't overreach or across yourself to get to the paint.

- Don't even think about painting anything until you have cleaned it thoroughly and allowed enough time for it to dry out.

- If the finish is solid and just old/faded etc, clean first to remove contaminants and then 'flat' down the surface with fine sandpaper to provide a good key (new paint won't stick to any shiny or glossy surfaces for very long). Sanding also flattens out any old brush marks and highlights any imperfections you might want to fill before continuing, (think, interior woodwork, furniture, crafts etc.).

- Remember you'll always need to fill holes, nail holes, dents etc. at least twice because filler always shrinks back, leaving dimples.

- You'll need a *very clean* working environment when replacing finishes, especially using slow drying oil-based paints and varnishes. This is because any movement causes dust to swirl around and settle onto your wet and sticky project, spoiling the results. Carefully vacuum the whole area and wipe down any horizontal surfaces with a slightly damp cloth before starting. Allow any dampness to dry before applying the finish.

- Put something on the floor. Seriously, you will drip paint at some point. The minimum is dust sheets/drop cloths, but you'll still need a large square of thick polythene under the actual paint tin, roller tray etc. as anything other than spatter will soak through fabric sheets...

- Be especially aware not to stand on any paint drips and then tread it all over the new wooden flooring in the next room. Oh, go on then, ask me how I learned that...

- If you're painting a project on a dusty floor in a garage/shed/etc. and you want a high gloss finish, you should consider putting down polythene or even damping down the floor with a fine spray from a garden sprayer (not so much it splashes when you walk on it).

- Spray guns (air or airless) are especially good for complex shapes such as staircase spindles or doors with panels etc.

- Obvious I know, but don't forget to protect any surfaces near where you're working if you're spraying or using aerosols. Paint inevitably seems to drift onto stuff that you don't want painting, (blame Mr Murphy again).

- Never work from the paint tin. Always 'decant' a smaller amount of paint into a small, manageable size pot, tin, mug, bucket, whatever.

- When pouring into the above receptacle, always pour from the front side of the paint tin/bucket. Then when the paint drips down the front and you wipe it away with a brush you won't paint over the instructions on the back of the tin (smart huh?).

- A great painting technique is to apply paint quickly and evenly with a small roller and then immediately go over it with a good quality large brush (called laying off) for a fast, really flat, and professional looking finish on all woodwork.

- Don't mix tools for paint types. A roller sleeve for water-based paints won't work very well on oil-based paints and vice versa.

- Seriously consider a very light sanding or flatting in between coats on woodwork projects, it can make all the difference to the smoothness of the final coat. Use a very fine sandpaper (maximum 240grit, preferably finer, say 400grit).

- Use a roller handle on large rollers, it'll help balance the weight of the roller head when it's full of paint, plus it makes rolling large areas much easier on your poor body.

- Be aware that you might get a little paint spatter from a roller, especially if you 'roll' too fast. Check horizontal surfaces such as the tops of skirting boards etc., for little paint dots. Slow down, use a finer roller 'nap' or use masking tape to protect areas.

- When painting a room, paint trims first, then the ceiling and then the walls... (opinions vary on this though...).

- Don't stop half way through an area, i.e. keep a wet edge going until you've completed a side/wall etc. Dry edges can be visible after.

- Be super methodical in your movements with a roller or brush, randomness has no place in painting, paint like a robot would...

- When dipping a brush in paint, dab the brush against the inside of the paint bucket a few times to remove the excess (not the rim).

- If the above tip doesn't work for you and you want to use the rim of the paint tin or bucket to remove the excess (it's a free country), always wipe in the same place to avoid covering the whole rim in paint (you'll get paint all over the brush handle if you do).

- Practise cutting in to vertical or horizontal corners, glass etc. with a good paintbrush. Masking up takes up a lot of time and isn't always necessary (or very effective, heavy paint easily creeps behind tape).

- If you do have to use masking tape, make sure you press the inner edge down well (closest to the paint) with a thin flexible scraper (not a finger). The outer edge can be floating, it'll make removal easier.

- Before removing masking tape off glass, lightly run a sharp blade along its edge to 'cut' the paint. But really, paint is very easily scraped off glass so learn to cut in without masking off and if you run a little paint onto the glass, don't panic, let it dry and use a blade mounted in a tool to easily scrape it off in seconds.

- When 'cutting in', don't run a fully loaded paint brush up to the edge, start a little further out and spread the paint along a little first, working down to the very edge with a lightly loaded brush.

- Don't wash water-based paint out of rollers every day. Wrap it tightly in plastic film to keep the air out. Wash the roller only when you've finished with that colour. Lasts a few days easily.

- Before washing a roller sleeve, squeeze the excess paint out of it. Stand the roller on the tray and run a paint scraper down the roller. Turn a little and repeat. A thick pile roller can hold a lot of paint!

- Don't clean oil-based paint off paintbrushes each day, store them in water (just covering the bristles). Water excludes the air that oil-based paint needs to dry. Brushes last a long time like this if you remember to check on the water level from time to time.

- To get the water out of the above brushes; in a small empty paint tin or bucket, hold the brush between slightly dampened palms, (how you do this is up to you, most folks use a little spit; I know, eww!), rotate the brush between your palms as fast as you can (like a boy scout starting a fire...). Done properly this flings out any water in the brush. Double check with the old 'brush above the shoulder and a couple of sharp flings down' technique (as if you're throwing a knife into the ground). Best do this outside though...

- Lastly, buy the best brushes you can find and look after them. It's a nightmare to get a good finish with cheap (throwaway) brushes and they'll shed bristles too, driving you crazy.

One danger you might not have heard about is spontaneous combustion, and no not the kind of thing you see in a horror movie, this is for real! Certain chemicals like oils, wood stains and varnishes etc. don't dry out through evaporation but by oxidisation. This means a tightly wadded up rag soaked in the some of the above-mentioned chemicals in a nice sheltered spot like in a bucket in your shed, is in a perfect spot to heat up to the point of combustion. And it happens all the time... Use a clean and empty metal paint tin with a lid to store dirty rags until you can throw them away properly. You should soak them under the tap, wring them out and then roll them tightly in a Ziploc plastic bag, sealing the top. I use my old rags to light fires in the workshop stove, which of course you should never do...

Now you've built up a little knowledge, and used your tools a few times to maintain a few things, you've fixed some broken stuff, ripped out a load of junk and improved a few areas of your home; you've even managed to assemble that IKEA bookcase that's been in the bedroom, like forever, (heady stuff I know...).

So, what's next? Making new stuff that's what! You still here? Get over there pronto... (points to the next page...)

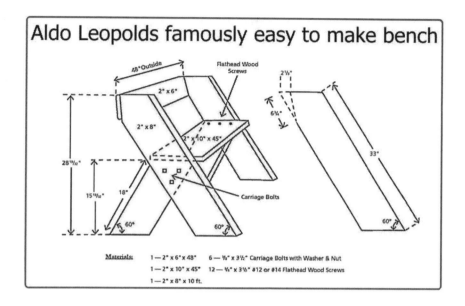

Aldo Leopolds famously easy to make bench

Arguably, the most artistic part about being handy is the ability to make your own stuff. Nothing beats the thrill of turning raw materials into an actual object, especially if you designed parts of it, because that makes it uniquely yours. If you've only ever tackled assembly of manufactured stuff, making stuff has one major difference; there are no instructions (Oh, the horror of it!) But don't panic, it's fine to cheat a little by borrowing someone else's design; how about Aldo Leopold's famous easy to make bench? It's simple enough joinery for beginners, plus it'll look great in the garden as well as being a perfect place for a coffee break.

Building something simple helps build familiarity with your tools and gets you used to buying, cutting, and fastening together some raw materials. Who knows, you might end up building a bookcase, a shed, a fence or even a house or a boat one day...

For example, me and my boy built a little plywood 'mouse' boat using freely available plans from the internet and Gavin Atkins book '*17 plywood boats anyone can build.*'. So simple, so cheap, and so, so much fun! Talk about a conversation starter when it's on the roof rack!

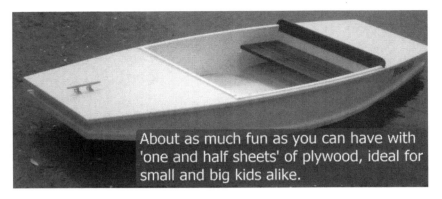

About as much fun as you can have with 'one and half sheets' of plywood, ideal for small and big kids alike.

WHAT TO BUILD AND SEEING IT THOUGH

If you've got this far in the book, I hope you've grasped the concept that you could, in theory build anything you want. Because you know to start small. You know to build on your existing skills, and how to learn new ones by utilising books, online videos and 'how to's' or by finding someone to give you the advice you need. The information is out there: detailed plans, designs, forums, clubs, websites, friends, neighbours. Utilize other people's experiences. It doesn't matter what you set out to build, be it a bookcase, boat or even a house, every project is just a series of small tasks, one after the other until it's finished. Just keep breaking the job down into ever smaller, ever more manageable tasks and keep making progress, however small.

My colleague used to say; 'a house is just a pile of mortar and bricks with a few planks of wood thrown in'. We build houses, even grand ones, one brick/block/plank at a time. In theory, this 'one at a time' method means anyone could do it. If you don't believe me, search online for 'self-build homes' and find thousands of houses, built by amateurs, all over the world, you can even buy kits to get you started.

Sure, building something large takes a lot of time, but what 'hobby' doesn't? If you can lay one brick perfectly (even if it takes a minute or two), potentially you can lay a thousand and so on until you've built your house. Tackle every practical task one piece at a time, one cut, one nail, one screw, one coat of paint etc. One easily *researched, learned, and practiced* technique at a time.

Breaking stuff down into small, individual tasks is the key to coping with the magnitude of larger jobs and learning the skills you need, one small step at a time. Even professionals like me need to mentally break down their projects, a joker of a client once pointed to a 20-ton pile of sand and a pile of 20,000 bricks then and said 'right, off you go then, move all that' as he handed me a small trowel... The only way you get through it, is to look at the work one wall at a time, or one day at a time, and on bad days, one brick at a time...

RESOURCES FOR PLANS

The more artistic amongst you might want to design your own stuff. But for everyone else, take a look at the many plans available online, both free and paid for. Although step-by-step instructions leave little to the imagination, they are a great starting point for you if you're a new in the handy game. Following a properly designed set of plans takes the guess work out of a project, especially if the plan supplier has an active support system like a forum where you can ask for help from others who are in the same boat (well, not literally; unless you're actually building a boat of course...). Working to a well-produced and detailed plan also gives you the confidence to try new techniques or tools for the first time, because you know the end result will fit and is a good design.

Working to plans might even allow you to tackle a project above your perceived skill level. For example, the vast majority of boat plans sell to people who have never built a boat before, although I'd recommend you aim more towards the bird box end of the scale to start off with, until you have a little more experience with your tools.

You'll also find plans and designs in magazines about your interests. Woodworking magazines for example, have many project ideas and additionally, lots of useful tips and advice sections that'll build up your knowledge over time. Check out your favourite magazines' website for any free plans they might have published for their readers. Magazines also often host a forum where you might find help you if you're stuck and need advice about something specialised or specific.

There are also plenty of books (and said magazines) in most libraries with ideas and plans for projects. Who knows, you could even write your own one-day, because when you look through the books in the library, you might think, 'I could do better than that.'

SOME GENERAL TIPS & TECHNIQUES

We've looked at a lot of skills in the previous chapters; such as using some simple tools, a little about glues and other ways to join stuff together, plus drilling holes in a variety of different materials. But to make something from scratch you're going to need a few more skills, so let's go over a few general things to fill in any gaps and take a brief look at a couple of common materials. Lastly, I'll mention upcycling as a great source of nearly free materials, including my personal favourite, pallets!

SETTING OUT

In the *Preparation and Plans* chapter earlier in the book, we looked at calculating the materials and tools you need for your project, but there is still one thing you need to do. Before starting with the actual materials, you need to spend some time setting out. I don't need to remind you that this is an area fraught with potential disaster, set out wrong and the whole job is off to a bad start. This applies whether your dividing a large bedroom into two smaller ones or tiling a wall. Start wrong, end wrong. Simple as that.

Invest plenty of time to think about "what you want to go where" before you start fixing materials. Take lots of measurements, re-read the *Discrepancies in the Fitting Area* in the *Assembling & Installing* chapter for tips on getting a 'heads up' about stuff which will trip you up later. Knowing about a potential problem is half the solution because you can make allowances. If a room isn't square for example (and you know about it) you know you'll need to adjust your angles to make stuff fit.

I once built some fitted wardrobes against a wall that was a mind boggling 30mm (1 ¼″) out of plumb. Had I not known about this I'd have had a pretty nasty shock when offering the wardrobe up to the wall.

Some setting out jobs need careful juggling of materials to achieve the best look. Symmetry and balance are important in nearly all cases. Tiling a wall is a classic example. You can't just start at one end and work left to right, it will look terrible, seriously, (unless you're very lucky with the spacing).

For example, if tiling a wall, measure or preferably set out dry tiles along each wall (or on the floor) starting in the middle of the wall and working out to the edges. If you end up with a small cut at the end, go back and start with a full tile in the middle instead and set out again to get a bigger cut at the edges. All tiling looks best if you avoid small pieces of tile, because they are difficult to cut. Sometimes you can 'roll' larger tile offcuts around the corner and carry on which looks good, but not if there is something else on the new wall which needs centring (see next paragraph). I know, it sounds complicated and that's because it is complicated; that's why you see terribly finished tiling everywhere...

If there is something on the wall, it's best to start in the middle of it so the cuts are the same each side (windows, doors, kitchen hob extractors, sinks, bathroom basins, toilets etc.). If there are several things on the same wall, such as a window and a door or a basin and a toilet, you've got some serious juggling to do to get it to look right. Choose the window usually or try centring the material at different points and chose the one which looks best to the eye. Never, and again I really do mean never, fix the first tile unless you know exactly where the last tile is going.

Another example, say you're fitting a new wooden floor and the room is wider one end than the other, you'll end up with a big tapered cut on the last row and maybe it's right where you'd see it entering the room. Find out exactly where the 'out of squareness' is located, (which corner, which wall etc.) and try adjusting your starting point to minimise the taper.

Maybe it's better to 'split the difference' and cut half the taper off the first row and then cut the other half of the taper off the last row? No, it still looks bad? Okay, maybe cut the whole taper off the first row at the back of the room and pull the bookcase away from the wall a little in the corner and use the sofa to help 'hide' the taper. This way the last row will be a straight cut and look good when you first come into the room. Always think about how it looks to your eye, if it looks good, it is good (regardless of what the tape measure or spirit level says).

Think three dimensionally too, for example, measure a room for squareness (from corner to corner), but also check for high points or dips and hollows. This could cause the above wooden floor to creak, or 'rock' over a high point or even come apart over a big hollow or dip in the substrate. You might need to find the highest point and either grind it down or raise the surrounding floor with a cementitious self-levelling compound. It's much easier to pre-flatten out a substrate or a wall, because trying to flatten things out 'as you go' using material (extra thick adhesive when tiling for example) is very difficult and time consuming. Working on flat or level surfaces is quick and easy. Oh, and with tiles, the large the tile, the flatter the substrate needs to be, i.e. small 150mm (6″) square tiles can 'flow' a little over gentle undulations, 900mm (3′) tiles, not so much...

MODULAR

Almost everything in construction is modular. By this, I mean that material sizes and spacing measurements are rarely random but designed to fit somewhere specific. For example...

- Two bricks side by side are the same length as one brick lengthways plus room for a joint, ideal for half bond walling...

- If you set out timber studs at 400mm or 600mm (16″ or 24″) centre-to-centre, then 2400mm × 1200mm (8′x4′) drywall sheets will fit perfectly.

- If you set out floor joists at 600mm centre-to-centre, then 2400mm × 600mm (8′x2′) chipboard flooring sheets fit perfectly. Although if you're gluing the joints (and you should be) then 'flying joints' are cool.

- Builders metalwork like joist hangers etc. will fit standard 47mm (2″) timbers (smaller and larger sizes are also available).

- Kitchen units come in a range of sizes based on 100mm (4″) so you'll see units in multiples of 100mm. i.e. 300, 400, 500, 600, 800, 1000mm etc. to name a few common ones.

- 600mm (24″) white goods such as dishwashers, washing machines and fridges etc. will fit into an exact 600mm (24″) gap between kitchen units (because all white goods are slightly undersized).

- Timber sizes run around 25mm (1″) or multiples thereof. So, you'll see timber 25, 50, 75, 100mm thick and the same in height, 25, 50, 75, 100, 125, 150, 175, 200, 225mm etc.

- Timber lengths run around 300mm (12″) units, so you'll commonly see 2400mm, 2700mm, 3000mm, 3300mm, 3600mm, 3900mm, 4200mm, 4500mm, 4800mm and sometimes 5100mm or more (8′, 9′, 10′, 11′, 12′, 13′, 14′, 15′, 16′, 17′ etc.).

NOTE: Make allowances for the fact that most timber is slightly under-sized to allow for regularising (making the timber a consistent size) so 50mm is more likely to actually measure 47mm and a 200mm deep floor joist might only actually be 195mm etc.

NOTE: Originally timber shipped in the random lengths which naturally occurred after sorting according to quality. You'll still see this occasionally in older, more traditional merchants and indeed some countries still do this. Norway is one of them and after decades of buying set length timber lengths in the UK, I must confess I do find it a nuisance (and wasteful)!

MODULAR MISHAPS

One thing to remember about modular stuff is that you need to make allowances for the first spacing. Using one of the above examples, if you set out a timber stud wall with the studs at 400mm centres, when you offer up your first drywall board you'll find you're a little short because you set out or started your spacing from the centre of the first stud and not the outside of the new wall. Always set the centre of the second stud 400mm (etc.) from the wall and not the middle of the first stud next to the wall. Or you can measure out 2400mm from the wall and place a stud central on your mark and work back towards the wall in 600mm spaces (or 400mm etc., to suit your boards/job). Remember it's likely you'll be half lapping your boards across the studs so keep any odd spacing's to the edges or you'll end up cutting boards to fit in the middle of the wall which is inefficient.

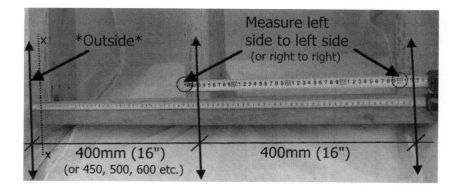

CENTRE-TO-CENTRE

Accurately set out first floor joists, ceiling joists, and studwork for example, to make it easy to fit subsequent materials such as drywall. With accurate and even spacing, the end of a drywall sheet falls exactly where you want them. If you randomly spaced them, you'd end up cutting every board... (very time consuming and expensive).

Working to centres is largely a figure of speech because although in theory, you're setting out centre-to-centre; in practise, it's difficult to measure from the middle of one thing to the middle of another.

It's mostly easiest to measure from the left side to the left side (if you're a righty handed person).

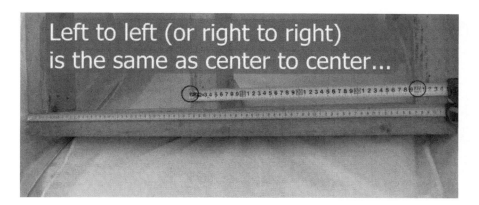

More likely you'll be measuring from the outside-to-outside or inside-to-inside, which when you think about it, is actually the same thing, as long as you start the first one in the right place. Couple of caveats: *you must always indicate with a cross, which side of your mark the item is to go!* And never measure in between things either; i.e., from the outside of one stud to the inside of the next stud, as this method will lead to inaccuracies because the width of studs will vary in thickness.

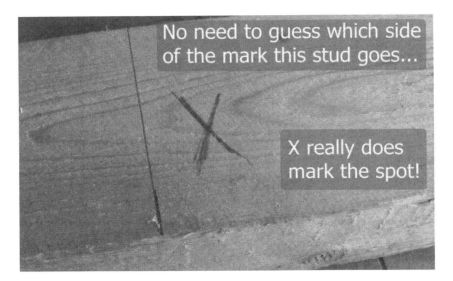

No need to guess which side of the mark this stud goes...

X really does mark the spot!

WORKING WITH TIMBER

Fortunately, timber is one of the easiest materials to cut, shape and sand using simple hand or power tools. However, the very things which make timber easy to work with, also make it easy to damage. It splits, snaps and it splinters like crazy if you use bad tools or techniques.

But even with the best tools and techniques, (unless you turn out to be utterly brilliant at this), occasionally you'll have to cut a second piece because the first one isn't a good fit. It happens to us all, and in my opinion, it's the willingness to repeatedly re-cut a less than perfect piece which separates poor quality work from high quality work. If you misjudge a cut, just pull another piece from the stack, and use what you learned from the first cut to improve the second. Say a mitre doesn't work out because you assumed a corner was 90° square, but it wasn't, (you should always check first), use the piece you've cut as a template, moving the new cut line to account for the out-of-squareness. Plus, the chances are the first workpiece will come in use somewhere else on the project, where you need smaller pieces etc., so very little is actually wasted in practise.

However, if it's a one off, special piece, then you'll need to exercise every possible care and give it 100% of your attention to ensure you don't make a mistake. Like a golfer's pre-swings next to the ball, you're going to have to double and triple check what you're doing is right. I've worked on $25,000 staircases where specially made components need final cutting before fitting. The consequences of screwing it up would be catastrophic (big bucks and long shipping times etc.), no pressure then...

CUTTING TIMBER

Timber is obviously not a 'man made' product as such, each piece is different and you'll need to check each piece for defects to ensure its suitability for the particular job in hand, (remember the *Timber* section in the *Buying Stuff* chapter?). Then depending on its size and length, decide how best to cut it and with what tool...

- A regular handsaw is fine for just about anything if you don't mind sweating a little! Gentle curves are possible too.

- Jigsaws are fair for straight cuts through thin material, good for rough (ish) square cuts and great for curves in flat panels etc.

- Hand held circular saws are good for straight cross or rip cuts in timber and panels. Be careful crosscutting smaller timbers as the blade can snatch dangerously (support the workpiece well).

- Cross cut or mitre saws are good for general cross cutting to length and of course mitre cuts.

- Table saws are great for resizing timber stock and panels.

- Plunge saws are good for panel work and cutting out square holes etc. Quick and easy to set up with great cut quality (minimal splintering due to the fine, multi toothed blade).

- Flip over saws combine a table saw and a mitre saw, making them a very versatile tool (it's my personal weapon of choice!).

We touched on supporting the workpiece properly in the *Mitre Saw* part in the *Developing Practical Skills* chapter I know; but the principles apply to most power tools. Most cutting problems arise from inadequate support, i.e. the timber moves and pinches the blade with unpredictable consequences. I seriously recommend you invest in a foldable workbench or some trestles to support your workpiece whilst working on it, oh and a 'quick clamp' or two is a good idea too to securely hold the workpiece down. Good support is especially important during those last few milliseconds of sawing to prevent pieces falling onto the floor and tearing away the corner. Trestles or old-fashioned sawhorses and two or three planks (scaffold boards, or lengths of stout timber) make a great impromptu workbench. Use two or three old bottle crates as minimum viable support.

If using a power saw, practise on some scrap first to learn how the tool 'takes' the timber. Power saws are, erm... powerful and can grab the workpiece, leading to things getting very dangerous, very quickly if improperly used. Remember also to use your ears, listen to the sound the blade makes, if the 'note' changes, it's getting tight somewhere, back off or slow down till the blade is running clear and sweetly again.

Learn which way the blade runs, and on which surface the blade will 'exit' the timber. The exit side is normally the side which chips the most. For example, a jigsaw or hand held circular saw will chip the top edge, whereas a table or bench saw will chip the bottom edge. Consider cutting from the backside or non-face side of your timber when using a circular saw.

You can use jigsaws from the backside too, but be wary of blade drift, because jigsaws have thin blades and are rather notorious for producing out of square cuts on thicker timbers. Incidentally, be aware that jigsaw blades wander quite badly generally, so only use very sharp blades and change them regularly (or look for thicker blades with a 'square cut' icon on them, being made from thicker metal, they drift much less). Better still, keep the jigsaw for thinner timber or curved cuts and use a handsaw or circular saw for thicker timber. You could consider buying special 'upside down' blades if you must work from the top or face side, but these can jump and chip, which rather defeats the object! If you must use upside down blades in your jigsaw, apply plenty of downward pressure whilst cutting and change them often.

If funds allow, look at *plunge saws* as these are brilliant for beginners and professionals alike because the saw sits and rides along a guide. They are not cheap and are quite sophisticated, but boy are they great for cutting sheet materials or even holes out of worktops etc. Simply mark where you want the cut, place the rubber edge of the guide on the pencil mark, set the depth of cut and lower the saw into the workpiece, gently slide along, release and lift. Fast, easy and a superior cut because of the fine multi-toothed blade.

Oh, and if you need to stop any power saw for any reason, pull the workpiece, or the saw back a little so the blades teeth won't snatch the wood and jump all over when you start up again.

SHAPING TIMBER

When it comes to removing wood and shaping it with a plane or a chisel etc, you need to look at the way the grain runs to avoid your tools 'tearing out'. Picture wood grain being like a handful of fibres roughly going the same direction, like a handful of straw. You must always be cutting down or with and across the fibres (grain), never up into or against them, otherwise the grain will 'tear' out bits of timber leaving an unsightly finish.

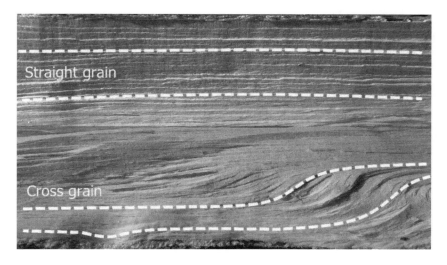

Straight grain

Cross grain

Experiment on scrap off-cuts first to get a feel of when the timber 'tears' and how it behaves under a plane or a chisel. Again, make sure the workpiece is secure, as pushing a plane exerts considerable force. Nail a thin 'stop' timber to the workbench and push the workpiece up to it; this will stop the workpiece sliding down the bench as you plane. Use a regular *quick clamp* if you're using a chisel etc.

Adjust the plane until it's taking little more than a whisper of timber away, if it digs in, you're trying to cut too deep or going into the grain. Think about the relationship between how much you are removing and how hard it is to push. Sometimes less really is more, because it's much easier and quicker to remove lots and lots of thin layers instead of pushing hard to remove a thicker layer, plus you'll get a finer finish. A properly sharp plane blade will leave a surface finish which needs little sanding.

Most often you'll find it easier to push the plane at a slight angle across the grain too. Hold the plane at a slight angle across the workpiece and push it straight down the timber following the grain.

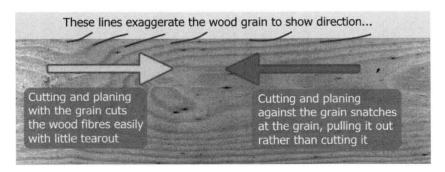

Hardness and grain direction varies from species to species and this affects the timbers 'workability'. Very hard timbers like seasoned oak or timber known for its gnarly grain like maple etc., require razor sharp edges on your tools and a good understanding of grain direction for success. Fortunately, the most commonly available 'white' timber you'll see in the store are some of the easiest to work with as they are soft and have relatively straight grain.

Cutting across the grain will cause breakout as the blade leaves the rear face. This will form splinters on the back edge with a saw blade. If you really don't want the back edge of a cut to splinter, try marking out using a sharp craft knife instead of a pencil. Cut on the waste side of the shallow cut/mark and any splinters shouldn't go past the shallow cut.

Plane blades are even worse and will break off a big lump of timber as it grabs the last bit of wood at the back edge on end grain. There are lots of ways to prevent this though, (first, make sure the blade is extremely sharp); but the three simplest ones are as follows...

1: Plane from each end towards the middle. Because the grain will tear up a little on the 'wrong' side, in practise this means you should plane mostly along the grain and then turn around near then end so that you're only planing against the grain for a short distance.

2: Plane a small 45° chamfer across the end of the workpiece and plane straight over it. Keep checking it's still there as it will reduce in size as you plane the end down, you might need to re-plane a new angle if you are taking a lot of material off the end of the workpiece.

3: Clamp some scrap wood on the backside of the workpiece to act as a sacrificial piece (i.e. it doesn't matter if it chips).

Plane over a piece of scrap wood clamped to the end

If you have a nice woodworking bench you should Google 'shooting boards' if you want to learn a really cool way of planing by sliding the plane on its side on the bench.

And lastly on grain, the next image shows a timber log which was difficult to split due to its complicated grain structure, see how torn up the fibres are? Imagine trying to plane this type of timber up!

Gnarly grained wood after splitting with a heavy maul

If you've drilled some holes you might need to use a wood chisel to square them up (on joints or to fit door locks and latches etc.). As with the hand plane, take a little at a time and make sure your chisel edge is very sharp. Wood chisels are one of the more difficult tools to master, so to start with, try pushing down on the chisel instead of hitting it with a mallet or hammer. This will teach you control and how the chisel behaves under pressure (chisels are flat on one side and bevelled on the other) and practise/experiment chiselling out wood up to a pencil line with the flat edge facing the line.

Sharpening cutting tools is a difficult skill all on its own which will take time to learn. It's doubtful you'll ever really master it without using a machine. I used to think I was an okay sharpener until I met a few guys who could get razor edges, (and I mean hair shaving sharp) on their tools and blades using stones and eyes alone. I gave up sharpening by hand at that point and bought a Tormek sharpening system and haven't looked back since. If you're determined to master hand sharpening, have a wander around online in the knife sharpening world, often linked to cooking or outdoor activities like hunting or survivalists etc. Many of the tips and techniques talked about in the knife world also apply to tool edges. And some of those chefs; wow, can they get an edge on a blade... scary sharp.

Finish timber projects off using sandpaper for a really nice surface, either by hand or on a machine. Detail or part sheet sanders use a flat, vibrating plate to remove material but a belt sander will remove large amounts of material. 40, 60 and 80 grits are aggressive for initial sanding with 120, 150 and 180 giving a smooth finish. 240 and up is for furniture work mostly and give a spectacularly fine finish. Personally, for most domestic construction use I get by with 40 grit for removing the worst and finishing up with 120 grit ready for the decorator, but then I am a hairy old builder and any cabinet makers reading this will have a heart attack at this recommendation... Basically, start coarse and gradually use finer and finer sandpaper (and yes, it takes ages...), oh, and don't forget your dust mask.

SHEET MATERIALS

I put his section here as they are mostly wood! Sheet materials are predictable, accurate in size, available in big sheets and are economical to buy, all impossible attributes for regular timber. That makes them perfect for anything that needs a stable, flat surface, (cabinets, shelves, book cases etc.). Quality and price range from cheap and ideal for hidden work, right up to marine plywood able to withstand anything the sea can throw it. There is of course a wide spread of costs, from hardboard cheap enough to use for covering down floors to oak veneered plywood where a mistake would be painfully costly. Let's go through some of the common ones...

- Chipboard (particle board). Essentially wood chips and glue, compressed in to a hard and rigid board perfect for flooring and furniture making.

- Melamine faced chipboard (laminated melamine particle board). Ideal for cabinets and furniture making. Mainly white but available in various colours.

- Plywood. Multiple thin veneers of real wood glued together in alternating grain directions to produce a hugely strong composite board. With a range of different face finishes, from melamine laminates to real-wood veneers such as oak, teak, birch, beech etc.

- Exterior grade plywood. As above but with weather proof glues.

- Marine plywood. As above but with waterproof glues.

- Hardboard. A very dense, highly compressed, usually thin fibreboard, popular in construction work for protecting floors, cutting templates and furniture making. Also available as a 'peg board', perforated with small holes.

- Laminated planks of various timber species. Blocks or strips of real timber are finger jointed and glued together to make wide boards. Often engineered out of small pieces of timber making it very stable and resistant to distortion.

- MDF Medium Density Fibreboard. The new standard in 'hobby' boards. Used everywhere. Now even available faced with real wood, melamine, and even an exterior grade.

- OSB Oriented Strand Board. Made from wood shavings glued and compressed. Makes a stronger board than chipboard. Common for any non-face work in construction from sheathing and roofing to hoardings around building sites.

- Composite boards. Used in the manufacture of stuff like caravans etc. Multiple materials laminated together, (e.g. polystyrene with an aluminium skin bonded on one side and thin plywood on the other). Strong and lightweight but very expensive.

- Technical boards. Exterior grade plywood with a range of different non-slip surfaces, often in a grid or mesh pattern. Perfect for use in trailers, scaffold platforms and other walkways, outdoor furniture and play equipment.

Sometimes sheet materials come in handy to reinforce regular timber. When ceramic floor tiling over floorboards for example. Ceramic tiles are hard and unyielding, but a wooden floor is not. Screw plywood sheets into the floor joists to spread the load and stick the tiles onto an *uncoupling membrane* to allow the floor to move but keep the tiles still.

WORKING WITH NEW DRYWALL

Say the roof has leaked and you need to replace a whole area with new drywall etc. First up is to remove all the old drywall (or lath and plaster) obviously, plus all the old fasteners, (remember you'll need to recycle drywall separately at most places). If you're only replacing part of a room, mark your cut lines, and use any old saw to cut through the ceiling keeping a watchful eye for anything hidden (wiring/pipes etc.). You'll see small drywall saws sold especially for this purpose, but an old timber saw will give you straighter and cleaner cuts. Save the small drywall saw for cutting out small holes for electricals etc. Start your cut by rubbing the very tip of the saw back and forth over your line until it goes through the board, widen the slot, and then put the saw through the board at an angle to follow the rest of your line.

Then take a moment to think if you need any new lights etc. in that space. For example, it's a great opportunity to get those fancy downlights you wanted, whilst the ceiling is down ...

New cables installed? Right then, before we go through some general installation techniques, let's look at the different types of drywall...

Call into your local supplier for a brochure and to see what they keep in stock. If they need to order it in, the chances are it's not a popular choice in your area. Logically the stuff in stock is what most folks are using. Arguably the 2.4m × 1.2m × 12.5mm (8′ × 4′ × ½″) sheet is the most common, but drywall is available in lots of different sizes and thicknesses. There are also boards made for lots of different situations such as...

- Sound blocking boards which are especially dense and heavy to minimise sound transfer.

- Heat resistant boards for cladding anything fire sensitive in a structure, such as steel beams or lintels.

- Moisture resistant boards for wet areas, i.e. behind most normal tiles (up to 10mm or ⅜″ thick or so). Heavy tiles like stone and thicker tiles need a cement-based backer board though...

- Drywall 'sandwiched to a rigid insulation of varying thicknesses for minimising heat loss.

- Foil backed (vapor barrier) board to resist moisture penetration (good for kitchen and bathroom ceilings).

- Super thin 6mm boards for renovation/over-boarding.

- 15mm thick boards for ceilings with wider joist spacing (no need to install noggins between joists to support the edges of the drywall).

- Tough, impact resistant boards for high traffic areas.

- Bendable boards for curved work on walls or columns.

- X-ray proof boards lined with lead, (no really!) for shielding many different types of medical machinery. (Ideal for stopping bothersome calls to your mobile. But don't expect your WIFI to work...)

THERE ARE TWO SYSTEMS OF DRYWALL...

In addition to the special types of drywall, there are two different finishing systems as well. Square edged where you need to plaster the whole surface and taper edged where you finish just the joints and screw holes.

Finish regular square edged boards, by sticking glassfibre joint tape over the joints and then plaster or 'skim' the whole surface with two thin coats of finish plaster to a thickness of 3 to 5mm (a good ⅛" or so), (UK etc.).

Alternatively, tapered edge boards have slightly thinner edges along the two long sides to allow you to stick tape (or glassfibre mesh) over the joints. Then you fill up the joints (and screw holes) with joint compound or 'mud', (arguably the proper drywall system, common in the USA). High quality work may have a thin layer of compound over the whole board as well.

In both systems, the drywall boards usually go across the timbers at 90°, (although in some situations, double boarding for example, they can go on parallel to the timbers for the first layer).

Note also that longer lengths of drywall may be available in your country. In the USA, longer lengths are available which might mean no butt joints at all in your rooms (that's good!).

The choice is up to you and for every five people you find that swear by tapered edged boards, you'll find another five who insist that square boards and finish plaster is the best way. I'm from the UK where square edged boards and finish plaster are the norm, (but I'm not bias... I do use tapered edge boards here in Norway).

DRYWALL INSTALLATION

The very first thing is to remember to mark where all your support timbers are onto the wall to indicate where the centre of each joist is, or on the floor if you're working on vertical timbers. This makes finding the timbers so much easier when you're fitting the boards (you can't see them remember).

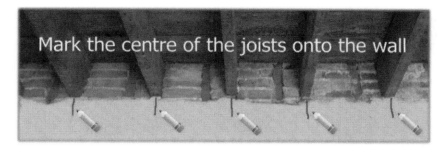

Mark the centre of the joists onto the wall

CUTTING AND FASTENING DRYWALL

Cutting drywall is extremely easy, mark the size you need (always remove a couple of millimetres or $^1/_{16}''$ or so for a fitting tolerance) and then lightly cut the top paper with a sharp craft knife against a thin straight edge (a plasterer's feather edge, aluminium strip, or a spirit level in a pinch). Pick up the board and stand it on its edge, bend the sheet away from your cut and the board will 'snap'. Then score the paper on the backside and bend the board again and you'll have two pieces.

Sometimes boards snap cleanly and sometimes they don't, either way sometimes you'll need to shave or trim a little off to get it to fit. The best tool for this is a simple surform. A small palm size one will do to rub over any rough edges or slightly reshape the boards cut edge.

Nails are defunct nowadays for fastening up drywall, so use drywalls screws as they hold much better. The most important skill to learn when installing drywall is... knowing when to stop driving in your screws!

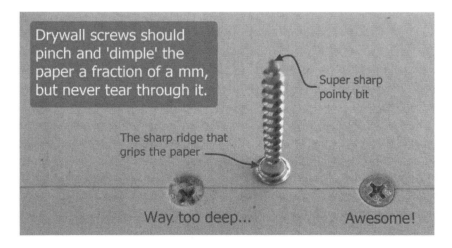

Drywall screws should pinch and 'dimple' the paper a fraction of a mm, but never tear through it.

Super sharp pointy bit

The sharp ridge that grips the paper

Way too deep...

Awesome!

A few more 'rules' for drywall fixings...

- On a paper bound long edge, go no closer than 10mm (⅜") to the edge of the drywall board with your screws.

- On a cut or short edge, go no closer than 12.5mm (½") to the edge of the drywall board with your screws.

- Butt joints on square edged drywall boards should end in the middle of the timber joist or stud.

- Angled screws are next to useless (they have little holding power). If your spacing is a little off and there is not much timber bearing to allow proper screw placement, screw an extra lath on the side of the timber to increase the bearing.

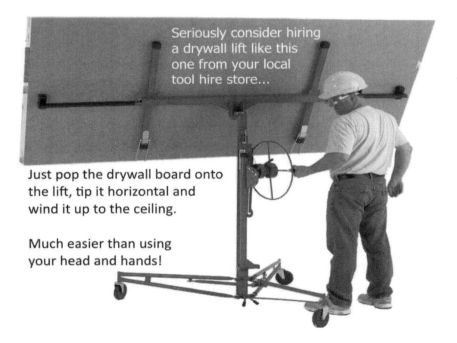

Seriously consider hiring a drywall lift like this one from your local tool hire store...

Just pop the drywall board onto the lift, tip it horizontal and wind it up to the ceiling.

Much easier than using your head and hands!

Regarding spacing of fasteners; aim for around 200mm (8") or less between screws for most drywall situations. On a standard 1.2m (4') wide board for example, I'll put a screw at each side and one in the middle (which is usually marked with a faint line or line of text etc). Then it's easy to 'fill in' the gaps either side of the centre screw with two more screws, dividing each side into three giving a spacing of around 200mm (8").

For some reason, it's easier for the eye to equally divide up space between two marks or objects than it is to judge or measure a set length.

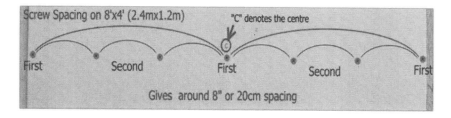

FINISHING TAPER EDGED BOARDS

Generally, the spacing of your timbers will enable the butt joints (short sides) to end in the middle of a timber (to save unnecessary cutting). However, the short sides of tapered edge boards have no taper (don't ask me why!). therefore, you'll need to choose. Either fit as per the square edged boards with the joint over a timber or go for recessed butt joints which go in the space between the timbers (hence often called flying or floating joints). You can make recessed butt joints several different ways. Ask in your local merchant to see if they stock a proprietary butt joint system, or add extra timber noggins recessed into the area, or make your own 'back-block' style 'butt boards' out of 150mm strips of plywood or OSB (Oriented strand board) with 3mm (⅛") packing strips at the edges. Or run the same strips through a table saw twice, to create a very shallow 2-3mm (⅛") depression in the middle of the board.

You tape and fill recessed butt joints exactly the same way as you do the long-tapered sides which saves time and material. Here is the propriety Buttboard system from Trim-Tex …

Buttboard™ from Trim-Tex Inc. in the USA

Or you can make up your own, here is two different ways…

Drywall 'flying joints' for tapered edge boards

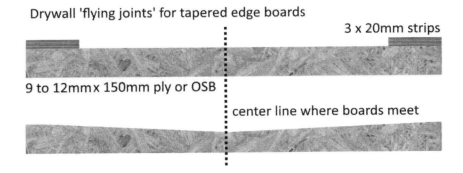

3 x 20mm strips

9 to 12mm x 150mm ply or OSB

center line where boards meet

Cover the joints with a paper tape set in joint compound (traditional) or a self-adhesive glassfibre mesh strip (easier) before filling them up with several layers of joint compound over successive days. Fill the joints in three sessions, (maybe only two layers for screw holes).

When it comes to joint compound, there are many different sorts, but in most cases for a DIY job, the standard all-purpose stuff is fine. Avoid anything that sets quickly (unless you know what you're doing) and make sure it's an 'easy to sand' version. Mix it up in the tub till it's smooth before using it on the first coat, but if you like, you can thin it a little for the subsequent coats to make it run little easier. Simply add a little water and mix it up using a 'potato' type masher or a paddle on a powerful electric drill, or at worst, a clean stick. You want a nice smooth and creamy consistency, but not too runny or soupy. Some folks describe it as somewhere between peanut butter and toothpaste if that helps! Proper drywall tools make the job easier and are worth the investment, as they'll save you hours of work and give you a superior finish. The process in brief...

- First coat, stick mesh over all the joints and run a strip of joint compound over the top or alternatively, set drywall tape into a thin layer of joint compound. Either way, smooth out and flatten the compound over the joint reinforcement using a wide bladed joint compound 'knife'.

- Fill all the screw holes. Dab and scrape.

- Second coat. The next day, fill the joint up to the top between the 'shoulders' of the tapered edge of the board with joint compound. Smooth out using a wide bladed joint compound 'knife'.

- Fill the screw holes for the second time (it always shrinks a little).

- Third coat. The next day again, run a very thin coat to fill up any shrinkage in the joint and further feather the joint onto the boards either side. Smooth out the joint with the widest joint compound 'knife' you have.

- Some folks lightly brush the very edges of the compound with a damp sponge to remove any lines, ridges etc., although any small imperfections are easy to sand out afterwards.

- Once the final coat is fully dry (24hrs at least, longer in low temps.), sand the filled areas flat with 120-grit paper on a flat block or a sanding pad on a pole.

- Further light sanding with a 150-180 grit sandpaper is best for those wanting really top-quality results.

- The more care you took putting the compound on, the less sanding you'll need to do. Stick to the big brand jointing compounds, because some of the cheap ones are horrible to use and seem to create more airborne dust.

If you're not using a recessed butt joint method the conventional way is to create a very shallow bump over butt joints. I'll not lie to you; this is tricky as you don't have the tapered edges to guide you...

In brief, here is the 'standard' butt joint...

- Trim back the paper alongside the joint making sure it's perfect, most go for a small 'V' shape here. This is because the paper edge doesn't wrap around the edge and loose, raggedy edges will thicken your joint and may even be visible in the finished joint.

- Stick your joint mesh over the joint as normal (or bed your tape).

- Make a thin, even run of compound central over the tape.

- Make two more thin, even runs, one either side of centre one over the mesh/tape. Leave it to dry.

- Once the first coat sets up, run two, wider layers of compound, one each side of the centre, ensure they cover the whole area.

- Sand the area to a feather edge being careful to not sand through to the tape.

- Repeat with more compound if necessary, to fill low spots and widen out the joint for better invisibility.

NOTE: Tapered edge boards have large areas of the original paper visible, so it's important to use a special drywall sealer over the surface before decorating or the drywall will act like blotting paper, soaking up all your expensive Farrow & Ball paint. High quality work might even apply a thin skim of compound over the whole wall to ensure and even texture etc.

FINISHING SQUARE EDGED BOARDS

Square edged boards are completely flat, so the entire surface of the boards needs covering in a finish or veneer plaster. Apply it in two thin coats giving a finished thickness just over 3-4mm (⅛″ or so). It's a 'wet' process and is messy, (some plasterers are better than others!). To access ceilings, use scaffolding (unless you're good on stilts) so you can easily reach the ceiling. Good access is vital as the wet plaster needs working over several times during and after application. The process in brief...

- Stick self-adhesive glassfibre tape over all joints.

- Thoroughly mix the powdered finish plaster until it's a very, very smooth, creamy consistency.

- Even a single lump in finish plaster is a nuisance. Site hygiene is important with finish plasters. Lumps in the mix will get large gobs of wet plaster thrown at you on site, along with some rather colourful vocabulary about your competence and parentage...

- Starting furthest away from any draughts (because open windows, doors etc. quickly dry out the plaster), apply the plaster to the boards in long even strokes using a plasterer's hawk and a plastering trowel. The key is to apply it quite evenly, smoothing it out a little as you go, which is easier than it sounds because it's quite a thin coat.

- Wait a few minutes for the plaster to firm up a little (after a cup of coffee say). Then apply the second coat 'wet on wet'. Professionals might 1st coat several walls before returning to 2nd coat the first one (but you'll need to be really fast and confident in your ability before copying this).

- Apply the second coat in the same manner as the first coat, although some plasterers put this one on at 90° to the first one.

- Once you have finished this second coat, it's a good idea for beginners to go back to the start and quickly run your trowel over it again to 'lay it in'. Watch the ceiling and see how the trowel is taking plaster from the high spots and depositing it in the low spots. Experiment with doing this at 90° to the direction you applied it. This will hopefully make trowelling up a little easier before the plaster starts to set up, giving you a flatter ceiling.

- Next up lies the secret. Wait. You need to wait now until the plaster has firmed up just enough so that working it over with a trowel doesn't leave deep lines from the trowel edges.

- Start working on the plaster too soon and the plaster will stay soggy and you'll not manage to get the plaster flat without lots of lines, you might even overwork it making it near impossible to finish properly.

- Leave it too long and you'll find it difficult because the plaster has set too hard to move/work.

- As you work the surface, the trowel should just pickup plaster from the high spots and deposit it into the low spots leaving the merest trace of trowel lines.

- With the plaster now flat, wait again for a few minutes. Once it's hardened off a little more, go over the plaster again with a wet trowel (have a big wet brush in your other hand). Wipe the trowel each time and even flick a little water onto the plaster on especially dry areas. The trowel shouldn't be picking up plaster at this point (well, not more than an occasional trace). The finish should be smooth and flat but not super glossy. So called 'polishing' is just not necessary (despite what the plasterers say).

- You don't need to sand new finish plaster (if it's done properly), in fact sanding will scratch the smooth surface the trowel made.

FINAL FINISHING

New plaster and joint compound is very absorbent, so it's a good idea to use a sealer before hanging wallpaper. If painting, use water-based paint and thin down the first coat a little (10% or so) to allow it to easily soak into the dry plaster. Use water-based paints on internal plasterwork.

When buying paint, always tell your paint supplier what room the paint is for and they'll advise on what's the most suitable for that area. Matt finishes are common generally, but special vinyl wipeable paints are more durable for kitchens and bathrooms as they cope better with moisture and grease etc. If you find particular walls get dirty quickly, you might consider upgrading the paint with a more durable type, so you can wipe or clean it more often. I always use a 'robust' style, wipeable paint in hallways and near back doors into gardens for example.

WORKING WITH MASONRY

Another brick in the wall

To extend your house you'll need materials to match the existing as nothing looks worse than mismatched materials. If you don't have any samples kicking around in the garden, take a good close up photo in good light and preferably one with you holding a tape measure or ruler underneath and up the side to indicate the size (if it's 'non-standard'). Modern bricks etc. are pretty much all the same modular size, but old bricks come in a variety of sizes and sometimes no two are the same!

As for colour; well, you'll have to go with the closest you can find because of course your originals may be decades (or even centuries) old and well weathered. There are various methods of prematurely aging new brickwork, some involving cow dung and milk; but unless you really know what you're doing, I'd strongly advise you to give that a miss unless you want to end up literally in the...

There are many hundreds of different bricks available and it's likely you'll need to 'special order' some from your local builder's merchant. Allow plenty extra for wastage and miscalculations, especially if you're having to pay for transport to ship them from some far distant brick 'library' or stockyard. Your local merchant should stock the most popular bricks for your area (probably not more than about 10 different ones though), so you might get lucky and find them already in the yard.

On landscaping projects in the garden, you might get away with a contrasting brick if you can't find an exact match. Or even a contrasting material stone/brick/concrete etc.

MIXING MORTAR

You might not think of mortar as 'glue', but mortar is an adhesive and it does stick bricks or blocks together (although some argue that it simply holds them apart...). Mortar is usually soft sand mixed with a binder; either lime in the case of older buildings or nowadays, Portland cement (or masonry cement) along with a few additives to make it workable and to slow down the setting reaction. In the trade, we call it, muck, mud, gobbo, pug etc. etc.

We touched on lime mortars in the *Repairing Masonry* section in the *Repairing stuff* chapter, but if you're building something new, it's more than likely you'll be using a cement-based mortar.

Try scraping a mortar joint on your house. If it's buff coloured and scrapes out relatively easily (and it's an old house) it's a lime putty and sharp sand mix. If the mortar is greyer coloured and hard (and the house is post WII) then it's more likely to be a cement and soft sand mix.

Of course, there are many different mixes within these two types and the exact mix of the mortar you should use depends on two factors, the strength of the brick/stone units themselves and the severity of their exposure to the elements or weather.

First, it's important your new mortar is slightly *weaker* than the units in the wall, because this allows the (slightly softer) joints to absorb any gentle movement of the structure as it settles onto its foundation under its own weight. If the mortar were stronger than the units in the wall, everything would be very rigid, and any movement would cause stress to build within the wall itself, cracking joints, and units alike.

Second, the mortar must be able to withstand many years of whatever the environment throws at it. Wind, rain, and freezing temperatures plus salt or other chemicals (acidic rain etc.). Ergo the mortar used to build a chimney in an exposed clifftop location in a cold climate needs to be much more durable than the mortar used to build a decorative fireplace in your lounge for example.

Also, don't mix and match mortars if possible. If you use a lime mortar on a modern building, you'll not hurt it, but if you use cement-based mortars on old buildings you could cause a few problems because it's far too rigid and it sets too hard to cope with the gentle meanderings of an old house. You could even end up creating problems with damp and damaging the bricks themselves (see *Repairing Masonry* in the *Repairing Stuff* chapter).

If in doubt, always get a sample of old mortar analysed to get an educated guess of the original mortar components before starting. But if you can't do this, a common lime mortar mix consisted of one-part lime mixed with two and a half parts sieved sharp sand (particle size from dust up to around a third of the average mortar joint height, 0.1mm to 3mm for example).

Lastly, you'll struggle with plain old mortar, it's coarse and dries out quickly. Additives in the form of either lime or a liquid plasticiser, improves the workability no end. Folks used to add a small squirt of dishwashing detergent, which made lovely creamy mortar, but that's not allowed anymore because it reduces the mortars durability. Add the recommended amount of mortar plasticiser exactly to the following mixes and you'll end up with soooo smooth mortar it will roll off your tools beautifully.

The following mortar mix ratios (or multiples thereof) will cover most building situations...

- **1:3** which is 1 cement to 3 building or bricklaying sand. Very strong mix, suitable for very hard materials such as blue bricks, concrete bricks or blocks or severe environmental conditions such as salty air, acid rain etc.

- **1:4** which is 1 cement to 4 building or bricklaying sand. Strong mix suitable for engineering bricks or hard bricks in general including exposed conditions such as chimneys or garden walls or below ground masonry etc.

- **1:5** which is 1 cement to 5 building or bricklaying sand. Medium strength mix suitable for most bricks exposed to normal conditions above ground.

- **1:6** which is 1 cement to 6 building or bricklaying sand. Soft mix suitable for sheltered or protected masonry and indoor work such as internal blockwork.

- **1:1:6** which is 1 cement, 1 lime and 6 building or bricklaying sand. A good general purpose, medium strength mix for bricks, block, and stone under normal conditions.

- **1:9** which is 1 cement to 9 building or bricklaying sand. A very weak mix, suitable for lightweight blocks and bedding items subject to some movement.

NOTE 1: The above mortars assume it's applied at normal thicknesses up to around 25mm (1″) or so. Any thicker than this and I'd replace one or two of the soft sand elements with a coarse or sharp sand, as this will strengthen the mix and give it more body, making it more suitable for the thicker applications such as bedding paving slabs etc.

NOTE 2: Masonry cement can replace the Portland cement and lime in the above mixes, except the first two (the strong ones).

NOTE 3: You can add lime to the other ratios in this list too as it acts as a good plasticiser, improving workability.

The most important thing to remember when mixing your own mortar is to MEASURE each component of the ratio. i.e. make it a *gauged mix*. If you throw it all in willy-nilly using a shovel, the actual mix ratio will be all over the place. No two mixes will be the same, different colour, different strength, different consistency, different durability. Don't do it. Use a small bucket, i.e. one bucket of cement, 6 buckets of sand for 1:6 ratio.

You will see folks just using a shovel and I'll be honest, I do (with great accuracy), but then I've mixed many, many, hundreds of tons of concrete and mortar by hand in a drum mixer. Gauging exact size shovels is an experienced skill, you look at each shovel and adjust the quantity before it goes in and balance the shovels (one slightly small is followed by one slightly big for example). Some of my apprentices got the hang of it in a week, but some never managed and stuck to the bucket method. Usually, folks starting out grab huge shovels of sand and then tiny shovels of cement (because it's dry and doesn't heap up like sand), which when you stop and think about it, throws the ratio of cement to sand right out of the window.

If all that seems like too much trouble, most DIY stores sell dry 'ready-mix' mortar in bags where you just need to add water. These are great for those smaller jobs as one bag mixes easily in a wheelbarrow with just a shovel.

Right, after all that we finally get to the mixing (sorry!). Mixing by hand is a matter of measuring the correct ratio of dry materials into a bucket or wheelbarrow and turning them over a few times to ensure the components are evenly mixed. Once the colour is even throughout, create a well in the middle (like making dough) and add some water and any admixtures you're using. Bring the dry materials into the water, moving it, chopping, and folding it with the shovel (or a hoe). Add more water and repeat. Keep adding water and mixing until the mixture is creamy and folds off the shovel smoothly. Not so wet it's runny and not so dry it's crumbly.

If you're using a drum mixer, first make sure your materials are in a logical position related to the drum. You need to avoid unnecessary bending and turning around. You should be able to insert the shovel into each material, lift and straight into the drum in one fluid move. Anything else is inefficient and will slow you down (and get you shouted at by 'muck' hungry bricklayers on site...). Oh, and allow room for you to stand on the side of the drum that's going down to avoid getting splashed (stack your materials in the right place). Splashes seem to curl out from the bottom of the drum up and follow the side heading upwards (mixers vary, you'll soon find out which side to stand!). It's a popular trick to get the new guy to stand on the wrong side of the mixer whilst explaining this; thus, perfectly illustrating the point...

Add some water to a clean drum first (important), then add around half of the aggregate (sand/stones) followed by the cement and then the rest of the aggregate. Adjust the water content to suit. If it's too wet it's fine to add more dry material BUT, remember you must keep to the ratio. If it's only a little too wet, use a trowel and put the materials into a bucket (1 trowel of cement, 6 trowels of sand, for a 1:6 mix etc) and then tip the bucket into the drum. Repeat as necessary. If the aggregates are wet (often are) sometimes the mix will get wetter the longer you leave it. Don't be in a hurry to add more water straight away, it takes a minute for the water level to stabilize.

GETTING MASONRY STRAIGHT AND PLUMB

You'll need the simplest of tools to get masonry straight; a spirit level and a length of string pulled very tight (look down the line to ensure it does not sag or dip). Set up a few bricks each end using the spirit level; the ends can be plain, stopped ends for a straight wall or corners if your building something square etc. depending on your project. Then, stretch the line over the two ends using line pins or a pair of *mason's corner blocks* exactly in line with the tops of the first two end bricks and you're good to go, the string line will show you where to lay each brick on that course. Be careful not to let the brick actually touch the line though (or it will push it out of line), just get each brick a hairs breadth away from the line each time. Move the line up the courses at the corner and repeat. When you 'run out' of corner bricks to guide you build the ends up again and repeat. If you don't have time to make corner blocks, wrap the line around a heavy object some ways past the end and higher than the wall you're building and place a brick or two on top of the course you want to build with the line underneath it.

If you want to build a curve you can buy special curved string lines (just kidding, no you can't) you set out your curve on the foundations and use the spirit level to 'plumb up' each brick, (or every other brick) at a time and yes, that's why you don't see curved walls too much, it's time consuming and expensive.

If you have a decent budget and want to build something a little bigger, consider investing in builder's profiles. These are pairs of tall box profiles which you bolt to the first section of walling. The profile has sliding parts to hold a tight line which enables you to slide it up the profile for each course and thus there is no need to build time consuming corners, although they can be a little fiddly to set up.

SOME GENERAL MASONRY TIPS

- Watch your running length, each brick needs to sit exactly half over the brick below (in the most common half bond) allowing a little for the vertical, cross joint.

- Keep a close eye on the line position. If it moves out of position, it'll throw out your bricklaying too (flick the line and watch it vibrate, if it doesn't it means something is touching it and pushing it out).

- Finish off your mortar joints regularly with the tool of your choice (half round or bucket handle being the most common in the UK). Don't leave it too long before finishing them off (especially if it's hot) or it will be hard work and you'll get poorly finished joints.

- After jointing up (finishing the joints) and at the end of the day's work, give the bricks a very light brushing with a soft brush to give it a final flourish in the quality department.

- If you get mortar on the bricks wait until you're finished and then apply a special brick cleaner, (it's a type of acid), followed by a good rinsing (personally I don't like the idea of splashing acid around, but then I've never needed to, because I keep my brickwork clean...).

- In the summer time 'greedy', softer, bricks might need soaking with water a few minutes before laying to counter their extreme suction.

- Cover your work down at the end of the day to protect it from the weather, especially if it's cold or wet. Mortar fleece and polythene are good, with a plank top and bottom to stop it blowing off.

WORKING WITH CONCRETE

Concrete is exciting stuff and I am always a little nervous waiting before a large pour. There is something about having tons of super heavy, wet sloppy stuff around that will set into 'stone' and knowing that nothing in the world can stop it. Twist your ankle? Nope, it's still going to set and you're going to have to get it done regardless.

If you need more than a cubic metre (35 cubic feet) you should call your local ready mixed concrete (RMC) guy to get a price for delivery. There are full sized machines, 6m³ to 8m³ (9 to 11 yrds³) and 'mini-mix' machines 3m³ (4yds³) or so. Remember there's often a part load cost, i.e. if you order half a truck load, they'll charge you a smaller amount for the remaining space to make up the company's minimum charge.

Another great alternative is the 'mix-on-site' or volumetric concrete mixing machines, perfect for any amount as they mix only what you need there and then (especially useful as there is no waste concrete to get rid of if you fluff the calculations). Most companies deliver from 1 to 12m³ (1 to 16yds³) making them perfect for most concrete pours.

Regarding which concrete to order, it's complicated, there are grades (from C7.5 to C60) but you also have *designated mixes* for specific purposes such as GEN1, 2 etc. (general works), PAV1,2 etc. (hard landscaping), FND etc. (foundations), RC 30, 40 etc. (reinforced concrete) etc. Then there are *prescribed mixes* which are replicable recipes for the concrete plant to follow. And even designer mixes for special applications. Oh, and *standard mixes* (ST1 to 5) for smaller jobs... (I told you it was complicated!)

Waaay too much to learn, and to be honest, you'll probably never need it, because on bigger jobs your architect will specify the mix, or the concrete supply company will recommend one. So rather than list the multitude of different concrete mixes (most of which you'll never need anyway) let's just say that when you order concrete, just tell them the following details about the proposed pour...

- Where it's going (foundations, floor slab, driveway etc.).

- If there will be contact with any contamination (sulphates in the ground, acidic ground water etc.)

- If it has any reinforcing mesh or rebar's etc.

- If you're going to pump it via a concrete pump (you can ask for additives to improve flow).

- If you need self-compacting concrete. Special additives make this flow like water, levelling out and needs no special compacting. Ideal to run around dense reinforcing bars in shuttering or for floors etc.

- If you need special additives: e.g. chemicals to slow down the initial set in hot weather to allow time for placement or speed up the initial set in cold weather to give some frost protection, or if you want to increase the waterproofing properties of the concrete or to increase its final strength by adding reinforcing plastic fibres.

- Any special conditions specified by the architect not mentioned above (lightweight, foamed, underwater, high heat, high strength, coloured etc. etc.).

Based on the above facts, they'll suggest and supply you with a suitable mix. It's as simple as that. Some common areas and usages requiring different concrete mixes are...

- Strip or normal foundations under garden walls, single story extensions, non-load bearing walls etc.

- Strip or normal foundations under higher or heavy walls, multiple stories, houses etc.

- Trench fill or mass fill foundations in difficult ground (clay etc.).

- Special foundations, i.e. rafts, piles, pads under columns etc.

- Anything containing reinforcement bars or mesh (over poor ground or weak spots etc.).

- Anything within a *shuttering* or *formwork*, columns, walls, etc.

- Floor slabs with a proposed screed on top etc.

- Finished floor slabs i.e. inside garages, workshops, etc.

- Domestic driveways and paths, i.e. foot and car traffic etc.

- Commercial driveways, i.e. lorries, forklift trucks etc.

- Around drains under buildings etc, to protect the pipes etc.

- Hard landscaping, paving, kerbstones etc. (usually a dry, weak mix).

In addition to all the above there is one last factor, slump. No, not what you do onto the sofa after moving a few tons of the stuff, but rather the amount of water you add to the mix for workability. Imagine making a sand castle with a bucket of concrete; slump is the amount the concrete castle sinks (slumps) when you lift away the bucket. Stiff concrete slumps hardly at all, has no flow capabilities and is very dry (which is ideal for laying kerbstones but hopeless inside a formwork around steel reinforcing). Really wet concrete, ideal for flowing around steelwork, would slump to a puddle, have excellent flow and levelling capabilities but be difficult to move by shovel (because it would drop off the sides!).

Official slump or *consistence* ratings are as follows: S1 is 10mm to 40mm (⅜″ to 1 ½″), S2 is 50mm to 90mm (2″ to 3 ½″), S3 is 100mm to 150mm (4″ to 6″), S4 is 160mm to 210mm (6 ½″ to 8 ½″), S5 is 210mm + or soup as it's called on site!

Different jobs require different slump. Pouring concrete into foundations or into formwork containing rebar's etc., you're going to need a higher slump to enable it to flow properly into every corner. Whereas a driveway for example needs a stiffer mix, avoiding too much water on the surface so you can tamp it flat with a straightedge and create a nice finish with a float, trowel or even a rotary machine called a power float (rubs the concrete to a super smooth surface).

Adjust the slump of your concrete on site, i.e. the concrete leaves the plant at the 'correct' slump for the grade of concrete you've asked for (usually S2). Most folks find this too dry (correct or otherwise) to be able to work the concrete easily and request the machine operator to add additional water. How much is up to you, but there is a line between improving workability and being silly and turning the concrete into soup just so it runs easily and makes short work of levelling it out.

The amount of water in the concrete mix determines the final strength, and too much water considerably weakens it, so don't go crazy, a little is okay, a lot is not. Some concrete pours I've witnessed (but was not controlling) were so thin (to flow around to awkward areas of foundation) that I was hesitant to stand on them the following day! That said, it was amazing that the watery soup I saw poured, set to the concrete I felt underneath my boots. The only reason the contractor got away with such poor-quality concrete is because it was almost 1m (3′) deep (trench fill) and probably had a large margin for error.

MIXING YOUR OWN CONCRETE

Mixing concrete yourself, up to 2 or 3 tons is fine and even larger quantities are still feasible. Buy or hire a small drum type concrete mixer (they are cheap), add a wheelbarrow, a shovel a few buckets and a stiff brush (for cleaning) and you're good to go. Smaller amounts you can mix in a wheelbarrow or even a large bucket with a trowel or a whisk on a powerful drill. Mixing concrete yourself has one great advantage and that's time. Mixing at your own pace means you'll always have a quantity you can handle, i.e. you can move, place, and finish it off in a reasonable time. Plus, you'll get the exact quality you want, i.e. it's never too wet or too dry; this makes levelling up and finishing off easier.

As I mentioned above, a concrete mix is a ratio of Portland cement, a fine aggregate, often called washed, sharp, or concreting sand (never soft building or bricklaying sand) and a coarse aggregate (crushed stone or gravel), mixed with enough water to hydrate the cement. In general, the thicker or larger the mass of concrete the less cement it needs. Mass fill projects like deep trench fill foundations will be a weaker mixture than you'd need for a garage floor for example. The ideal ratio of materials aims to fill any voids in the mixture. For example, too much sand will make weak concrete, too much stone will leave weakening voids, and as already mentioned, using too much water will also weaken the final strength.

Some places sell a very convenient 'all in ballast' aggregate (ballast for short) which is a mix of stone and sharp, concreting sand in one. Simply add cement and water to make concrete.

Always use cement before the use by date on the bag expires (within reason, it's not lettuce!) and the bag must be dry. I wouldn't use any bag full of lumps. These four mix ratios will cover most situations and they are comprised as follows...

- **1:1.5:2.5** which is one cement, 1.5 sand and 2.5 stone. (or **1:4** cement and ballast). Very strong mix suitable for reinforced concrete and padstones or areas needing great strength or water resistance etc. Similar to C35 RMC.

- **1:2:4** which is one cement, 2 sand and 4 stone (or **1:6** cement and ballast). Good general strength mix for slabs, paths, floors etc. Similar to C20 RMC.

- **1:2.5:5.5** which is one cement, 2.5 sand and 5.5 stone. (**1:8** cement and ballast). Slightly weaker mix good for foundations in good ground, fence posts, etc. Similar to C15 RMC.

- **1:3.5:6.5** lean mix which is one cement, 4 sand and 8 stone (**1:10** cement and ballast). Weak mix for cavity fill, soft spot infill, blinding, certain hard landscaping work etc. Similar to C7.5 RMC.

For those reading this book straight through, here's a warning; you might experience a déjà vu moment here from the mortar section (you may jump to the next heading, as it's more or less the same principle...)

The most important thing to remember when mixing your own concrete is to MEASURE each component of the ratio. i.e. make it a *gauged mix*. If you throw it all in willy-nilly using a shovel, the actual mix ratio will be correspondingly all over the place. No two mixes will be the same, different colour, different strength, different slump, different durability. Don't do it. Use a small bucket, i.e. one bucket of cement, 2 buckets of sand and 4 buckets of stones for 1:2:4.

You will see folks just using a shovel and I'll be honest, I do (with great accuracy), but then I've mixed many, many, hundreds of tons of concrete and mortar by hand in a drum mixer. Gauging exact size shovels is an experienced skill, you look at each shovel and adjust the quantity before it goes in and balance the shovels (one slightly small is followed by one slightly big for example). Some of my apprentices got the hang of it in a week, but some never managed and stuck to the bucket method. Usually, folks starting out grab huge shovels of sand and then tiny shovels of cement and stones (because they don't heap up like sand), which when you think about it, throws the ratio of cement to sand/stone right out of the window.

If all that seems like too much trouble, most DIY stores sell dry 'ready-mix' concrete in bags where you just need to add water. These are great for those smaller jobs as one bag mixes easily in a wheelbarrow with just a shovel.

Right, after all that we finally get to the mixing (sorry!). Mixing by hand is a matter of measuring the correct ratio of dry materials into a bucket or wheelbarrow and turning them over a few times to ensure the components are evenly mixed. Once the colour is even throughout, create a well in the middle (like making dough) and add some water. Bring the dry materials into the water, moving it, chopping, and folding it with the shovel (or a hoe). Add more water and repeat. Keep adding water and mixing until the mixture is creamy and folds off the shovel smoothly. Not so wet it's runny and not so dry it's crumbly.

If you're using a drum mixer, first make sure your materials are in a logical position related to the drum. You need to avoid unnecessary bending and turning around. You should be able to insert the shovel into each material, lift and straight into the drum in one fluid move. Anything else is inefficient and will slow you down (and get you shouted at by the guys placing the concrete on site...). Oh, and stand on the side of the drum that's going down to avoid getting splashed (adjust your materials accordingly). Splashes seem to curl out from the bottom of the drum up and follow the side heading upwards (mixers vary, you'll soon find out which side to stand!). It's a popular trick to get the new guy to stand on the wrong side of the mixer whilst explaining this; thus perfectly illustrating the point...

Add some water to the drum first (important), then add around half of the aggregates followed by the cement and then the rest of the aggregates. Adjust the water content to suit. If it's too wet it's fine to add more dry materials BUT, remember you must keep to the ratio. To add a little to dry up a wet mix, use a trowel and put the materials into a bucket (1 trowel of cement, 2 trowels of sand, and 4 trowels of stones for a 1:2:4 mix etc) and then tip the bucket into the drum. Repeat as necessary until the mix has dried up. If the aggregates are wet (often are) sometimes the mix will get wetter the longer you leave it. Don't be in a hurry to add more water straight away, it takes a minute for the water level to stabilize.

PLACING AND FINISHING CONCRETE

Before we look at placing concrete we need to ensure where it is going is strong enough to support it. This usually means removing the softer top layers or strata of earth. The uppermost stratum, often called *top soil* is largely made up of soft humus (dark, organic material) and has virtually no bearing capacity. The *subsoil* underneath might hold light stuff such as paving etc. and light garden walls if you're well into the subsoil. But you'll need to go further down, through the subsoil and into the substratum to achieve true bearing capacity. This means at least 1m or around 3 feet deep in many areas (dig a trial hole first and watch for colour changes as you go down).

Driveways and floor slabs etc. need compacted layers of crushed stone or clean rubble underneath to build up the levels after removing soft soils. Never pour concrete on soft or uncompact material and preferably always pour onto polythene to stop the water draining straight out of the concrete mix and into the ground (the slower it sets the better).

If you're going for RMC, remember that concrete lorries are big and heavy trucks. Often over 2.4m (8') wide and a fully loaded 6m³ barrel truck can weigh 25 tons or more! Plenty enough to make a mess of asphalt and even concrete driveways etc... Remember grass is easier to repair than hard landscaping... (if it hasn't rained in a while...). You're going to need good access routes to the drop off points enabling the truck to pour the concrete exactly where you need it. Always ask for advice (or even a site visit) from the RMC company if the access is tight to your pouring spot.

Plan your concrete pour so you're handling the concrete as little as possible. The best scenario for all concreting jobs is to drop the concrete exactly where you need it, preferably from multiple or moving drop points to spread out the load. Standard RMC machines need to be close to the pouring location (2m to 3m or 6' to 10'), although some concrete plants have mixers with a built-in conveyor system enabling them to place concrete some distance away. Alternatively, you can hire a lorry mounted concrete pump with a long movable boom (cost effective for larger loads or difficult locations). Be aware you need space for two trucks though...

If that's not possible, ask the company if the truck will pour directly into wheelbarrows for you, there may be a small charge for this (it takes a little longer) but it's miles better than the next option...

Try to avoid dropping the concrete onto a sheet of polythene out front and then shovelling the concrete into barrows and wheeling it into the job (believe me, I've had more than my fair share of doing this on tight jobs). If you can't avoid it; just make sure you have...

- Lots of strong polythene or a tarpaulin to cover down. Concrete spreads into a large area, especially if you add water to improve workability.

- Build solid ramps up to any step, no matter how small, you don't need any bumps at all with a wheelbarrow with 100kgs of wet concrete in it, trust me...

- Tack timber strips on any door frames you're running barrows though, just in case...

- More than enough folks on hand to get the concrete barrowed into place within 30 to 45mins for slabs and an hour for foundations. Any longer and you're in danger of the concrete starting its initial set or 'going off' before you've got it in place and tamped level.

- Allow a maximum of $1m^3$ ($1yd^3$) of concrete per person/ wheelbarrow and more if the barrow 'run' is far away (or it's in the middle of the summer).

- Plenty of shovels (save the spades for gardening), sturdy rakes or 'come alongs' (like a rake, only with a blade) to pull and push the concrete into place.

  Make your own tools such as, 'come alongs', tamps etc. out of scraps of timber. Easily customised to fit the job in hand.

Having an extra person on hand to mop sweating brows and hand out cups of cold water is a good idea in hot weather (and you think I'm joking, ha, ha, not this time!) Oh, and self-levelling concretes, screeds or really wet mixes need to go straight into their final place for obvious reasons (it'll run down the street if you try to pour it on polythene...).

Related to not handling the concrete more than you need to, is setting out your levels before the pour. This means that during the actual pour, you can concentrate on getting the concrete exactly where you need it, (because it's instantly obvious when it's correct).

For example, never try to level up wet concrete in the bottom of a footing trench with a spirit level; instead, hammer in a wooden peg (or rebar), at the exact level you need (measured from a known point such as the DPC or ground level etc.**).** Then add more pegs 1 metre or so apart and use your best spirit level (or laser/site level etc.) to ensure all the pegs are perfectly level with each other. Then the actual concrete pour is simplicity itself because you're just looking for the tops of the pegs. Rake the concrete around until you see the very top of the peg just visible in the concrete ('fish' around for them!). Drag away excess concrete from high spots to low spots.

In general, freehand work on fresh concrete takes longer than you have time for before it starts to stiffen up and set. You'll be happier working to predetermined level markers. Ideally you want to be throwing the concrete down as quick as possible and concentrate on levelling out and compacting.

Don't forget you must finish off the top of the concrete once you've levelled it all out using rakes, concrete come-along tools and shovels to drag, level out and compact the concrete. The above example in a footing trench is probably good enough finished off with the flat head of a rake or come along (if the slump was a little wet). Simply walk along the edge of the trench with the tool held vertically so the head is horizontal and work the very top of the concrete, flattening and smoothing out the surface.

Floor slabs, driveways etc. need a better finish. Always have hard edges to work your straight edge from; as with the trench, you don't want to be messing around with your spirit level at the concrete pouring stage. Set up exact levels beforehand using either walls, timber or a proprietary metal and peg system of shuttering. Use these levels to determine the final level of the concrete using a long straight edge or 'screeding' board. Roughly level out the concrete with the rakes, come alongs, and shovels and then tamp a section of the concrete with the straightedge (bounce it up and down on the surface). Withdraw to the beginning again and then 'saw' the surface of the concrete, back and forth until you feel the shuttering or masonry underneath the straight edge. Remove the excess in front of the straight edge and drop it into a low spot. Repeat across the whole slab. You might need to do this a couple of times to get the slab properly flat.

Compaction is important to remove the air which becomes entrained during the mixing and placing. Compacting concrete removes this air and increases final strength. There are several ways to do this...

- Tamps. From a length of straight timber to an aluminium straight edge. Bounce up and down followed by dragging, scraping, plus 'sawing' back and forth to both level and compact as you go.

- Compact smaller amounts of concrete with whatever you're moving it with. Rakes, shovels, rebar, or even a length of timber. Pumping them up and down as the concrete is going in will dispel air.

- Vibrating pokers are brilliant and it's amazing how much concrete will 'settle' out once this powerful little tool gets going. They help to move the concrete along and level out too. As the name suggests it's a long flexible rod connected to a vibrating engine. Dip the running poker into and around the concrete. Good for any concreting job and essential for any pour including mesh or bar reinforcing.

- Vibrate the edges of any timber shuttering by using the poker, or tapping with a small hammer, length of re-bar or similar.

There are of course machines available for hire to help with all these jobs. Including vibrating screed bars and trowels, right up to huge (and amazing to watch) laser guided boom screeders for big concrete pours.

Once the slab is flat and compacted, finish off the surface as you like (usually after waiting for a little while for any surface water to disappear). Wooden or plastic floats are a popular choice to get the slab flat, as they rub off micro high spots and fill in corresponding low spots. Either leave as a swirly, slightly rough, finish. Dragging a brush in straight lines across the wet concrete is also popular as is following on with a metal trowel once the concrete has further dried a little. Like plastering, a lot about concrete is in the timing. Go back too soon and it's too wet to work, leaving lines everywhere. But leave it too long and you're; well, in a lot of trouble to be honest!

In addition to flat trowels, you'll find round ended trowels (bull trowels) which don't leave lines, plus all sorts of edging trowels to create small round edges, border, or margin trowels, grooving trowels to allow or induce the concrete to crack from the bottom of the groove (looks better than a random hairline crack across the slab).

One last thing, if you're using mesh or rebar in the concrete, it's important to keep it away from the surfaces of the concrete (top, bottom, and sides) to prevent water penetrating far enough to accelerate corrosion. You can buy little plastic gizmos to clip to the reinforcement to hold it in the right place (or little concrete spacer blocks to sit the reinforcement on). Cover all reinforcing with the following thickness of concrete...

- 75mm (3") when on or in contact with the ground (footings or a driveway for example).

- 50mm (2") anything exposed and outdoors, driveways/paths etc.

- 40mm (1 9/16″) if on a DPM (damp proof membrane) on a sand blinding (ground floor slab for example).

- 25mm (1″) if indoors or covered (columns, lintels, or beams etc).

CURING CONCRETE

Wet concrete contains a large amount of water which will evaporate as the concrete cures or dries. The slower this happens the better it is for the concrete. Rapid water loss compromises the final strength of the concrete i.e. it's weaker. Wind and warm weather will dry out concrete very quickly (especially slabs). It is critical to slow down water loss by keeping it damp for a week (longer is even better). After the initial set, (which occurs after a few hours), concrete continues to strengthen and harden, reaching 90% or so after around a month, depending on the location and weather. After this period concrete continues to harden but very slowly over many years. Old concrete is often very hard indeed.

Fortunately, it's easy to slow down this water loss. Once the concrete surface is firm (a few hours), cover it up with polythene and weigh down the edges (bricks, planks, sand bags etc.), to stop the wind getting underneath. Wetting underneath and/or on top of the polythene holds the polythene in place too. Keep an eye on the surface colour of the concrete under the sheet, it should look dark and wet, if it's light grey and dry, add more water quick.

UPCYCLING

And lastly, although technically these materials are not 'new', (making it difficult to decide where to put this in the book), I think here is as good as anywhere because upcycling is making something 'new' out of something old and often unwanted. Upcycling is the latest buzzword to hit the DIY scene and centres around reusing something in a way not intended by the manufacturer. Here are a few projects to ponder...

- Old, unwanted furniture often makes wonderfully cheap and unique projects. Screw old drawers to the wall as shelves etc.

- Make furniture from unwanted stuff, turn an old door into a coffee table for example.

- Transform a by-product or waste material into new materials or products for creative use. Keep an eye on local businesses near you to see what they routinely throw away.

- Re-use unwanted items and fashion them into art. Sculptures from scrap metal or pictures from bottle caps or clocks out of cycle wheels or swings out of tyres and so on...

- And the most popular of all (with me at least), turning old pallets into furniture, chicken coops, potting benches and so on...

Working in East Africa, I learned that even humble tin cans have a useful life, long after storing my favourite baked beans. So don't throw too much away, it will come in handy one day... I promise.

Congratulations and welcome to the DIY hall of fame, you're now ready to work with real materials and use real tools to build something fantastic from scratch (even if it's just a nest box to start off with). From a blank piece of paper to a finished article is now possible because you know (in theory) you can build anything you want. You know to start small. You know to build on your existing skills, and how to learn new ones by utilising books, online videos and 'how to's' or by finding someone to give you the advice you need. You know the information is out there: look for detailed plans, designs, forums, clubs, websites, and don't forget your friends and neighbours.

It doesn't matter whether it's a bookcase, a boat, or a house, you understand every project is just a series of small steps, one, easily *researched, learned, and practiced* technique or task at a time. You know it takes time (what 'hobby' doesn't?) to build up skills and competence, but you also know that time rarely matters in the end. The only thing that matters is producing work of a good enough quality to make you happy with the end results.

Take short cuts, find, and follow plans if you want to be sure your projects come together with no problems. Otherwise, the whole world is out there to inspire you to make stuff, any kind of stuff. In fact, that's the problem with being able to make whatever you want; i.e. you have unlimited choices! There are almost too many variables when building from scratch (shape, material, colour, function etc.); it is more akin to art than science. So, go and create something wonderful... but first here is that pesky *Health and Safety* chapter I keep telling you to go to, there's no escaping it now...

Here goes; gently turn the page, you don't want to get a paper cut now...

HEALTH AND SAFETY

'No man was ever wise by chance'

Seneca

Don't take a chance with your health, always put...

Safety First!

Ouch! (although most folks use other words in these situations, some also with four letters...). Arguably, when you work with tools and materials, small injuries are almost inevitable, because even the most careful and cautious folks will occasionally catch their hand on something, trap a finger or slip with a tool. However, serious injuries are a different matter. You can reduce the risk significantly by *adopting safe working practises, every time...no exceptions.* Sorry to go on about this, but it's *really* important! Remember you're literally gambling with *your life* (or other peoples), if you *choose to*...

- ...succumb to pressure and cut corners to finish quickly.

- ...work with the wrong tool for the job.

- ...work without proper protective gear.

- ...work on unsafe or inappropriate support/ scaffolding.

- ...use unfamiliar tools without studying and practising first.

- ...make *any* decision that ignores your personal safety.

- ...make *any* decision that ignores the safety of others.

...because sooner or later, *you will have an 'accident'*, I put quotes around the word accident because true accidents are rare, most 'accidents' are a result of a bad choice or a poor judgement call.

There's no doubt that tackling some DIY jobs means using potentially dangerous tools or heavy materials plus difficult situations either in or on the ground or at considerable height. These situations require specific safety measures as mistakes can easily be fatal. Working from ladders being particularly dangerous statistically. You must take this stuff seriously because your first mistake could also be your last...

YOU ARE EVERYTHING!

Sweet I know, but you really are everything! So never forget the most important thing in your world is you. Everything and I mean everything else is unimportant compared to your health and safety. Because if you get hurt, injured or dead, you won't be able to finish the job and that will never do! A true handy person always works safely, because injuries slow you down and might delay the start of the next fun project...

If you're reading this as a 'young un', i.e. someone under say 30 (ancient I know!) you might be scoffing at all this stuff. I'm as fit as a butcher's dog you might say, watch me bounce ping-pong balls off my abs. But believe this. What you *do today*, affects what you *can do tomorrow*.

I know because I used to be that hero on the building site; running about on rooftops unsecured, abusing ladders and lifting what I now know to be insane weights; steel beams, oak beams, concrete lintels, timber etc. Not to mention thousands of tons of other smaller materials over the years, all by hand. Stupid and definitely not clever. Ask my knees now, go on ask... Oh, I'm sorry, they can't hear you over the creaking, clicking and groans of pain...

Human beings are not forklift trucks, *(that's why we have forklift trucks...)* If you repeatedly abuse something i.e. your body, it will eventually wear out, and 50 ain't that old, it's the new 40, hadn't you heard?

WARNING: Ignoring this advice may have serious consequences for your long-term health! When you're older *and* wiser *and* more experienced *and* more skilled, *and* (hopefully) wealthier, you'll still want to be active, so start the habit now, always work safe... every time.

KEEPING YOUR BLOOD WHERE IT BELONGS...

A few tips to help you stay safe...

TAKE YOUR TIME

Rushing about to finish quickly will eventually cause you to lose some skin or even some precious blood. Why? Because safety concerns are not your first priority, getting the project finished is. Working safely should always be uppermost in your mind, no matter how urgent the project is. Rushing to finish quickly could even *finish you*, it happens believe me, more often than you think. I've seen one person die on the job and that's one too many, but I've seen plenty of stupid accidents, some of them my own.

Even if you only hurt yourself a little bit, you'll slow yourself down. This is a big problem for a professional. Most of the curses that fly when we injure ourselves are because our dumb mistake will hamper and slow us down for days afterwards, costing us time off work and money.

Also, think about who's benefiting from you taking risks or short cuts. Mostly it's someone else! If your other half (or the client if it's your own business,) is complaining about how long a job is taking, remind them that top quality work always takes a little longer, think Rolls Royce not Trabant!

USE PROPER PERSONAL PROTECTION EQUIPMENT

Most are no-brainers; you *know* this stuff, so use them okay?

- Avoid wearing lose clothing near rotary machines and don't wear any jewellery whilst working, even rings (free!).

- Use safety glasses when using tools that could cause sparks or debris to fly, they are effective, and easy to use, there's no logical reason not to use them. Plus, they are as comfortable as sunglasses these days, gone are the hopeless misting goggles of yore (very cheap).

- Wear gloves when handling materials and when using club hammers and cold chisels etc. to protect your hands (cheap). Gloves also prevent getting rough skin, which might snag stockings, either your own or someone else's (priceless).

- Wear coveralls etc. when using chemicals or irritating stuff like insulation. Plus, they're handy against regular dust too (cheap).

- Hard hats, if there is a 'reasonable risk' of falling debris and always if there are people and/ or loose material above you (cheap).

- Wear high visibility (Hi-Vis) clothing if working with others or in a busy location (cheap).

- Wear a facemask when working in dusty conditions, with insulation materials or cutting treated timber etc. Disposables or even better, a proper filtered facemask (cheap).

- Wear ear protection when using loud tools, tools in enclosed spaces or for any extended length of time. Tiny and cheap foam plugs as a minimum or better, proper over the head ear defenders (cheap).

- Use steel toe capped boots if handling heavy stuff. Good ankle protection too (medium cost).

- Wear a good thick leather belt to support your back. Helpful if you have a lot of heavy lifting to do; some folks even swear by a weight-lifter's belt to support a hard working back (medium cost).

- Having an accident and injuring yourself because you didn't bother with any of the above (very, very expensive).

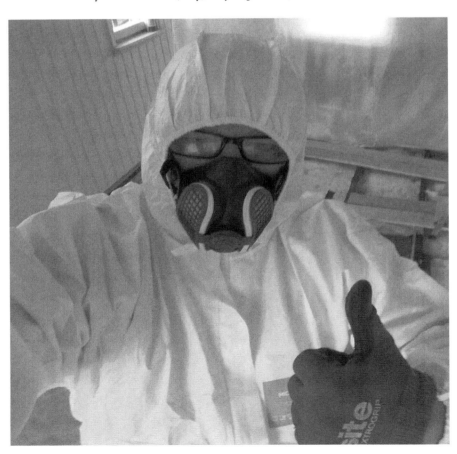

FITNESS

I mentioned earlier that DIY can be a part of your keep fit regime by keeping you active. Keep in mind your current level of fitness though, because some DIY tasks are very strenuous. You wouldn't embark on a 10-mile run if you'd only ever done 2-mile walks, would you? No, so don't make the first project a biggie in the garden. Like everything else we've looked in this book, start small and work your way up, slowly.

POOR JUDGEMENT OR DECISIONS

Remember no one wakes up in the morning intending to have an accident that day. Accidents are the consequences arising from a poor judgement call.

But maybe one day you're pressed for time, so you decide to take a 'short cut' or do something you wouldn't normally do. But always ask yourself first; what are the implications? What are the consequences of this decision? Make every decision you make a conscious one.

But if you misjudged the risk or danger, or played them down, *because* you were pressed for time. Then your decision could, and probably would, lead to an accident. For example, at the town dump, if you get pierced by a nail sticking out of a piece of skirting board, it's because at some point you made the decision to leave the nails sticking out when you took the skirting board off the wall (to save a few seconds). And that is a very mild example, believe me, I've seen much, much worse...

USING THE WRONG TOOL FOR THE JOB

A hammer is a hammer and a wrench is not. Don't expect a wrench to do the job of a hammer without getting you into trouble. I know it's a nuisance when you're working in the attic and you need yet another tool from the shed/car/downstairs/etc.; but reaching for the wrong tool can cost you dearly in terms of blood or damage to the workpiece.

Before you start up the stairs, out into the garden or head for the scaffold with your bucket of tools, take a moment, close your eyes if you need to, and conjure up a mental image of the task in hand. Picture yourself doing the work and what tools you need. Mentally walk through it. Do you have everything you might need in your bucket?

THINKING, IT'LL ONLY TAKE A MINUTE

That tiny job to put one screw in, or push something into place, is not an excuse to take short cuts with your safety. It only takes a fraction of a second to slip, fall, cut, or catch yourself. The length of the job is never an excuse to take short cuts with safe working practises.

USING THE WRONG MATERIALS OR FIXINGS

Always make the extra effort to use the right thing for the job you're doing. A nail will only do a screws job for so long before it fails. If the job calls for specific fixings, use them. When fixings fail, things fall apart and someone might get hurt, not to mention your pride...

Always follow the manufacturer's instructions. For example, if the instructions say the glue isn't water resistant, don't expect it to last very long if you use it outside. Oh, and don't build a boat with interior grade plywood, even if you paint it well, (and yes, I know the proper marine ply is expensive) unless you're a really good swimmer etc...

THINKING, A LADDER IS FINE

According to the World Health Organisation (WHO), 424,000 people die from falling, plus another 37.3 million falls are severe enough to need medical attention (globally). Every... single... year. This makes falling the second biggest cause of accidental death after motoring accidents.

If you don't want to join them, always use proper scaffolding with safety rails when doing anything at any kind of height i.e. over 2m (6' or so.) Using a platform will enable you to work much quicker compared with working off a ladder because you'll have more space and a much better reach.

When I first started out, I used to take crazy risks on ladders because I thought hiring scaffolding was expensive.

I soon realised the only person benefitting was my customer because I was billing for labour, materials, and access equipment 'as used'. So essentially, I *risked my life for nothing*. If you can't afford to do the job with safe access, then forget it, let the darn thing fall down. It's dumb to risk your life for a house.

IT WON'T HAPPEN TO ME...

Don't tell me you weren't thinking that because I know you were (because everyone does). No one gets up in the morning with the intention of having an accident, no one, ever. You're probably thinking, 'Oh, I'll be all right, it wouldn't happen to me because I know what I'm doing, I'm careful, I know what's an acceptable risk.' Come on admit it, you're thinking those guys must have been a tiny bit dumb to have an accident; you've seen the YouTube videos, right? Well, maybe that's true, but more likely they were regular guys getting on with the job thinking, *'I'll be all right, it won't happen to me because I know what I am doing, I'm careful'*... just... like... you...

FIRST AID KIT

If you're not used to working with your hands, the concept of getting hurt and seeing yourself bleed might come as a bit of a shock the first time. Prepare yourself, put together a simple first aid kit before you start. No need to buy anything fancy. If you need anything fancy, then arguably you should be calling for an ambulance to take you to the hospital...

You can buy over the counter first aid kits from any pharmacy or you can put together your own to cover the main types of accidents. This is what I keep in my own kits, (car, home and at work... and yes, that's three kits!).

- Antiseptic wipes and sprays (ouch, okay they hurt a bit, but think about the how dirty that wound is. It's important to avoid infection.

- Pair of round nose medical scissors for cutting bandages etc. and for cutting clothing from more serious injuries.

- A pair of good tweezers and a medium size sewing needle (for splinters) Wipe everything with an antiseptic wipe first.

- Capsules of sterile water. Twist off the top to rinse wounds. For debris in the eye, pierce the top with needle and gently squeeze capsule and use the thin stream to rinse debris out of the eye.

- Plasters to protect small damage (minor blood loss). Personally, I don't use them for cuts as the non-sticky part/pad allows the cut to open and close as you move around. In most cases, I like to 'stitch' a cut closed with tape or steri-strips, this closes the cut and keeps it closed allowing the body to repair the damage (always clean first).

- Thin adhesive tape or 'steri-strips' (butterfly stitches) for medium size cuts (medium blood loss). Close wound and stick them straight across the cut, spaced at around 1cm ($^3/_8''$) intervals (after cleaning thoroughly of course).

- Small compress pads for medium cuts or skin damage (serious, scary looking blood loss)

- Medium compress pads for large damage (very serious, very scary looking blood loss)

- Large absorbent compress pads plus roll and triangular bandages for serious damage (call an ambulance kind of blood loss!)

- Roll of 25mm (1") adhesive tape to hold compress pads in place.

- A proper, clearly marked first aid bag to put it all in.

I might just add a few extra things into my car first aid kit like a blanket, disposable gloves, a one-way resuscitation valve and a torch with spare batteries. The theory being that the better the first aid kit, the less likely you are to need one! Also, don't forget that it might not be you that needs it, so always make sure it's obvious what it is, easy to see and easily accessible for everyone.

ON THE LIGHTER SIDE

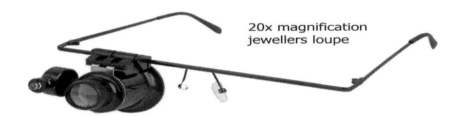

20x magnification jewellers loupe

Splinters.

You're going to get them for sure, and rather than digging around blindly with blunt tools, get yourself a jeweller's loupe or magnifier. They cost next to nothing and will miraculously turn that miniscule, annoying sliver of wood (or metal, glass, thorn etc.) into a massive tree trunk, which you can gently and much less painfully negotiate out, using a clean needle and a pair of tweezers. Trust me on this, it'll be the best thing you buy for your kit.

I use magnifying type shown in the previous image; they are awesome... Oh, and don't worry, you'll get really good at 'operating' on yourself...

It's really quite a shame that no one wants to talk about Health and Safety and in fact the very phrase elicits groans of derision and ridicule. It's shocking that something as important as keeping us safe has become a byword for 'dumb rules'. Rules to treat as 'unreasonable' and 'restrictive' and fair game for selective interpretation. Worse still, rules seen as 'unnecessary' and perfectly okay to avoid and ignore.

But you must be sensible when it comes to construction, because far too many people, every single year, are injured, plus of course those who make their last mistake and actually die (and I'll bet that 99.9% were not intending to die that particular day...). Many of the deaths happen to those employed in the industry, i.e. professionals. So, if professionals are getting into trouble, have a think about how careful *you* need to be to stay safe, sobering huh?

Remember that you are not immortal, and you're not big and clever (yes, even if you're under 25). You will hurt yourself (or worse) if you do stupid things. It's cause and effect; yin and yang, action and reaction, or karma; whatever you call it, these are the unbreakable laws of the universe. Do stupid things now, pay later, (or now, you can never tell when payment is due with the laws of the universe) and pay them you must. Don't be that hero, lifting stupidly heavy things or reaching off the ladder or balancing on the roof edge.

So I repeat, (because it's that important), take your time, (no short cuts), and always wear the proper protective equipment for the job in hand. Use the right tools for the job and never ignore common sense and think "oh, it'll only take a minute". Sometimes it only takes a split second, let alone a minute to have a serious accident.

Never think "it won't happen to me" (because it can), hospitals are full of people whose life has been forever changed (and never for the better) after a split-second incident. So be paranoid, be afraid, always think the worst, be a pessimist when it comes to your health and safety, it might just save your life.

Oh, and always, and I really mean always, keep a half decent first aid kit easily accessible, hang it on a nail if you must. Don't forget it might not be you who needs to find and use it. If it's you lying on the floor, bleeding out or unconscious, you'd better hope whoever finds you can see the kit and that it has the right things in it...

Jeeze, tough love huh!

EPILOGUE (ENOUGH NOW...GO FORTH AND BE HANDY!)

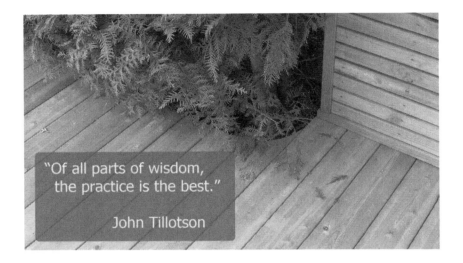

"Of all parts of wisdom,
the practice is the best."

John Tillotson

Phew; it's been quite a journey hasn't it! This has been a theoretical book about a practical subject, but now you have some theory under your belt, it's time to start the real learning process and get your hands dirty. It's like learning to drive; you start learning for real the first time out on your own after passing the driving test. Being practical is no different. Real practise will promote understanding which will make being handy intuitive to you over time (so you have to persevere). Approach being practical with the right attitude, remember the RELEARN method, and it'll come, like everything else you know how to do. Remember what Walter Scott said; 'For success, *attitude* is equally as important as ability.' And you already got attitude!

REPEAT AFTER ME... (DON'T BE SHY...)

- I can learn how to do some of the maintenance or improvement jobs in and around my home.

- I can learn how to make some small repairs to my stuff.

- I'm going to do some research and learn some interesting and useful things I can use on my projects...

- At last, I have realised the importance of reading instructions...

- I have prepared and polished up my tool kit... (such as it is).
- I'm already gathering the materials I need to make something super exciting...
- I now understand the importance of allowing plenty of time so I can make a great job.
- I already have a few small things in mind that I know I can do...
- I've already cleared the house of unnecessary distractions...
- I've put beer in the fridge to celebrate when I've completed the project and made a fabulous job... (or wine, if you're a little bit posh).
- I've sent Ian some chocolate, 'liked' him on Facebook and bought extra copies of this book to give all my friends come Christmas... *wink* *wink*...

REMEMBER...

Seriously though; when your project is in front of you...

- Don't panic, go slowly and carefully.
- Stop the second you're not sure, seek reassurance by re-reading the instructions, going over your research or getting advice from others.
- Think back to what you've learned from past experience.

Don't be afraid to ask for help at *any* time. DIY isn't like asking for directions, you are not lost; you just need some specific info to help you out of an unfamiliar situation. There is no shame in asking for that. I hope you've found the book useful, but most of all I hope it's inspired you to have a go at your own DIY jobs around the home or even to build something just for fun.

Bye for now, and...

Good Luck!

How did you get on, what do you think?
Are you inspired to have a go at DIY?

If you think this book will help others,
I'd love it if you'd leave a review for me...

It's taken me over 30 years working on the tools to gain enough experience to write this book, that's over 50,000 hours. Phew. Still it'll only take you a few minutes to leave a review won't it. *wink*, *wink*...

author.to/iananderson (amazon.co.uk)
amazon.com/author/iananderson
goodreads.com/ian-anderson

For insults, typos you noticed, suggestions for revisions or general mud-slinging, I'll look forward to hearing from you at ian@handycrowd.com

But wait, don't get your coat just yet, there is still a little more stuff to come in the appendices... (and just when you thought you'd finished...)

As you were...

APPENDICES ONE (ONLINE RESOURCES)

Here are some online resources I've personally found useful. But please bear in mind that things change, and links break all the time... (let me know if you hit a broken link or want to suggest a new one).

Some of the links are very people 'unfriendly' so to save your poor typing fingers, I've copied these pages and put the links online here: handycrowd.com/links so you can just click them... you're welcome!

BUILDING RELATED TOPICS

Askjeff.co.uk: Popular newspaper columnist, builder by trade, now teaching and writing to help others better look after their homes.

Brick.org.uk: UK based brick resource.

British-gypsum.com: Great installation guides for drywall and plasters in the UK.

Calderlead.co.uk/wp-content/uploads/2011/07/Calder-Guide-to-Good-Leadwork.pdf: For a great leadwork guide.

Diydoctor.org.uk: Popular place for DIY information and advice articles plus a forum.

Diynot.com: DIY encyclopaedia and active forum covering a wide range of topics.

Gobrick.com: USA based brick resource.

Gov.uk/government/uploads/system/uploads/attach-ment_data/file/516238/160413_Householder_Technical_Guid-ance.pdf: Permitted development notes in the UK.

Homebuilding.co.uk: Physical magazine with an online presence. Lots of how to and tips articles.

Idostuff.co.uk: Informal DIY advice and tips.

Ihbconline.co.uk/caring: Great resource for older homes from The Institute of Historic Building Conservation, accessed via the little 'hamburger' icon in the top left-hand corner.

Leadsheetassociation.org.uk: All you need to know to make the most out of lead as a good, long lasting building material.

Lime.org.uk: All about lime and its proper use.

Nhbc.co.uk: National House Building Council who are responsible for new housing standards in the UK.

Nps.gov/tps/how-to-preserve/briefs/2-repoint-mortar-joints.htm: How to re-point the mortar joints on your house using the correct materials.

Periodliving.co.uk: Magazine based DIY advice with an old house flavour.

Planningportal.co.uk: Advice and procedures related to UK planning and building regulations

Pointmaster.co.uk: Pumps mortar into empty joints in brick/paving via a nozzle.

Ultimatehandyman.co.uk: Over 50,000 pages of DIY info and an active forum.

Wickes.co.uk: UK based home DIY supplier.

En.wikipedia.org/wiki/Electrical_wiring: To fully understand just how ridiculously complex cable colours are in domestic wiring.

COMPUTER RELATED TOPICS

Dropbox.com: Dropbox automatically saves your stuff to a server in the 'cloud'. First 2GB free.

Dummies.com: Excerpts from the Dummies guide books (there are other topics too).

Fixyourownprinter.com: How to fix your own printer (printers have all sorts of hidden menus you can exploit for repairs...).

Help.lockergnome.com: A great online forum about computer problems.

Howtogeek.com: Brilliant place to get help with computer problems.

Onedrive.live.com: Like Dropbox, OneDrive is a cloud-based storage facility from Microsoft with first 5GB free.

Pcworld.com: Lots of how to articles and advice.

Primopdf.com: The No1 free PDF converter. Simple to convert documents to PDF format for easy and safe distribution.

Processlibrary.com: The place to go to find out what that process is running on your computer.

Speedtest.net: Check your internet connection speeds, uploads and downloads, (contact your provider for not keeping their promise!)

Techguy.org: Free tech support...heaven! Although they won't say no to a small donation.

Technibble.com: A vibrant community of Computer Technicians sharing their knowledge with each other and you.

Techrepublic.com: Top resource for the IT trade, lots of useful tips and tweaks.

Thewindowsclub.com: Large community for windows support with active forum and many useful articles to help you get the most out of windows.

FUN STUFF

Climbingarborist.com: Great tree climbing resource from Dan Holiday a trained arborist.

Craftster.org: Online community where people share hip, offbeat, crafty projects. 'No tea cosies without irony' is the tag line...

Duckworksbbs.com/plans/gavin/mouse: Free plans to build a mouse boat, one of the simplest boats to build in the world.

Fornobravo.com/pompeii_oven: Free plans to build a wood fired pizza oven!

For-wild.org: Plans to build an Aldo Leopold bench, probably the easiest cool looking bench to build there is.

Glen-L.com: The holy grail for home boat builders!

Lifehacker.com: Tips to get you through life with a twist of humour and the faintly ridiculous!

Stormdrane.blogspot.com: For anything you need to make out of paracord, surely one of the most useful materials.

Treehousesupplies.com: Inspiration, for building that tree house you always wanted?

Treetopbuilders.net: More treehouses!

Woodenboat.com: Great help for anyone contemplating building or owning a wooden boat. New or old.

Ziplinegear.com/manual: Everything you need to know about building the kids a Zip line or flying fox.

GENERAL TOPICS

About.com: 'Need. Know. Accomplish.' Say the people at about.com, a huge online resource of practical information.

Blog.makezine.com: Community of resourceful people who undertake amazing projects.

Bongous.com: Gives you an address in the USA for delivery purposes, (if your supplier doesn't ship internationally) Bongo then forwards it to you for a small fee plus actual delivery costs.

Justanswer.com: A paid 'ask an expert' service. Over 100 categories and you don't pay until they have answered to your satisfaction.

Handycrowd.com: Me, of course! Companion to this book. Come in, I'll go and put the kettle on...

Multimedia.3m.com/mws/media/3724890/adhesives-and-tapes-design-guide.pdf: Hundreds of 3M bonding solutions PDF.

Popularmechanics.com: Great general practical info on a wide range of topics. Been around a long time! Classic and helpful magazine too.

Selfsufficientish.com: Urban homesteading on a budget. Good advice on making stuff and saving money.

Wikipedia.org: Background reading for pretty much everything!

Youtube.com/watch?v=f2O6mQkFiiw: Learn what happens what happens to your brain when you practise.

MAINTENANCE AND REPAIR RELATED TOPICS

Buildingconservation.com: Conservation information about methods, products, and services for historic buildings.

Cadw.wales.gov.uk/historicenvironment: Information about looking after old buildings and conservation in general. Available from the Welsh Gov.at

Ereplacementparts.com: Great place to find parts and repair advice with videos, forum, and active Facebook resources.

Howtomendit.com: Wide ranging 'How To' site.

Ifixit.com: Free, editable online repair manual.

maintenancematterswales.org: Advice about looking after an older home including sections on planning your maintenance properly and keeping records. From the Welsh Gov.

PLASTIC RELATED TOPICS

http://info.craftechind.com/download-the-full-guide-to-gluing-plastics: Guide to gluing plastics.

Microfluidics.cnsi.ucsb.edu/processing/237471_LT2197_Plastic_Guide_v6_LR7911911.pdf. Loctite, a guide to binding the 30 most common plastics.

Nerfhaven.com: Intro to solvent welding plastics. Available at Nerfhaven.com/forums/topic/18527-intro-to-solvent-welding-plastic

Polyvance.com/identify.php: Best plastic identification and how to repair plastic table on the net.

Weldguru.com/plasticrepair.html: All about welding plastics.

TIMBER RELATED TOPICS

Finewoodworking.com: Leading magazine and TV based info.

Nzffa.org.nz/specialty-timber-market/glossary-of-timber-terms/ Great list of all the terms used in timber production.

Salford.gov.uk/media/385493/inform-insect-attack.pdf: Great introduction to wood boring insect attacks.

Timberworkforums.com: Ozzie based timberwork forum with loads of good advice and a friendly crowd.

TOOLS AND HARDWARE RELATED TOPICS

Boltdepot.com: Lots of fastener related information.

Custompartnet.com/drill-size-chart: Chart for HSS drill bit sizes by gauge, inch, and metric.

Heinnie.com: Because every handy person needs a good, reliable knife. Biggest and best.

Rawlplug.co.uk/downloads: Detailed instructions on using anchors.

Screwfix.com: A UK supplier of building materials with a great multi trade forum with many professionals and a few nuts!

TooledUp.com: UK based supplier of tools and equipment.

VEHICLE RELATED TOPICS

Autorepair.about.com: Simple car maintenance advice and tutorials.

Autotrader.co.uk: Reviews are great for finding potential problems with your car.

Fuelly.com: Track your fuel consumption because increased consumption is an early warning that your motor needs a tune up.

Obd-codes.com: On board, diagnostic stuff, OBD2 or OBDII to work out what fault codes mean on your car.

Parkers.co.uk/cars/reviews: Reviews are great for finding potential problems with your car.

Theaa.com/motoring-advice: Motoring related advice on a wider range of topics.

Usedcarexpert.co.uk: Used car experts for general info etc.

Wisebuyers.co.uk: First call for car related reviews, prices, and specifications.

APPENDICES TWO (STUFF THERE WASN'T ROOM FOR...)

HOME MAINTENANCE GUIDE

Now we all know how important it is to maintain the house we live in to stop it falling apart around our ears and generally being a nuisance. Here is an easy introductory guide to looking after your home with some very simple maintenance. Available for free download from...

handycrowd.com/easy-home-maintenance-guide

Where you can read it, download it, or print it out.

ESTIMATE COSTS OF A NEW EXTENSION OR BUILDING

To avoid nasty surprises in your building budget you'll need to do some sums. As a professional builder, my estimate of costs determines my profitability, I need to get it right. It might look laborious, but going through the project step by step will teach you lots about your project, you might even remember a few things you'd forgotten to allow for... Available for free download from...

handycrowd.com/workbook

Where you can read it, download it, or print it out.

A VERY HANDY PERSONAL INFORMATION TEMPLATE

Imagine if you lost your house and everything in it. Now, imagine how you would sort out the aftermath with only sketchy details about your accounts! What happens if you die? (sorry, but it happens......). You owe it to your family to have your affairs in order. They would have enough to deal with if you don't make it. This simple template easily stores all the information you might need in an emergency or even as an everyday reference. Available for free download from...

handycrowd.com/information-template

Where you can read it, download it, or print it out.

ODD TIPS (I thought about afterwards!)

- **Callipers:** Use an adjustable wrench as a crude calliper to measure the diameter of small round things (bolts, drill bits etc.). Then use the jaws to find a suitable drill bit for a bolt hole for example.

- **Door holder:** Take a short piece of 50mm × 100mm (2″ × 4″) timber, around 600mm (2′) long and cut a 35mm deep slot through it, just wider than a door. Lay the door into the slot and secure it with a long, tapered wedge (cut from the side of the timber), it works even better if you match the angle of the wedge on one side of the slot.

Hot Glue: Use hot glue to temporarily hold stuff. Ideal for stuff too small for regular clamps. Tap to remove and residue cleans off easily.

Ladders: Put a pair of old gloves onto the top of the ladder to protect the surface its leaning on. Don't forget ladders rub because they move up and down slightly when you climb on them.

Measure: Don't use a tape measure if you don't have to. Hold up the workpiece and mark the size directly onto it. Great for small trims.

Moving heavy stuff: Move heavy items by lifting them up one end and laying a sheet underneath them. Lift up the other end and pull the sheet through so it's totally underneath the item. Make sure the floor is clean and grit free if its wooden. Grab good handfuls of the sheet and pull. The whole thing will slide easily on the sheet.

Pointing paving: Keep the paving clean, cut a square of thick polythene (or lino) 300mm or 12" or so and cut a slit or narrow slot in it about 200mm or 8" long. Position the cut over the joint and drop the mortar through it. Scrape off excess mortar, move the guide along and repeat. Go back and finish off the joint surface as you wish.

Sanding: Use a wire brush or even an old paint scraper to unclog, clogged sandpaper, (it clogs up easily with oils etc.).

String: Screw an old funnel to the shed wall and pop a ball of string into it. Thread the string down through the funnel. You can even rivet a razor blade to the funnel to cut the string on.

Wiring: An easy way to expose the inner wires in a cable is by pulling the bare earth wire. Grab the bare earth wire with your pliers and pull down at an angle. The earth wire 'cuts' through the outer sheathing, opening it up safely and without 'nicking' the other wires.

GLOSSARY

Here are some of the more unusual terms I used in this book. Please head over to dictionary.reference.com or wikipedia.org for more info...

ARCING

The proper description of an electrical arc gets a bit complicated with plasma discharges and so on, but for us, it simply means when electricity jumps across a gap, causing burning and sooty deposits.

CAPTIVE NUTS

Where the inside of an item is inaccessible, manufacturers will weld a nut to the inside of the casing. Problems occur when the nut breaks free because of corrosion, making removal of the bolt pretty near impossible because you can't stop the captive nut from turning.

CENTRE PUNCH

A metal marking device consisting of a pointed bar placed exactly centre of where you need a hole and then tapped with a hammer. The small depression created locates the drill bit and stops it wandering on start up.

CHUCK

A drill chuck is a self-centring, (usually with three-jaws) mechanism to hold a drill bit in a drill. Lathes also have a chuck which also holds the workpiece.

CHURN BRUSH

A brush with downward pointing stiff bristles, originally for cleaning the inside of milk churns. Now popular for finishing off lime mortar joints as well as for cleaning of a mason's tools (mixers, shovels, trowels, wheelbarrows, etc.)

CURING

Curing helps concrete develop its full strength and durability. Curing starts as soon as the concrete is in place and involves keeping it moist for at least three days, preferably a week and ideally 28 days.

FALL

A predetermined fall or drop from absolute level. Usually expressed as a ratio, or in degrees or as a percentage from horizontal. For example, a shower floor falling at 1:64 or 0.9° or 1.57% means for every 640mm (25") along, the fall is 10mm (⅜"). The opposite of a rise.

FACE SIDE

The best or most visible side of the workpiece. Usually the top or front. Often marked with a light pencil 'squiggle' (so you know to protect it).

FASTENERS

Fasteners (or fixings in the UK). A generic term that covers any mechanical item holding two or more things together. E.g. screws, nails, nuts and bolts, rivets, clips, clamps, pins, ties etc.

FEED

The pressure applied during a machining operation. Practically, this translates to how hard you push the tool. Drilling steel requires high feed and drilling soft-wood requires very little feed for example.

FERROUS METAL

Ferrous metals contain a percentage of iron. Steel is made from iron with the addition of carbon and other substances. Heavily recycled but with a much lower value than non-ferrous metals like copper, brass, and aluminium.

FIXINGS

Same as fasteners in most places.

FLASHINGS

Thin metal covers between different parts of a building to keep the weather out. Typically, around stuff that comes through the roof like chimneys. Also where a roof abuts a wall or other roof. Made from lead, copper, galvanised steel, tin, or even plastic-coated steel etc.

FLOOR JOISTS (FIRST FLOOR)

Large structural timbers situated in-between the different levels in your house. Fasten the ceiling material to the underside of the floor joists. Pipes and wiring run through holes drilled in the centre of the joist (spacing, size and location rules apply) or on top in notches (size and location rules apply). Fasten floor-boards to the topside.

FLUX

For the solder to bond properly to metal, the surfaces need to be very clean. Flux is essentially an acid-based cleaner used to prime components ready to receive molten solder.

FOOTINGS

Often called a strip foundation. A deep trench in the ground partially filled with concrete to provide a foundation for a wall. In the UK, typically around 1m (40") deep and 600mm (24") wide. Concrete thickness is not less than 150mm (6") but I usually go for 300mm, (12") or more.

FOOTING COURSES

Common before the use of concrete in foundations became the norm. Footing courses are the first few brick courses laid deep in the ground. They start off wide and then narrowed as the wall proceeded upwards towards ground level. They help spread the load of the wall over a wider area

FORMWORK
See Shuttering.

FRAMING
See Stud Wall.

FUSEBOX
Where the power comes into the property and where all power cables radiate out and around the property. Also, the normal home for the electricity meter. Alternative names are: breakers, circuit breakers, consumer unit, distribution board, electrical panel, fuse board, fuse panel, junction box, service panel to give you a few...

GABLE END
Generally triangular shaped walls at the ends of a double pitched roof.

GASKET
A gasket is a seal between the mating surfaces of two different components. Usually highly compressed via fasteners through the components to prevent leakage of either liquid (antifreeze, water, fuel, oil, etc), or air, which passes between the joined components.

GEARS
Usually round discs with teeth around the outer edge on a shaft. Placed side by side with other gears and shafts to transfer rotary action from one place to another, often altering the speed and power transmitted. A small gear running against a large gear will cause the big gears shaft to turn slower (than the shaft driving the small gear) and with more torque (the force or power).

GRAIN
Describes the lay or direction of wood fibres. For example: with the grain (planes along timber cleanly); against the grain (planes along timber but snags and tears out); across the grain (planes across the fibres, with or against); end grain (planes at right angles to the grain, such as the end of a piece of timber)

GAUGE
Imperial screw thicknesses or 'gauge' indicates screw thickness, (6, 8 and 10 being common), the larger the number the thicker the gauge. Metric screw thicknesses are in millimetres. By coincidence, the size of an imperial screw head in 'mm' also roughly equates to the imperial gauge. For example, an 8-gauge screw has an 8mm wide head.

HARDCORE

The name given to stone material used as infill under floors, driveways, paths etc. to provide a firm base. Crushed limestone, 50mm (or 75mm) down to dust being common. Broken down masonry is okay under garden landscaping.

HOME

Yes, I know it's where you live, but also home means something which is fully inserted. i.e. all the way home etc. (pipes, fittings, screws etc.).

ISOLATING VALVE

A small valve to switch off the water feed to a single appliance or tap. Can be on the hot and/or cold supply and often operated with a large flat screwdriver. Usually turned through 90° to open and close the valve. Better quality ones and many washing machine valves come with their own little lever.

KEY

(surface preparation). The process of slightly roughening the surface of an object, usually with fine sandpaper. This removes any smoothness or gloss that might prevent the new finish from sticking to the old layers.

(engineering). A key is a small block of metal which stops movement between a component (usually a gear, pulley, wheel etc.) and a rotating shaft. Half the key sits in a groove in the shaft called a key seat and the other half of the key sits in a corresponding slot called a keyway in the component on the shaft. Small half-moon shape keys, called 'woodruff keys' are common.

LEAD HOLE

A small hole that acts as a lead for a much larger hole when drilling with HSS bits. Start with a small bit and follow with the larger drill, which then naturally follows the smaller hole. Don't confuse this with a 'pilot hole'.

MASON'S CORNER BLOCKS

Small wooden or plastic 'L' shaped blocks with a slot to take a mason's string line. Wrap the line around the block to secure it. Pulling on the line creates enough tension to hold the blocks in place when positioned on the corner of a brick. Position the line at the exact top of a brick each end and heavily tension the line to avoid line sag.

MARKING GAUGE

An adjustable tool for marking parallel lines on the workpiece (single or double), consisting of a beam with a lockable headstock to set the width. The end of the beam has a marking method, typically a pin, blade, wheel, or pencil.

MESH
Either a network of wire or thread (metal reinforcing etc.) or when the teeth of a gearwheel engage with another gearwheel.

MURPHY'S LAW
A popular saying or philosophy that maintains "Anything that can possibly go wrong will go wrong and usually in the most inconvenient manner".

NOGGIN
A noggin (or nogs, or nogging), or dwang, or blocking, are bracing pieces used between wall studs or floor joists to add rigidity. Mostly made of timber in stud walls. In between floor joists a proprietary system made from steel, or aluminium or a metal banding commonly replaces timber nogs.

NON-FERROUS METAL
A non-ferrous metal usually means one that does not rust or contain any appreciable amount of iron. For example, Aluminium, Copper, and Lead plus some alloys such as Brass (Copper & Tin alloy). Non-ferrous metals have a high value and are 'weighed in' at local recycling centres in exchange for cash.

OPEN CIRCUIT
The electrical opposite of a short circuit is an 'open circuit', which is an infinite resistance between two nodes, i.e. the current cannot flow around the circuit and the item cannot work. Open circuits are common on damaged flex where internal wires break. Sometimes on/off or intermittent circuits form as the ends of the wire touch together in the moving flex.

PADSTONES
Strong concrete or brick blocks placed under the ends of lintels and beams to spread the high crushing load over a larger area to prevent damaging the softer walling material. Cast-in-situ or built with blocks and strong mortar.

PECKING
Term used to describe repeatedly backing off or partially withdrawing a drill bit when drilling holes to clear swarf.

PILOT HOLE
Small hole drilled, (usually into timber) which stops a fastener splitting the material. Don't confuse this with lead holes used to start a much larger hole.

PIPE
Mostly used to transport fluids or gas, virtually always round and are available in larger sizes than tube. Sized by measuring the internal dimension and usually available in a range of different wall thicknesses.

PLANE

A *plane* is a flat, two-dimensional surface, or a hand tool used to smooth rough timber or the aircraft that takes you on your holidays. As opposed to *plain* which means something simple or low-lying land. All pronounced exactly the same... (Oh, the English language).

RISE

A predetermined rise from absolute level. Usually expressed as a ratio, or in degrees or as a percentage from horizontal. For example, a wheelchair ramp rising at 1:12 or 4.8° or 8.39% means that for every 120mm (5″) along, the rise is 10mm (⅜″). The opposite of a fall.

RIVET

A soft metal pin (usually aluminium) which goes through holes in two or more plates or pieces and pulled up tight to hold them together.

RSJ

A Rolled Steel Joist (RSJ) or Universal Beam (UB). Commonly called an 'I' beam due to their cross-sectional shape. The horizontal parts of the 'I' are flanges, and the vertical part is the web. Often quoted as a given weight per M which relates to the thicknesses of the flanges and web.

SETTLEMENT

Minor movement of a structure caused by weight, seasonal variations in temperature affecting materials, seasonal shifts in the ground supporting the structure or even materials drying out and shrinking.

SHAKE PROOF WASHERS AND NUTS

Special washers that go onto a bolt before adding a nut. Have 'spikes' internally or externally to bite into the metal component and nut. Also a 'split ring' style, which is a spring steel washer cut through and twisted open slightly to add tension to the nut once tightened. A shake proof nut has a plastic insert in the top of the nut that grips the bolt when tightened. Most are officially considered single use.

SHORT CIRCUIT

A short circuit is where an electrical current has travelled along an unintended path and usually results in a blown fuse or tripped circuit breaker. There may also be a loud bang and smoke plus a scorched area at the short circuit site.

SHUTTERING

Temporary concrete mould, edge, or perimeter forms to hold wet concrete in place until it sets. Made from timber, metal, or sheet material etc. Often treated with a release agent to stop the concrete from sticking to it. Usually removed after a few days.

SLATE RIP

A long thin tool with a handle on one end and a hook on the other. Slid up under slates and yanked sharply downwards to cut or pull out the nails holding the slates.

SOLDER

Solder is a low melting point fusible metal alloy used to join metal workpieces together using a soldering iron. Common in electronics on PCB's and to connect pipes in plumbing. Looks like a thick, silver/grey soft bendable wire. Needs a special flux during the heating phase to chemically clean the parts.

STOPCOCK

A way of isolating or switching off the water supply where it comes into your property. Usually a large tap like valve that you turn clockwise until it stops. Remember when switching the water back on; to open the valve fully and then wind it back in a little (half a turn or so). This stops the valve sticking in the fully open position. Don't confuse this with an isolating valve which isolates a single appliance.

STUD WALL

Often called framing. Lightweight and usually non-load bearing walls made from timber. A specially dried timber with rounded edges called CLS is popular. Some common sizes are 38mm × 63mm (1 ½″ × 2 ½″) or 38mm × 89mm (1 ½″ × 3 ½″) or 48mm × 73mm (2″ × 3″) or 48mm × 89mm (2″ × 4″). Standard 'rough sawn' timber is also common, 48mm × 73mm (2″ × 3″) or 48mm × 98mm (2″ × 4″). Consists of a top or head plate, a bottom or base plate with vertical timbers in between. Short crosspieces/ 'noggings' or 'dwangs' and any 'blockings' are fixed between the vertical 'studs.' The whole wall is then clad, usually with drywall (or timber shiplap etc., sheet material etc.). A lightweight metal stud system is also common.

SUBSIDENCE

A downward movement of the ground underneath the foundation of a wall or floor. Usually causes movement of the structure creating cracks. Large trees close to walls and leaking drains are the main culprits.

SWARF

The debris or waste resulting from drilling or machining. Also known as chips, turnings, filings, or shavings; usually metal although it can also be wood or plastic.

TARNISH

Tarnish is a thin layer of corrosion that forms on the surface of non-ferrous and other similar metals as their outermost layer reacts chemically, usually with air, water, or oils in your skin.

TIMBER

Timber (or sometimes lumber) is wood from a tree cut and prepared into a range of sizes ready for construction use, (definition varies from region to region, no one can agree 100%!)

TUBE

Mostly used for building structural things and is stronger than pipe. Tube can be **square**, **rectangular** or **round**. Sized by measuring the external dimension and various different wall thicknesses.

UNCOUPLING MEMBRANE

A separating layer under floor tiles to allow substrates such as wooden flooring to move without damaging the tiles.

WALL PLATE

A wall plate is a horizontal, structural, load-bearing timber (usually 50mm × 100mm or 2″ × 4″) bedded in mortar, on top of a wall and strapped down the walls. Roof members sit on and are fixed to it.

WOOD

Wood is the hard, fibrous material forming the main substance of trees. Once felled, the sawmill transforms wood into timber for construction.

WORK HARDENING

Also called strain hardening or cold working. A strengthening of a metal caused by plastic deformation. Bending metal moves the crystal structure within the metal increasing its hardness. Can be a positive or a negative attribute.

WORKPIECE

Generic name given to whatever you're working on; it can be anything from a piece of timber to a sheet of glass etc.

WORKPLACE

Generic name for any place where you're working, from a bench in the garage to the spare bedroom. Don't confuse this with the other workplace where you go to earn your wages...

GETTING IN TOUCH

Please remember you're not alone. If you have questions, suggestions, or want to point out spelling mistakes or you just want to tell me about a better way. Please feel free to get in touch and I'll get back to you ......

CONTACT DETAILS

I'm happy to stand behind this book (and not only to avoid any eggs!) Of course, if the book makes the bestseller lists, I'll be far too busy with Oprah to talk to you personally, but in that case, I promise I'll have one of my minions handle your enquiry...

For the foreseeable future however, I'd be delighted to hear from you. I'm always open to feedback and I'd love to read any constructive criticism you might have. Since it's pretty much the point of this book, I've taught myself everything I needed to learn to publish this book, so any errors you see are definitely my own. If you're a spammer though, or overly rude, I'll have my men track you down...

You can email me at ian@handycrowd.com, or
catch up with me on most flavours of social media...

facebook.com/handycrowd
twitter.com/handycrowd
pinterest.com/handycrowd
linkedin.com/in/ianmanderson

COMPANION WEBSITE

You'll also find me pottering about on handycrowd.com where I'll be writing more 'how to' articles and answering your emails or comments.

Come on in, I'll go and put the kettle on!

NEWSLETTER

You can also register for updates and newsletters and I promise not to abuse your email address. I'll only write when there's something interesting or useful for you, Christmas's, and birthdays etc...

ABOUT THE AUTHOR

Hang on a sec. I'm not going to write this in the more traditional 'third person', because it's just me here after all, so that would be just silly, right? So, what about little old me then? Well, I'm a simple English builder, and I've been self-employed since the tender age of 18 (i.e. a very long time...).

About a hundred years ago I was awarded a silver trowel at college for my skills with a trowel, as well as the silver medal, first prize for surveying and levelling. Nowadays, I'm a Licentiate member of the City and Guilds Institute of London and a few years ago I took a Master of Science degree in Trauma and Disaster Management from the University of Lincoln in the UK.

Practically and physically, I've built new houses, extensions, restored period houses using lime mortars, underpinned ancient foundations, and restored centuries old roofing, as well as carrying out routine repairs and maintenance work on a variety of properties in the UK. I'm also a keen home mechanic and love classic cars. Oh, and I love recycling and repurposing stuff, especially pallets, my standard 'go-to' resource.

I'm a keen humanitarian and have lived and worked in various East African countries. In Uganda, I taught local artisans and built health units in remote rural areas, plus the restoration of a couple of hospitals. I also helped to set up projects in Rwanda as part of a British Conservative Party initiative by David Cameron for his international development team under Andrew Mitchell MP (project Umubano).

To balance things out I was a househusband or 'Mr Mom' for a couple of years; looking after 3 acres of wild New Zealand scrub, two chickens and of course my Norwegian wife, and two fantastic children.

I'm a 'try anything' handyman (or should that be 'repair-person' these days?) and it's my goal to learn something new every day. This I find very easy to do, as I'm writing, inventing, developing products and webmastering (all self-taught of course), close to the beach in Norway. And yes, of course, the days are never long enough...

Stay well and I wish you well in all your own endeavours...